South Korea
a country study

Federal Research Division
Library of Congress
Edited by
Andrea Matles Savada
and William Shaw
Research Completed
June 1990

On the cover: North Watchtower, Suwŏn Castle

Fourth Edition, First Printing, 1992.

Library of Congress Cataloging-in-Publication Data

South Korea : a country study / Federal Research Division, Library
   of Congress ; edited by Andrea Matles Savada and William
   Shaw.—4th ed.
      p.   cm. — (Area handbook series, ISSN 1057-5294) (DA
pam ; 550-41)
      "Research completed July 1990."
      Includes bibliographical references (pp. 347-375) and index.
      ISBN 0-8444-0736-4
      1. Korea (South).   I. Savada, Andrea Matles, 1950-
II. Shaw, William, 1944-   . III. Library of Congress. Federal
Research Division. IV. Series. V. Series: DA pam ; 550-41.
DS902.S68   1992   91-39109
951.95—dc20   CIP

Headquarters, Department of the Army
DA Pam 550-41

For sale by the Superintendent of Documents, U.S. Government Printing Office
Washington, D.C. 20402

Foreword

This volume is one in a continuing series of books prepared by the Federal Research Division of the Library of Congress under the Country Studies—Area Handbook Program sponsored by the Department of the Army. The last page of this book lists the other published studies.

Most books in the series deal with a particular foreign country, describing and analyzing its political, economic, social, and national security systems and institutions, and examining the interrelationships of those systems and the ways they are shaped by cultural factors. Each study is written by a multidisciplinary team of social scientists. The authors seek to provide a basic understanding of the observed society, striving for a dynamic rather than a static portrayal. Particular attention is devoted to the people who make up the society, their origins, dominant beliefs and values, their common interests and the issues on which they are divided, the nature and extent of their involvement with national institutions, and their attitudes toward each other and toward their social system and political order.

The books represent the analysis of the authors and should not be construed as an expression of an official United States government position, policy, or decision. The authors have sought to adhere to accepted standards of scholarly objectivity. Corrections, additions, and suggestions for changes from readers will be welcomed for use in future editions.

Louis R. Mortimer
Chief
Federal Research Division
Library of Congress
Washington, D.C. 20540

Acknowledgments

This edition supercedes *South Korea: A Country Study* published in 1982. The authors wish to acknowledge their use of portions of that edition in the preparation of the current book.

Various members of the staff of the Federal Research Division of the Library of Congress assisted in the preparation of the book. Sandra W. Meditz made helpful suggestions during her review of all parts of the book. Robert L. Worden also reviewed parts of the book and made numerous suggestions and points of clarification. Timothy L. Merrill assisted in the preparation of some of the maps, checked the content of all of the maps, and reviewed the sections on geography and telecommunications. Thanks also go to David P. Cabitto, who designed the cover and chapter art and provided graphics support; Marilyn L. Majeska, who managed editing and production and edited portions of the manuscript; Andrea T. Merrill, who provided invaluable assistance with regard to tables and figures; and Barbara Edgerton, Alberta Jones King, and Izella Watson, who performed word processing.

The authors also are grateful to individuals in various United States government agencies who gave their time and special knowledge to provide information and perspective. These individuals include Ralph K. Benesch, who oversees the Country Studies-Area Handbook Program for the Department of the Army; Cho Sung Yoon, Far Eastern Law Division, Library of Congress, who reviewed the sections of the manuscript on the judiciary and the legal system; and John Merrill of the Department of State, who reviewed the text and also offered suggestions and points of clarification.

The editors are also grateful to several academic experts on Korea: Gari K. Ledyard, Robert Ramsey, and Donald N. Clark. Although they provided advice on specific issues, they are in no way responsible for the views found in the book. In addition, the editors wish to thank various members of the staff of the Embassy of the Republic of Korea in Washington for their assistance.

Others who contributed were Harriett R. Blood and Greenhorne and O'Mara, who assisted in the preparation of maps and charts; Katherine Young, who edited portions of the manuscript; Catherine Schwartzstein, who performed final prepublication editorial review, and Joan C. Cook, who prepared the index. Linda Peterson and Malinda B. Neale of the Library of Congress Composing Unit prepared camera-ready copy, under the direction of Peggy Pixley. The inclusion of photographs was made possible by the generosity of various individuals and public and private agencies.

Contents

Chapter 2. The Society and Its Environment 67
Donald M. Seekins

Preface

Like its predecessor, this study attempts to review the history and treat in a concise and objective manner the dominant social, political, economic, and military aspects of South Korea. Under Roh Tae Woo, who was elected president of the Sixth Republic in 1987 (as well as under the previous president, Chun Doo Hwan, 1980–87), South Korea has been struggling to maintain its economic successes. Movement in more democratic directions has been much slower than economic development. Political unrest, labor strikes, and student agitation continued to challenge the government in the early 1990s.

Sources of information included books, scholarly journals, foreign and domestic newspapers, official reports of governments and international organizations, and numerous periodicals on Korean and East Asian affairs. Chapter bibliographies appear at the end of the book, and brief comments on some of the more valuable sources recommended for further reading appear at the end of each chapter. A Glossary also is included.

Spellings of place-names used in the book are in most cases those approved by the United States Board on Geographic Names. However, the generic parts appended to some geographic names have been dropped and their English equivalents substituted: for example, Cheju Island, not Cheju-do, and South Ch'ungch'ŏng Province, not Ch'ungch'ŏng-namdo. The name South Korea has been used where appropriate in place of the official name, Republic of Korea. The McCune-Reischauer system of transliteration has been employed, except in cases of the names of some prominent national figures, internationally recognized corporations, and the city of Seoul, where the more familiar journalistic equivalent is used. The names of Korean authors writing in English are spelled as given.

Measurements are given in the metric system. A conversion table is provided to assist those readers who are unfamiliar with metric measurements (see table 1, Appendix).

The body of the text reflects information available as of June 1990. Certain other portions of the text, however, have been updated: the Introduction discusses significant events that have occurred since the completion of research, and the Bibliography includes recently published sources thought to be particularly helpful to the reader.

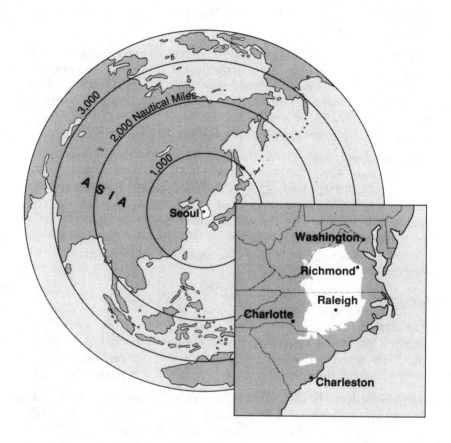

Country

Formal Name: Republic of Korea.

Short Form: South Korea.

Term for Citizens: Korean(s).

Capital: Seoul.

Date of Independence: August 15, 1948.

Geography

Location and Size: Strategic location in waters of the Sea of Japan, Korea Strait, and Yellow Sea. Total land area of Korean Peninsula, including islands, 220,847 square kilometers; approximately 98,477 square kilometers (44.6 percent) constitutes territory of South Korea.

Land Boundary: 238 kilometers with North Korea.

Disputes: Demarcation Line with North Korea; Liancourt Rocks claimed by Japan.

Topography and Drainage: Approximately 70 percent of land area mountains and uplands. Principal ranges—T'aebaek and Sobaek range and Chiri Massif. Tallest mountain—Mount Halla at 1,950 meters, a volcanic cone located on Cheju Island. Longest rivers—Naktong River, 521 kilometers; Han River, which flows through Seoul, 514 kilometers; and Kŭm River, 401 kilometers.

Climate: Long, cold, dry winters; short, hot, humid summers with late monsoon rains, flooding. Seoul's January mean temperature − 5°C to − 2.5°C; July, 22.5°C to 25°C. Cheju Island warmer, milder weather than other parts of South Korea. Annual rainfall varies from year to year but usually averages more than 100 centimeters; two-thirds of precipitation falls between June and September. Droughts, particularly in southwest; approximately one every eight years.

Society

Population: 1980 census reports total population of 37,448,836. January 1989 estimate 42.2 million. Population in 1985 of two largest cities, Seoul and Pusan, 9.6 million and 3.5 million, respectively. Population growth rate in late 1980s less than 1 percent.

Language: Korean the national language. No significant linguistic minorities. Regional dialects of Korean mutually intelligible with exception of that spoken on Cheju Island. Written language uses Chinese characters and Korean *han'gŭl* script, or *han'gŭl* alone.

Education and Literacy: Adult literacy rate in late 1980s approximately 93 percent. Primary school education compulsory (grades one through six). Approximately 95 percent of population age-group in secondary schools (middle and high schools); 83 percent in academic high schools; 17 percent in vocational high schools in 1987. About 35 percent of student age-group attended colleges and universities in 1989—one of world's highest rates.

Religion: Great diversity of religious traditions include Buddhism, Confucianism, Ch'ŏndogyo, Catholicism, and Protestantism, and as many as 300 new religions incorporating elements of these mainstream religions. Shamanism, oldest religious tradition.

Health: Increase in life expectancy from 51.1 years for men and 54.2 years for women in late 1950s to 66 years for men and 73 years for women in 1990 reflects dramatic improvements in health conditions. Death rate declined significantly from 13.8 deaths per 1,000 in late 1950s to 6 per 1,000 in 1990. Infant mortality 23 deaths per 1,000 live births as of mid-1990. Health personnel and facilities largely concentrated in large cities, particularly Seoul and Pusan. Serious public health problems caused by environmental pollution and poor sanitation. No unified national health insurance system but medical insurance benefits available to almost all South Koreans.

Economy

General Character: Export oriented although domestic market increasing source of growth in late 1980s; real growth 12.5 percent 1986–88; 6.5 percent, 1989. Dominated by *chaebŏl,* or business conglomerates. Most industries, except mining, in urban areas of northwest and southeast. Heavy industry generally in south. World's tenth largest steel producer in 1989. Major electronics producer. Automobiles and automotive parts major domestic growth and export industry of 1980s. Armaments also manufactured for domestic use and export. Construction critical source of foreign currency and invisible export earnings. Textiles, clothing, and leather products important. Growing labor movement affects production and costs.

Gross National Product (GNP): In 1989 US$204 billion, US$4,830 per capita, 6.5 percent annual growth rate.

Gross Domestic Product (GDP): US$211.9 billion at market prices, 1989; real annual growth 6.1 percent. Average growth 6.1 percent 1986–90; high, 12.4 percent in 1986; low, 6.1 percent in 1989.

Industry: Main growth sector, produced 46 percent of GDP and employed 35 percent of work force in 1988.

Resources: Minimal resources. Mineral deposits mostly small, except for tungsten. Anthracite coal most important mineral product by volume and value, but also imported. Most energy needs met by nuclear power, coal, and crude petroleum imports.

Agriculture, Forestry, and Fishing: Employed approximately 21 percent of work force in 1989; generated 10.2 percent of GDP. Relative importance declining since mid-1960s; production grew 5.9 percent in first half of 1989. Major crops rice and barley, also millet, corn, sorghum, buckwheat, soybeans, and potatoes. Fishery products popular food and important export commodity. Inadequate forestry resources.

Foreign Trade: Annual trade in 1988 more than US$100 billion; first time world's tenth largest trading nation. Major trading partners United States and Japan. Main exports textiles, clothing, electronic and electrical equipment, footwear, machinery, steel, ships, automobiles and automotive parts, rubber tires and tubes, plywood, and fishery products. Main imports machinery, electronics and electronic equipment, petroleum and petroleum products, steel, grains, transport equipment, raw materials, chemicals, machinery, timber and pulp, raw cotton, and cereals. Balance of payments affected by oil imports and raw materials needs; surplus of US$4.6 billion in 1989, but deficit of US$1.9 billion, 1990.

Currency and Exchange Rate: January 1990, US$1 = 683.4 wŏn (W).

Fiscal Year: January 1 through December 31.

Transportation and Telecommunications

Roads: 51,000 kilometers of roadways; 46.3 percent paved in 1988; 1,539 kilometers express highways, more under construction; 845,000 passenger cars and 748,000 commercial vehicles in 1987. Intercity bus system; subway system in Seoul.

Railroads: State-run Korean National Railroad with 6,340-kilometer network; 761.8 kilometers double track; 1,023 kilometers electric railroads. Suburban lines connect to Seoul subway system.

Major Ports: Pusan, Inch'ŏn, Kunsan, Mokp'o, and Ulsan.

Civil Aviation: International airports at Seoul, Pusan, and Cheju. Two airlines serve major domestic cities: Asiana Airlines and Korean Air. Korean Air international service includes routes to Japan, North America, Middle East, Soviet Union, and Western Europe.

Telecommunications: Adequate domestic and international services; approximately 9.2 million telephones in 1987; 42 million radio receivers; by 1989 there were 79 AM and 46 FM radio stations; 256 television stations (57 of 1 kilowatt or greater) and 8.6 million television sets; four satellite earth stations.

Government and Politics

System of Government: Constitution of Sixth Republic approved October 1987; effective February 1988. Strong presidency; president elected for one five-year-term by direct popular vote. 224 members of 299-member National Assembly elected by popular vote for four-year-term in April 1988; rest appointed by political parties according to proportional formula.

Justice: Administration of justice as function of courts established under Constitution and amended Court Organization Law of 1949. Supreme Court highest organ of court system; appellate courts and district courts. Constitution Court decides constitutionality of a law, dissolution of a political party, impeachment, petitions relating to Constitution, disputes between state agencies, or between state agencies and local governments. Family Court adjudicates domestic affairs and juvenile delinquency. Courts-martial have jurisdiction over offenses committed by armed forces personnel and civilian military employees.

Administrative Divisions: Nine provinces and six provincial-level cities. Provinces divided into counties and ordinary cities; counties into townships and towns; townships into villages. Mostly part of central government; increasing self-government.

Politics: Multiparty system, but political parties with contrary aims or activities may be dissolved by Constitution Court.

Foreign Affairs: Member of most international organizations but no formal membership in United Nations in mid-1990. Mutual defense treaty with United States, which along with Japan, one of two most important foreign policy partners. Relations with Democratic People's Republic of Korea (North Korea) treated as "internal" rather than "foreign"; public and private contacts increasing.

National Security

Armed Forces: Active-duty personnel 650,000 (June 1989). Component services: army, 575,000 (including 25,000 marines); air force, 40,000; navy, 35,000. Reserve forces about 1.2 million in 1990. Compulsory service in army, navy, and air force, thirty to thirty-six months.

Combat Units and Major Equipment: Ground Forces: three army headquarters; equipment inventory includes 1,560 tanks and 1,550 armored personnel carriers, 12 surface-to-surface missiles. Air Force: includes twenty-two ground attack/intercept squadrons and one reconnaissance squadron; inventory includes 500 combat aircraft. Navy: three fleet commands, one aviation command, one amphibious command with minisubmarines, destroyers, frigates, missile-attack craft, minesweepers, patrol boats, and amphibious craft.

Military Budget: 5 percent GNP, US$10 billion, 1989 estimate.

Military Production: Domestic defense industry begun in early 1970s provides approximately 70 percent of weapons, ammunition, communication and other equipment, vehicles, clothing, and other supplies to armed forces.

Internal Security Forces: Agency for National Security Planning (ANSP), Defense Security Command, Korean National Police collect domestic intelligence. Korean National Police strength 130,000 in 1989.

Foreign Military Treaties: Signatory to Republic of Korea-United States of America Mutual Defense Treaty (1954).

Figure 1. Administrative Divisions of South Korea, 1990

Introduction

FOR NEARLY A HALF-CENTURY, the Republic of Korea (South Korea) and the United States have maintained a close relationship. Since the mid-1980s, South Korea has been the seventh or eighth largest trading partner of the United States, and the United States has ranked as South Korea's first or second trading partner. In 1990, nearly four decades after the end of the Korean War (1950–53), Washington retained more than 45,000 troops on the Korean Peninsula committed to the defense of South Korea. During the 1991 conflict in the Persian Gulf, Seoul joined other coalition partners of the United States and provided a military medical team and several hundred million dollars in support of the campaign to end the Iraqi occupation of Kuwait.

Ties between the two countries extend to language, education, and culture. In 1991 English was the primary foreign language studied in South Korea, and for some time it has been popularly said that more Ph.Ds from American universities work for the South Korean government than for the United States government. Hundred of thousands of United States servicemen, businessmen, Peace Corps volunteers, and missionaries have lived and worked in South Korea, and as many as 1.5 million South Koreans—one fourth of all overseas Koreans—have emigrated to the United States.

The Korean Peninsula has been inhabited since paleolithic times, and Korean historians trace the ethnic roots of the Korean people at least as far back as the pottery-using cultures of the fourth and third centuries B.C. Early tribal groups formed numerous federations, and over the centuries these combined into larger state-like entities. Sometime before the fourth century B.C., at least one of these entities had begun to refer to its leaders by the Chinese title for king, *wang*. Three of these states, boasting an aristocratic social structure and centralized institutions of government, had come to dominate Korea by the early centuries of the present era, conducting trade and intermittent warfare with each other and with China. Stretching down from Manchuria in the north was the kingdom of Koguryŏ; in the southwest and southeast, respectively, the kingdoms of Paekche and Silla held sway. Korean political, cultural, and linguistic unity dates back to the unification of these three kingdoms under Silla in the seventh century A.D., making Korea, despite its present temporary division into two states, one of the oldest unified nations in the world.

Geographically poised between China and Japan, Korea developed its own social and cultural patterns. More deeply influenced than Japan by Chinese culture, Korea adopted the Chinese model of monarchy and successive dynasties, rather than developing a single imperial line from its early tribal federations. Yet Korea retained its native preference for a strongly aristocratic social order based on hereditary lineages. Korea also served as one of several cultural bridges between its two regional neighbors, taking pride in passing along advanced Chinese political, philosophical, religious, and literary ideas and models to what Koreans consistently perceived as a less well-developed Japan.

Korea's geographic position often made it a focal point for regional conflict. Recovering from two Japanese invasions in the late sixteenth century and Manchu incursions several decades later, Korea's last traditional dynasty—the kingdom of Chosŏn (1392–1910)—withdrew into self-protective isolation, strictly regulating travel and commerce with Japan while maintaining its tributary status with China. This policy was increasingly challenged, however, during the nineteenth century, when Western diplomats, traders, and adventurers sought to open all of East Asia, including what they termed the Korean "Hermit Kingdom," to European-style trade and diplomatic relations. In the end, Japan forced open the Korean door, imposing a Western-style "unequal treaty" on Korea in 1876.

At the turn of the century, Korea was the object of two wars as China and Japan in turn fought to maintain footholds on the peninsula and to exclude a Russia keenly interested in Korea's warm-water ports. In the first half of the twentieth century, Korea was victimized by several decades of colonization by Japan (1910–45), becoming by the 1930s a stepping stone and industrial base for Japanese military expansion into Manchuria and northern China. Although many Koreans fought for independence from Japanese rule, Korea's liberation in 1945 was brought about not by Korean efforts but by the Allied victory over Japan and by the division of Korea into two zones of occupation by the United States and the Soviet Union. In the southern zone, the United States Army Military Government in Korea lasted for three years before the establishment of the Republic of Korea. South Korea's immediate postwar fate was dominated not only by the Cold War antagonism of the two great powers but also by seemingly irreconcilable political differences among Koreans themselves. Separate and antagonistic states controlled the two halves of the peninsula by 1948, setting the stage for the considerable civil conflict that led to the Korean War (1950–53).

Given the tragic and bitter legacy of the loss of national independence under Japanese colonial rule, the experience of national partition in 1945, and the ensuing civil war, educational authorities in South Korea have emphasized areas of national identity in schoolbook treatments of Korean history and language. Despite many differences among South Koreans, this carefully nourished national consciousness centered perceptions on national independence and the place of Korea on the stage of world history. Such thinking underlies much of the vigorously pursued economic development of the past three decades and also carried on a long tradition of modern Korean thought. For example, after Japan seized control of Korean foreign relations and military affairs in 1905, Korean historian Ch'oe Nam-sŏn compared the nation's parlous condition with the glories of ancient Korean dynasties and asked, "How long will it take us to accomplish the goal of flying our sacred national flag above the world?" As energetic national preparations for the 1988 Seoul Olympics—under the slogan "Korea to the world, the world to Korea"—demonstrated, toward the end of the century South Koreans still were striving for national success and an international reputation in response to that same impulse.

South Korean urbanization—which increased by a rate of more than 4 percent annually during the 1960s and 1970s—continued at a slightly slower rate of 3 percent per year in the 1980s. According to the 1990 census, Seoul was one of the world's largest cities. Its more than 10.6 million people accounted for almost one quarter of the country's 43.5 million people. The concentration of the population in Seoul prompted efforts by city planners to decentralize government and other functions by moving some ministries and agencies to Taejŏn. The growth of Seoul and other cities, although partly caused by interurban migration, also was accompanied by a reduction of the rural farming population, especially in the poorer areas of the southwest. This migration was reflected in Seoul by the numerous restaurants that offered regional specialties and by the electoral districts that produced bloc votes for presidential candidates from one or another province in the December 1987 presidential election.

Another social change with political implications was the increased emphasis on higher education during the 1980s. When army General Chun Doo Hwan took power in 1980, he approved a plan to double college and university enrollments within four years. Perhaps, as some observers said, the change was intended to submerge traditional student protest in a sea of aspiring professionals and white-collar workers. Yet planners also knew that broader education was vital to continued economic growth, inasmuch as the country's exports faced increasing competition from labor-rich Third World countries and Seoul sought to shift to knowledge-intensive and high-technology industries. By 1990, according to a Ministry of Education study, one South Korean in four was a student. The number of South Koreans in college by the late 1980s comprised some 35 percent of the relevant age-group, a higher percentage than Japan or any country in the world except the United States and the Philippines.

The changes in higher education corroded old political patterns and in several ways may have set the stage for the political and constitutional reforms of the late 1980s. With the spread of scientific and technical education and the continued growth of a new managerial elite, the military's claim—heard especially in the high-growth years of the 1960s and early 1970s—to managerial and technical leadership became increasingly irrelevant. The more educated populace also seemed less tolerant of press censorship and other authoritarian practices. Meanwhile, increasing student enrollments and the consequent rise in the number of college graduates in the job pool created even greater discontent among many unemployed and underemployed graduates and provided a setting in which a small but increasingly radical student dissident movement—often financed with sizable student association fees—could find its voice.

The steady modernization and urbanization of society were accompanied by a continued growth in nostalgia for Korea's past. Even in the countryside, the 1980s saw a continuation of the late 1970s revival of folk arts, often supported by generous government subsidies for regional festivals and "living cultural treasures"—experts in traditional technologies, crafts, and arts, such as architecture, temple painting, or traditional *p'ansori* folk opera. Shamanism, ignored by modernizing elites in the 1950s and 1960s, was much more openly practiced in the 1970s and 1980s, when it was not unusual to see a new office building or major tourist hotel formally opened with shamanistic rites. Many urban professionals enjoyed taking their children to visit the Folk Village near Seoul where they could examine a well-scrubbed reconstruction of nineteenth-century country life and try to imagine a quieter, less hurried time. The revival of traditional culture in the 1970s and 1980s cut across class and political lines. It had a political dimension as well, seen both in dissident student adaptations of traditional anti-aristocratic mask dramas that lampooned the social and political establishment and in government promotion of school trips to the shrine of sixteenth-century naval hero Yi Sun-sin.

Religious commitment was strong for many South Koreans, nearly half of whom were affiliated with an organized religious community in the 1980s. About 20 percent of the population was Buddhist, whereas a somewhat larger and more rapidly growing Christian community gave South Korea the second largest proportion of Christians in Asia, following the Philippines. Although conservative on the whole, the country's Christian population also included some of the most active elements of the political dissident movement.

Confucianism was dominant during the last dynasty (1392–1910) but declined in force as a political philosophy following the loss of independence to Japan in 1910. Nevertheless, it retained a lingering impact on social relations even in the early 1990s. Attempts to revive Confucian ethical values, whether through the Park Chung Hee government's campaign for filial piety and loyalty in the 1970s or in occasional public seminars or newspaper editorials through the early 1990s, reflected both a decline in the practice of Confucianism as a living creed and the feeling of many South Koreans that rapid modernization and the growth of materialism had created an ethical vacuum.

Population policies begun in the 1960s continued their momentum through the 1980s. Tax and medical insurance benefits for smaller families, for example, provided additional incentives for family planning in the early 1980s. The government also distributed posters, such as one featuring an attractive young couple and the slogan, "Have one child and raise it well." The effect of such efforts continued to be felt in a decline in the number of primary and middle school students; the number of middle school students alone dropped by half a million during the 1980s. The success of the family planning program was suggested by the desire of other Asian countries to send officials to Seoul for training.

As the number of births per couple reached 1.9 in 1990, the population growth rate dropped to just over 0.9 percent from almost 1.6 a decade earlier, causing the Economic Planning Board to predict serious labor shortages and to authorize importing increased numbers of foreign workers. Many factories already had been compensating for such shortfalls by hiring illegal immigrants (1,000 such workers were deported in 1990), or by breaking prevailing patterns to hire married women in substantial numbers. By 1991 South Koreans also were beginning to reflect on the social and policy implications of two emerging problems: a possible male-female imbalance by the end of the 1990s, resulting from a continuing preference for sons and use of family planning techniques; and projections of a steadily increasing proportion of elderly in the population over the coming two decades.

South Korea's economic growth continued to be driven by the import of raw materials and semi-finished components (the latter proportionally declining in the late 1980s) and the export of finished industrial products. Manufacturing accounted for more than 30 percent of the gross domestic product (GDP—see Glossary), aided by the rapid modernization of technology and the continuous reinvestment of trade proceeds. By the end of the 1980s, the Republic of Korea was the world's tenth largest steel producer and had made major strides in mastering the production technologies required for the home electronics and semiconductor industries. South Korean-made televisions, personal computers, videocassette recorders, and microwave ovens increasingly became known under their own brand names, although dependence on Japan for key components and some assembly production for Japanese companies also continued.

The automotive industry gained a firmer footing under close government direction following overexpansion in the late 1970s. Most of the growth in the early 1980s was fueled by overseas sales, which began to boom in 1985, but also was stabilized by a rapidly growing domestic market by the end of the decade. Textiles and construction, both staples among the export industries in the 1970s, continued to play an important role through the 1980s. As South Korea's comparative advantage in labor became increasingly subject to challenge from developing economies in Asia and elsewhere, however, planners looked to even greater social investment in high-technology fields, such as materials science, biotechnology, electronics, and aerospace, and to an economy that would become technology-intensive sometime during the 1990s.

Growth in the service sector, comprising real estate, supply services, entertainment, the hotel industry, and other services, continued in the late 1980s, outpacing increases in manufacturing. The number of workers in service industries increased by 8 percent between 1988 and 1989, amounting to more than twice the rate of increase in manufacturing-sector employees during the same period. In the first half of 1990, the total number of workers in manufacturing declined for the first time since the early 1960s. In 1990 the Economic Planning Board, concerned over this trend and a projected shortfall of 69,000 new manufacturing workers for the year, announced its Industrial Manpower Supply Program. The program was designed to stem the exodus of skilled manpower from manufacturing industries by offering long-term workers preferred admission to college and university night-school programs. The government also prepared to use tax penalties and higher utility rates to slow the growth in what it viewed as unproductive "consumption industries."

As South Korea continued to industrialize and urbanize during the 1980s, the agricultural sector drifted into stepchild status. Official support for rice prices dropped behind the rate of inflation in the mid-1980s as Seoul attempted to reduce government costs. Urban growth contributed to a series of problems. Young people were sent to the cities for education or left the farms to seek employment and left behind a smaller and increasingly older farm population. Young bachelor farmers had greater difficulty in finding wives willing to undergo the rigors of rural life. Productivity gains failed to keep up with changes in population, leading to greater imports of wheat and soybeans. Rising land prices caused by the housing squeeze and commercial and industrial construction gave an impression of increased farmers' assets, even as modern machinery costs and increased use of consumer credit contributed to higher farm indebtedness. Tenancy increased from 21 percent to more than 30 percent during the decade, as urban investors and the larger scale farming encouraged by the government absorbed increasingly scarce and costly farm lands. Average farm incomes had fallen well below urban incomes by the end of the decade. By 1990 many farmers could agree with the statement of the founder of a matchmaking center for bachelor farmers that it was "time to turn the government's attention to farmers' life and welfare."

Part of increasing farm indebtedness during the second half of the 1980s was used to finance consumer durables that brought farm families closer to national standards, even as the gap between rural and urban incomes was increasing. A 1990 report of the Ministry of Agriculture and Fisheries indicated that more than 90 percent of rural households had refrigerators, electric rice cookers, and propane gas ranges. Even more significant were major increases in rural ownership of consumer goods, such as telephones and color television sets, which served to link rural families with national and international developments and issues. Such linkage, in turn, may have contributed both to an increasing awareness of the growing rural-urban gap and to the politicization of farmers' movements in response to foreign pressures to liberalize agricultural markets.

In political life, South Korea began the 1980s with an old pattern. For the third time in two decades, a military leader or former military leader declared a state of political crisis, rewrote the constitution, and drove prominent civilian politicians from government through farfetched legal charges or under the guise of "political purification." Re-elected president in electoral college voting in February 1981, former General Chun Doo Hwan consolidated his control through dominance over the court system, use of the state security apparatus, and tight restriction of the media. By the second half of the decade, however, Chun's government had lost considerable political capital. In the National Assembly elections of 1985, Chun's Democratic Justice Party was able to retain control of the legislature only through a system of proportionality that converted its scant 35 percent of the popular vote into 54 percent of the seats. Polls taken in 1986 showed that only 41 percent of people queried expressed confidence in political leaders and that less than 50 percent of respondents were satisfied with the kind of society in which they lived. Dissatisfaction with government control of the media was especially strong and was evident in newspaper editorials and a popular campaign to withhold payment of compulsory viewers' fees to the state-run television network.

The gradual reemergence of banned political figures, such as Kim Dae Jung and Kim Young Sam, began in 1985 and culminated in the full restoration of political rights to all former politicians in a political compromise between the ruling and opposition political parties that followed severe civil disturbances in June 1987. Subsequent events marked a watershed in South Korean politics. First, the government removed virtually all restrictions on the media. Next, in late 1987, the Constitution was revised—the first constitutional revision since 1960 that was drafted through a process of multiparty discussions. The 1987 revision promised substantial changes in the unequal power relationships among the three branches of government that had prevailed at least since the inception of the *yusin* constitution in 1972. Under the new fundamental law, the president lost the power to rule through emergency decrees and to dissolve the legislature. The National Assembly gained new rights to investigate state affairs, to hold longer annual sessions, and to approve Supreme Court appointments. These and other constitutional provisions pointed to more potential autonomy for the legislature, the court system, and for the constitutional review of legislation.

The presidential election of December 1987 placed a former army general, Roh Tae Woo of the ruling Democratic Justice Party, in the Blue House, or presidential mansion. A minority president, he won only 36 percent of the votes cast. Kim Young Sam and Kim Dae Jung, who together accounted for 54 percent of the votes, accused Roh's party of election fraud, while apologizing to the public for their failure to agree between themselves on a unified opposition candidacy. The charge of fraud on a scale great enough to have swung the election was undermined at the time by the fragmentary and anecdotal evidence presented and by the insistence of each of the two Kims that he was the one who would have prevailed in the absence of government misconduct. In 1990, however, the government admitted to one serious legal breach— the diversion of more than US$14 million dollars from the 1987 national budget to support Roh's election campaign. For some observers, it remained an open question whether other large-scale irregularities may have occurred, or what further steps the government might have taken to ensure victory had the two major opposition candidates been unified.

In the National Assembly elections held in April 1988, the ruling party lost a working majority for the first time in South Korea's history. The new balance of forces in the legislature made a reality of the separation of powers provided for in the new Constitution when opposition assembly members joined forces to reject President Roh's first appointment for chief justice of the Supreme Court in the summer of 1988. Through the rest of 1988 and 1989, additional signs of the new order were seen in the distribution of committee chairmanships among the ruling and opposition parties and in the process of compromise, as floor leaders of the four principal parties periodically met to negotiate working agendas for the legislature and its committees. As 1989 ended, Roh's party was engaged in secret negotiations with two of the three opposition parties to bring this process of compromise under firmer control.

As a result of these talks, Roh's party merged with Kim Young Sam's Reunification Democratic Party and Kim Chong-p'il's New Democratic Republican Party to create a new Democratic Liberal Party (DLP) in January 1990. Some observers likened the resulting coalition to Japan's Liberal Democratic Party. Each of the former opposition party leaders clearly hoped to become an important power broker within the ruling party and perhaps also to become the party's candidate for the 1992 presidential election.

In the short term, the formation of the DLP provided the president with a substantial majority in the National Assembly, while politically isolating his most uncompromising political opponent, Kim Dae Jung. Seen in longer-term perspective, the merger curtailed the broader processes of compromise and cooperation in the National Assembly that had included even Kim's Party for Peace and Democracy (PPD) in 1988 and 1989. It further put the new ruling party in the awkward position of having to pass important legislation in the absence of opposition politicians, who boycotted the legislature on several occasions during 1990. The merger also complicated factional politics within the ruling party.

Although politicians were permitted to change parties under the 1987 Constitution and related laws, Kim Dae Jung immediately labelled the move a "coup d'état against representative politics" and called, unsuccessfully, for new elections. A small number of legislators from Kim Young Sam's party also objected to the new super-party and eventually formed the small Democratic Party. Kim Dae Jung's isolated Party for Peace and Democracy spent much of 1990 and early 1991 fulminating against the DLP and attempting to embarrass the government politically by boycotting National Assembly sessions or attempting to resign. The disengagement of the PPD often seemed to leave it marginalized and unable to contribute to major legislation or even to influence issues in which it had an immediate political interest, such as the scheduling of small district local elections in March 1991. Awareness of the costs of intransigence may have prompted a more moderate approach in the second half of 1991. In private talks with President Roh in September, Kim Dae Jung successfully lobbied for several regional development projects in the Chŏlla region.

By mid-1991 the DLP coalition was beginning to show signs of strain, brought about by differences over questions such as the timing of the upcoming 1992 presidential and National Assembly elections and disagreement over how the party's presidential candidate would be chosen. On most such issues, Kim Chong-p'il and President Roh formed a mini-coalition within the party, opposed by Kim Young Sam and his followers. Competition for the party's presidential nomination reintensified after National Assembly elections in March 1992, in which the DLP won slightly less than 50 percent of the seats. The DLP was able to recover a bare majority by absorbing several members who had run as independents.

Kim Dae Jung's party encountered major defeats in local elections in March and June 1991. It subsequently absorbed small numbers of opposition lawmakers, becoming in turn the New Democratic Party and finally, under Kim's joint leadership with Yi Ki-t'aek, the Democratic Party (DP) in September. The DP, which included some members from outside the Chŏlla region, continued to fight the ruling DLP across a variety of issues, including tax and budget policy, hyperinflation in urban land prices, and corruption. Like the Kim Young Sam faction within the DLP, the DP opposed possible revision of the Constitution to create a parliamentary system of government. In National Assembly elections in March 1992, the DP won a respectable 31.1 percent of the seats.

Outside the world of the parties, other features of political life changed during the 1980s. Professional associations and interest groups, long under the domination of the state, began to strive for more autonomy. Farmers' associations—traditionally little more than mechanisms for communicating government policies—began to proliferate and to protest trade liberalization measures. Professional associations of university teachers, journalists, and lawyers also became increasingly outspoken on political issues. The major business conglomerates—*chaebŏl*—sought a greater role in economic policy formation. The voices of industrial associations were heard more clearly as the respective economic ministries began to gain influence within a less centralized state planning structure. At the fringes of politics, an extremist wing of the leftist student movement conducted sporadic violence through the 1980s. The violence peaked in dozens of arson or Molotov cocktail assaults against government offices, commercial establishments, police boxes, and United States diplomatic and cultural facilities in late 1988 and 1989.

South Korea's diplomacy during the 1980s, while remaining oriented toward the West, also aggressively pursued closer ties with China, the Soviet Union, and East European countries. Trade with these countries, obscured by Seoul's nonpublication of the relevant import-export statistics, continued to grow throughout the decade, and was matched by a variety of other contacts, culminating in the participation of the Soviet Union, China, and all the major East European countries in the 1988 Seoul Olympics. These efforts, which South Korea termed *pukpang chŏngch'aek,* meaning "Nordpolitik" or northern policy, were intended to diversify the country's global trade relations and to give Seoul greater leverage in its difficult relationship with the Democratic People's Republic of Korea (North Korea).

Seoul's northern policy alone would probably have accomplished little without the dramatic liberalizing reforms in East European countries, which made it possible for South Korea to establish diplomatic relations with all nations of Eastern Europe by the end of the 1980s. The opening of diplomatic relations with the Soviet Union in September 1990 followed a series of high-level bilateral meetings in 1989 and early 1990.

South Korea's two-way trade with communist countries increased by one-third in 1990 to reach an estimated US$5.6 billion. Increased trade relations with the Soviet Union followed closely on the heels of the 1988 Seoul Olympics, driven by Moscow's perception that South Korea could play an important role in the development of the Soviet Far East. As with other East European countries, South Korea's exports to the Soviet Union were heavily concentrated in electrical and electronic appliances. During 1990 and early 1991, news of bilateral exchanges, civil aviation agreements, and pending commercial deals between the *chaebŏl* and the Soviet Union filled the South Korean press. By the end of 1991, South Korea had paid or approved slightly more than half of a promised US$3 billion package of loans, commodity credits, and project assistance to the Soviet Union, and it was expected that Seoul's aid program would continue with the new Commonwealth of Independent States.

Trade with China, which began with quiet transactions in the late 1970s, was estimated to have reached US$1 billion in 1985 and more than US$5 billion in 1991. The importance of the Seoul-Beijing economic relationship was demonstrated in the establishment of trade offices with limited consular functions in the two capitals in October 1991 and a trade agreement two months later, in which South Korea and China exchanged most-favored-nation status. The political component in such trade remained prominent, as evidenced in Seoul's tolerance for sustained balance of payments deficits. In the case of trade with China, such deficits grew from US$1.2 billion in 1989 to a projected US$2 billion for 1991.

Probably because China remained more sensitive than the Soviet Union to North Korea's reactions, progress in moving toward diplomatic relations between Seoul and Beijing was slower than the moves establishing formal trade ties. In the mid-1980s, the two countries had increased quasi-diplomatic contacts to include a number of negotiations to resolve a series of sea and air incidents, and China permitted South Korea's attendance at international conferences and meetings of United Nations organizations in China. The two countries also participated jointly in a variety of athletic competitions and sports exchanges. In September 1990, China extended courtesy diplomatic status to South Korean athletic officials attending the Asian Games in Beijing; and by mutual agreement senior diplomats in the trade representative offices held formal diplomatic immunities and privileges under the Vienna Convention, reportedly performing consular as well as commercial duties. Beijing sent a vice foreign minister to the Seoul meeting of the United Nations Economic and Social Commission for Asia and the Pacific in April 1991; South Korean-Chinese discussions during the meeting provided the highest level official contact to that date between the two countries. In May 1991, when it became clear that China would no longer support its North Korean ally by vetoing South Korea's membership in the United Nations, some observers believed that the two countries had moved even closer to establishing formal diplomatic ties.

Over the past two decades, South Korea's relations with North Korea have been characterized by alternating periods of tension and dialogue. A joint communiqué issued by the two countries on July 4, 1972, agreed to continue discussions concerning political and military questions and confidence-building measures to be implemented through a North-South Coordinating Committee and Red Cross channels. Through the 1970s, however, further discussions stalled as each side reaffirmed its position in an effort to claim and retain the initiative and to deny legitimacy to the other side.

In early 1980, the two countries for the first time referred to each other by their official names and agreed to work toward prime ministers' talks. By the following year, negotiations stalled again after P'yŏngyang made a number of political demands on the Chun Doo Hwan government—including withdrawal of United States troops from South Korea—as a precondition for further talks and also sponsored an abortive attempt to have Chun assassinated by two Canadian gangsters. A second attempt—a bombing in October 1983—failed to kill the South Korean president but killed four cabinet ministers and thirteen other officials during a state visit to Rangoon, Burma. In 1984 Seoul rejected P'yŏngyang's proposals for three-way talks that would have included Washington but excluded South Korea from key discussions on military topics. Bilateral discussions during the same year concerning a joint Olympics team failed to achieve results in time for the Los Angeles Olympics in July.

After South Korean acceptance of North Korean rice, cement, and medicine for southern flood victims in September 1984, the two sides conducted talks and some exchanges on a range of issues for a sixteen-month period through early 1986. These discussions in the mid-1980s were sometimes acrimonious and frequently interrupted, each side presenting proposals, as one observer noted, that almost seemed intended to provoke rejection by the other or to play to the galleries of world opinion. In retrospect, however, it can be seen that the mid-1980s discussions were successful in establishing institutions for dialogue on both sides and in laying down multiple channels of contact and communication that continued to function through the early 1990s.

A series of talks to reunite families separated by national division and the war took dozens of Red Cross representatives and even more journalists from each side across the Demarcation Line during three visits in 1984. In September 1985, several dozen North Koreans and South Koreans met with separated family members, and a similar number of folk art performers from each side gave concerts in the two capitals.

In the area of economic cooperation, vice-ministerial level conferences met at P'anmunjŏm on a number of occasions during 1984 and 1985, exploring for the first time specific trade, transportation, and other joint projects. South Korean and North Korean legislators met twice in July 1985 to explore political issues. Bilateral discussions began in 1984 concerning a North Korean proposal to cohost the 1988 Seoul Olympic Games. After an interlude following the North Korean bombing of a South Korean airliner over the Andaman Sea in November 1987, Olympic talks continued through mid-1988, when they broke down in disagreement over the number of games to be hosted in P'yŏngyang.

The two Koreas continued to talk past each other concerning broader political issues during much of 1988 and 1989. President Roh's July 1988 proposal for freer contacts and expanded exchanges between the two Koreas and the eventual establishment of a Korean commonwealth was met with North Korean reiteration of Kim Il Sung's 1972 proposal for a transitional Democratic Confederal Republic of Korea. Meanwhile, Seoul began to disclose the existence of a quiet trade relationship between the two countries and in early 1989 allowed a major industrialist to travel to P'yŏngyang to discuss additional forms of economic cooperation. North Korea generally welcomed these steps but also continued to demand abrogation of South Korea's National Security Act, under which Seoul prosecuted several unauthorized South Korean travellers to North Korea.

An important breakthrough in relations between the two Koreas began in 1990, which saw the beginning of a series of prime ministerial talks. Held alternately in Seoul and P'yŏngyang, these garnered substantial publicity but little progress until mid-1991, when it became clear that Seoul had won China's support for its plan to have both Koreas simultaneously admitted to the United Nations. That event took place in September. During the fourth round of prime ministers' talks in P'yŏngyang in October, the two Koreas agreed to work on a nonaggression accord. This document, the Agreement on Reconciliation, Nonaggression, Exchange and Cooperation, was signed in Seoul on December 13, 1991. It took effect in mid-February 1992, at the time of the sixth round of prime ministerial talks in P'yŏngyang. In late December 1991, the two Koreas signed a separate agreement barring either side from having or using nuclear weapons.

Although the new agreement was in itself a landmark, observers noted that it was essentially a promissory note, in which the two Koreas pledged to cease negative actions toward each other and to continue to work toward resolution of several important issues. These issues included a declaration of nonaggression, a separate peace treaty, and measures to promote free travel and correspondence. The question of mutual inspection of nuclear facilities, which South Korea held to be of overriding importance, still was being discussed by working-level negotiators in late March 1992.

South Korea's relationship with the United States increasingly was focused on bilateral economic issues, spurred by a current account surplus that began in the mid-1980s and increasing United States pressures to open South Korean markets for agricultural and industrial products as well as telecommunications and finance services. These issues posed a problem not only for South Korean diplomacy, but also contributed to often tumultuous domestic criticism of Seoul whenever it appeared to show signs of weakness in negotiations with Washington.

An important issue in South Korean-United States relations during the 1980s was the joint security relationship. This relationship not only encompassed technical issues such as the size, composition, financial support, and legal status of United States forces stationed in South Korea, but also included a psychological dimension because of the popularly perceived role of the joint United States-Republic of Korea Combined Forces Command in the brutal killings of civilians in Kwangju in May 1980 during the coup d'état of Chun Doo Hwan. Facts surrounding the Kwangju incident—deliberately distorted under Chun Doo Hwan's martial law authorities—remained unclarified until the United States government issued a detailed statement on the subject in 1989. The statement, prepared in response to a South Korean National Assembly query, showed that the United States had not approved the coup and that the troops used in Kwangju in 1980 were not under operational control of the Combined Forces Command but had taken their orders from South Korean army authorities under General Chun.

The Korean War permanently enhanced the role of the military in South Korean society and politics as well as in the defense of the nation. Although South Korean military officers did not seek to intervene actively in politics under the rule of President Syngman Rhee (1948–60), the coups d'état of generals Park Chung Hee in 1961 and Chun Doo Hwan in 1980 demonstrated that some elements in the army believed that the nation's security demanded periodic corrections in the course of politics as well as preparedness against North Korea. The army's influence on society and politics during the 1980s continued to be seen in the laws that prevented the news media from freely covering political-military issues, mandatory student participation in the college-level Student Defense Corps, the custom of preferential placement of retired senior officers in the civil service and in state-run corporations, and in the frequent practice of punitively drafting students expelled for demonstrating against the government. At an even broader level, harsh discipline within the military probably provided the most significant political socialization for the more than 75 percent of South Korean males who served in the regular army, the reserves, or the Homeland Reserve Force.

Many of these practices were the subject of reforms outlined in the Ministry of National Defense White Paper in 1988, when the Roh administration abolished the Student Defense Corps and made efforts to standardize conscription practices and to provide some protection to the rights of recruits. As opinion surveys conducted in 1990 indicated, however, the public continued to support reforms that would improve conditions of service, eliminate preferential placement of retired military officers in the civil service, and move military installations away from populated areas. In the same year, the government promulgated additional regulations intended to reduce the more severe aspects of military life and protect the basic rights of recruits.

As the 1990s began, however, some observers believed that change in many military practices would come slowly. One of the most outspoken criticisms, voiced in a South Korean army publication in 1990, was by an army major general who charged that "a trend characterized by assaults, abusive language and torture prevails in the barracks." He called upon the army to reform itself to regain the trust of the public. The charges were given additional credence two months later when a former marine corps officer was convicted on charges of torturing a subordinate. In October 1990, the minister of national defense was relieved of his position after a former undercover agent of the Defense Security Command disclosed that the military counterintelligence organization had continued to maintain dossiers and conduct surveillance on some 1,300 prominent civilians, including politicians, clergymen, and journalists. The government pledged its efforts to return the Defense Security Command to its original function. The following year, however, the government admitted as true new media charges that the DSC was investigating several student activists.

Under President Chun Doo Hwan's force modernization program, military spending increased dramatically during the 1980s, exceeding estimated North Korean military spending during most of the decade and nearly doubling to US$10 billion a year by 1990. As a result of improvements in the defense industrial base that began in the mid-1970s, 70 percent of the equipment and weaponry used by the armed forces was being produced by domestic defense industries by the late 1980s.

At the end of the 1980s, the armed forces numbered about 650,000. The army continued to divide responsibilities among three commands. The First Army and the Third Army defended the country from the threat of North Korean attack in their positions along the Demilitarized Zone. The Second Army, positioned well south of Seoul, was charged with logistical and training responsibilities and managing the military reserve system. Some of the country's forward defense was also provided by the marine corps, which was charged with defense of the Han River estuary and five islands located close to North Korea. Specialized army units, such as the Capital Defense Command, defended the seat of government, while the Defense Security Command in Seoul was responsible for military counterintelligence and monitoring politics within and outside of the military.

The air force expanded its fighter squadrons during the 1980s, operating almost 700 combat, transport, and training aircraft under its three commands. In wartime, it assumed control of civilian airports and sections of major highways adapted for use as runways. During the 1980s, the air force added the F–16 and the Republic of Korea-United States coproduced F–5 to its fighter inventory. The smaller navy also modernized during the decade, focusing on antisubmarine warfare and the deployment of new, domestically produced submarines, frigates, fast-attack craft, and patrol boats.

In 1990 Roh moved the headquarters of the army and air force (with navy to follow) to Taejŏn in an effort to promote more effective interservice cooperation and more efficient command and control of the armed forces during wartime. In that same year, the armed forces began a three- to five-year plan to reorganize the command structure. Under the Armed Forces Organization Act passed in July and promulgated in October, the joint chiefs of staff system in use since the Korean War would be replaced with a more centralized Joint Chiefs of Staff headquarters in which operational control of the military forces would be centralized in the hands of the chairman of the Joint Chiefs of Staff. The new Joint Chiefs of Staff structure was designed to give Seoul a wartime command structure separate from the United States-Republic of Korea Combined Forces Command.

Fundamental to the restructuring was the separation of the operational and administrative functions immediately below the minister of national defense. Under the reorganization, which took effect on Armed Forces Day, October 1, 1990, the minister of national defense defined military policy, consolidated planning, and allocated resources. The newly invigorated Joint Chiefs of Staff had the authority to employ military units of all the military services, including task forces organization for joint operations. Unified operations, strategic planning, intelligence, and logistic directorates consolidated functions previously controlled by the separate services, and the service headquarters were reduced to maintenance, support, logistics, personnel, and administrative functions. The services were to have reduced intelligence organizations, but most of their intelligence assets were to be transferred to the newly created Joint Chiefs of Staff Defense Intelligence Command.

The 45,000 United States troops in Korea in 1990 included a small contingent at P'anmunjŏm with the United Nations Command, some 32,000 United States Army members under the Eighth Army, and 12,000 United States Air Force personnel under the Seventh Air Force. Military issues relating to the Combined Forces Command and other topics were discussed in annual bilateral Security Consultative Meetings and in other joint talks. In April 1990, the United States Department of Defense announced a program to shift gradually the United States military presence in South Korea to a smaller and more supportive role as international political conditions and strengthened South Korean defense capabilities permitted. As part of this program, the United States and South Korea also agreed to disband the United States-Republic of Korea Combined Field Army and to separate the Ground Component Command from the Combined Forces Command during the 1991–93 period. The two countries further agreed to appoint a South Korean senior officer as commander of the Ground Component Command and to replace the senior member of the United Nations Command to the Military Armistice Commission (MAC)—who had been a United States officer since the signing of the armistice in 1953—with a South Korean general. The appointment of a South Korean army major general to the senior MAC position was made in March 1991.

At the twenty-second Security Consultative Meeting in November 1990, Seoul agreed to increase its financial support for United States forces stationed in South Korea from US$2.7 billion in 1990 to US$2.8 billion the following year. This figure includes valuations for contributions in real estate, logistics support, discounted costs, and tax. Other issues discussed included Seoul's requests for eased United States restrictions on its exports of coproduced military hardware and improved terms for United States Foreign Military Sales to South Korea. Discussions also occurred concerning possible reductions in the Team Spirit exercise scheduled for 1991, in part because of United States military commitments in the Persian Gulf and in part because of budgetary reasons. The exercise was reduced in scale in 1990 and 1991 and cancelled in 1992

In January 1991, South Korea and the United States signed an amended Status of Forces Agreement (SOFA) governing the legal position of United States forces in South Korea. This agreement, the first major revision of the 1966 SOFA, expanded Seoul's criminal jurisdiction over United States personnel. Other provisions of the agreement concerned customs procedures and the disposition of property no longer used by United States forces in South Korea.

In 1991 President Bush announced that the United States would withdraw its nuclear weapons from the Korean Peninsula, and later in the year, in a statement accepted by United States authorities, President Roh Tae Woo declared that the country was free of such weapons. In 1989 the United States had stated that North Korea had a plutonium reprocessing facility theoretically capable of supporting nuclear weapons development. By mid-1991, United States, Japanese, and South Korean estimates held that North Korea was much closer to producing a nuclear weapon than previously realized. By the end of the year, North Korea, which had signed the Treaty on the Nonproliferation of Nuclear Weapons in 1985, still had not set a date for on-site inspections of nuclear facilities by the International Atomic Energy Agency. In the joint statement issued after the close of the twenty-third United States-Republic of Korea Security Consultative Meeting in November 1991, both countries declared that they had "agreed to postpone the second stage reduction of United States forces in Korea until such time as the North Korean threat and uncertainties of developing nuclear weapons have disappeared and the security in this region is fully guaranteed." This fact meant that withdrawals would stop once United States forces were drawn down to the 36,000 target for stage one. It was also confirmed at the meeting that the United States-Republic of Korea Combined Field Army would be dissolved and that a Korean general would be made Combined Forces Command ground component commander in 1992, further decreasing the United States profile.

March 31, 1992   William Shaw

Chapter 1. Historical Setting

Panghwasuru Pavilion, port of Suwŏn Castle

A SMALL COUNTRY, approximately the size of Britain, Korea is located on a peninsula that protrudes southward from the northeastern corner of the Asian continent. It is an old country, whose people evolved as one nation from the seventh century until 1945, when the country was divided by the United States and the Soviet Union at the end of World War II. The ensuing cold war created two Korean governments, one in the north known as the Democratic People's Republic of Korea (DPRK), and another in the south known as the Republic of Korea (ROK). The two Koreas engaged in a bitter war between 1950 and 1953 and remained divided as of 1990, even though the two governments began to talk to each other in 1971.

South Korea and North Korea took distinctly different paths of development after they were divided. By 1990 North Korea had emerged as a staunch communist society, while South Korea was evolving into a liberal democracy after many years of military dictatorship. The two societies, however, shared a common tradition and culture.

Origins of the Korean Nation

As is true of all countries, Korea's geography was a major factor in shaping its history; geography also influenced the manner in which the inhabitants of the peninsula emerged as a people sharing the common feeling of being Koreans (see Physical Environment, ch. 2). The Korean Peninsula protrudes southward from the northeastern corner of the Asian continent and is surrounded on three sides by large expanses of water. Although Japan is not far from the southern tip of this landmass, in ancient times events on the peninsula were affected far more by the civilizations and political developments on the contiguous Asian continent than by those in Japan (see fig. 1).

Because the Yalu and Tumen rivers have long been recognized as the border between Korea and China, it is easy to assume that these rivers have always constituted Korea's northern limits. But such was not the case in the ancient period. Neither of the rivers was considered to be sacrosanct by the ancient tribes that dotted the plains of Manchuria and the Korean Peninsula. Because the rivers freeze in the winter, large armies were able to traverse them with ease. Even when the rivers were not frozen, armies equipped with iron tools could easily build ships to cross them.

The Korean people trace their origins to the founding of the state of Chosŏn. Chosŏn rose on the banks of the Taedong River in the northwestern corner of the peninsula and prospered as a civilization possessing a code of law and a bronze culture. The Chosŏn people gradually extended their influence not only over other tribes in the vicinity, but also to the north, conquering most of the Liaodong Basin. However, the rising power of the feudal state of Yen in northern China (1122–225 B.C.) not only checked Chosŏn's growth, but eventually pushed it back to the territory south of the Ch'ŏngch'ŏn River, located midway between the Yalu and Taedong rivers. The Chinese had discovered iron by this time and used it extensively in farming and warfare; the Chosŏn people were not able to match them. Yen became established in the territory vacated by Chosŏn.

Meanwhile, much of what subsequently came to constitute China proper had been unified for the first time under Qin Shi Huangdi. Subsequently, Yen fell to the Qin state; the Qin Dynasty (221–207 B.C.) was in turn replaced by a new dynasty, the Han (206 B.C.–A.D. 220). In 195 B.C. a former officer of Yen took over the throne of Chosŏn by trickery, after which he and his descendants ruled the kingdom for eighty years; but in 109–108 B.C. China attacked Chosŏn and destroyed it as a political entity. The Han Chinese then ruled the territory north of the Han River as the Four Eastern Districts; the original territory of Chosŏn became Lolang (or Nangnang in Korean). (North Korean historians have argued that the Lolang District was located more to the northwest of the Korean Peninsula, perhaps near Beijing. This theory, however, has not been universally accepted.) Until the Han period, the Korean Peninsula had been a veritable Chinese colony. During some 400 years, Lolang, the core of the colony, had become a great center of Chinese art, philosophy, industry, and commerce. Many Chinese immigrated into the area; the influence of China extended beyond the territory it administered. The tribal states south of the Han River paid tribute to the Chinese and patterned much of their civilization and government after Chinese models.

The Three Kingdoms Period

The territory south of the Han River is relatively distant from the Asian continent; hence, the people living there were initially able to develop independently, without much involvement with events on the continent. The early settlers of this region gradually organized themselves into some seventy clan states that were in turn grouped into three tribal confederations known as Chinhan, Mahan, and Pyŏnhan. Chinhan was situated in the middle part of the peninsula, Mahan in the southwest, and Pyŏnhan in the southeast. Their economies were predominantly agricultural, and their level of development was such that they built reservoirs and irrigation facilities. These tribal states began to be affected by what was happening in the region north of the Han River around the first century B.C.

About the middle of the third century A.D., the Chinese threat began to serve as a unifying political force among the loose confederations of tribes in the southern part of the peninsula. Adopting the Chinese political system as a model, the tribes eventually merged into two kingdoms, thereby increasing their chances of survival against Chinese expansionism. The two kingdoms eventually came to play an important role in Korean history.

Geographic features of the southern parts of the land, in particular the configuration of mountain ranges, caused two kingdoms to emerge rather than one. In the central part of Korea, the main mountain range, the T'aebaek Range, runs north to south along the edge of the Sea of Japan, which lies off the east coast of the peninsula. Approximately three-fourths of the way down the peninsula, however, at roughly the thirty-seventh parallel, the mountain range veers southwest, dividing the peninsula almost in the middle. This extension, the Sobaek Range, proved politically significant; the tribes west of it were not shielded by any natural barriers against the Chinese-occupied portion of the peninsula, whereas those to the southeast were protected. Moreover, the presence of the mountains prevented the tribes in the two regions from establishing close contacts.

The tribal states in the southwest were the first to unite, calling their centralized kingdom Paekche. This process occurred in the mid-third century A.D., after the Chinese army of the Wei Dynasty (A.D. 220–65), which controlled Lolang, threatened the tribes in A.D. 245. The Silla Kingdom evolved in the southeast. Silla historians traced the kingdom's origin to 57 B.C., but contemporary historians regard King Naemul (A.D. 356–402) as having been the earliest ruler. Some of the tribal states in the area of the lower Naktong River, along the south central coast of the peninsula, did not join either of these kingdoms. Under the name Kaya, they formed a league of walled city-states that conducted extensive coastal trade and also maintained close ties with the tribal states in western Japan. Sandwiched between the more powerful Silla and Paekche, Kaya eventually was absorbed by its neighbors during the sixth century (see fig. 2).

The northern kingdom of Koguryŏ emerged from among the indigenous people along the banks of the Yalu River. The Han

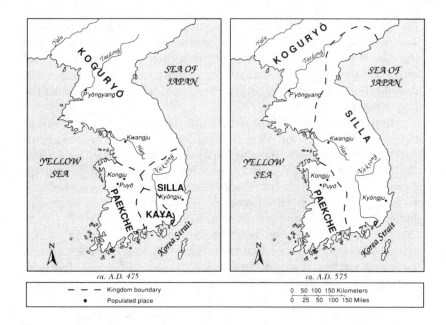

ca. A.D. 475   ca. A.D. 575

— — — — Kingdom boundary
• Populated place

0 50 100 150 Kilometers
0 25 50 100 150 Miles

Figure 2. Korea During the Three Kingdoms Period, Fifth to Sixth Centuries A.D.

Chinese seized the area in 108 B.C., but from the beginning Chinese rulers confronted many uprisings against their rule. Starting from a point along the Hun River (a tributary of the Yalu), the rebels expanded their activities to the north, south, and southeast, increasingly menacing Chinese authority. By A.D. 53 Koguryŏ had coalesced into an independent centralized kingdom; the subsequent fall of the Han Dynasty and ensuing political divisions in China enabled Koguryŏ to consolidate and extend its power. Despite repeated attacks by Chinese and other opposition forces, by 391 the kingdom's rulers had achieved undisputed control of all of Manchuria east of the Liao River as well as of the northern and central regions of the Korean Peninsula. Koguryŏ's best-known ruler, King Kwanggaet'o—whose name literally means "broad expander of territory"—lived to be only thirty-nine years of age, but reigned twenty-one years, from 391 to 412. During that period, Kwanggaet'o conquered 65 walled cities and 1,400 villages, in addition to aiding Silla when it was attacked by the Japanese. His accomplishments are recorded on a monument erected in 414 in southern Manchuria. Koguryŏ moved its capital to P'yŏngyang in 427 and ruled the territory north of the Han River. But Koguryŏ's

6

expansion caused it to come into conflict with the Sui Dynasty of China (581–617) in the west and Silla, which was beginning to expand northward, in the south.

Although Koguryŏ had been strong enough to repulse the forces of the Sui Dynasty, combined attacks by Silla and the Tang Dynasty of China (618–907) proved too formidable. Koguryŏ's ally in the southwest, Paekche, fell before Tang and Silla in 660; the victorious allies continued their assault on Koguryŏ for the next eight years and eventually vanquished the weary kingdom, which had been suffering from a series of famines and internal strife.

Silla thus unified Korea in 668, but the kingdom's reliance on China's Tang Dynasty had its price. Eventually Silla had to forcibly resist the imposition of Chinese rule over the entire peninsula, which Silla's rulers did, but their strength did not extend beyond the Taedong River. Much of the former Koguryŏ territory was given up to the Chinese and to other tribal states. It remained for later dynasties to push the border northward to the Yalu and Tumen rivers.

The Evolution of Korean Society

After the Three Kingdoms period, Korea witnessed the rise and fall of three dynasties—unified Silla (668–935), Koryŏ (918–1392), and Chosŏn (1392–1910). Each of these dynasties was marked by initial periods of consolidation, the flourishing of civilization, and eventual decline.

Silla

The first 215 years of the Silla Dynasty were marked by the establishment of new political, legal, and education institutions of considerable vigor. Domestic and foreign trade (with Tang China and Japan) prospered. Scholarship in Confucian learning, mathematics, astronomy, and medicine also flourished. Buddhism, introduced to the peninsula in A.D. 372, reached its zenith (see Religion, ch. 2).

Silla began to decline, however, in the latter part of the eighth century when rebellions began to shake its foundations. By the latter half of the ninth century, two rivals had emerged. The chaotic situation eventually led to the emergence of a new Koryŏ Dynasty in 918 under a former officer, Wang Kŏn.

Koryŏ

The founder of Koryŏ and his heirs consolidated control over the peninsula and strengthened its political and economic foundations by more closely following the bureaucratic and land-grant systems of Tang China. The rise of the Kitan Liao tribe in the north, however, threatened the new dynasty. The Liao invaded in 1010; Koryŏ was engulfed in devastating wars for a decade. After peace was restored, Koryŏ's inhabitants witnessed nearly a century of thriving commercial, intellectual, and artistic activities parallel to those taking place under the Song Dynasty (960–1279) in China. The Koryŏ leaders actively sought to imitate the Song's advanced culture and technology. In turn, the Song looked upon Koryŏ as a potential ally against the tribal invaders to whom it had been forced to abandon northern China in 1127. Stimulated by the rise of printing in Song China, Koryŏ also made great headway in printing and publication, leading to the invention of movable metal type in 1234, two centuries before the introduction of movable type in Europe.

By the twelfth century, Koryŏ was plagued by internal and external problems. Power struggles and avariciousness among the ruling classes led to revolts by their subjects. The situation was aggravated by the rise in the north of the Mongols, who launched a massive invasion in 1231. The Koryŏ armies put up fierce resistance but were no match for the highly organized mounted troops from the north, whose forces swept most of the Eurasian continent during this period.

The Mongol Empire under Khubilai Khan enlisted Koryŏ in its expeditions against Japan, mustering thousands of Korean men and ships for ill-fated invasions in 1274 and 1281. In each instance, seasonal typhoons shattered the Mongol-Koryŏ fleets, giving rise to the myth of kamikaze, or the "divine wind." Korea, in the meantime, was completely under Mongol domination. Koryŏ kings married Mongol princesses. Only in the early fourteenth century, when the Mongol Empire began to disintegrate and the Ming Dynasty (1368–1644)—founded by a former Chinese peasant—pushed the Mongols back to the north, did Koryŏ regain its independence. In 1359 and 1361, however, Koryŏ suffered invasions by a large number of Chinese rebel armies, known as the Red Banner Bandits, who sacked and burned the capital at Kaesong, just north of the mouth of the Han River. The country was left in ruins.

As the Mongols retreated to the north and the Ming established a garrison in the northeastern part of the Korean Peninsula, the Koryŏ court was torn between pro-Ming and pro-Mongol factions. General Yi Sŏng-gye, who had been sent to attack the Ming forces in the Liaodong region of Manchuria, revolted at the Yalu and turned his army against his own capital, seizing it with ease. Yi took the throne in 1392, founding Korea's most enduring dynasty. The new state was named Chosŏn, the same name used by the first Korean kingdom fifteen centuries earlier, although the later entity

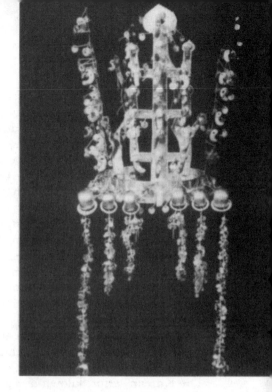

Fifth- or sixth-century gold crown excavated from a Silla Dynasty tomb Courtesy Embassy of the Republic of Korea, Washington

usually has been called simply the Chosŏn Dynasty or the Yi Dynasty. The capital of Chosŏn was at Seoul.

The Chosŏn Dynasty

The Koryŏ Dynasty had suffered from a number of internal problems; Yi and his followers implemented drastic reforms to place the new dynasty on firmer ground. One of these problems revolved around the deterioration of land administration, a basic issue in a predominantly agrarian society. Contrary to the law specifying public (governmental) ownership of land, powerful clans and Buddhist temples had acquired a sizable proportion of farmland. By exacting a disproportionate share of crops in the form of rents, the "landlords" were causing economic destitution and social discontent among the peasants. By illicitly removing the farms from tax rolls, these clans and temples reduced the government's income, thus straining the treasury. Yi had sided with reformists even before he took power, hence it was natural for him to rectify past inequities after ascending to the throne.

The reform of the land system, however, had direct repercussions on the practice of Buddhism because Buddhist temples and monks had been among those exacerbating the land problem. The economic influence of the temples was eliminated when they lost vast lands. The rectification went beyond economic reform, however, because the dominant forces in the new dynasty were

9

devout Confucianists who regarded Buddhism as a false creed. The fact that Buddhist monks had wielded a strong influence in politics, the economy, and society during the latter part of the Koryŏ Dynasty—and that many of them had been corrupted by power and money—strengthened the opposition to Buddhism. Accordingly, the new dynasty launched a sweeping attack on Buddhism and its institutions, an attack that had profound and enduring effects on the character of civilization on the peninsula.

Many of the outstanding temples were permitted to remain intact; indeed, a few Chosŏn monarchs were devout Buddhists. Nevertheless, Buddhism exerted little influence over the religious life of Korea under the Chosŏn Dynasty; nor did any organized religion replace it. Although many people adhered to shamanism, geomancy, fortunetelling, and superstitions, Korea effectively became a secular society.

The Chosŏn Dynasty had an auspicious beginning. During the reign of the fourth monarch, King Sejong (1418–50), a Buddhist, enormous strides were made in the arts, science, and technology. The Korean script, known as *han'gŭl* (see Glossary), which eventually came into common usage in the twentieth century, was developed by scholars at that time.

After Sejong, however, the dynasty fell into the hands of lesser men, and in the late fifteenth century the country began a long decline. Succession to the throne often caused long and bitter struggles, particularly when a ruler did not leave behind an heir who had reached the age of majority. Members of the Confucian-educated, scholar-official elite *yangban* (see Glossary) class quarreled over minor points of Confucian ritual and etiquette, especially the proper period of mourning upon the death of a royal personage. Factional groups began vying for power, frequently going to the extreme of exterminating the members of defeated factions. The civil service examination became a sham, and corruption ran rampant. Royal relatives and members of powerful factions increased their landholdings, which became exempt from taxes and thereby reduced the dynasty's sources of revenue. The farmers suffered more and more from tax burdens and other extractions imposed by greedy officials and landlords. In short, the country was not being effectively governed. To make matters worse, Japanese attacks in 1592 and 1597 and Manchu assaults in 1627 and 1636 ravaged the country's economy and turned much of the farmland to waste for a long period thereafter.

The resulting social and economic depression of the seventeenth and eighteenth centuries fostered the rise of a new intellectual movement advocating the practical use of human knowledge. Pioneered by a Confucian scholar named Yi Su-kwang, the new thought—soon to be called Sirhak (practical learning)—was partly inspired by the firsthand knowledge of occidental sciences that Yi Su-kwang had acquired while on official visits to Beijing. As historian Ki-baik Lee has noted, Sirhak thought encompassed a variety of intellectual activities and several diverse viewpoints. These included proposals for refinement of the traditional administrative and land systems, advocacy of commercial and manufacturing activity, and a renewed interest in Korean history and language. Brought to maturity in the late eighteenth century by Chǒng Yag-yong, the Sirhak Movement was supported by a group of discontented scholars, petty officials, former bureaucrats, and commoners.

The Sirhak Movement found itself in direct confrontation with the dominant trend in neo-Confucian thought, which stressed the metaphysical and abstract teachings of the renowned Chinese philosopher Zhu Xi (see Traditional Social Structure, ch. 2). Neither the efforts of such wise and able kings as Yǒngjo (1725–75) and Chǒngjo (1776–1800), nor those of the Sirhak scholars, were able to reverse the trend against empirical studies and good government.

Western ideas, including Christianity, reached Korea through China in the seventeenth century. By 1785, however, the government had become incensed over the rejection of ancestor worship by Roman Catholic missionaries, and it banned all forms of Western learning. Western ships began to approach Korean shores after 1801, seeking trade and other contacts, but the government rejected all overtures from abroad. When news of the Opium War in China (1839–42) reached Korea, the dynasty had all the more reason to shut the doors tightly against Western "barbarians." In the meantime, the Chosǒn Dynasty suffered from a series of natural calamities including floods, famines, and epidemics, as well as large-scale revolts of the masses in the northwest (1811–12) and southwest (1862 and 1894–95).

The expansion of Western powers in East Asia in the nineteenth century significantly altered the established order, in which Korea had been dominated by China. China under the Qing Dynasty (1644–1911) was in decline; its power waned rapidly under the concerted attacks of such Western nations as France, Britain, and Russia. Stimulated by these events, Japan proceeded to modernize after having been forced to open its ports by Commodore Matthew C. Perry of the United States Navy in 1853–54. Korea, however, remained dormant, having closed itself to all outside contacts in the early eighteenth century.

The Japanese were the first foreign power in recent history to succeed in penetrating Korea's isolation. After a warlike Japanese

11

provocation against Korea in 1875 (when China failed to come to Korea's aid), the Japanese forced an unequal treaty on Korea in February 1876. The treaty gave Japanese nationals extraterritorial rights and opened up three Korean ports to Japanese trade. In retaliation, China sought to counter Japan by extending Korea's external relations and playing off one Western power against another. Accordingly, Korea signed treaties with the United States, Britain, Italy, Russia, and other countries within the decade after the one with Japan.

Internally, the Korean court split into rival pro-Chinese, pro-Japanese, and pro-Russian factions, the latter two having more reformist and modernizing orientations. In 1895 the Japanese minister to Korea masterminded the assassination of the Korean queen, who with her clan had opposed reform-oriented, Japanese-supported leaders. The Korean king, however, rejected not only Japan but also the various reform measures and turned for support to one of Japan's adversaries—Russia. The king fled to the Russian legation in Seoul to avoid possible Japanese plots against him and conducted the nation's business from there. The Japanese blunder had served the Russians well.

In the meantime, under the leadership of Sŏ Chae-p'il, who had exiled himself to the United States after participating in an unsuccessful palace coup in 1884, a massive campaign was launched to advocate Korean independence from foreign influence and controls. As well as supporting Korean independence, Sŏ also advocated reform in Korea's politics and customs in line with Western practices. Upon his return to Korea in 1896, Sŏ published *Tongnip simmun* (The Independent), the first newspaper to use the *hangŭl* writing system and the vernacular language, which attracted an ever-growing audience (see The Korean Language, ch. 2). He also organized the Independence Club to introduce Korea's elite to Western ideas and practices. Under his impetus and the influence of education provided by Protestant mission schools, hundreds of young men held mass meetings on the streets and plazas demanding democratic reforms and an end to Russian and Japanese domination. But the conservative forces proved to be too deeply entrenched for the progressive reformers, who trashed the paper's offices. The reformers, including Syngman Rhee, then a student leader, were jailed. Sŏ was compelled to return to the United States in 1898, and under one pretext or another the government suppressed both the reform movement and its newspaper.

The revolt of 1894–95, known as the Tonghak Rebellion, had international repercussions. Like the Taiping rebels in China thirty years earlier, the Tonghak (see Glossary) participants were fired

Statue of King Sejong (1418–50), Tŏksu Palace, Seoul
Courtesy Oren Hadar

by religious fervor as well as by indignation about the corrupt and oppressive government. The rebellion spread from the southwest to the central region of the peninsula, menacing Seoul. The Korean court apparently felt unable to cope with the rebels and invited China to send troops to quell the rebellion. This move gave Japan a pretext to dispatch troops to Korea. The two countries soon engaged in the First Sino-Japanese War (1894–95), which accelerated the demise of the Qing Dynasty in China.

The victorious Japanese established their hegemony over Korea via the Treaty of Shimonoseki (1895) and dictated to the Korean government a wide-ranging series of measures to prevent further domestic disturbances. In response, the government promulgated various reforms, including the abolition of class distinctions, the liberation of slaves, the abolition of the ritualistic civil service examination system, and the adoption of a new tax system.

Russian influence had been on the rise in East Asia, in direct conflict with the Japanese desire for expansion. In alliance with France and Germany, Russia had just forced Japan to return the Liaodong Peninsula to China (which Japan had seized during the First Sino-Japanese War) and then promptly leased the territory from China. The secret Sino-Russian treaty signed in 1896 also gave the Russians the right to build and operate the Chinese Eastern Railway across northern Manchuria, which served as a link in the Russian Trans-Siberian Railway to Vladivostok. Russia proceeded to acquire numerous concessions over Korea's forests and mines.

The strategic rivalry between Russia and Japan exploded in the Russo-Japanese War of 1904–5, won by Japan. Under the peace treaty signed in September 1905, Russia acknowledged Japan's "paramount political, military, and economic interest" in Korea. A separate agreement signed in secret between the United States and Japan at this time subsequently aroused anti-American sentiment among Koreans. The Taft-Katsura Agreement was cynical by modern standards, exchanging what amounted to a lack of interest and military capability in Korea on the part of the United States (Japan was given a free hand in Korea) for a lack of interest or capability in the Philippines on the part of Japan (Japanese imperialism was diverted from the Philippines). Given the diplomatic conventions of the times, however, the agreement was a much weaker endorsement of the Japanese presence in Korea than either the Russo-Japanese peace treaty or a separate Anglo-Japanese accord. Two months later, Korea was obliged to become a Japanese protectorate. Thereafter, a large number of Koreans organized themselves in education and reform movements, but by then Japanese dominance in Korea was a reality. Japan annexed Korea as a colony on August 22, 1910.

Characteristics of Society under the Dynasties

Cultural Expression

Koreans, like the other East Asian peoples, have a highly developed aesthetic sense and over the centuries have created a great number of paintings, sculptures, and handicrafts of extraordinary beauty. Among the very earliest are the paintings found on the walls of tombs of the Koguryŏ Kingdom (located in what is now North Korea) and around the China-North Korea border area. These paintings are colorful representations of birds, animals, and human figures that possess remarkable vitality and animation. Similar, though less spectacular, tombs are found around the old capitals of the kingdoms of Paekche and Silla in present-day South Korea. A number of gold objects, including a gold crown of great delicacy and sophistication dating from the Three Kingdoms period, have been found in South Korea.

Buddhism was the dominant artistic influence during the later Three Kingdoms period and the Silla and Koryŏ dynasties. Themes and motifs that had originated in India passed to Korea through Central Asia and China. A number of bronze images of Buddha and the Bodhisattvas were made during the sixth, seventh, and eighth centuries. The images are not mere copies of Indian or north Chinese models, but possess a distinctly ''Korean'' spirit that one critic has described as ''as indifference to sophistication and artificiality and a predisposition toward nature.'' The striking stone Buddha found in the Sŏkkuram Grotto, a cave temple located near Kyŏngju in North Kyŏngsang Province, was carved during the Silla Dynasty and is considered to be the finest of Korean stone carvings. During the centuries of Buddhism's ascendancy, a large number of stone pagodas and temples were built, one of the most famous being the Pulguksa Temple near Kŏyngju.

The Koryŏ Dynasty is best remembered for its celadons, or bluish-green porcelains, considered by many specialists to be the best in the world, surpassing even the Chinese porcelains upon which they were originally modeled. Many have intricate designs of birds, flowers, and other figures rendered in light and dark-colored clay on the blue-green background; some are delicately formed into the shapes of flowers, animals, and objects. Chosŏn Dynasty pottery tended to be simpler and more rustic and had a great influence on the development of Japanese artistic appreciation from the late sixteenth century on. After the attempted Japanese invasions of Korea in the 1590s, Korean potters were taken back to Japan.

During the Chosŏn Dynasty, Buddhism was no longer a source of artistic inspiration. The art, music, and literature of the *yangban* were deeply influenced by Chinese models, yet exhibited a distinctively Korean style. Korean scholar-officials cultivated their skills in the arts of Confucian culture—Chinese poetry, calligraphy, and landscape painting. Poetry was considered to be the most important of these arts; men who lacked poetic ability could not pass the civil service examinations. Scholars were expected to refine their skill in using the brush both in calligraphy, the ornamental writing of Chinese characters that was considered an art in itself, and in landscape painting, which borrowed Chinese themes and styles. However, scholarly calligraphers and landscape painters were considered amateurs. Professional artists were members of the *chungin* (see Glossary) class and were of low status, not only because their painting tended to diverge from the style favored by the upper class but because it was too realistic. Particularly among the *yangban,* Chinese dominance of cultural expression was assured by the fact that Korean intellectual discourse was largely dependent on Chinese loanwords. Scholars preferred to write in Chinese rather than in native Korean script.

One uniquely Korean style of painting that developed during this period was found in the usually anonymous folk-paintings (*minhwa*), which depicted the daily life of the common people and used genuine Korean rather than idealized or Chinese settings. Other folk paintings had shamanistic themes and frequently depicted hermits and mountain deities.

A distinctive position in traditional Korean literature is occupied by a type of poem known as the *sijo*—a poetic form that began to develop in the twelfth century. It is composed of three couplets and characterized by great simplicity and expressiveness:

> My body is mortal, commonly mortal.
> My bones end in dust, soul or no soul.
> My lord owns my heart, though, and that cannot
> change.

This poem is by Chŏng Mong-ju (1337–92), a Koryŏ Dynasty loyalist who was assassinated at the foundation of the Yi Dynasty. The poet refers to his political choice not to side with the new government.

Many of these poems reveal a sensitivity to the beauties of nature, delight in life's pleasures, and a tendency toward philosophical contemplation that together produce a sense of serenity and, sometimes, loneliness. Frequently the poems reveal a preoccupation with purity, symbolized by whiteness:

> Do not enter, snowy heron, in the valley where the
> crows are quarreling.
> Such angry crows are envious of your whiteness,
> And I fear that they will soil the body you have
> washed in the pure stream.

The development of a Korean alphabet (today known as *han'gŭl*) in the fifteenth century gave rise to a vernacular, or popular, literature. Although the native alphabet was looked down upon by the *yangban* elite, historical works, poetry, travelogues, biographies, and fiction written in a mixed script of Chinese characters and *han'gŭl* were widely circulated. Some vernacular literature had what could be interpreted as social protest themes. Probably the earliest of these was *The Tale of Hong Kil-tong* by Hŏ Kyun. The protagonist, Hong Kil-tong, was the son of a nobleman and his concubine; his ambition to become a great official was frustrated because of his mother's lowly background. He became a Robin Hood figure, stole from the rich to give to the poor, and eventually left Korea in order to establish a small kingdom in the south. Other vernacular writers included Kim Man-jung, who wrote *The Nine Cloud Dream*, which dealt with Buddhist themes of karma and destiny, and *The Story of Lady Sa*. Pak Chi-wŏn's *Tale of a Yangban* gave a realistic account of social life in eighteenth-century Korea. In 1980 Korean scholars discovered a nineteenth-century vernacular novel that told of the complicated relationships among members of four *yangban* and commoner clans over five generations in a very detailed and realistic manner. At 235 volumes, this work is one of the longest novels ever written.

P'ansori combine music and literary expression in ballad-form stories, which are both recited and sung by a performer accompanied by a drummer who sets the rhythms—a kind of ''one-man opera'' in the words of one observer. *P'ansori* usually are inspired by myths or folk tales and have Confucian, Buddhist, or folkloric themes. In the 1970s and 1980s, dissident students often drew on the techniques of traditional folk drama to satirize contemporary politics.

Korean folk tales are closely tied to religious traditions and usually have shamanistic, Buddhist, or Confucian themes. While Confucian tales tend to be moralistic and didactic, Buddhist and shamanistic tales are highly imaginative and colorful, depicting the relationships among spirits, ghosts, gods, and men in many different and often humorous ways.

Korean Identity

That the Korean kingdoms were strongly affected by Chinese civilization and its institutions was not surprising. Not only were the Chinese far more numerous and often more powerful militarily than the Koreans, but they also had a more advanced technology and culture. Chinese supremacy in these realms was acknowledged not only by the Koreans, who were militarily inferior, but also by those who were powerful enough to conquer China, such as the Kitan Liao, who ruled parts of northern China, Manchuria, and Mongolia between 907 and 1127; the Mongols who ruled China from 1279 to 1368; the Jurchen tribes, who later seized northern Manchuria; and the Manchus, who ruled China between 1644 and 1911. The adoption of Chinese culture was more than simply an expression of submission to China, it also was the indispensable condition of being civilized in the East Asian context. This situation continued until the inroads of Western civilization substantially altered the political and cultural map of Asia in the latter part of the nineteenth century.

The adoption of Chinese culture and institutions by the Korean kingdoms, however, did not obliterate the identity of the Korean people. Koguryŏ had risen against the Chinese conquerors, and Silla had stubbornly resisted Chinese attempts to turn it into a colony. While Silla and subsequent dynasties were obliged to pay tribute to the various Chinese, Mongol, and Jurchen dynasties, and although Korea was subjected to direct overlordship by the Mongols for a century, the Korean kingdoms were able to survive as independent entities, enabling their citizens to maintain an identity as a separate people.

Further contributing to the maintenance of this identity was the Korean language, which linguists generally agree belongs to the Altaic language family of Inner Asia. There is no doubt that the indigenous language was deeply affected by the country's long contact with China. Not only did its written form rely on Chinese characters until the fifteenth century, but about half of its vocabulary was of Chinese origin. Nevertheless, the language is very different from Chinese in its lexicon, phonology, and grammar. Although at one time the ruling classes were set apart from the rest of the population by their knowledge of Chinese characters and their ability to use Chinese in its written form, since the unification of the peninsula by the Silla Dynasty all Koreans have shared the same spoken language.

Political and Social Institutions

Despite the fact that Korea would undergo numerous reforms, palace coups, and two dynastic changes after the Silla period, many of the political and social systems and practices instituted during the Silla Dynasty persisted until the nineteenth century. Their Chinese inspiration, of course, had much to do with the durability of these systems. One lasting principle was that of centralized rule. From the time of the Koguryŏ, Paekche, and Silla states of the Three Kingdoms period, royal houses always governed their domains directly, without granting autonomous powers to local administrators. The effectiveness of the central government varied from dynasty to dynasty and from period to period, but the principle of centralization—involving a system of provinces, districts, towns, and villages—was never modified.

Another feature that endured for centuries was the existence of a stratified social system characterized by a clear distinction between the rulers and the ruled. Under the Silla Dynasty, society was rigidly organized into a hereditary caste system. The Koryŏ Dynasty, which succeeded Silla, instituted a system of social classes according to which the rest of the population was subordinate to an elite composed of scholar-officials. By passing the higher civil service examination and becoming a government official a commoner could become a member of the elite, but since examinations presupposed both the time and wealth for education, upward mobility was not the rule. This system continued during the Chosŏn Dynasty. The strength of the aristocratic tradition may have been one factor contributing to the relative weakness of the Korean monarchy, in which the king usually presided over a council of senior officials as primus inter pares, rather than governing as absolute ruler.

During the Chosŏn Dynasty, family and lineage groups came to occupy tremendous importance. Because one's social and political status in society was largely determined by birth and lineage, it was only natural that a great deal of emphasis was placed on family. Each family maintained a genealogical table with meticulous care. Only male offspring could prolong the family, and clan lines and theirs were the only names registered in the genealogical tables; therefore, the birth of a son was regarded as an occasion of great joy. The Confucian stress on the family reinforced the importance Koreans attached to the family.

The Confucian principle of Five Relationships (see Glossary) governing social behavior became the norm of Korean society. Righteousness toward the sovereign, filial piety, deference to older and superior persons, and benevolence to the younger and inferior became inviolable rules of conduct. Transgressors of these rules were regarded as uncultured beings unfit to be members of society. Whether in the family or society at large, people in positions of authority or occupying superior status commanded respect.

Still another enduring feature of traditional society under the Chosŏn Dynasty was the dominance of the *yangban* class. The *yangban* not only held power but also controlled the national wealth in the form of land. The court permitted the *yangban* to collect revenues on the land as remuneration for their services. Because much commercial activity was related to tributary missions to China or to government procurements, the wealth of the merchants often was dependent upon the discretion of the *yangban*.

Finally, because under the Chosŏn Dynasty one could enter into the scholar-official elite by passing examinations based on Confucian writings and penmanship, the entire society stressed classical education. The arts of war were accorded a lesser status, even though the founders of both the Koryŏ and Chosŏn dynasties were generals and despite the fact that the country had suffered from numerous foreign invasions.

Korea under Japanese Rule

Korea underwent drastic changes under Japanese rule. Even before the country was formally annexed by Japan in 1910, the Japanese caused the last ruling monarch, King Kojong, to abdicate the throne in 1907 in favor of his feeble son, who was soon married off to a Japanese woman and given a Japanese peerage. Japan then governed Korea under a residency general and subsequently under a governor general directly subordinate to Japanese prime ministers. All of the governor generals were high-ranking Japanese military officers.

In theory the Koreans, as subjects of the Japanese emperor, enjoyed the same status as the Japanese; but in fact the Japanese government treated the Koreans as a conquered people. Until 1921 they were not allowed to publish their own newspapers or to organize political or intellectual groups.

Nationalist sentiments gave rise to a Korean student demonstration in Japan, and on March 1, 1919, to a Proclamation of Independence by a small group of leaders in Seoul. With the consolidation of what became known as the March First Movement, street demonstrations led by Christian and Ch'ŏndogyo (a movement that evolved from Tonghak) groups erupted throughout the country to protest Japanese rule.

Kyŏngbok Palace, Seoul
Courtesy Oren Hadar

In the wake of the protest, Japan granted considerable latitude to Korea. As historians have noted, the ensuing intellectual and social ferment of the 1920s marked a seminal period in modern Korean history. Many developments of the period, including the organization of labor unions and other social and economic movements, had continuing influence into the postliberation period. In the 1930s, however, the ascendancy of the military in Japanese politics reversed the change. Particularly after 1937, when Japan launched the Second Sino-Japanese War (1937–45) against China, the colonial government decided on a policy of mobilizing the entire country for the cause of the war. Not only was the economy reorganized onto a war footing, but the Koreans were to be totally assimilated as Japanese. The government also began to enlist Korean youths in the Japanese army as volunteers in 1938 and as conscripts in 1943. Worship at Shinto shrines became mandatory, and every attempt at preserving Korean identity was discouraged.

The Korean economy also underwent significant change. Japan's initial colonial policy was to increase agricultural production in Korea to meet Japan's growing need for rice. Japan had also begun to build large-scale industries in Korea in the 1930s as part of the empire-wide program of economic self-sufficiency and war preparation. Between 1939 and 1941, the manufacturing sector represented 29 percent of Korea's total economic production. The primary industries—agriculture, fishing, and forestry—occupied only 49.6 percent of total economic production during that period, in contrast to having provided 84.6 percent of total production between 1910 and 1912.

The economic development taking place under Japanese rule, however, brought little benefit to the Koreans. Virtually all industries were owned either by Japan-based corporations or by Japanese corporations in Korea (see The Japanese Role in Korea's Economic Development, ch. 3). As of 1942, Korean capital constituted only 1.5 percent of the total capital invested in Korean industries. Korean entrepreneurs were charged interest rates 25 percent higher than their Japanese counterparts, so it was difficult for Korean enterprises to emerge. More and more farmland was taken over by the Japanese, and an increasing proportion of Korean farmers either became sharecroppers or migrated to Japan or Manchuria. As greater quantities of Korean rice were exported to Japan, per capita consumption of rice among the Koreans declined; between 1932 and 1936, per capita consumption of rice declined to half the level consumed between 1912 and 1916. Although the government imported coarse grains from Manchuria to augment the Korean food supply, per capita consumption of food grains in 1944 was 35 percent below that of 1912 to 1916.

Under Japanese rule, intellectual influences different from traditional Buddhist, Confucianist, and shamanistic beliefs flooded the country. Western-style painting was introduced, and literary trends, even among writers who emphasized themes of social protest and national independence, tended to follow Japanese and European models, particularly those developed during the late nineteenth and early twentieth centuries. The works of Russian, German, French, British, American, and Japanese authors were read by the more educated Koreans, and Korean writers increasingly adopted Western ideas and literary forms. Social and political themes were prominent. *Tears of Blood,* the first of the "new novels," published by Yi In-jik in serial form in a magazine in 1906, stressed the need for social reform and cultural enlightenment, following Western and Japanese models. Yi Kwang-su's *The Heartless,* published in 1917, stressed the need for mass education, Western science, and the repudiation of the old family and social system. Ch'ae Mansik's *Ready Made Life,* published in 1934, protested the injustices of colonial society.

In the 1920s and 1930s, socialist ideas began to influence the development of literature. In 1925 left-wing artists, rejecting the romanticism of many contemporary writers, established the Korean

Proletarian Artists' Federation, which continued until it was suppressed by Japanese authorities in 1935. One of the best representatives of this group was Yi Ki-yŏng, whose 1936 novel *Home* tells of the misery of villagers under Japanese rule and the efforts of the protagonist, a student, to organize them. Poets during the colonial period included Yi Sang-hwa, Kim So-wŏl, and Han Yong-un. But the beginning of the Second Sino-Japanese War marked a period of unprecedented repression in the cultural sphere by Japanese authorities, which continued until Korea's liberation in 1945.

From the late 1930s until 1945, the colonial government pursued a policy of assimilation whose primary goal was to force the Koreans to speak Japanese and to consider themselves Japanese subjects. In 1937 the Japanese governor general ordered that all instruction in Korean schools be in Japanese and that students not be allowed to speak Korean either inside or outside of school. In 1939 another decree "encouraged" Koreans to adopt Japanese names, and by the following year it was reported that 84 percent of all Korean families had done so. During the war years, Korean-language newspapers and magazines were shut down. Belief in the divinity of the Japanese emperor was encouraged, and Shinto shrines were built throughout the country. Had Japanese rule not

23

ended in 1945, the fate of indigenous Korean language, culture, and religious practices would have been extremely uncertain (see Korea and Japan, ch. 2).

Japanese rule was harsh, particularly after the Japanese militarists began their expansionist drive in the 1930s. Internal Korean resistance, however, virtually ceased in the 1930s as the police and the military gendarmes imposed strict surveillance over all people suspected of subversive inclinations and meted out severe punishment against recalcitrants. Most Koreans opted to pay lip service to the colonial government. Others actively collaborated with the Japanese. The treatment of collaborators became a sensitive and sometimes violent issue during the years immediately following liberation.

World War II and Korea

On August 8, 1945, during the final days of World War II, the Soviet Union declared war against Japan and launched an invasion of Manchuria and Korea. By then, Japan had been depleted by the drawn-out war against the United States and its Allies, and Japanese forces were in no position to stave off the Soviets. The dropping of atomic bombs on Hiroshima and Nagasaki on August 6 and August 9, respectively, had led the Japanese government to search for ways to end the war. On August 15, 1945, Japan surrendered unconditionally.

The Japanese surrender and the Soviet landing on the Korean Peninsula totally altered the history of contemporary Korea. At the Cairo Conference of December 1943, the Allies had decided to strip Japan of all the territories it had acquired since 1894, the beginning of Japan's expansionist drive abroad. The United States, China, and Britain had agreed at Cairo that Korea would be allowed to become free and independent in due course after the Allied victory. The Soviet Union agreed to the same principle in its declaration of war against Japan.

Although the United States president, Franklin D. Roosevelt, and Marshal Josef V. Stalin of the Soviet Union had agreed to establish an international trusteeship for Korea at the Yalta Conference of February 1945, no decision had been made on the exact formula for governing the nation in the aftermath of Allied victory. The landing of Soviet forces, however, compelled the United States government to improvise a formula for Korea. Unless an agreement were reached, the Soviets could very well occupy the entire peninsula and place Korea under their control. Thus, on August 15, 1945, President Harry S Truman proposed to Stalin the division of Korea at the thirty-eighth parallel. The next day Stalin agreed. Evidently Stalin did not wish to confront the United States by occupying the entire peninsula. He may also have hoped that the United States, in return, would permit the Soviet Union to occupy the northern half of the northernmost major Japanese island, Hokkaidō (see fig. 3).

The Allied foreign ministers subsequently met in Moscow on December 7, 1945, and decided to establish a trusteeship for a five-year period, during which a Korean provisional government would prepare for full independence; they also agreed to form a joint United States-Soviet commission to assist in organizing a single ''provisional Korean democratic government.'' The trusteeship proposal was immediately opposed by nearly all Koreans, especially the Korean right under Syngman Rhee, who used the issue to consolidate his domestic political base. The Korean communists objected at first, but quickly changed their position under Soviet direction.

The joint commission met intermittently in Seoul from March 1946 until it adjourned indefinitely in October 1947. The Soviet insistence that only those ''democratic'' parties and social organizations upholding the trusteeship plan be allowed to participate in the formation of an all-Korean government was unacceptable to the United States. The United States argued that the Soviet formula, if accepted, would put the communists in controlling positions throughout Korea.

South Korea under United States Occupation, 1945-48

The three-year occupation by the United States of the area approximating present-day South Korea, following the liberation of Korea from Japan, was characterized by uncertainty and confusion. This difficult situation stemmed largely from the absence of a clearly formulated United States policy for Korea, the intensification of the confrontation between the United States and the Soviet Union, and the polarization of Korean politics between left and right. Although the United States had maintained diplomatic ties with the Chosŏn Dynasty between 1882 and 1905, Korea in 1945 still was a remote country known only to a small number of missionaries and adventurous businessmen, holding little importance in the official scheme of things. And although the United States had proposed the thirty-eighth parallel as a dividing line between the two occupation armies, United States policymakers still were unsure of the strategic value of South Korea. United States policy

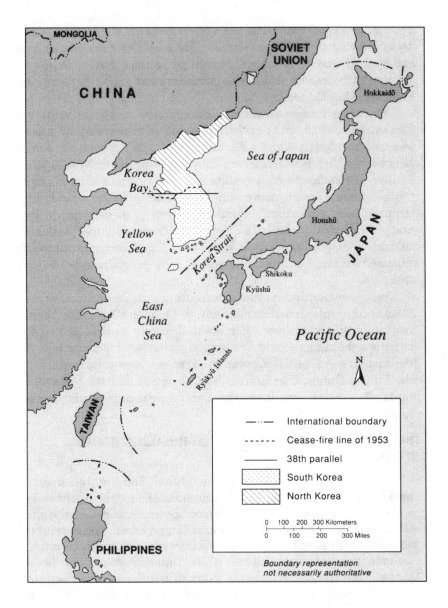

CHINA

MONGOLIA

SOVIET UNION

Hokkaidō

Sea of Japan

Korea Bay

Honshū

Yellow Sea

Korea Strait

Shikoku

Kyūshū

East China Sea

Pacific Ocean

N

Ryūkyū Islands

TAIWAN

JAPAN

PHILIPPINES

—··— International boundary

------ Cease-fire line of 1953

——— 38th parallel

South Korea

North Korea

0 100 200 300 Kilometers
0 100 200 300 Miles

Boundary representation
not necessarily authoritative

Figure 3. South Korea in Its Asian Setting, 1990

toward Korea became more uncertain after the deadlock of the
United States-Soviet joint commission. While United States officials
were pessimistic about resolving their differences with the Soviet
Union, they remained committed to the December 1945 decision

of the Allied foreign ministers (made during their Moscow meeting) that a trusteeship under four powers, including China, should be established with a view toward Korea's eventual independence. Thus, United States officials were slow to draw up long-range alternative plans for South Korea.

Moreover, as the Soviet Union consolidated its power in North Korea and the Nationalist Party (Guomindang or Kuomintang— KMT) government of Chiang Kai-shek began to falter in China, United States strategists began to question the long-run defensibility of South Korea. By 1947 it appeared that South Korea would become the only area of mainland Northeast Asia not under communist control. According to one highly placed official, this was an "exposed, unsound military position, one that [was] doing no good."

Lieutenant General John R. Hodge, commander of the United States occupation forces in Korea, was obliged to work under a severe handicap—a mission of maintaining peace and order until the international conflict over Korea was resolved. Possessing very limited resources, Hodge was expected to pursue the "ultimate objective" of fostering "conditions which would bring about the establishment of a free and independent nation."

General Hodge had to contend with hostile Korean political groups. Before United States forces had landed in Korea in September 1945, the Koreans had established self-governing bodies, or people's committees. The leaders of these committees had organized the Central People's Committee, which proclaimed the establishment of the "Korean People's Republic" on September 6, 1945. Exiles abroad, mainly in China, had organized the "Korean Provisional Government" in Shanghai as early as 1919 and had sustained a skeletal organization in other parts of China until 1945.

The United States recognized neither the republic nor the provisional government. The provisional government was headed by Syngman Rhee, its first president, and Kim Ku and Kim Kyusik, premier and vice premier, respectively. The United States would not recognize any group as a government until an agreement was reached among the Western Allies. The exiles were mollified by the favorable treatment they received when they returned to South Korea, but were incensed by the order to disband issued by the United States Army Military Government in Korea. The military government that administered the American-occupied zone proceeded to disband the local people's committees and impose direct rule, assigning military personnel who lacked language skills and knowledge of Korea as governors at various levels.

The Korean Communist Party, resuscitated in October 1945, had been a major force behind the Central People's Committee and the "Korean People's Republic" and quickly built a substantial following among the workers, farmers, and students. The party eventually changed its stance on trusteeship and came out in support of it on January 3, 1946. Because the party was under the control of the Soviet command in P'yŏngyang, it came into direct confrontation with the United States Army military government.

The situation was exacerbated in December 1945 when the decision to establish a trusteeship was announced. To the Koreans, who had anticipated immediate independence, the decision to implement a five-year trusteeship was humiliating, and the initially warm welcome to United States troops as liberators cooled. By early 1946, the United States Army military government had come to rely heavily on the advice and counsel of ideologically conservative elements, including landlords and other propertied persons.

The United States initially supported the returned exiles and the conservative elements, but between May 1946 and April 1947, the military government tried to mobilize support behind a coalition between the moderate left represented by Yŏ Un-hyŏng (or Lyuh Woon Hyung), who had been the figurehead of the Central People's Committee, and the moderate right, represented by Kim Kyu-sik, vice premier of the exiled government. This attempt only intensified splits within the left-wing and right-wing camps without producing any positive results. The moderates' argument that the Koreans should oppose the trusteeship was unacceptable to the other parties. Communist leaders, on the other hand, were driven underground in May 1946 after the discovery of a currency-counterfeiting operation run by the party. The left-wing and right-wing groups, in the meantime, frequently engaged in violent clashes not only on ideological grounds, but also because of their opposing views about the trusteeship decision.

In December 1946, the military government established the South Korean Interim Legislative Assembly to formulate draft laws to be used as "the basis for political, economic, and social reforms." South Korea's problems, however, required solutions at a much higher level. The left-wing political groups, consolidated under the rubric of the South Korean Workers' Party, ignored the assembly. The conservative Korean Democratic Party, supported by landlords and small-business owners, opposed the assembly because their principal leaders were excluded from it. Although many of the assembly's forty-five elected members were conservatives, most of the forty-five appointed members were moderates nominated by Kim Kyu-sik, who had emerged as Hodge's choice for political leadership. Unfortunately, Kim lacked dynamism and broad support among the masses.

Economy and Society

These circumstances had thrown South Korea's economy into complete chaos. Even if the occupation forces had arrived with a carefully laid economic plan, the situation would have been difficult because the Japanese had developed Korea's economy as an integral part of their empire, linking Korea to Japan and Manchuria.

The division of Korea into two zones at an arbitrary line further aggravated the situation. There were many inherent problems in building a self-sufficient economy in the southern half of the peninsula. Most of the heavy industrial facilities were located in northern Korea—the Soviet zone—including the chemical plants that produced necessary agricultural fertilizers. Light industries in southern Korea had been dependent on electricity from the hydraulic generators located on the Yalu River on the Korean-Manchurian border; electric generating facilities in the south supplied only 9 percent of the total need. Railroads and industries in the south also had been dependent upon bituminous coal imported from Manchuria, Japan, and the north (although the south had been exporting some excess anthracite to the north).

The problems were compounded by the fact that most of Korea's mines and industries had been owned and operated by Japan. As the United States Army military government let the 700,000 Japanese depart from South Korea in the months following the start of the American occupation, almost all of the mines and factories—now enemy properties vested in the military government—were without managers, technicians, and capital resources. This situation led to severe problems of unemployment and material shortages.

The months after the arrival of occupation forces also witnessed a vast inflow of population. South Korea's population, estimated at just over 16 million in 1945, grew by 21 percent during the next year. By 1950 more than 1 million workers had returned from Japan, 120,000 from China and Manchuria, and 1.8 million from the north. The annual rate of increase of births over deaths continued at about 3.1 percent. Since rural areas were inhospitable to newcomers, most of the refugees settled in urban areas; Seoul received upwards of one-third of the total. The situation was further aggravated by scarcities of food and other commodities and by runaway inflation, caused in part by the fact that the departing Japanese had flooded Korea with newly printed yen.

The social unrest created by these developments can be easily surmised. By 1947 only about half the labor force of 10 million was gainfully employed. Labor strikes and work stoppages were recurrent phenomena, and demonstrations against the United States Army military government's policies drew large crowds. Temporary stoppages of electricity—supplied from the northern areas—in the early part of 1946 and late 1947 plunged the southern region into darkness on each occasion, deepening the despair of the populace. The disillusioned and disconcerted people paid keen attention to political leaders of various persuasions who offered new ways of solving the Korean problem.

Establishment of the Republic of Korea

In this atmosphere, the United States scuttled an earlier plan to provide US$500 million over five years for South Korean development. It then submitted the Korean problem to the United Nations (UN) in September 1947. In November the UN General Assembly recognized Korea's claim to independence and made preparations for the establishment of a government and the withdrawal of occupation forces. The United Nations Temporary Commission on Korea arrived to supervise the election of a national assembly, which was held in May 1948. The Soviet Union, however, objected to the UN resolution and refused to admit the commission to the Soviet-controlled zone in the north. It was becoming increasingly clear that two separate regimes would be established on the peninsula.

The prospect of perpetuating the division of Korea catapulted some of the southern political leaders to action, significantly altering the political configuration there. The choice they faced was between immediate independence at the price of indefinite division, or postponement of independence until the deadlock between the United States and the Soviet Union was resolved. Rhee had campaigned actively within Korea and the United States for the first alternative since June 1946. Other major figures in the right-wing camp, including Kim Ku and Kim Kyu-sik, decided to oppose the "separate elections" in the south, hoping to resolve the international impasse by holding talks with their northern counterparts. The group led by the two Kims made their way to P'yŏngyang, the future capital of North Korea, in April 1948, boycotted the May 1948 elections, and were discredited when P'yŏngyang cut off electricity, leaving Rhee a clear field although he lacked grass roots support apart from the Korean Democratic Party. By this time, the communists in the south had lost much of their political following, particularly after a serious riot in October 1946; most of their leaders congregated in the north. The moderate left-wing camp was in disarray after their leader, Yŏ Un-hyŏng, was assassinated in July 1947. Kim Kyu-sik had been the clear choice of the

United States Army military government, but he could not be dissuaded from his fruitless trip to P'yŏngyang.

The National Assembly elected in May 1948 adopted a constitution setting forth a presidential form of government and specifying a four-year term for the presidency. Syngman Rhee, whose supporters had won the elections, became head of the new assembly. On this basis, when on August 15, 1948, the Republic of Korea (South Korea) was proclaimed, Rhee assumed the presidency. Four days after the proclamation, communist authorities completed the severing of north-south ties by shutting off power transmission to the south. Within less than a month, a communist regime, the Democratic People's Republic of Korea (North Korea), was proclaimed under Premier Kim Il Sung, who claimed authority over the entire country by virtue of elections conducted in the north and the underground elections allegedly held in the south. Rhee scarcely had time to put his political house in order before North Korea launched its attack on South Korea in June 1950.

The South Korean army had come into being in September 1948 (see The South Korean Army after World War II, ch. 5). A communist-led revolt of army regiments in the southern part of the peninsula in October of the same year, known as the Yŏsu-Sunch'ŏn rebellion, had consumed much of the army's attention and resources, however, and a massive purge in the aftermath of that revolt weakened the entire military establishment. Given South Korea's precarious future and the communist victory in China, the United States was not eager to provide support. By June 29, 1949, United States occupation forces had been withdrawn, save for a handful of military advisers, and Korea had been placed outside of the United States defense perimeter.

The Korean War, 1950-53

In the meantime, the communists had built a formidable political and military structure in North Korea under the aegis of the Soviet command. They had created a regional Five-Province Administrative Bureau in October 1945, which was reorganized into the North Korean Provisional People's Committee in February 1946 and shed the "Provisional" component of its name twelve months later. The communists also expanded and consolidated their party's strength by merging all of the left-wing groups into the North Korean Workers' Party in August 1946. Beginning in 1946, the armed forces also were organized and reinforced. Between 1946 and 1949, large numbers of North Korean youths—at least 10,000—were taken to the Soviet Union for military training. A draft was instituted, and in 1949 two divisions—40,000 troops—

31

of the former Korean Volunteer Army in China, who had trained under the Chinese communists and had participated in the Chinese civil war (1945-49), returned to North Korea.

By June 1950, North Korean forces numbered between 150,000 and 200,000 troops, organized into ten infantry divisions, one tank division, and one air force division. Soviet equipment, including automatic weapons of various types, T-34 tanks, and Yak fighter planes, had also been pouring into North Korea in early 1950. These forces were to fight the ill-equipped South Korean army of less than 100,000 men—an army lacking in tanks, heavy artillery, and combat airplanes—plus a coast guard of 4,000 men and a police force of 45,000 men.

The events following the June 1950 invasion proved the superiority of North Korean military forces and the soundness of their overall invasion strategy. South Korea's army was simply overwhelmed; Seoul fell within three days. By early August, South Korean forces were confined in the southeastern corner of the peninsula to a territory 140 kilometers long and 90 kilometers wide. The rest of the territory was completely in the hands of the North Korean army.

The only unforeseen event complicating North Korea's strategy was the swift decision by the United States to commit forces in support of South Korea. On June 26, 1950, Truman ordered the use of United States planes and naval vessels against North Korean forces, and on June 30 United States ground troops were dispatched. The United States, fearing that inaction in Korea would be interpreted as appeasement of communist aggression elsewhere in the world, was determined that South Korea should not be overwhelmed and asked the UN Security Council to intervene. When Douglas MacArthur, the commanding general of the United Nations forces in Korea, launched his amphibious attack and landed at Inch'ŏn on September 15, the course of the war changed abruptly. Much of North Korea was taken by United States and South Korean forces before Chinese "volunteers" intervened in October, enabling North Korea to eventually restore its authority over its domain. The war lasted until July 27, 1953, when a ceasefire agreement was signed at P'anmunjŏm. By then, the war had involved China and the Soviet Union, which had dispatched air force divisions to Manchuria in support of North Korea and had furnished the Chinese and North Koreans with arms, tanks, military supplies, fuel, foodstuffs, and medicine. Fifteen member-nations of the United Nations had contributed armed forces and medical units to South Korea.

The war left indelible marks on the Korean Peninsula and the world surrounding it. The entire peninsula was reduced to rubble;

casualties on both sides were enormous. The chances for peaceful unification had been remote even before 1950, but the war dashed all such hopes. Sizable numbers of South Koreans who either had been sympathetic or indifferent to communism before the war became avowed anticommunists afterwards. The war also intensified hostilities between the communist and noncommunist camps in the accelerating East-West arms race. Moreover, a large number of Chinese volunteer troops remained in North Korea until October 1958, and China began to play an increasingly important role in Korean affairs. Because tension on the Korean Peninsula remained high, the United States continued to station troops in South Korea over the strenuous objections of North Korean leaders. The war also spurred Japan's industrial recovery and the United States' decision to rearm Japan.

The Syngman Rhee Era, 1948–60

The Political Environment

Even though Syngman Rhee had been handily elected president by the National Assembly in 1948—with 180 of the 196 votes cast in his favor—he quickly ran into difficulties. South Korean politics during Rhee's regime (1948–60) essentially revolved around Rhee's struggle to remain in power and the opposition's efforts to unseat him. Constitutional provisions concerning the presidency became the focal point.

Because Rhee's four-year term of office was to end in August 1952 under the 1948 constitution, and because he had no prospect of being reelected by the National Assembly, he supported a constitutional amendment, introduced in November 1951, to elect the president by popular vote. The proposal was resoundingly defeated by a vote of 143 to 19, prompting Rhee to marshal his supporters into the Liberal Party. Four months later, in April 1952, the opposition introduced another motion calling for a parliamentary form of government. Rhee declared martial law in May, rounded up the assembly members by force, and called for another vote. His constitutional amendment to elect the president by popular vote was railroaded through, passing with 163 votes of the 166 assembly members present. In the subsequent popular election in August, Rhee was reelected by 72 percent of the voters.

The constitution, however, limited the president to only two terms. Hence, when the end of Rhee's second term of office approached, the constitution again was amended (in November 1954) by the use of fraudulent tactics that allowed Rhee to succeed himself indefinitely.

In the meantime, South Korea's citizens, particularly the urban masses, had become more politically conscious. The press frequently exposed government ineptitude and corruption and attacked Rhee's authoritarian rule. The Democratic Party capitalized on these particulars; in the May 1956 presidential election, Rhee won only 55 percent of the votes, even though his principal opponent, Sin Ik-hŭi, had died of a heart attack ten days before the election. Rhee's running mate, Yi Ki-bung, fared much worse, losing to the Democratic Party candidate, Chang Myŏn (John M. Chang). Since Rhee was already eighty-one years old in 1956, Chang's victory caused a major tremor among Rhee's supporters.

Thereafter, the issue of Rhee's age and the goal of electing Yi Ki-bung became an obsession. The administration became increasingly repressive as Liberal Party leaders came to dominate the political arena, including government operations, around 1958. Yi, formerly Rhee's personal secretary, and his wife (Mrs. Rhee's confidant and a power-behind-the-scenes) had convinced the childless Rhee to adopt their son as his legal heir. For fear that Rhee's health might be impaired, he was carefully shielded from all information that might upset him. Thus, the aged and secluded president became a captive of the system he had built, rather than its master.

In March 1960, the Liberal Party managed to reelect Rhee and to elect Yi Ki-bung vice president by the blatant use of force. Rhee was reelected by default because his principal opponent had died while receiving medical treatment in the United States just before the election. As for Yi, he was largely confined to his sickbed—a cause of public anger—but "won" 8.3 million votes as against 1.8 million votes for Chang Myŏn. The fraudulent election touched off civil disorders, known and celebrated as the April 19 Student Revolution, during which 142 students were killed by the police. As a result, Rhee resigned on April 26, 1960. The next day all four members of the Yi family died in a suicide pact. This account has been challenged by some who believed Yi's family was killed by his bodyguards in hopes of enabling Rhee to stay on.

Rhee, a self-righteous man convinced of his indispensability to Korea, loathed his critics and opponents and equated criticism with treason. Although his record as a national hero and his skill in handling United States-Korean relations won him admiration during the immediate years after the Korean War, Rhee became a captive of the people surrounding him. In the late 1950s, his policies were largely without results as rapid changes in the economy and society deeply affected South Korea's system.

Society under Rhee

The transformation of South Korean society during the Rhee era was of revolutionary proportions because of the convergence of a number of forces. A major impetus for social change was the greatly enhanced opportunity for education. Although Japan had introduced a modern education system to Korea, opportunities for Koreans were purposely limited, particularly at the secondary and university levels. Educational opportunities were greatly expanded immediately after the Japanese defeat, and the trend continued through the Korean War and afterwards. Higher education provided more opportunities for upward mobility to a large number of young people. This opening also meant greater political awakening among the young, particularly in view of the strong emphasis placed on democratic values and ideas by teachers and intellectuals. For the first time, Korean youths were provided open access to democratic ideas both at school and through the mass media. These Western ideas became the norm against which to judge the government in power when the exigencies of the war period were removed.

A land reform law enacted in June 1949 also had a leveling effect on Korean society. Under this law, nearly 1 million sharecroppers, or approximately 40 percent of total farm households, became small landowners. The reform also brought about the decline of the landlord class that had formed the backbone of traditional Korean society for centuries. Because big business and industrial groups did not emerge until the late 1950s and early 1960s, almost everyone in society was placed on an equal footing.

The Korean War had the most significant effect on the social system. The movement of large armies up and down the length of the peninsula was accompanied by civilian refugees. People of diverse backgrounds intermingled for prolonged periods, deeply affecting everyone's way of life. The indiscriminate destruction of property during the war also had the effect of homogenizing Korean society.

The war caused hundreds of thousands of young men from rural areas to enlist in the army, exposing them to modern organization, technologies, and a new world outlook. The war also gave rise to a large officer corps that later developed into an increasingly significant social group.

Better education and the government's postwar economic policies contributed to accelerated urbanization. Reconstruction projects created jobs in the cities, while the government's effort to control the prices of farm products made it unprofitable to till small farm plots. The urban population increased rapidly from 11.6 percent in 1940 to 24.4 percent in 1955 and 28.3 percent in 1960. These changes had a direct impact on politics because the better-educated and urbanized elements became increasingly vocal and more independent in their political judgments.

The Postwar Economy

The war had destroyed most of South Korea's production facilities. The South Korean government began rehabilitation as soon as the battle zone near the thirty-eighth parallel stabilized in 1952. The United Nations Korean Reconstruction Agency and members of the UN, principally the United States, also provided badly needed financial assistance. Seoul depended heavily on foreign aid, not only for defense, but also for other expenditures. Foreign aid constituted a third of total budget in 1954, rose to 58.4 percent in 1956, and was approximately 38 percent of the budget in 1960. The first annual United States economic aid bill after the armistice was US$200 million; aid peaked at US$365 million in 1956 and was then maintained at the US$200 million level annually until the mid-1960s.

The scarcity of raw materials and the need to maintain a large army caused a high rate of inflation, but by 1958 prices had stabilized. The government also intensified its effort to increase industrial production, emphasizing power generation and textile and cement production. In order to reduce dependence on imports, such principal items as fertilizer and steel began to be produced domestically.

The average rise in the gross national product (GNP—see Glossary) was 5.5 percent from 1954 through 1958. Industrial production led the advance, growing by nearly 14 percent per year. The tightening of fiscal and monetary policies in 1958, coupled with the phasing out of the United Nations Korean Reconstruction Agency program and the reduction in direct aid from the United States in 1957, caused a shortage of raw materials for import-dependent industries and led to an overall economic decline. By 1958 Liberal Party leaders paid more attention to political survival than to economic development. The government adopted a comprehensive Seven-Year Economic Development Plan in January 1960, but before the plan could be implemented, the student revolution brought down the government.

The Democratic Interlude

Rhee's resignation left a political void subsequently filled by Ho Chong, whom Rhee had appointed foreign minister the day before he resigned. Although Ho was a lifelong friend of Rhee, he had maintained amicable relations with Democratic Party leaders and thus was acceptable to all concerned. Between April and July 1960, Ho's transitional government maintained order, exiled Rhee and his wife to Hawaii, and prepared for a new general election of the National Assembly in July. That body revised the constitution on June 15, instituting a parliamentary form of government with a bicameral legislature. In the July election, the Democratic Party won 175 of the 233 seats in the lower house of the National Assembly. The second largest group, the independents, won forty-nine seats. The Liberal Party won only two seats. In the upper house, the Democratic Party won thirty-one of the fifty-eight seats.

The Democratic Party had been a coalition of two divergent elements that had merged in 1955 to oppose Rhee. When the common enemy—Rhee and his Liberal Party—had been removed from the scene and opportunities for power were presented, each group sought to obtain the spoils for itself.

The Democratic Party candidate for the presidency in the March 1960 election, Cho Pyŏng-ok, died of illness shortly before the election, just as his predecessor, Sin Ik-hŭi, had in 1956. The two groups openly struggled against each other during the July elections for the National Assembly. Although they agreed on Yun Po-sŏn as presidential candidate and Chang Myŏn as their choice for premier, neither had strong leadership qualities nor commanded the respect of the majority of the party elite. Yun and Chang could not agree on the composition of the cabinet. Chang attempted to hold the coalition together by reshuffling cabinet positions three times within a five-month period. In November 1960, the group led by Yun left the Democratic Party and formed the New Democratic Party (*Simmindang*).

In the meantime, the tasks confronting the new government were daunting. The economy suffered from mismanagement and corruption. The army and police needed to be purged of the political appointees who had buttressed the dictatorship. The students, to whom the Democratic Party owed its power, filled the streets almost daily, making numerous wide-ranging demands for political and economic reforms, but the Democratic Party had no ready-made programs. Law and order could not be maintained because the police, long an instrument of the Rhee government, were demoralized and totally discredited by the public. Continued factional wrangling caused the public to turn away from the party.

This situation provided a fertile ground for a military coup. Whereas Rhee had been able to control the military because of his personal prestige, his skill in manipulating the generals, and the control mechanisms he had instituted, Chang lacked all these advantages. When the demands of the young army officers under Major General Park Chung Hee were rebuffed, and as political power appeared to be increasingly hanging in the balance with no one clearly in charge, the army carried out a coup d'état on May 16, 1961. Chang's own army chief of staff, Chang To-yŏng, joined the junta, and Chang's fragile government was toppled. (The junta subsequently tried and convicted General Chang for attempting to take over the junta.) The young officers' initial complaint had been that Chang Myŏn had not kept a campaign pledge to weed out corrupt generals from the South Korean army, and some Korean sources attributed this failure to the intervention of high-ranking United States military officers, who feared the weakening of South Korea's national security.

Yun Po-sŏn sided with the junta and persuaded the United States Eighth Army and the commanders of various South Korean army units not to interfere with the new rulers. Yun stayed on as president for ten months after the military junta took over power, thereby legitimizing the coup. A small number of young officers commanding 3,600 men had succeeded in toppling a government with authority over an army of 600,000.

South Korea under Park Chung Hee, 1961–79

The junta under Park Chung Hee quickly consolidated its power, removed those it considered corrupt and unqualified from government and army positions, and laid plans for the future. The thirty-two-member Supreme Council for National Reconstruction (SCNR) became all-powerful.

The Korean Central Intelligence Agency (KCIA) was created in June 1961 to prevent a countercoup and to suppress all potential enemies. It was to have not only investigative power, but also the power to arrest and detain anyone suspected of wrongdoing or harboring antijunta sentiments. The KCIA extended its power to economic and foreign affairs under its first director, Colonel (retired) Kim Chong-p'il, a relative of Park, and one of the original planners of the coup against Chang.

In May 1961, the junta pledged to make an all-out effort to build a self-reliant economy and to carry out a "great human revolution" by wiping out all corruption and evil practices in the government and by introducing a "fresh and clean morality." The National Assembly was dissolved, and high-level civilian officials were replaced by military officers. By 1963 the junta's economic policies had not produced any favorable results.

The KCIA under Kim Chong-p'il was involved in a number of scandals that considerably tarnished the junta's image. The military leaders had worked actively to establish a political party, later known as the Democratic Republican Party (DRP), which existed from 1963 to 1980, in preparation for the return of politics to the civilians. Former politicians, however, were prohibited from engaging in organizational activities. Although Park had announced in February 1963 that he would not participate in civilian politics, the following month he announced a popular referendum to decide whether the junta should extend its rule for another four years. Facing stiff opposition from both the South Korean public and the United States, the plan for a referendum was canceled.

The Military in Politics

The junta had drawn up a new constitution and had put it before a popular referendum in December 1962, receiving 78.8 percent of the vote. Under the new constitution, the president was to be elected by direct popular vote and have strong powers—including the authority to appoint the premier and cabinet members without legislative consent and to order emergency financial and economic measures. Under United States pressure, Park, who had held the position of acting president following Yun's resignation in March 1962, retired from the army as a four-star general and ran as the DRP candidate in the October 1963 presidential election. He was elected by a narrow margin, winning 46.6 percent of the vote, as compared with 45.1 percent for Yun Po-sŏn, the New Democratic Party candidate. In the subsequent election for the unicameral legislature, held in November 1963, the government won 110 of the 175 seats.

Until 1971 South Korea operated under the political framework it had adopted in 1963. Even though Park imposed some restrictions on members of the press, intellectuals, and opposition politicians, these groups were permitted considerable latitude to criticize the government and to engage in organizational activities. Although there were numerous student demonstrations, particularly in 1965 when the government normalized its relations with Japan and sent 45,000 combat troops to support the Republic of Vietnam in response to a request from the United States, the students were controlled and there were no casualties in confrontations with the police. The presidential and National Assembly elections in 1967 and 1971 were closely contested but won by Park. In order to succeed himself for the third time in 1971, Park amended the constitution in 1969.

In December 1971, Park again tightened his control over the country. He proclaimed a national emergency and forced through the National Assembly a bill granting him complete power to control, regulate, and mobilize the people, the economy, the press, and everything else in the public domain. In October 1972, he proclaimed martial law, dissolved the National Assembly, closed all universities and colleges, imposed strict press censorship, and suspended political activities. Within a few days he "submitted" a new draft constitution—designated the *yusin* (revitalization) constitution—to a national referendum. The 1972 constitution allowed Park to succeed himself indefinitely, to appoint one-third of the National Assembly's members, and to exercise emergency powers at will. The president was to be chosen by the more than 2,000 locally elected deputies of the supposedly nonpartisan National Conference for Unification, who were to cast their votes as an electoral college without debate.

Students and intellectuals conducted a national campaign to revise the 1972 constitution in the fall of 1973. As the student campaign began to gather momentum, the president issued his first emergency decree in January 1974 outlawing all such campaigns. Successive emergency measures imposed further restrictions on other segments of society, but the harshest and most comprehensive restrictions were imposed by Emergency Measure Number Nine, issued in May 1975, which made it a crime either to criticize the constitution or to provide press coverage of such an activity, subject to a penalty of more than a year's imprisonment. Student participation in politics or coverage of student political activities in the press were subject to the same punishment. The president justified the harsh measures by citing the need for national unity in the face of an alleged threat of attack from North Korea.

Having concentrated all power around himself, Park suppressed his opponents harshly. KCIA agents abducted Kim Dae Jung, Park's opponent in the 1971 presidential elections, from a hotel in Tokyo in August 1973, precipitating a major crisis in South Korean-Japanese relations. Kim had been abroad after the election and remained there after Park declared martial law, traveling between Japan and the United States and conducting anti-Park activities. Students demonstrating against the *yusin* constitution were summarily incarcerated. In March 1976, prominent political leaders, including former President Yun and presidential candidate Kim, issued the Democratic Declaration calling for the restoration of democracy. Park had them arrested and sentenced to five to eight years in prison.

In the meantime, Park narrowly avoided an assassination attempt by a South Korean youth (resident in Japan), whose stray bullets killed the president's wife instead in August 1974. After this incident, Park became more reclusive and came to rely more and more on his chief bodyguard, Ch'a Chi-ch'ŏl, of the Presidential Security Force.

Force alone could not sustain the authoritarian system. Park's strongest defense against his critics had been the high rate of economic growth under his leadership (see The Government Role in Economic Development, ch. 3). By 1978, however, the growth rate had begun to decline, and inflation had become a serious problem. Seoul successfully weathered the first "oil shock" when Middle Eastern suppliers drastically raised prices in 1973, but was hard hit by the second shock in 1978–79. In December 1978, Park belatedly adopted a stabilization plan to cool down the economy, but the plan caused a serious recession, leading to a succession of bankruptcies and increased unemployment.

The first overt manifestation of workers' discontent appeared in August 1979 with demonstrations by 200 women employees of the Y.H. Industrial Company, which had just gone bankrupt. Women workers occupied the headquarters of the opposition New Democratic Party and demanded the right to manage the company themselves. When the workers refused to obey the government's order to disperse, some 1,000 riot policemen raided the building. Pandemonium occurred, and one of the workers died—it was unknown whether she had jumped, was pushed, or was jostled to her death. Despite the government's efforts, the "Y.H. Incident" became a rallying cry of the opposition.

Aside from the visible social unrest caused by political suppression and economic recession, the opposition camp had reason to become emboldened in its criticism of the government in 1979. Disaffection was particularly severe in urban areas. Although the New Democratic Party was suffering from internal dissension, it won a plurality in the December 1978 general elections for the National Assembly, the first general elections to be held since 1973. In the 1978 elections, the Democratic Republican Party won only 30.9 percent of the popular vote, a decline of 7.8 percent from 1973. In contrast, the opposition obtained 34.7 percent, an increase of 2.2 percent from 1973. Independent candidates won 27.2 percent of the vote (twenty-two seats in the National Assembly); fifteen of the twenty-two subsequently joined the New Democratic Party, although three were "persuaded" to switch to the government party. Because one-third of the National Assembly's members were government-appointed, the opposition could not command a majority.

The new leader of the New Democratic Party, Kim Young Sam, began his challenge to the government in June 1979. He announced to the foreign press his readiness to meet with Kim Il Sung, the North Korean president, to discuss matters relating to unification and delivered a scathing attack on the government in the National Assembly. He argued that the government had been in power too long and had been clearly discredited by the elections; that Emergency Measure Number Nine suffocated peoples' freedom and was clearly unconstitutional; that Seoul had colluded with hoodlums to assault the New Democratic Party headquarters and to harass him; that the suppression of human rights had become an international disgrace; that the people should be permitted to elect their own president through direct elections and be allowed to live without fear; and that a fair distribution of wealth should be permitted without government interference. The government immediately retaliated and ousted Kim from the National Assembly. In a show of solidarity, all opposition members of the National Assembly resigned on October 13, 1979.

The Y.H. Incident and the harsh confrontation between the government and the opposition parties agitated the college students. Students in Taegu and Seoul staged campus rallies and demonstrations in September 1979. In mid-October, students in Pusan poured into the streets and clashed with police, leading the government to declare martial law in that city. In late October, students in Masan launched a demonstration. The government placed the city under ''garrison decree,'' and the army took over the responsibility for public order.

Close Park associates such as Kim Chong-p'il were reported to have counseled the president to meet some of the student demands and reduce repression, but were opposed by presidential security chief Ch'a Chi-ch'ŏl. Ch'a also sharply disagreed with Kim Chae-gyu, the director of the KCIA, who had counseled moderation in the government's handling of the student protesters. On October 26, 1979, the nation's most powerful figures—Park, Ch'a, and Kim Chae-gyu—met in a KCIA safe house restaurant for dinner to discuss, among other things, the Pusan situation. In the sharply divided discussion that followed, Kim gunned down Park, Ch'a, and their bodyguards.

It could be argued that Park had created his own dilemma by instituting the *yusin* constitution and by assuming unlimited powers. If he had loosened control, however, the demand for reforms might have spread, proving impossible to contain. The system had provided for neither a pressure-release valve nor an escape hatch.

In his eighteen years in power (1961–79), Park had been obsessed with ushering the country into the ranks of developed nations, had pursued his goal relentlessly, and had achieved considerable results. Having been trained under the Japanese, he closely patterned his development strategies after Japan's, where a feudal society had been turned into a modern nation between the 1860s and 1930s.

The Japanese leaders of the Meiji era (1868–1912), however, possessed two advantages over Park. First, they had operated in a period when the masses were less politically conscious and authoritarian control was more easily accepted. This was not the situation in South Korea, where students had already toppled a government in 1960. Second, the Japanese also had a built-in system of checks and balances because the top-echelon leaders operated in a council where different leaders interacted among themselves as equals. Park, by contrast, operated on a one-man-rule basis, unchecked by constraints on his own decision-making powers.

Economic Development

South Korea's economy grew rapidly under Park. The military leaders, with little previous political or administrative experience, and lacking a developmental program, later turned to the economists and planners for assistance. The Economic Planning Board was established in 1961. A program of rapid industrialization based on exports was launched. The shift in orientation was reflected in the First Five-Year Economic Development Plan (1962–66), and the subsequent second (1967–71), third (1972–76), and fourth (1977–81) five-year economic development plans.

Park's policies encouraged private entrepreneurs. Businesses were given powerful incentives to export, including preferential treatment in obtaining low-interest bank loans, import privileges, permission to borrow from foreign sources, and tax benefits. Some of these businesses later became the *chaebŏl* (see Glossary; The Origins and Development of Chaebŏl, ch. 3).

Toward these ends, the currency was drastically devalued in 1961 and 1964, and import quotas for raw materials eased. Private saving was encouraged by raising interest rates, and funds were borrowed from abroad. Exports also were encouraged by direct subsidies; all taxes and restrictions on the import of intermediate goods that were to be used to produce export products were removed. As the existing industries—textiles, clothing, and electrical machinery, among others—had been stagnant because of a lack of imported raw materials, these policies produced immediate results.

These developmental programs required enormous amounts of capital. As the level of United States assistance stabilized, the Park regime turned to "financial diplomacy" with other countries. The normalization of relations with Japan in 1965 brought Japanese funds in the form of loans and compensation for the damages suffered during the colonial era. Park made a state visit to the Federal Republic of Germany in 1964 that resulted in the extension of government aid and commercial credits. The availability of funds and the increasing level of exports elevated Seoul's credit rating, making it possible to increase borrowing in the open international market. Further, the conflict in Indochina stimulated economic growth. Seoul's export drive also owed much to the availability of an educated labor force and a favorable international market.

South Korean businesses discovered that they could successfully compete abroad. As idle capacity was used up and the demand for new manufacturing investment rose, increasing numbers of foreign investors were attracted to South Korea.

Foreign exchange earnings improved as export and foreign receipts rose. The government also took steps to increase tax revenues and stabilize consumer prices. Much of the price stabilization program was carried out at the expense of farmers, who were forced to accept the government's policy of low grain prices. Agricultural development lagged behind until 1971, when the government shifted to a policy of high grain prices and inaugurated the Saemaŭl undong (New Community Movement) aimed at improving the farm village environment and increasing agricultural production and income (see The Agricultural Crisis of the Late 1980s, ch. 3).

Official statistics indicated rapid economic growth. Substantial successes were achieved under the first two five-year economic development plans. The manufacturing sector provided the main stimulus, growing by 15 percent and 21 percent, respectively, during the two plans. Domestic savings rates grew and exports expanded significantly (see Economic Plans, ch. 3). A new economic strategy emphasizing diversification in production and trade proved generally successful in the 1970s. Under the third plan, the government made a bold move to expand South Korea's heavy and chemical industries, investing in steel, machinery, shipbuilding, electronics, chemicals, and nonferrous metals. South Korea's capability for steel production and oil refining rose most notably. Refineries for zinc and copper and modern shipbuilding facilities were constructed; automobiles began to be exported to a few markets. The plan sought to better prepare South Korea for competition in the world market and to facilitate domestic production of weaponry.

The quadrupling of oil prices beginning in 1973 severely threatened the South Korean economy, which depended heavily on imported oil for energy production. Construction contracts in the Middle East, however, provided the necessary foreign exchange to forestall a balance-of-payments crisis and to continue the high rate of growth.

The growth-oriented economic strategy emphasizing exports inevitably produced side effects. Although the government previously had been able to manage these side effects and effectively surmount various economic crises, the situation began to deteriorate in 1978. The emphasis on exports had produced a shortage of domestic consumer goods that was exacerbated by the increasing demands brought about by rising wages and the advance in living standards. Price controls imposed on producers of consumer goods discouraged the manufacture of these goods. Meanwhile, the inflow of dollars rapidly expanded the money supply and inflation became a serious problem. According to a Bank of Korea report, consumer prices rose only 14.4 percent in 1978, but most observers agreed that the actual rate was near 30 percent.

The high rate of inflation continued into 1979. According to a report issued by the Economic Planning Board in August 1979, the average household's cost of living had gone up 26.3 percent from the previous year. Although wages had been rising rapidly during the previous several years—spurred by shortages of skilled and semiskilled workers—the rise in wages began to slow down. The average wage increased 12 percent during the year preceding August 1979.

To address these ills, Park had replaced the economic team in the cabinet in December 1978 and adopted stabilization measures entailing the lowering of the growth rate: a stringent tight-money policy; a switch of investment capital planned for heavy industries to light industries producing consumer products; a reduction of price controls to encourage more production of consumer goods; and assistance for the poor. But these measures caused a recession, produced a succession of bankruptcies among small and medium loan-dependent enterprises, and increased unemployment.

Society under Park

The rapid pace of industrialization not only changed much of the South Korean landscape, as farmlands were converted into highways and factory sites, but also profoundly modified social structure, social values, and behavior. As late as 1965, some 58.7 percent of the labor force was engaged in agriculture and fishery, but the percentage declined to 50.4 percent in 1970 and 38.4 percent in 1978. The percentage of workers engaged in secondary industries, including mining and manufacturing, rose from 10.3 percent in 1965 to 35.2 percent in 1970 and 38.4 percent in 1978. Industrialization led to a rapid increase in South Korea's urban population, which rose from 28.3 percent of the total in 1960 to 54.9 percent in 1979. Rapid urbanization compounded the problems of housing, transportation, sanitation, and pollution, and exacerbated other social problems.

Improved living standards and ever-increasing job opportunities accelerated the desire among South Koreans for education, particularly at secondary schools and institutions of higher learning. In 1960 about one-third of children between twelve and fourteen years of age attended middle schools; that proportion increased to 53.3 percent in 1970 and 74.0 percent in 1975. In 1960 some 19.9 percent of the population between fifteen and seventeen years of age attended high schools; that proportion increased to 29.3 percent in 1970 and 40.5 percent in 1975. By 1970 about 9.3 percent of college-age youths attended colleges and universities, and the number of university graduates exceeded 30,000 a year. Eight years later, 41,680 students graduated from four-year institutions of higher learning (see Education, ch. 2).

Most workers with higher education qualifications were absorbed by the rapidly growing industrial and commercial sectors, joining the ranks of the growing middle class. Demands and rewards for people in the more prestigious fields—doctors, lawyers, economists, scientists, and managers—were increasing. The number of white-collar workers in commerce, industry, banking, civil service, and the teaching profession also rose, as did the number of small entrepreneurs and retailers.

A high proportion of those people who regarded themselves as middle class resided in Seoul, the locale for much of the nation's wealth, talent, and many of its cultural resources. As beneficiaries of the rapidly expanding economy, much of the middle class either was content with its situation or indifferent to politics. Many highly educated persons in this group who found themselves in less well-paid positions than they would have liked remained dissatisfied, and together with students and intellectuals they formed the core of opposition to the Park regime.

Rural villages also underwent changes of revolutionary proportions, particularly after 1971. As the government had emphasized industrial growth and slighted the agrarian sector, agricultural production lagged; its annual rate of growth during the 1967–72 period was only about 2.5 percent. With overall GNP growing at over 10 percent a year during the same period, the rural economy steadily lost ground, until by 1969 farm income was only a little more than half that earned by urban workers. This situation contributed to the high rate of migration to the cities and eroded political support for the president (see Agriculture, ch. 3).

This situation led the government to take active measures to increase farm productivity and income in 1971. Government subsidies to farmers were increased by setting relatively high prices for grains. Higher-yield rice varieties were introduced. Advanced agricultural technology was made more widely available through extension services, and more fertilizers and credits were provided. As a result of these measures, farm productivity and farm income increased very rapidly during the ensuing years, and the rate of emigration to the cities tapered off.

The Saemaŭl Movement was instituted with great fanfare by Park in the fall of 1971. The movement was envisioned as a highly organized, intensively administered campaign to improve the "environment" quality of rural life through projects undertaken by the villagers themselves with government assistance. The bureaucracy, particularly at the regional and local levels, was mobilized on a massive scale to ensure that the program would be carried through to completion in all 36,000 villages. The initial emphasis was on improving village roads and bridges and replacing thatch with tile or composition roofs.

The momentum was maintained and increased in subsequent years as the Saemaŭl Movement evolved into a major ideological campaign aimed at the psychological mobilization of the entire country in support of "nation building." During the first two or three years, emphasis continued to be on improving the village environment, but later focus was shifted toward projects designed to raise agricultural productivity and farm income.

As local government officials were jolted out of their traditional lethargy by the continuing insistence of higher authorities that essential services be delivered to farmers, the farmers began to have ready access to agricultural extension services, rural credit, and market information. The result of improved services and increased resource allocation was that farmers became more confident of their ability to improve the village environment through their own cooperative efforts and became more convinced of the usefulness of outside official help. As a result of the Saemaŭl Movement, about 85 percent of villages had electricity, and about 60 percent of farm households had television sets by the late 1970s. Some 85 percent of rural children continued from free, obligatory primary schooling to middle school, and over 50 percent of these middle school pupils were entering high schools. Many farmers also acquired modern amenities that had been available only to city dwellers just a decade earlier, such as sewing machines, radios, irons, and wall clocks.

Namdaemun, or South Gate, Seoul, showing the contrast
of the old city with the new
Courtesy Oren Hadar

Foreign Relations

Relations with North Korea

Even though the Korean War ended in a truce agreement in July 1953, a high level of tension remained between the two countries. Although North Korea presented numerous proposals for peaceful unification after signing the truce, none was premised on the notion of the continuation of the existing South Korean government, which made the proposals unacceptable to Seoul.

Throughout the Park era, relations with North Korea were marked by mutual distrust and discord, with only a brief respite between July 1972 and June 1973 when the two sides engaged in high-level negotiations. Hopes were raised that tensions might be reduced and a way toward unification of the divided nation found. Entrenched suspicions made the contentious issues separating the two sides even more difficult to solve, and the talks were broken off (see Relations with North Korea, ch. 4). Meanwhile, the armed confrontation continued (see The Threat from the North, ch. 5).

The continuing failure of the negotiations reflected the depth of the gap separating the two Koreas—particularly noteworthy in view of the mellowing international environment evidenced, for example, by China's much-improved relations with both the United States and Japan. There were indications that both China and the United States exerted considerable influence on the Korean negotiations, but without marked effect. Leaders in the north and the south found their ideologies and aims totally incompatible. South Korea's leaders were determined to keep their society free from communism, while North Korea's leaders were committed to the cause of bringing "people's democratic revolution" to the south.

Relations with Japan

The most important development in South Korea's diplomacy under Park was the normalization of relations with Japan. Although South Korea had traded with Japan since 1948 and the two countries had engaged in negotiations since 1951, disagreement on a number of issues had prevented diplomatic ties. The junta under Park actively sought to normalize relations. Negotiations resumed in October 1961, culminating in an agreement in June 1965 to establish diplomatic relations (see Relations with Japan, ch. 4). Park settled for a fraction of the "reparations" earlier demanded by Rhee, and Japanese fishermen were given access to South Korean waters outside of the three-mile territorial limit (Rhee had prohibited Japanese fishermen from coming any closer than the medial line between Japan and Korea). Under the treaty, the Japanese government was to provide the capital necessary for an industrialization program and to open up ever-increasing loans, investments (both public and private), and trade (see Foreign Economic Relations, ch. 3). The treaty normalizing relations was denounced as a sellout by the opposition and the intellectuals and touched off prolonged, widespread student demonstrations.

South Korean-Japanese relations since normalization have been amicable, but were considerably strained by the abduction from Tokyo of Kim Dae Jung in August 1973, which resulted in long and embarrassing negotiations. In 1979 South Korean-Japanese relations entered a new era as the two countries began informal ties on defense matters, such as the establishment of the Korean-Japanese Parliamentary Conference on Security Affairs.

Relations with the United States

South Korea continued to depend on United States military assistance. In spite of initial United States hesitation about supporting Park in 1961, the two countries maintained close economic, military, and diplomatic ties. South Korea dispatched combat troops to the Republic of Vietnam (South Vietnam) in 1965 to augment United States forces there, and President Lyndon B. Johnson paid a personal visit to Seoul in October 1966 to show his appreciation.

Friction began to develop in the Washington-Seoul relationship after the United States withdrew one of its two divisions from South Korea in 1971 and intensified after Park instituted rigorous authoritarian measures under his 1972 constitution. This tension led to an accelerated effort by the Park government to gain support in the United States Congress. The methods used by Seoul's lobbyists ultimately resulted in the embarrassing "Koreagate" affair of 1977, involving former Ambassador Kim Dong-jo and rice dealer Park Tong Sun. Investigations by the Ethics Committee and by the Subcommittee on International Organizations of the Committee on International Relations of the United States House of Representatives received much press coverage and weakened United States support for South Korea.

During his presidential election campaign in 1976, Jimmy Carter pledged, if elected, to withdraw all combat troops from South Korea. His victory aggravated United States-South Korean relations considerably (see Relations with The United States, ch. 4). In March 1977, the United States decided to withdraw its ground combat forces over a four-to-five year period. Some 3,600 troops subsequently were withdrawn, but further reductions were suspended in 1979. In the meantime, President Carter and the Congress continued to press for the improvement of the human rights climate in South Korea. Relations between the two countries were at a low point in 1979, just before Park's assassination. In early 1981, President Ronald Reagan's administration announced that further withdrawals were not being considered.

The Transition

Soon after Park's October 26, 1979 assassination, South Korea went through kaleidoscopic changes—intense and open competition for power, student upheavals, a military takeover, a gruesome massacre, and the emergence of a new authoritarian order. Since Park had concentrated virtually all political power around himself, his assassination created a political vacuum. One of his main pillars of power, the director of the Presidential Security Force, was assassinated with him; the director of the other major political instrument, the KCIA, was quickly arrested by the Martial Law Command for conducting the assassinations. In addition, the National Assembly, one-third of its members presidential appointees, had been rendered impotent by the *yusin* constitution.

Ch'oe Kyu-ha, premier under Park, was elected president in December 1979 by the National Conference for Unification, a rubber stamp electoral college. Ch'oe had no independent political base. He reaffirmed the need for a new constitution in his December 21 inaugural speech, stating that a new constitution supported by a majority of the people would be adopted within a year and that a fair general election would be held soon afterward.

Even before his inauguration, Ch'oe, as acting president, had abolished Emergency Measure Number Nine. Several hundred individuals serving prison terms or being investigated on charges of violating that decree were released on December 8. One of those benefiting from the release was Kim Dae Jung, who had been under house arrest and whose civil rights were to be restored on February 29, 1980. Also affected were student activists who had been arrested for staging campus demonstrations.

Lieutenant General Chun Doo Hwan, the head of the Defense Security Command, was responsible for conducting the investigation of Park's assassination. Chun used the factionalism rife within the military to assert his control over the army on December 12, 1979. He promptly set about uprooting the Park-era power elite and building a new political base. This power play, combined with increasing social and labor unrest, economic instability, and the factionalism within and between the ruling and opposition parties, set the scene for the military's consolidation of power and culminated in Chun's assumption of the presidency in August 1980.

Politics in South Korea in 1980 mainly revolved around framing a new constitution. The principal opposition party, the New Democratic Party under Kim Young Sam, advocated concluding the process by August 15, but President Ch'oe, evidently under military pressure, was not ready to expedite the constitutional process. The scheduling issue led to a major student upheaval in May 1980, followed by a military takeover.

The Democratic Republican Party

In the meantime, the country underwent a brisk process of political realignment. Although Park had organized and headed the Democratic Republican Party in 1963 to mobilize mass support behind his regime, by 1972 he had discarded it when he imposed the *yusin* constitution. As a result, the DRP had only a nominal existence at the time of Park's death. It was incumbent upon the new president of the DRP, Kim Chong-p'il, to revive the party. The DRP had suffered a disastrous loss in the December 1978 National Assembly elections. This situation led to a call for "rectification" (*chŏngp'ung*) within the party, which meant removing certain top leaders who had attracted notoriety for illicit wealth and undemocratic political behavior.

The New Democratic Party

The New Democratic Party (NDP), the principal opposition party, also had its share of problems. Kim Young Sam was elected as NDP leader for three years in 1979, so his position would have been secure had not the Ch'oe government restored Kim Dae Jung's civil rights. Even though Kim Dae Jung, the NDP presidential candidate in 1971, had been out of the political arena for more than seven years, he commanded a large political following. Because the NDP was expected to win the forthcoming election by a wide margin, the presidency of the republic was at stake in the negotiations for Kim Dae Jung's reinstatement in the party. In the end, negotiations broke off, and on April 7, 1980, Kim Dae Jung declared that he would no longer seek to rejoin the NDP.

Although Kim Young Sam and his supporters had waged a fierce political struggle against President Park toward the end of his rule, many of those in leadership positions in the NDP had tended to be accommodating to the Park regime. Kim Dae Jung and his followers, on the other hand, represented the active dissident students, intellectuals, and progressive Christians who had engaged in direct struggle against the Park regime. The *chaeya seryŏk* (literally, forces in the field, but the term also means an opposing political force) were more radical in orientation. Kim Dae Jung and his group wished to expedite the process of restoring democracy, even if it meant forcing the hands of Ch'oe and his supporters.

Students in 1980

While professional politicians engaged in the struggle for realignment, college students were restless for action. The students initially were concerned with campus affairs. As soon as the new semester began in March 1980, students on various campuses began to demand the removal of professors with close ties to the Park regime and of university owner-presidents who had amassed fortunes by operating their institutions. They also demanded autonomy from government control. The students held rallies and on-campus demonstrations and in some cases occupied college offices. As a result of the unrest, many university presidents resigned.

In early May 1980, however, the students' slogans began to change. Students demanded that martial law be lifted immediately and that the "remnants of the *yusin* system," including Chun, be removed. They also demanded the guarantee of labor rights, the removal of "compradore capital," and the protection of farmers' rights. Although student demonstrations had been confined to their campuses when the issues raised concerned institutional matters, they now began to spill out into the streets.

The massive demonstrations by the students continued until May 16, when Premier Sin Hyŏn-hwak promised that the government would attempt to speed up the process of adopting a new constitution. Ch'oe even shortened his Middle Eastern trip by a day and returned home on the evening of May 17. Student demonstrations paralyzed the nation and sent politicians and government leaders to their council meetings. According to an unconfirmed report, Sin even offered his resignation to the president upon his return and advised the president to remove Chun.

General Chun Doo Hwan Takes Over

Whatever counsel the civilian leaders may have offered Ch'oe, the military's position prevailed. Chun Doo Hwan, as head of the Defense Security Command, had already replaced the army chief of staff in December 1979 and had taken the command of the KCIA in April 1980.

Chun's methodical and speedy actions after May 17 clearly revealed that he had a well-laid plan. He issued a decree closing down the colleges and universities and prohibiting all political gatherings. All publications and broadcasts were to receive prior censorship, criticism of the incumbent and past presidents was outlawed, and the manufacture and spreading of rumors were forbidden.

Chun's plan aimed not only at quelling demonstrations but also at destroying the power base of all existing political figures and groups.

The arrest of Kim Dae Jung and other arch enemies of Park was to be expected as soon as the military stepped in on May 17. But the arrest of Kim Chong-p'il and other people who had been influential under Park came as a total surprise.

The Kwangju Uprising

Chun's hard-line policy led to a confrontation in Kwangju, a city of 600,000 people located 170 miles south of Seoul, in South Chŏlla Province, the scene of an uprising and bloodbath between May 18 and 27. As noted in a report issued by the Martial Law Command, the students and "hot-blooded young soldiers" confronted each other; angry citizens joined in, driven by alleged rumors that the "soldiers of Kyŏngsang Province origin came to exterminate the seeds of the Chŏlla people."

The Kwangju massacre was to became an important landmark in the struggle for South Korean democracy. It heightened provincial hostility and marked the beginning of the rise of anti-American sentiment in South Korea.

According to the report, the sequence of events was triggered by student demonstrations on the morning of May 18 in defiance of the new edict. Some 200 Chŏnnam University students began demonstrating in the morning, and by 2:00 P.M. they had been joined by more than 800 additional demonstrators. City police were unable to control the crowd. At about 4:00 P.M., the Martial Law Command dispatched a Special Forces detachment consisting of paratroopers trained for assault missions. The report did not mention it, but the paratroopers killed a large number of people.

On May 20, some 10,000 people demonstrated in Kwangju. On May 21, the Special Forces were withdrawn, and the city was left to the rioters. A memorial service was held on May 24, with approximately 15,000 citizens in attendance.

On May 25, approximately 50,000 people gathered for a rally and adopted a resolution calling for the abolition of martial law and the release of Kim Dae Jung. A committee of leading citizens was organized on May 23 to try to settle the impasse, but "impure elements" and "maneuverers behind the scene" allegedly obstructed an effective solution. On May 27, at 3:30 A.M., an army division that had been circling the city for three days launched an attack. After light skirmishes, the army quashed the revolt in less than two hours. The army arrested 1,740 rioters, of whom 730 were detained for investigation.

A number of conclusions can be drawn from the Martial Law Command's account. The uprising started with student demonstrations. The Martial Law Command dispatched assault troops whose random killings angered citizens who had not participated in the initial student demonstrations. According to later reports by the command, nearly 200 persons were killed, including 22 soldiers and 4 policemen; of the civilians killed, only 17 died on the final day of assault. And, regardless of who spread the "wanton rumors," they evidently were credible enough to prompt the gathering of 50,000 Kwangju citizens.

Chun, touring the city after the revolt had ended, told the people of Kwangju not to make an issue of what had happened, but to learn from it. The specter of Kwangju, however, was to haunt him for years to come.

There were several aftereffects resulting from the Kwangju incident. It deepened the chasm that had existed between the Kyŏngsang provinces (from which Park and Chun originated) and the Chŏlla provinces, of which Kwangju is a capital and from which the opposition leader Kim Dae Jung came (see Population Settlement Patterns, ch. 2). The United States' role also was controversial. General John A. Wickham, Jr. had released South Korean troops from the South Korea-United States Combined Forces Command to end the rebellion, and President Reagan had strongly endorsed Chun's actions (see Relations with the United States, ch. 4).

The Chun Regime

Having suppressed the Kwangju uprising with brute force, General Chun Doo Hwan further tightened his grip on the government. He and three of his close associates served as the core of the junta committee, known as the Special Committee for National Security Measures. The three were Lieutenant General Ch'a Kyuhŏn (deputy chief of staff of the army), Major General Roh Tae Woo (commander of the Capital Garrison Command), and Major General Chŏng Ho-yong (commander of the Special Forces). The junta vested in itself the authority to pass laws and to make all decisions affecting the state until a new National Assembly came into being.

On August 5, 1980, Chun promoted himself from lieutenant general to full general in preparation for retiring from the army on August 22. On August 27 he was elected president by the National Conference for Unification, receiving 2,524 of the 2,525 votes cast. The single dissenting vote was invalidated for an unknown reason.

Chun presented his objective at his September 1, 1980, inauguration: to create a new society where all past corrupt practices would be replaced by mutual trust and justice. In order to accomplish this goal, he planned to remove the old politicians from the scene; only those certified as "clean" would be permitted to participate in building the new order.

In the economic field, Chun intended to do away with excessive protection of industries and to encourage creativity. An increase in employment opportunities would be facilitated, and cooperation and coprosperity between labor and management would be brought about. Farmers' income would be increased by continuing the Saemaŭl Movement.

The 1980 Constitution

One of Chun's inaugural promises was the promulgation of a new constitution and the holding of a national referendum to approve it. On September 29, 1980, the government announced the draft of a constitution that in many ways was the most democratic South Korea had ever had—except for the supplementary provisions and the procedure for presidential election. The guarantee of peoples' democratic rights was absolute, including the right to privacy in communications, the prohibition of torture, and the inadmissability in court trials of confessions obtained by force. The president, who was to be elected by an electoral college and to serve a single seven-year term, was given strong powers, including the right to dissolve the National Assembly, which in turn could bring down cabinets but not the president. In the event that the constitution was amended to extend the president's term of office, such changes were not to be applied to the incumbent. The document received the overwhelming approval of the voters—91.6 percent—at the national referendum held on October 22, 1980.

The constitution, however, was a "promissory note." Until the new National Assembly was elected and inaugurated, the Legislative Council for National Security, to be appointed by Chun, would enact all laws. A supplementary provision in the constitution also called for the dissolution of all existing political parties. In effect, by offering to bring in a democratic government by June 1981, Chun had obtained a mandate to change the political landscape in whatever form he chose. The new constitution placed South Korea under a constitutional dictatorship from October 1980 to June 1981.

Purges

Chun zealously pushed his campaign to weed out corruption.

The clean-up campaign began in May 1980 when Kim Chong-p'il and others were forced to give up their wealth and retire from politics. In June some 300 senior KCIA agents were dismissed. In July 1980, more than 230 senior officials, including former cabinet officers, were dismissed on corruption charges. The ax also fell on 4,760 low-level officials in the government, state-owned firms, and banks, with the proviso that the former officials not be rehired by such firms within two years. The Martial Law Command arrested 17 prominent politicians of both the government and opposition parties for investigation and removed some 400 bank officials, including 4 bank presidents and 21 vice presidents. The government also announced the dismissal of 1,819 officials of public enterprises and affiliated agencies, including 39 (some 25 percent) of the presidents and vice presidents of such enterprises and banks and 128 board directors (more than 22 percent).

The "clean-up campaign" also extended to the mass media. On July 31, 1980, the 172 periodicals that allegedly caused "social decay and juvenile delinquency" were summarily abolished, among them some of the finest intellectual magazines of liberal inclination and prestigious journals for general audiences. This action resulted in the dismissal of hundreds of journalists and staff. The daily newspapers not affected by the purge also were directed to weed out "corrupting," that is, liberal writers (see The Media, ch. 4).

Chun's "Cultural Revolution"

In the wake of Chun's purge, the government also launched a massive reeducation program for the nation's elites. High government officials, judges, prosecutors, business executives, college professors, and their spouses—32,000 persons in all—were brought together for an intensive three-day training program at Saemaǔl's New Community Training Centers in Suwŏn and elsewhere. The training regimen included morning exercises, environmental cleanup, lectures on the New Community Movement, and discussion sessions on "the proper way of life."

This training program, initiated under Park's regime, eventually was to be extended to the general public. In August 1980, the government launched another massive propaganda campaign, organizing "Bright Society Rallies" in major cities where tens of thousands of citizens were mobilized to hear speeches. In addition, "Cleansing Committees" were established at all levels of government down to the local ward (*ri* and *dong*) levels (see Local Administration, ch. 4).

Economic Performance

The new regime inherited an economy suffering from all the side effects of Park's export-oriented development program and policy of expanding heavy and chemical industries (see Economic Development, this ch.; Industrial Policies, ch. 3). The international economic environment of the early 1980s was extremely unfavorable, a situation that further restricted South Korea's exports. It was necessary, therefore, for the Chun regime to concentrate on stabilization, and it devoted its first two years to controlling inflation while attempting to bring about economic recovery. Investment was redirected from the capital-intensive heavy and chemical industries towards labor-intensive light industries that produced consumer goods. Import restrictions were lifted.

The economy began to improve in 1983 because of stringent anti-inflationary measures and the upturn in the world economy. While South Korea had suffered a negative growth rate in 1980, it attained an 8.1 percent growth rate in 1983. Exports began increasing in mid-1983 and the economy began to gain strength. A good harvest in 1983 also helped. South Korea attained its 1983 export target of US$23.5 billion, a 7.6 percent increase from 1982.

In December 1983, Seoul unveiled its revised Fifth Five-Year Economic and Social Development Plan. The plan called for steady growth for the next three years, low inflation, and sharply reduced foreign borrowing. Exports were to rise by 15 percent a year, inflation was projected to be held at 1.8 percent, and per capita GNP was to rise to US$2,325 by 1986. The annual growth rate was planned to average 7.5 percent though the actual performance was higher. The real GNP growth rate was 7 percent in 1985, but for the next three years 12.9 percent, 12.8 percent, and 12.2 percent, respectively.

Foreign Policy

United States

One of the most salient elements of the Chun regime was its close ties with the Reagan administration. The ties were in sharp contrast to the strained Washington-Seoul relationship under presidents Carter and Park, when the United States government had criticized Park's dictatorial policies and attempted to implement Carter's campaign pledge to withdraw United States ground combat troops from South Korea. The relationship also had been strained because of the 1977 Koreagate scandal.

Reagan provided unmitigated support to Chun and to South

Korea's security. Chun was Reagan's first official guest in the White House. Reagan reaffirmed his support of Chun by visiting Seoul in November 1983.

While Reagan's support considerably buttressed Chun's stature in domestic politics and the international arena, it also fueled the subculture of anti-Americanism. The opposition forces in South Korea, suffering from the government's stringent suppression, denounced United States' support for the Chun regime as a callous disregard for human rights and questioned the United States' motives in Korea. The past image of the United States as a staunch supporter of democracy in South Korea was replaced with that of defender of its own interests, a policy impervious to injustices committed in South Korea. This view was accentuated by the fact that Chun's White House visit occurred only several months after the Martial Law Command had brutally suppressed the student uprising in Kwangju. (It was later revealed by Richard V. Allen, National Security Advisor to President Reagan, that Chun's visit was part of Washington's diplomatic effort to spare the life of Kim Dae Jung, who had been sentenced to death.) This atmosphere led some of South Korea's radical elements to take extreme measures, such as arson committed at the United States Information Service building in Pusan in March 1982 and the occupation of the United States Information Service Library in Seoul in May 1985. Students who demonstrated against the Chun government invariably carried anti-American slogans.

Japan

The Chun government also brought about a significant change in South Korea's relations with Japan. In 1981 Chun utilized the United States' support and its strategy of allocating greater responsibility to Japan in the East Asian region to persuade Tokyo to grant Seoul a large public loan. The negotiations lasted until early 1983 and aroused many conflicting emotions in both countries. However, Chun was able to obtain a US$4 billion low-interest loan that significantly contributed to boosting South Korea's credit rating and to accelerating its economic recovery; Seoul's foreign debt had reached US$41 billion at the end of 1983 and was badly in need of an improved credit rating. Japanese prime minister Nakasone Yasuhiro capped the negotiation process by paying a state visit to Seoul in January 1983. Whereas other Japanese prime ministers had visited Seoul for inaugurations or funerals, this was the first state visit to South Korea by a Japanese leader since the country was liberated from Japan in 1945.

China and the Soviet Union

Chun continued Park's policy of improving relations with China and the Soviet Union and attached considerable importance to these two countries, long the allies of North Korea. Beijing and Moscow were thought to have much influence in charting the future of the Korean Peninsula and were thus a part of Nordpolitik (see Relations with the Soviet Union; Relations with China, ch. 4).

Seoul's official contact with Beijing was facilitated by the landing of a hijacked Chinese civilian airliner in May 1983. China sent a delegation of thirty-three officials to Seoul to negotiate the return of the airliner, marking the beginning of frequent exchanges of personnel. For example, in March 1984, a South Korean tennis team visited Kunming for a Davis Cup match with a Chinese team. In April 1984, a thirty-four-member Chinese basketball team arrived in Seoul to participate in the Eighth Asian Junior Basketball Championships. Some Chinese officials reportedly paid quiet visits to South Korea to inspect its industries, and South Korean officials visited China to attend various international conferences. Since China and South Korea began indirect trade in 1975, the volume has steadily increased (see Foreign Trade Policy, ch. 3).

The Soviet Union's unofficial relationship with South Korea began in 1973, when it permitted South Koreans to attend an international conference held in the Soviet Union. In October 1982, a Soviet official attended an international conference in South Korea on the preservation of cultural relics. The uproar following the Korean Air (KAL) 007 incident in September 1983, when the Soviet air force shot down the KAL passenger airplane, brought about a hiatus in contacts, but the unofficial relationship resumed in 1988.

The Demise of the Chun Regime

Even though Chun Doo Hwan's government had attained considerable results in economy and diplomacy, his government failed to win public trust or support. In spite of Chun's lofty pronouncements, the public basically regarded Chun as a usurper of power who had deprived South Korea of its opportunity to restore democracy. Chun lacked political credentials; his access to power derived from his position as the head of the Defense Security Command—the army's nerve center of political intelligence—and his ability to bring together his generals in the front lines.

Chun and his military followers failed to overcome the stigma of the Kwangju incident, and the new ''just society'' that he promised did not materialize. In fact, between 1982 and 1983, at least two of the major financial scandals in South Korea involved

Chun's in-laws. The Chun government's slogans became hollow. While Park had gained respect and popularity through the record-breaking pace of economic development, Chun could not repeat such a feat. In the 1985 National Assembly elections, opposition parties together won more votes than the government party, clearly indicating that the public wanted a change. Moreover, increasing numbers of people had become more sympathetic to the students, who presented increasingly radical demands.

One of the most serious problems the government faced was that the argument for restricting democracy became less and less credible. The people had long been tolerant of various restrictions imposed by succeeding governments because of the perceived threat from the north, but the consensus eroded as the international environment moderated. More and more people became cynical about repeated government pronouncements, viewing them as self-serving propaganda by those in power. This tendency was particularly pronounced among the post-Korean War generation that constituted a majority of the South Korean population.

The unpopular Chun regime and its constitutional framework was brought down in 1987 largely by the student agitation that beset the regime. Student activists set the tone and agenda of the society as a whole because the government and the government-controlled press had lost their credibility. The opposition parties worked with the students, although they disagreed on the ultimate aim—the politicians wanted reform, while the students demanded revolution. The opposition politicians wanted constitutional reform to replace the existing system of electing the president through the handpicked electoral college with direct popular election. The students attacked not only the military leaders in power but also the entire socio-political and economic establishment.

A small number of confirmed radicals led the student movement. They argued that the basic cause for the political and social malaise in South Korea was "American imperialism," which they believed had dominated South Korea ever since it was liberated from Japan in 1945. In their view, "American imperialism" buttressed the military dictatorship and the exploitative capitalist system; the struggle against the military dictatorship and American imperialism was inseparable. This position was the same argument that North Korea had been advancing since 1946, but a more important source of intellectual persuasion came from the revisionist school of historiography that swept United States academia during the 1970s.

The revisionist argument was very similar to that of Lenin on imperialism. The Cold War was seen as the inevitable outcome of the United States capitalist system's need for continuous economic expansion abroad. United States participation in the Korean War and the subsequent stationing of United States forces in South Korea satisfied such a need, according to this perspective. For the revisionists, it was irrelevant that the United States had decided to abandon Korea in September-October 1947, or that the United States had withdrawn its occupation forces from South Korea in 1949. The communist countries, whether the Soviet Union or North Korea, were seen as passive entities reacting against the aggressive actions of "American imperialists" rather than pursuing their own goals. The fact that the United States had interjected itself into the Korean War in 1950, and that it continued to station its troops in South Korea after the war, was evidence enough.

The revisionist arguments found a fertile soil among the university students. The inquisitive students had long viewed the one-sided anticommunist propaganda emanating from official and established sources as stifling and as leaving too many questions unanswered. The new arguments sounded logical and convincing, particularly when some of the revisionists took liberty with historical evidence. Increasing numbers of students took to the streets to denounce the military dictatorship and American imperialism.

Initially, the public was apathetic to the confrontation between the student demonstrators and government, but the daily fracas on the streets and the never-ending smell of tear gas aroused their ire. The news about the torture and death of a student, Pak Chong-ch'ŏl, by the police touched the sore nerves of the people. President Chun attempted to squash the opposition by issuing a declaration on April 13, 1987, to suspend the "wasteful debate" about constitutional reform until a new government was installed at the end of his seven-year term. The declaration was, instead, his regime's swan song. Chun wanted to have his successor "elected" by his handpicked supporters; the public greeted the declaration with universal outrage. Even the Reagan administration, which had been taciturn about South Korea's internal politics, urged the Chun government not to ignore the outrage. Finally, on June 29, 1987, Roh Tae Woo, the government party's choice as Chun's successor, made a dramatic announcement in favor of a new democratic constitution that embodied all the opposition's demands.

* * *

Extensive literature is available in English on all the subjects covered in this chapter. Ki-baik Lee's *A New History of Korea* is the best account of Korean history available in English. The following sources are also helpful: Han Woo-kuen's *The History of Korea;*

William Henthorn's *A History of Korea;* *The History of Korea* by Sohn Pow-key, Kim Chol-choon, and Hong Yi-sup; and *East Asia: Tradition and Transformation,* coauthored by John K. Fairbank, Edwin O. Reischauer, and Albert M. Craig.

Aspects of the Chosŏn Dynasty are dealt with in JaHyun Kim Haboush's *A Heritage of Kings,* William Shaw's *Legal Norms in a Confucian State,* and Young-ho Ch'oe's *The Civil Examinations and the Social Structure in Early Yi Dynasty Korea.* Late nineteenth-century developments are covered in Vipan Chandra's *Imperialism, Resistance, and Reform in Late Nineteenth-Century Korea,* James B. Palais's *Politics and Policy in Traditional Korea,* and C.I. Eugene Kim and Han-Kyo Kim's *Korea and the Politics of Imperialism, 1876–1910.*

Various aspects of Japanese rule are detailed in Andrew J. Grajdanzev's *Modern Korea* and Chong-Sik Lee's *Japan and Korea: The Political Dimension.* Korea's reaction to Japanese colonialism is recounted in Chong-Sik Lee's *The Politics of Korean Nationalism.* George McAfee McCune's *Korea Today* is particularly valuable for the period between 1945 and 1948. The period of Japanese colonial rule is also treated in Dennis L. McNamara's *The Colonial Origins of Korean Enterprise* and Michael Edson Robinson's *Cultural Nationalism in Colonial Korea, 1920–1925.*

Among the numerous works that have taken advantage of declassified documents concerning the period leading up the Korean War are James Irving Matray's *The Reluctant Crusade,* the second volume of Bruce Cuming's work on that period, *The Roaring of the Cataract, 1947–50,* and Peter Lowe's *The Origins of the Korea War.*

Information about Korea under Syngman Rhee can be found in Gregory Henderson's book, *Korea: The Politics of the Vortex;* in Joungwon Alexander Kim's *Divided Korea: The Politics of Development, 1945–1972;* and in Chi-young Pak's *Political Opposition in Korea, 1945–1960.* Robert T. Oliver, a close associate of Rhee, explains Rhee's actions in *Syngman Rhee and American Involvement in Korea, 1942–1960.* Lee Hahn-Been's *Korea: Time, Change, and Administration* analyzes governmental performance under Rhee and subsequent regimes. Han Sung-Joo's *The Failure of Democracy in South Korea* provides an incisive analysis of both the Rhee regime and the Chang Myŏn government.

A number of books treat Korea in the modern era, although most of them emphasize the political aspect of the society. Gregory Henderson's book is particularly valuable for its treatment of modern and contemporary periods through the late 1960s. The 1961 coup d'état and the government under Park Chung Hee are discussed in Kim Se-Jin's *The Politics of Military Revolution in Korea,*

John Kie-Chiang Oh's *Korea: Democracy on Trial,* David C. Cole and Princeton N. Lyman's *Korean Development: The Interplay of Politics and Economics,* Young Whan Kihl's *Politics and Policies in Divided Korea,* Sung Chul Yang's *Korea and Two Regimes,* and *The Economic and Social Modernization of the Republic of Korea* by Edward S. Mason and others. For the government under Chun Doo Hwan, see Harold C. Hinton's *Korea under New Leadership;* for South Korea's foreign policy, see Youngnok Koo and Sung-joo Han's *Foreign Policy of the Republic of Korea* and Byung Chul Koh's *The Foreign Policy Systems of North and South Korea.* South Korea's relations with North Korea are treated in detail by Robert A. Scalapino and Chong-Sik Lee's *Communism in Korea* and Ralph N. Clough's *Embattled Korea.*

Studies on Korea: A Scholar's Guide, edited by Kim Han-Kyo, lists numerous books and articles; many items are annotated. *Far Eastern Economic Review, Journal of Northeast Asian Studies, Asian Wall Street Journal,* and *Asian Survey* regularly provide analyses of South Korea's politics and economy. A comprehensive source of publications dealing with Korean history is the Association for Asian Studies' annual *Bibliography of Asian Studies.* (For further information and complete citations, see Bibliography.)

Chapter 2. The Society and Its Environment

North Watergate, Suwŏn Castle, has a stone bridge with seven arches spanning the Namch'on River.

FEW SOCIETIES HAVE CHANGED as rapidly or as dramatically since the end of World War II as that of the Republic of Korea (South Korea). When the war ended in 1945, the great majority of the people living in the southern half of the Korean Peninsula were poor peasants. The Japanese colonial regime from 1910 to 1945 had promoted modernization of the economy and society. The regime's efforts, however, had a limited, and mainly negative, impact on most Koreans inasmuch as the main intent of the modernization program was to serve Japan. The poverty and distress of the South Koreans were deepened by the Korean War of 1950–53 when numerous people died and cities and towns were devastated. During the next four decades, however, South Korea evolved into a dynamic, industrial society. By 1990 educational and public health standards were high, most people lived in urban areas, and a complex structure of social classes had emerged that resembled the social structures of developed Western countries or Japan. The country also was making substantial progress in its evolution from a military dictatorship similar to that of many Third World regimes to a democratic, pluralistic political system. In the mid-1950s, few observers could have imagined that Seoul, the country's capital, would emerge from the devastation of war to become one of the world's most vibrant metropolitan centers—rivaling Tokyo, Hong Kong, and Los Angeles.

Colonial occupation, war, and the tragedy of national division fostered abrupt social changes. Rapid economic growth engendered profound changes in values and human relationships. Yet there also was continuity with the past. Confucian and neo-Confucian ideas and institutions, which flourished during the Chosŏn Dynasty (1392–1910), continued to have an important impact in 1990. The Confucian influence was most evident in the tremendous value placed on education, a major factor in South Korea's economic progress. Equally evident was the persistence of hierarchical, often authoritarian, modes of human interaction that reflected neo-Confucianism's emphasis on inequality.

The complex kinship structures of the past, sanctified by Confucianism, had eroded because of urbanization but did not disappear. In 1990 Koreans were more likely to live in nuclear families than their parents or grandparents, but old Confucian ideas of filial piety still were strong. At the same time, contemporary social values were influenced by traditional but non-Confucian Korean values, such as shamanism and Buddhism, and by ideas brought into the country from the West and Japan.

The population of the Korean Peninsula, sharing a common language, ethnic identity, and culture, was one of the world's most homogeneous. Although there were significant regional differences even within the relatively small land area of South Korea, neither the Democratic People's Republic of Korea (North Korea) nor South Korea had significant non-Korean ethnic minorities. This homogeneity, and the sense of a shared historical experience that it promoted, gave the people of South Korea a strong sense of national purpose. However, the years of Japanese colonial rule, the division of the peninsula after World War II, the establishment of two antagonistic states in the north and south, and the profound changes in the economy and society caused by industrialization and urbanization since the 1950s led many South Koreans to search anew for their national identity and place in the world. Often, the concern for identity expressed itself as xenophobia, the creation of a "national mythology" that was given official or semiofficial sanction, or the search for the special and unique "essence" of Korean culture.

Physical Environment

Land Area and Borders

The Korean Peninsula extends for about 1,000 kilometers southward from the northeast part of the Asian continental landmass. The Japanese islands of Honshū and Kyūshū are located some 200 kilometers to the southeast across the Korea Strait; the Shandong Peninsula of China lies 190 kilometers to the west. The west coast of the peninsula is bordered by the Korea Bay to the north and the Yellow Sea to the south; the east coast is bordered by the Sea of Japan (known in Korea as the East Sea). The 8,640-kilometer coastline is highly indented. Some 3,579 islands lie adjacent to the peninsula. Most of them are found along the south and west coasts.

The northern land border of the Korean Peninsula is formed by the Yalu and Tumen rivers, which separate Korea from the provinces of Jilin and Liaoning in China. The original border between the two Korean states was the thirty-eighth parallel of latitude. After the Korean War, the Demilitarized Zone (DMZ—see Glossary) formed the boundary between the two. The DMZ is a heavily guarded, 4,000-meter-wide strip of land that runs along the line of cease-fire, the Demarcation Line (see Glossary), from the east to the west coasts for a distance of 241 kilometers (238 kilometers of that line form the land boundary with North Korea).

The total land area of the peninsula, including the islands, is 220,847 square kilometers. Some 44.6 percent (98,477 square kilometers) of this total, excluding the area within the DMZ, constitutes the territory of the Republic of Korea. The combined territories of North Korea and South Korea are about the same size as the state of Minnesota. South Korea alone is about the size of Portugal or Hungary and is slightly larger than the state of Indiana.

The largest island, Cheju, lies off the southwest corner of the peninsula and has a land area of 1,825 square kilometers. Other important islands include Ullŭng in the Sea of Japan and Kanghwa Island at the mouth of the Han River. Although the eastern coastline of South Korea is generally unindented, the southern and western coasts are jagged and irregular. The difference is caused by the fact that the eastern coast is gradually rising, while the southern and western coasts are subsiding.

Lacking formidable land or sea barriers along its borders and occupying a central position among East Asian nations, the Korean Peninsula has served as a cultural bridge between the mainland and the Japanese archipelago. Korea contributed greatly to the development of Japan by transmitting both Indian Buddhist and Chinese Confucian culture, art, and religion. At the same time, Korea's exposed geographical position left it vulnerable to invasion by its stronger neighbors. When, in the late nineteenth century, British statesman Lord George Curzon described Korea as a "sort of political Tom Tiddler's ground between China, Russia, and Japan," he was describing a situation that had prevailed for several millennia, as would be tragically apparent during the twentieth century.

Topography and Drainage

Early European visitors to Korea remarked that the land resembled "a sea in a heavy gale" because of the large number of successive mountain ranges that crisscross the peninsula. The tallest mountains are in North Korea. The tallest mountain in South Korea is Mount Halla (1,950 meters), which is the cone of a volcanic formation constituting Cheju Island. There are three major mountain ranges within South Korea: the T'aebaek and Sobaek ranges and the Chiri Massif (see fig. 4).

Unlike Japan or the northern provinces of China, the Korean Peninsula is geologically stable. There are no active volcanoes, and there have been no strong earthquakes. Historical records, however, describe volcanic activity on Mount Halla during the Koryŏ Dynasty (918–1392 A.D.).

Over the centuries, Korea's inhabitants have cut down most of the ancient Korean forests, with the exception of a few remote, mountainous areas. The disappearance of the forests has been a major cause of soil erosion and flooding. Because of successful reforestation programs and the declining use of firewood as a source of energy since the 1960s, however, most of South Korea's hills in the 1980s were amply covered with foliage. South Korea has no extensive plains; its lowlands are the product of mountain erosion. Approximately 30 percent of the area of South Korea consists of lowlands, with the rest consisting of uplands and mountains. The great majority of the lowland area lies along the coasts, particularly the west coast, and along the major rivers. The most important lowlands are the Han River plain around Seoul, the P'yŏngt'aek coastal plain southwest of Seoul, the Kŭm River basin, the Naktong River basin, and the Yŏngsan and the Honam plains in the southwest. A narrow littoral plain extends along the east coast.

The Naktong is South Korea's longest river (521 kilometers). The Han River, which flows through Seoul, is 514 kilometers long, and the Kŭm River is 401 kilometers long. Other major rivers include the Imjin, which flows through both North Korea and South Korea and forms an estuary with the Han River; the Pukhan, a tributary of the Han that also flows out of North Korea; and the Sŏmjin. The major rivers flow north to south or east to west and empty into the Yellow Sea or the Korea Strait. They tend to be broad and shallow and to have wide seasonal variations in water flow.

News that North Korea was constructing a huge multipurpose dam at the base of Mount Kŭmgang (1,638 meters) north of the DMZ caused considerable consternation in South Korea during the mid-1980s. South Korean authorities feared that once it was completed, a sudden release of the dam's waters into the Pukhan River during north-south hostilities could flood Seoul and paralyze the capital region. During 1987 the Kŭmgang-san Dam was a major issue that Seoul sought to raise in talks with P'yŏngyang. Although Seoul completed a "Peace Dam" on the Pukhan River to counteract the potential threat of P'yŏngyang's dam project before the 1988 Olympics, the North Korean project apparently still was in its initial stages of construction in 1990.

Climate

Part of the East Asian monsoonal region, South Korea has a temperate climate with four distinct seasons. The movement of air masses from the Asian continent exerts greater influence on South Korea's weather than does air movement from the Pacific Ocean.

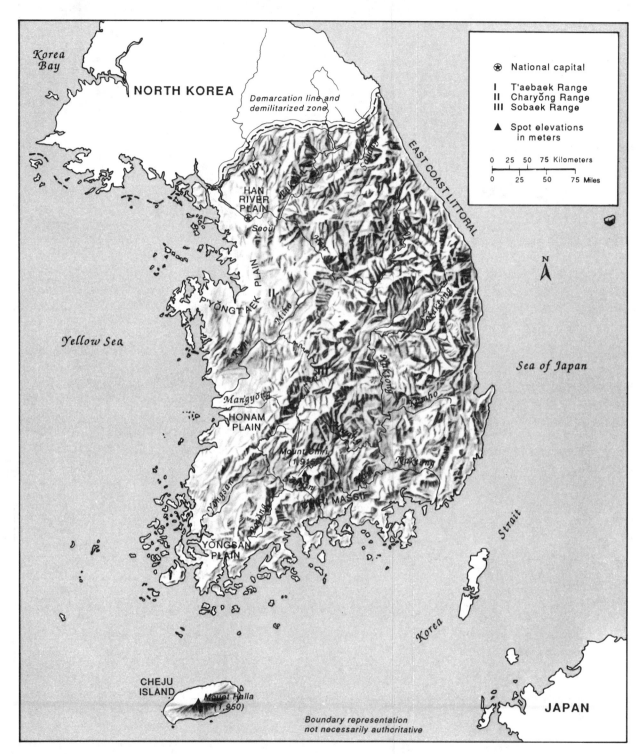

Figure 4. Topography and Drainage

Winters are usually long, cold, and dry, whereas summers are short, hot, and humid. Spring and autumn are pleasant but short in duration. Seoul's mean temperature in January is −5°C to −2.5°C; in July the mean temperature is about 22.5°C to 25°C. Because of its southern and seagirt location, Cheju Island has warmer and milder weather than other parts of South Korea. Mean temperatures on Cheju range from 2.5°C in January to 25°C in July.

The country generally has sufficient rainfall to sustain its agriculture. Rarely does less than 75 centimeters of rain fall in any given year; for the most part, rainfall is over 100 centimeters. Amounts of precipitation, however, can vary from year to year. Serious droughts occur about once every eight years, especially in the rice-producing southwestern part of the country. About two-thirds of the annual precipitation occurs between June and September.

South Korea is less vulnerable to typhoons than Japan, Taiwan, the east coast of China, or the Philippines. From one to three typhoons can be expected per year. Typhoons usually pass over South Korea in late summer, especially in August, and bring torrential rains (see fig. 5). Flooding occasionally causes considerable damage. In September 1984, record floods caused the deaths of 190 people and left 200,000 homeless. This disaster prompted the North Korean government to make an unprecedented offer of humanitarian aid in the form of rice, medicine, clothes, and building materials. South Korea accepted these items and distributed them to flood victims.

Population

Although a variety of different Asian peoples had migrated to the Korean Peninsula in past centuries, very few have remained permanently. Hence, by 1990 both South Korea and North Korea were among the world's most ethnically homogeneous nations. The number of indigenous minorities was negligible. In South Korea, people of foreign origin, including Westerners, Chinese, and Japanese, were a small percentage of the population, whose residence was generally temporary. Like their Japanese neighbors, Koreans tend to equate nationality or citizenship with membership in a single, homogeneous ethnic group or "race" (*minjok,* in Korean). A common language and culture also are viewed as important elements in Korean identity. The idea of multiracial or multiethnic nations, like India or the United States, strikes many Koreans as odd or even contradictory. Consciousness of homogeneity is a major reason why Koreans on both sides of the DMZ viewed their country's division as an unnatural and unnecessary tragedy.

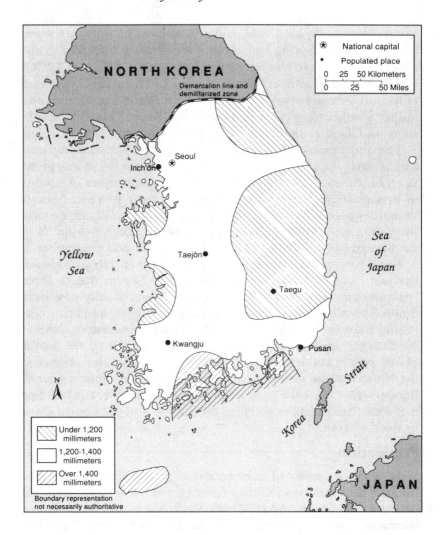

Figure 5. Average Annual Rainfall

Against the background of ethnic homogeneity, however, significant regional differences exist. Within South Korea, the most important regional difference is between the Kyŏngsang region, embracing North Kyŏngsang and South Kyŏngsang provinces in the southeast, and the Chŏlla region, embracing North Chŏlla and South Chŏlla provinces in the southwest. The two regions, separated by the Chiri Massif, nurture a rivalry said to reach back to the Three Kingdoms Period, which lasted from the fourth century to the seventh century A.D., when the kingdoms of Paekche and Silla struggled for control of the peninsula (see The Origins of the Korean Nation, ch. 1; fig. 2). Observers noted that interregional marriages are rare, and that as of 1990 a new four-lane highway completed in 1984 between Kwangju and Taegu, the capitals of South Chŏlla and North Kyŏngsang provinces, respectively, had not been successful in promoting travel between the two areas.

South Korea's political elite, including presidents Park Chung Hee, Chun Doo Hwan, and Roh Tae Woo, have come largely from the Kyŏngsang region. As a result, Kyŏngsang has been a special beneficiary of government development assistance. By contrast, the Chŏlla region has remained comparatively rural, undeveloped, and poor. Chronically disaffected, its people rightly or wrongly have a reputation for rebelliousness. Regional bitterness was intensified by the May 1980 Kwangju incident, in which about 200 and perhaps many more inhabitants of the capital of South Chŏlla Province were killed by government troops sent to quell an insurrection. Many of the troops reportedly were from the Kyŏngsang region (see Students in 1980, ch. 1; United States Forces in South Korea, ch. 5).

Regional stereotypes, like regional dialects, have been breaking down under the influence of centralized education, nationwide media, and the several decades of population movement since the Korean War. Stereotypes remain important, however, in the eyes of many South Koreans. For example, the people of Kyŏnggi Province, surrounding Seoul, are often described as being cultured, and Ch'ungch'ŏng people, inhabiting the region embracing North Ch'ungch'ŏng and South Ch'ungch'ŏng provinces, are thought to be mild-mannered, manifesting true *yangban* virtues (see Traditional Social Structure, this ch.). The people of Kangwŏn Province in the northeast are viewed as poor and stolid, whereas Koreans from the northern provinces of P'yŏngan, Hwanghae, and Hamgyŏng, now in North Korea, are perceived as being diligent and aggressive. Cheju Island is famous for its strong-minded and independent women.

Population Trends

The population of South Korea has grown rapidly since the republic's establishment in 1948. In the first official census, taken in 1949, the total population of South Korea was calculated at 20,188,641 people. The 1985 census total was 40,466,577. Population growth was slow, averaging about 1.1 percent annually during the period from 1949 to 1955, when the population registered at 21.5 million. Growth accelerated between 1955 and 1966 to 29.2

million or an annual average of 2.8 percent, but declined significantly during the period 1966 to 1985 to an annual average of 1.7 percent (see fig. 6). Thereafter, the annual average growth rate was estimated to be less than 1 percent, similar to the low growth rates of most industrialized countries and to the target figure set by the Ministry of Health and Social Affairs for the 1990s. As of January 1, 1989, the population of South Korea was estimated to be approximately 42.2 million.

The proportion of the total population under fifteen years of age has risen and fallen with the growth rate. In 1955 approximately 41.2 percent of the population was under fifteen years of age, a percentage that rose to 43.5 percent in 1966 before falling to 38.3 percent in 1975, 34.2 percent in 1980, and 29.9 percent in 1985. In the past, the large proportion of children relative to the total population put great strains on the country's economy, particularly because substantial resources were invested in education facilities (see Primary and Secondary Schools, this ch.). With the slowdown in the population growth rate and a rise in the median age (from 18.7 years to 21.8 years between 1960 and 1980), the age structure of the population has begun to resemble the columnar pattern typical of developed countries, rather than the pyramidal pattern found in most parts of the Third World.

The decline in the population growth rate and in the proportion of people under fifteen years of age after 1966 reflected the success of official and unofficial birth control programs. The government of President Syngman Rhee (1948–60) was conservative in such matters. Although Christian churches initiated a family planning campaign in 1957, it was not until 1962 that the government of Park Chung Hee, alarmed at the way in which the rapidly increasing population was undermining economic growth, began a nationwide family planning program. Other factors that contributed to a slowdown in population growth included urbanization, later marriage ages for both men and women, higher education levels, a greater number of women in the labor force, and better health standards (see Public Health and Welfare, this ch.).

Public and private agencies involved in family planning included the Ministry of Health and Social Affairs, the Ministry of Home Affairs, the Planned Parenthood Federation of Korea, and the Korea Institute of Family Planning. In the late 1980s, their activities included distribution of free birth control devices and information, classes for women on family planning methods, and the granting of special subsidies and privileges (such as low-interest housing loans) to parents who agreed to undergo sterilization. There were 502,000 South Koreans sterilized in 1984, as compared with 426,000 in the previous year.

The 1973 Maternal and Child Health Law legalized abortion. In 1983 the government began suspending medical insurance benefits for maternal care for pregnant women with three or more children. It also denied tax deductions for education expenses to parents with two or more children.

As in China, cultural attitudes pose problems for family planning programs. A strong preference for sons—who in Korea's Confucian value system are expected to care for their parents in old age and carry on the family name—means that parents with only daughters usually continue to have children until a son is born. The government has encouraged married couples to have only one child. Such encouragement has been a prominent theme in public service advertising, which stresses "have a single child and raise it well."

Total fertility rates (the average number of births a woman will have during her lifetime) fell from 6.1 births per female in 1960 to 4.2 in 1970, 2.8 in 1980, and 2.4 in 1984. The number of live births, recorded as 711,810 in 1978, grew to a high of 917,860 in 1982. This development stirred apprehensions among family planning experts of a new "baby boom." By 1986, however, the number of live births had declined to 806,041.

Given the size and age structure of the population in 1990, however, substantial increases are expected over the next few decades. According to the government's Economic Planning Board, the country's population will increase to between 46 and 48 million by the end of the twentieth century, with growth rates ranging between 0.9 and 1.2 percent. The population is expected to stabilize (that is, cease to grow) in the year 2023 at around 52.6 million people. In the words of *Asiaweek* magazine, the "stabilized tally will approximate the number of Filipinos in 1983, but squeezed into less than a third of their [the Philippines'] space."

Population Settlement Patterns

South Korea was one of the world's most densely populated countries, with an estimated 425 people per square kilometer in 1989—over sixteen times the average population density of the United States in the late 1980s. By comparison, China had an estimated 114 people, the Federal Republic of Germany (West Germany) 246 people, and Japan 323 people per square kilometer in the late 1980s. Because about 70 percent of South Korea's land area is mountainous and the population is concentrated in the lowland areas, actual population densities were in general greater than the

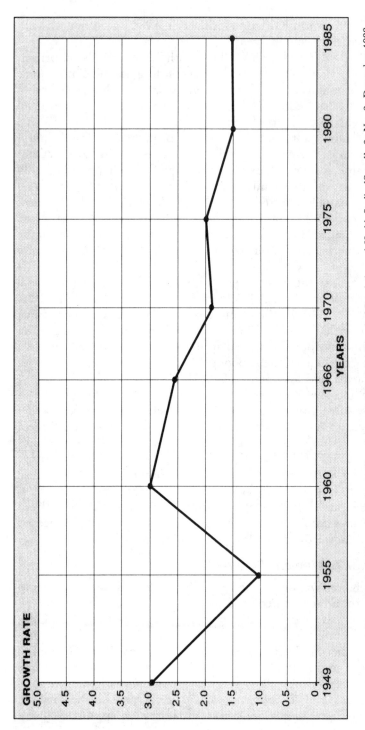

Source: Based on information from Korea Institute for Population and Health, *Journal of Population and Health Studies* [Seoul], 8, No. 2, December 1988, 11; and Republic of Korea, National Bureau of Statistics, Economic Planning Board, *Korea Statistical Handbook, 1987*, Seoul, 1987, 8.

Figure 6. Population Growth Rate, Selected Years, 1949–85

average. As early as 1975, it was estimated that the density of South Korea's thirty-five cities, each of which had a population of 50,000 or more inhabitants, was 3,700 people per square kilometer. Because of continued migration to urban areas, the figure was doubtless higher in the late 1980s.

In 1988 Seoul had a population density of 17,030 people per square kilometer as compared with 13,816 people per square kilometer in 1980. The second largest city, Pusan, had a density of 8,504 people per square kilometer in 1988 as compared with 7,272 people in 1980. Kyŏnggi Province, which surrounds the capital and contains Inch'ŏn, the country's fourth largest city, was the most densely populated province; Kangwŏn Province in the northeast was the least densely populated province.

The extreme crowding in South Korea in 1990 was a major factor not only in economic development and in the standard of living but also in the development of social attitudes and human relationships. More than most other peoples, South Koreans have had to learn to live peacefully with each other in small, crowded spaces, in which the competition for limited resources, including space itself, is intense. Continued population growth means that the shortage of space for living and working will grow more severe. According to the government's Economic Planning Board, the population density will be 530 people per square kilometer by 2023, the year the population is expected to stabilize.

Urbanization

Like other newly industrializing economies, South Korea experienced rapid growth of urban areas caused by the migration of large numbers of people from the countryside. In the eighteenth and nineteenth centuries, Seoul, by far the largest urban settlement, had a population of about 190,000 people. There was a striking contrast with Japan, where Edo (Tokyo) had as many as 1 million inhabitants and the urban population comprised as much as 10 to 15 percent of the total during the Tokugawa Period (1600–1868). During the closing years of the Chosŏn Dynasty and the first years of Japanese colonial rule, the urban population of Korea was no more than 3 percent of the total. After 1930, when the Japanese began industrial development on the Korean Peninsula, particularly in the northern provinces adjacent to Manchuria, the urban portion of the population began to grow, reaching 11.6 percent for all of Korea in 1940.

Between 1945 and 1985, the urban population of South Korea grew from 14.5 percent to 65.4 percent of the total population (see fig. 7). In 1988 the Economic Planning Board estimated that the

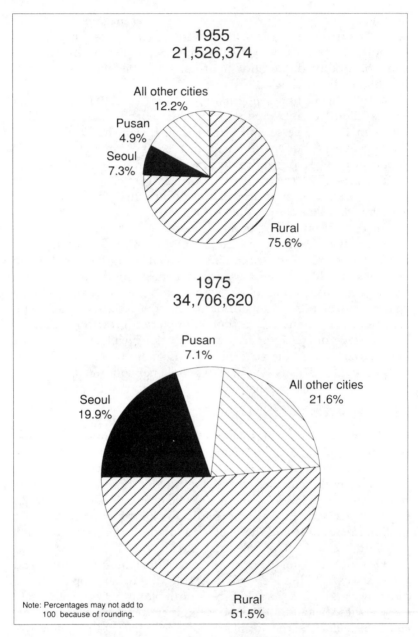

Source: Based on information from Korea Institute for Population and Health, *Journal of Population and Health Studies* [Seoul], 8, No. 2, December 1988, 19, 22.

Figure 7. Rural and Urban Population Distribution, Selected Years, 1955–85

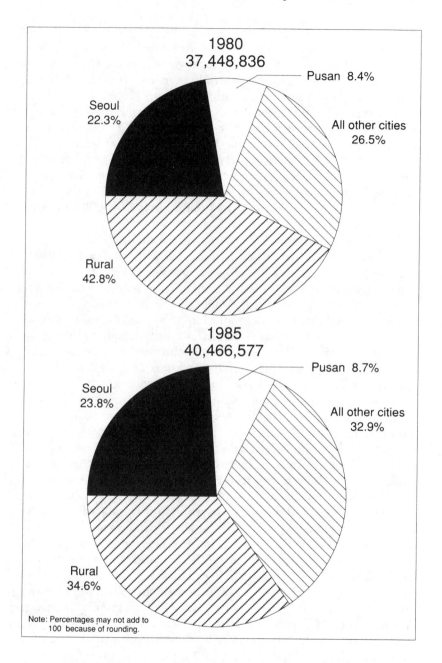

1980
37,448,836

Pusan 8.4%

Seoul
22.3%

All other cities
26.5%

Rural
42.8%

1985
40,466,577

Pusan 8.7%

Seoul
23.8%

All other cities
32.9%

Rural
34.6%

Note: Percentages may not add to
100 because of rounding.

urban portion of the population will reach 78.3 percent by the end of the twentieth century. Most of this urban increase was attributable to migration rather than to natural growth of the urban population. Urban birth rates have generally been lower than the national average. The extent of urbanization in South Korea, however, is not fully revealed in these statistics. Urban population was defined in the national census as being restricted to those municipalities with 50,000 or more inhabitants. Although many settlements with fewer than 50,000 inhabitants were satellite towns of Seoul or other large cities or mining communities in northeastern Kangwŏn Province, which would be considered urban in terms of the living conditions and occupations of the inhabitants, they still were officially classified as rural.

The dislocation caused by the Korean War accounted for the rapid increase in urban population during the early 1950s. Hundreds of thousands of refugees, many of them from North Korea, streamed into the cities. During the post-Korean War period, rural people left their ancestral villages in search of greater economic and educational opportunities in the cities. By the late 1960s, migration had become a serious problem, not only because cities were terribly overcrowded, but also because the rural areas were losing the most youthful and productive members of their labor force.

In the early 1970s, the Park Chung Hee government launched the Saemaŭl undong (New Community Movement) as a rural reconstruction and self-help movement to improve economic conditions in the villages, close the wide gap in income between rural and urban areas, and stem urban migration—as well as to build a political base. Despite a huge amount of government-sponsored publicity, especially during the Park era, it was not clear by the late 1980s that the Saemaŭl undong had achieved its objectives. By that time many, if not most, farming and fishing villages consisted of older persons; relatively few able-bodied men and women remained to work in the fields or to fish. This trend was apparent in government statistics for the 1986–87 period: the proportion of people fifty years old or older living in farming communities grew from 28.7 percent in 1986 to 30.6 percent in 1987, whereas the number of people in their twenties living in farming communities declined from 11.3 percent to 10.8 percent. The nationwide percentages for people fifty years old or older and in their twenties were, in 1986, 14.9 percent and 20.2 percent, respectively (see Agriculture, ch. 3).

In 1985 the largest cities were Seoul (9,645,932 inhabitants), Pusan (3,516,807), Taegu (2,030,672), Inch'ŏn (1,387,491), Kwangju (906,129), and Taejŏn (866,695). According to government statistics, the population of Seoul, one of the world's largest cities, surpassed 10 million people in late 1988. Seoul's average annual population growth rate during the late 1980s was more than 3 percent. Two-thirds of this growth was attributable to migration rather than to natural increase. Surveys revealed that "new employment or seeking a new job," "job transfer," and "business" were major reasons given by new immigrants for coming to the capital. Other factors cited by immigrants included "education" and "a more convenient area to live." To alleviate overcrowding in Seoul's downtown area, the city government drew up a master plan in the mid-1980s that envisioned the development of four "core zones" by 2000: the original downtown area, Yongdŭngp'o-Yŏido, Yŏngdong, and Ch'amsil. Satellite towns also would be established or expanded. In the late 1980s, statistics revealed that the daytime or commuter population of downtown Seoul was as much as six times the officially registered population. If the master plan is successful, many commuters will travel to work in a core area nearer their homes, and the downtown area's daytime population will decrease. Many government ministries have been moved out of Seoul, and the army, navy, and air force headquarters have been relocated to Taejŏn.

In 1985 the population of Seoul constituted 23.8 percent of the national total. Provincial cities, however, experienced equal and, in many cases, greater expansion than the capital. Growth was particularly spectacular in the southeastern coastal region, which encompasses the port cities of Pusan, Masan, Yŏsu, Chinhae, Ulsan, and P'ohang. Census figures show that Ulsan's population increased eighteenfold, growing from 30,000 to 551,300 inhabitants between 1960 and 1985. With the exception of Yŏsu, all of these cities are in South Kyŏngsang Province, a region that has been an especially favored recipient of government development projects. By comparison, the population of Kwangju, capital of South Chŏlla Province, increased less than threefold between 1960 and 1985, growing from 315,000 to 906,129 inhabitants.

Rapid urban growth has brought familiar problems to developed and developing countries alike. The construction of large numbers of high-rise apartment complexes in Seoul and other large cities alleviated housing shortages to some extent. But it also imposed hardship on the tens of thousands of people who were obliged to relocate from their old neighborhoods because they could not afford the rents in the new buildings. In the late 1980s, squatter areas consisting of one-story shacks still existed in some parts of Seoul. Housing for all but the wealthiest was generally cramped. The concentration of factories in urban areas, the rapid growth of motorized traffic, and the widespread use of coal for heating during the severe winter months have caused dangerous levels of air and water pollution. Although environmental awareness is increasing, a polluted environment will adversely affect the quality of life in the cities for some time to come.

Koreans Living Overseas

Large-scale emigration from Korea began around 1904 and continued until the end of World War II. During the Japanese colonial occupation, many Koreans emigrated to Manchuria (present-day China's northeastern provinces of Liaoning, Jilin, and Heilongjiang), other parts of China, the Soviet Union, Hawaii, and the continental United States. Most emigrated for economic reasons; employment opportunities were scarce, and many Korean farmers lost their land after the Japanese introduced a system of land registration and private land tenure, imposed higher land taxes, and promoted the growth of an absentee landlord class charging exorbitant rents. Koreans from the northern provinces of Korea went mainly to Manchuria, China, and Siberia. Many people from the southern provinces went to Japan. Koreans were conscripted into Japanese labor battalions or the Japanese army, especially during World War II. In the 1940–44 period, nearly 2 million Koreans lived in Japan, 1.4 million in Manchuria, 600,000 in Siberia, and 130,000 in China. An estimated 40,000 Koreans were scattered among other countries. At the end of World War II, approximately 2 million Koreans were repatriated from Japan and Manchuria.

More than 4 million ethnic Koreans lived outside the peninsula during the early 1980s. The largest group, about 1.7 million people, lived in China. Most had assumed Chinese citizenship. The Soviet Union had about 430,000 ethnic Koreans. One observer noted that Koreans had been so successful in running collective farms in Soviet Central Asia that being Korean was often associated by other Soviets with being rich.

By contrast, many of Japan's approximately 700,000 Koreans had below-average standards of living. This situation occurred partly because of discrimination by the Japanese majority and partly because of the fact that a large number of resident Koreans, loyal to the North Korean regime of Kim Il Sung, preferred to remain separate from and hostile to the Japanese mainstream. The pro-North Korea Chōsen sōren (General Association of Korean Residents in Japan) initially was more successful than the pro-South Korea Mindan (Association for Korean Residents in Japan) in attracting adherents among residents in Japan. Since diplomatic relations were established between Seoul and Tokyo in 1965, however,

Typical housing outside the city wall, Seoul, 1904
Courtesy Prints and Photographs Division, Library of Congress
Typical housing, Seoul, 1989
Courtesy Oren Hadar

87

the South Korean government has taken an active role in promoting the interests of their residents in Japan in negotiations with the Japanese government (see Relations with Japan, ch. 4). It also has provided subsidies to Korean schools in Japan and other community activities.

By the end of 1988, there were over 2 million South Korean overseas residents. North America was the preferred destination—the choice of over 1.2 million of these residents. Korean immigrants in the United States and Canada gained a reputation for hard work and economic success. South Koreans also were overseas residents of Japan (at least 680,000), Central America and South America (85,000), the Middle East (62,000), Western Europe (40,000), other Asian countries (27,000), and Africa (25,000). A limited number of South Korean government-sponsored migrants settled in Chile, Argentina, and other Latin American countries. Because of South Korea's rapid economic expansion, an increasing number of its citizens resided abroad on a temporary basis as business executives, technical personnel, foreign students, and construction workers. A small number of overseas South Koreans had migrated back to South Korea, primarily because of the much improved economic conditions and the difficulties in adjusting to living abroad.

Social Structure and Values

The social values of contemporary South Korea reflect the synthesis and development of diverse influences, both indigenous and foreign. Probably the most important of these is the neo-Confucian doctrine of the Chinese philosopher Zhu Xi (1130–1200), first introduced into Korea during the closing years of the Koryŏ Dynasty (918–1392). The rulers of the Chosŏn Dynasty (1392–1910) adopted it as their state ideology. The most important Korean neo-Confucian philosopher, Yi Hwang, also known as Yi T'oe-gye (1501–70), had a great influence on later generations of Confucianists not only in Korea but also in Japan.

Neo-Confucianism combines the social ethics of the classical Chinese philosophers Confucius (Kong Zi, 551–479 B.C.) and Mencius (Meng Zi, 372–289 B.C.) with Taoist, or Daoist, and Buddhist metaphysics. One of the doctrine's basic ideas is that the institutions and practices of the ideal human community are an expression of the immutable principles or laws that govern the movements of the cosmos. Through correct social practice, as defined by the Confucian sages and their commentators, individuals can achieve a kind of spiritual unity with heaven. Neo-Confucianism defines formal social relations on all levels of society. Social relations are not conceived of in terms of the happiness or satisfaction of the individuals involved, but in terms of the harmonious integration of individuals into a collective whole that mirrors the harmony of the natural order.

Neo-Confucianism in Korea was becoming rigid and increasingly conservative by the mid-1500s. The practice of neo-Confucianism emphasized hierarchy in human relations and self-control on the individual level. Society was defined in terms of the Five Relationships (*o ryun* in Korean; *wu lun* in Chinese) that had been formulated by classical Chinese thinkers, such as Mencius, and subsequently sanctified by the neo-Confucian metaphysicians: "between father and son there should be affection; between ruler and minister there should be righteousness; between husband and wife there should be attention to their separate functions; between old and young there should be a proper order; and between friends there should be faithfulness." Only the last was a relationship between equals. The others were based on authority and subordination, including the first relationship, which involved not so much mutual love as the unquestioning subordination of the son to the will of his father.

Throughout traditional Korean society, from the royal palace and central government offices in Seoul to the humblest household in the provinces, the themes of hierarchy and inequality were pervasive. Persons were expected to nurture "sincere" attitudes, which meant not so much expressing what one "really" felt as "reflecting on" or "clarifying" one's thoughts and feelings until they conformed to traditional norms. There was no concept of the rights of the individual. The ideal man or woman was one who controlled his or her passions or emotions in order to fulfill to the letter a host of exacting social obligations.

In the context of wider society, a well-defined elite of scholar-officials versed in neo-Confucian orthodoxy was legitimized in terms of the traditional ethical distinction between the educated "superior man" or "gentleman" and the "small man" who seeks only profit. The distinction was a central theme in the writings of Confucius and Mencius. Confucianism as a political theory proposed a benevolent paternalism: the masses had no role in government, but the scholar-officials were supposed to look after them as fathers look after their children.

Just as the father commanded unquestioning obedience in the household and the scholar-official elite did so in the nation as a whole, there was also a hierarchy in international relations. China, the homeland of neo-Confucianism and the most powerful nation in the region, was the center of Chosŏn Korea's cultural universe for most of the dynasty's duration.

Foreign observers have been impressed with the diversity of the

Korean character as expressed in day-to-day human relations. There is, on one hand, the image of Koreans as self-controlled, deferential, and meticulous in the fulfillment of their social obligations; on the other hand, there is the Korean reputation for volatility and emotionalism, for being the "Irish of the East." The ecstasy and euphoria of shamanistic religious practices, one of Korea's most characteristic cultural expressions, contrasts sharply with the austere self-control of Confucian ancestor rituals (see Religion, this ch.).

Although relatively minor themes in the history of Korean ethics and social thought, the concepts of equality and respect for individuals are not entirely lacking. The doctrines of Ch'ŏndogyo (see Glossary), an indigenous religion that originated in the nineteenth century and combines elements of Buddhism, Taoism, shamanism, Confucianism, and Catholicism, teach that every human "bears divinity" and that one must "treat man as god."

Western social and political values such as democracy, individualism, the equality of the sexes (also seen in Ch'ŏndogyo), and national self-determination were introduced by late nineteenth-century Korean reformers and by West European and North American missionaries, who had a profound effect upon the development of Korean education and political values. These concepts have played an increasingly prominent role in South Korean life in recent decades.

Although by no means democratic, the Confucian tradition itself contains anti-authoritarian themes. Mencius taught that the sovereign and his officials must concern themselves with the welfare of the people and that a king who misuses his power loses the right to rule—the doctrine of the Mandate of Heaven. In Korean as well as Chinese history, there were many Confucian statesmen who, often at the cost of their own lives, opposed the misuse of power by those in authority. The tradition of political protest in South Korea, particularly by university students, owes as much to this aspect of the Confucian tradition as it does to democratic and Marxist concepts imported from the West. Just as out-of-power "rustic literati," or *sarim*, pursued purely moral and academic studies and disdained government service at various times during the Chosŏn period, so modern-day university students, claiming to be the "conscience of the nation," have opposed the bureaucratic and professional elite in government and private business.

Thus, to depict traditional Korean social values in terms of an authoritarian Confucian tradition is overly simplistic. A more comprehensive account of social values might describe them in terms of interacting dualities, a kind of yin-yang opposition and synthesis. There is the tension, for example, between self-control and solemnity, on the one hand, and almost explosive volatility at the level of individual behavior, on the other; between the duty-bound austerity of Confucian family life and ritualism, and the ecstasy and abandon of shamanistic rites; between the conservatism of agricultural villages and the looser social organization of fishing communities; between the orthodox concept of male supremacy and the reality of much "hidden" female power; between the "higher" rationalized, humanistic, or scientific culture imported from China, Japan, or the West, and much older indigenous or native cultural themes; between hierarchy and equality; and between slavish deference to authority and principled resistance.

Traditional Social Structure

In Chosŏn Dynasty Korea, four rather distinct social strata developed: the scholar-officials, collectively referred to as the *yangban;* the *chungin* (literally "middle people"), technicians and administrators subordinate to the *yangban;* the *sangmin,* or commoners, a large group composed of farmers, craftsmen, and merchants; and the *ch'ŏmmin* (despised people)," at the bottom of society. To ensure stability, the government devised a system of personal tallies in order to identify people according to their status.

In the strictest sense of the term, *yangban* referred to government officials or officeholders who had passed the civil service examinations that tested knowledge of the Confucian classics and their neo-Confucian interpreters. They were the Korean counterparts of the scholar-officials, or mandarins, of imperial China. The term *yangban,* first used during the Koryŏ Dynasty, means literally "two groups," that is, civil and military officials. Over the centuries, however, its usage became rather vague, so that the term can be said to have several overlapping meanings. Strictly speaking, a *yangban* lineage was one that consistently combined examination success with appointments to government office over a period of some generations. During the Chosŏn period, examination candidates had to show several generations of such ancestry on both sides to be admitted to the civil service examinations. A broader use of the term included within the *yangban* two other groups that could be considered associated with, but outside of, the ruling elite. The first group included those scholars who had passed the preliminary civil service examination and sometimes the higher examinations but had failed to secure government appointment. In the late Chosŏn Dynasty, there were many more successful examination candidates than there were positions. The second group included the more remote relatives and descendants of government officials. Even if these people were poor and did not themselves serve in the government, they were considered members of a *"yangban* family" and thus shared the aura of the elite as long as they retained Confucian culture and rituals.

An interesting development in the social history of the Chosŏn Dynasty occurred after the government began to sell honorary patents of office to people who were not *yangban* to raise revenue following the dislocations of the Hideyoshi invasions. Wealthy commoners sometimes went beyond such status symbols to commission forged genealogies or to take on other trappings of *yangban* status. This form of social climbing was highly irritating to traditional *yangban* families of the types mentioned above. Probably even more common were former *yangban* families that had drifted down into genteel poverty and commoner status. Both developments show that the Chosŏn Dynasty class system was beginning to lose some of its rigidity on the eve of the momentous changes of the late nineteenth century.

Yangban serving as officials could enrich themselves because they were given royal grants of land and had many opportunities for graft; but unemployed scholars and local gentry often were poor. They were a kind of "twilight elite" that was both feared and yet often mocked in peasant entertainments. In his satirical *Tale of a Yangban,* the writer Pak Chi-wŏn (1737–1805) describes the life of a *yangban,* however poor, as one of enforced idleness, exacerbated by the need to maintain appearances. A *yangban* had to study Confucian literature and pass at least the preliminary examinations. He was prohibited from engaging in manual labor or commerce and had to present an image of poise and self-control. A *yangban* could not, among other things, "poke and play with his chopsticks," "eat raw onions," or "puff hard on his pipe, pulling in his cheeks." Yet he exercised much arbitrary power in his own village. In principle, the *yangban* were a meritocratic elite. They gained their positions through educational achievement. Certain groups of persons (artisans, merchants, shamans, slaves, Buddhist monks, and others) were prohibited from taking the higher civil service examinations, but these formed only a small minority of the population. In theory, the examinations were open to the large majority of people who were farmers. In the early years of the Chosŏn Dynasty, some commoners may have been able to attain high positions by passing the examinations and advancing on sheer talent. In later years, talent was a necessary but not sufficient prerequisite for entry into the core elite because of the surplus of successful examinees. Influential family connections were virtually indispensable for obtaining high official positions. Moreover, special posts called "protection appointments" were inherited by descendants of the

Chosŏn royal family and certain high officials. Despite the emphasis on educational merit, the *yangban* became in a very real sense a hereditary elite.

Below the *yangban* yet superior to the commoners were the *chungin*, a small group of technical and administrative officials. They included astronomers, physicians, interpreters, and professional military officers, as well as artists. Local functionaries, who were members of a lower hereditary class, were an important and frequently oppressive link between the *yangban* and the common people. They were often the de facto rulers of a local region.

The commoners, or *sangmin*, composed about 75 percent of the total population. These farmers, craftsmen, and merchants alone bore the burden of taxation and were subject to military conscription. Farmers had higher prestige than merchants, but lived a hard life. Below the commoners, the "base people," or *ch'ŏmmin*, did what was considered vile or low-prestige work. They included servants and slaves in government offices and resthouses, jailkeepers and convicts, shamans, actors, female entertainers (*kisaeng*), professional mourners, shoemakers, executioners, and, for a time at least, Buddhist monks and nuns. Also included in this category were the *paekchŏng*, apparently descended from Inner Asian nomads, who dealt with meat and the hides of animals, were considered "unclean," and lived in segregated communities. Slaves were treated as chattels but could own property and even other slaves. Although numerous at the beginning of the Chosŏn Dynasty, their numbers had dwindled by the time slavery was officially abolished at the end of the nineteenth century.

During their invasions in 1592 and 1597, the armies of the Japanese warlord Toyotomi Hideyoshi destroyed many genealogical records, making it difficult to determine who was and who was not a member of a *yangban* family. Also, as Japanese armies were approaching Seoul, slaves in the capital rose up and burned documentary evidence of their servitude. By the late eighteenth and nineteenth centuries, the old social distinctions were breaking down. During the early Chosŏn Dynasty, commoners did not have family names or class affiliations (see Traditional Family Life, this ch.). However, they began to adopt names in order to avoid the stigma of low status. Counterfeit genealogies could frequently be purchased, and commoners sometimes attached their names to *yangban* genealogies to avoid military service taxes. Other late Chosŏn Dynasty social changes included the gradual shift of agricultural labor from slave status to contractual arrangements and the emergence of "entrepreneurial farmers"—commoners who earned small surpluses through innovative agricultural techniques.

The Emergence of a Modern Society

In 1894 a program of social reforms, known as the Kabo Reforms, was initiated by pro-Japanese Korean officials. *Yangban* and commoners were made equal before the law, the old Confucian civil service examinations were abolished, and slavery and *ch'ŏmmin* status was ended. Modern forms of government and administration, largely borrowed from Japan, were adopted. In the years before annexation, a self-strengthening movement and government reforms attempted to regain Korean control of the pace and direction of change. However, it was only following the Japanese annexation in 1910 that the rapid social transformation of Korea began.

Rural society was radically transformed. Traditionally, all land belonged to the king and was granted by him to his subjects. Although specific parcels of land tended to remain within the same family from generation to generation (including communal land owned by clans and lineages), land occupancy, use, and ownership patterns often were legally ambiguous and widely divergent from one part of the country to another. There was no institution of private property during the Chosŏn Dynasty. The Japanese, however, conducted a comprehensive land survey between 1910 and 1920 in order to place landownership on a modern legal footing. Farmers whose families had tilled the same soil for generations but could not prove ownership in a way satisfactory to the colonial authorities had their land confiscated. Such land came into the hands of the colonial government, to be sold to Japanese land companies, such as the Oriental Development Company, or to Japanese immigrants. As research by Edward Graegert has shown, however, the survey also helped to confirm, or in some cases even to improve, the position of some members of the existing Korean landlord class. Many were former *yangban* who cooperated with the Japanese. Those *yangban* who remained aloof from their country's new overlord often fell into poverty. The farmers themselves either became tenants or were forced to leave the land. During the depression of the 1930s, thousands emigrated to the cities or overseas. Many others fled to the hills to become ''fire-field'' (slash-and-burn) farmers, living under extremely harsh and primitive conditions. By 1936 this last group numbered more than 1.5 million people.

The Japanese built railroads, highways, schools, and hospitals and established a modern system of administration. These changes were intended to link the colonial economy more effectively to that of Japan. The new, modern sector required technically trained experts. Although the top positions were invariably occupied by Japanese, Koreans worked on the lower levels as secondary technical and administrative personnel. Thus, while the number of Korean high officials in the colonial administration increased from only 354 to 442 people between 1915 and 1942, the number of junior officials increased from 15,543 to 29,998 in the same period. Japan's industrial development policies during the 1930s and 1940s, although concentrated in the northern half of the peninsula adjacent to Manchuria, created a new class of workers and lower-level industrial managers who played an important role in the industrial development of South Korea after 1945.

The great majority of Koreans suffered under Japanese rule. A large number of farmers were forced off their land after 1910; industrial workers and miners working for Japanese-owned firms were often treated little better than slaves. Under colonial agricultural policies, rice cultivation was maximized, although most rice was grown for consumption in Japan.

Nevertheless, development under Japanese colonial rule provided some foundation, however unintentionally, for South Korea's impressive post-1945 economic growth (see Korea under Japanese Rule, ch. 1). A small group of Korean entrepreneurs emerged who fostered close ties with the colonial government, and Japanese business interests established family-held firms that were the precursors of South Korea's present-day *chaebŏl,* or business conglomerates. It is a tribute to their acumen that these entrepreneurs were able to survive and prosper in a colonial economy dominated overwhelmingly by Japanese capital.

Three developments after 1945 were particularly important for South Korea's social modernization. The first was the land reform carried out by United States and South Korean authorities between 1945 and 1950. The institution of private property was retained, but the American occupation authorities confiscated and redistributed all land held by the Japanese colonial government, Japanese companies, and individual Japanese colonists. The Korean government also carried out a reform whereby Koreans with large landholdings were obliged to divest most of their land. A new class of independent, family proprietors was created.

The second development was the great influx from North Korea and other countries of repatriates and refugees. In the 1945–49 period, between 1.5 million and 2 million Koreans returned to South Korea from Japan, the northeast provinces of China, and other foreign countries. With the establishment of a communist state in North Korea, a large number of refugees fled to South Korea and were joined by many more during the Korean War. A conservative estimate of the total number of refugees from the north is 1.2 million.

Most of the northerners settled in the cities—new recruits for the country's industrial labor force.

The third development was a direct result of the Korean War. Traditionally Koreans, like their Chinese and unlike their Japanese neighbors, considered the military to be a low-status occupation. Korea did not have its own armed forces during the colonial period, although some Koreans served in the Japanese military, especially after 1941, and a handful, such as former President Park Chung Hee, received officer's training. The North Korean invasion of June 1950 and the three years of fighting that followed cast the South Korean military establishment into the role of savior of the country. And since the coup d'état of May 1961 that established Park Chung Hee, the military establishment has held considerable political power. Roh Tae Woo, elected president in 1987, was a retired general with close connections to the military elite.

Universal military conscription of men has played an important role in South Korea's development, both in political socialization and in integrating a society divided by strong regional prejudices. It also has exposed the nation's young men to technical training and to a disciplined way of life.

During the three decades after Park's 1961 coup d'état, the goal of the military elite was to create a harmonious, disciplined society that was both technically advanced and economically efficient. Economic modernization, however, has brought social changes—especially in education and urbanization—that have had a corrosive effect on the military's authoritarian view of society and have promoted the emergence of a more contentious, pluralistic society than many in the military have found desirable.

Social Classes in Contemporary South Korea

Rapid economic growth, industrialization, and urbanization have caused a profound transformation in the class structure of South Korean society since the end of the Korean War. One of the most important changes has been the emergence of a "new" middle class consisting of civil servants, salaried white-collar workers in large private companies, and professionals with specialized training, such as engineers, health care professionals, university professors, architects, and journalists. The number of factory workers also has grown impressively. According to figures provided by Kim Kyong-Dong, a sociologist at Seoul National University, the portion of the population that can be labeled "new middle class" (excluding self-employed professionals) grew from 6.6 percent to 17.7 percent between 1960 and 1980. The proportion of industrial workers expanded from 8.9 percent to 22.6 percent of the labor force during the same period. Independent farmers and members of the rural lower class, including agricultural laborers, experienced corresponding declines in percentage: together, they accounted for 64 percent of the population in 1960 but only 31.3 percent in 1980.

The urban lower class, consisting to a great extent of recent arrivals from rural parts of the country living in squatter areas, composed an estimated 6.6 percent of the population in 1960 and 5.9 percent in 1980. An "old" middle class consisting of shopkeepers and small business proprietors in urban and rural areas, self-employed professionals, and self-employed craftsmen grew modestly from 13 percent to 20.8 percent of the population between 1960 and 1980. Kim's figures also include what he euphemistically calls an "upper-middle" class—the country's economic and social elites, whose numbers grew from 0.9 percent to 1.8 percent of the population between 1960 and 1980.

Another way of viewing contemporary South Korean society is to consider the sources of social inequality. In a 1988 article, Korea specialist David I. Steinberg focused on several of these sources, which include the disparity in living standards between urban and rural areas—the main motivation behind sustained urban migration. Although the Saemaŭl Movement was successful in narrowing the gap between rural and urban incomes during the mid-1970s, disparities subsequently reemerged. Steinberg also noted that despite the land reform of the late 1940s, tenancy has grown, and that by 1981 as many as 46 percent of all farmers were "full or partial tenants."

Discrimination on both the community and individual levels against the people of North Chŏlla and South Chŏlla provinces remains a second important source of inequality. Disparities in per capita income between Seoul and the provinces of North and South Kyŏngsang had virtually disappeared by the early 1980s, but per capita incomes in the capital were still 1.8 times those in the Chŏlla region in 1983. As in most other Asian (and most Western) countries, gender differences remain another source of major inequalities (see Changing Role of Women, this ch.).

Government control of the financial system has created substantial inequalities between the favored *chaebŏl,* which at least until the late 1980s had access to credit at low rates, and capital-starved smaller businesses that had to rely on nonbank sources of credit. Official support of the *chaebŏl* as the engines of South Korean economic growth and industrialization was clearly reflected in the differences between salaries and working conditions of employees in large and small enterprises. Also, the Park and Chun regimes' hostile policies toward labor unions kept workers' wages low—and internationally competitive. In Steinberg's words, "The Korean worker has been asked to suffer for the good of society as a whole . . . ." Activists who tried to organize independent unions were harassed, arrested, imprisoned, and frequently tortured by the authorities. During the liberalization that began in 1987, however, the government permitted the establishment of independent labor unions and assumed a new attitude, at times approaching neutrality in labor-management disputes (see Interest Groups, ch. 4).

Education remained the single most important factor affecting social mobility in the 1990s. With the exception of the military, whose top echelons were educated at the Korea Military Academy, the postwar elites of South Korea shared one characteristic: they were graduates of the most prestigious universities. There was a well-defined hierarchy of such schools, starting with Seoul National University at the top and followed by Yŏnse University and Koryŏ University (more commonly known as Korea University in English). Ehwa Woman's University was the top institution for women (see Education, this ch.).

A survey conducted in the mid-1970s by the Korea Development Institute, a research organization funded by the government but having considerable operational independence, revealed that 25 percent of a sample of entrepreneurs and 35 percent of a sample of higher civil servants had attended Seoul National University. The university's control of entry into the government and business elites is comparable to that exercised by the University of Tokyo in Japan. One major difference, however, is that for a Japanese student an extended period of study or residence abroad is not considered advisable because it interrupts one's career "track" within a single bureaucracy or corporation; many prominent South Koreans, however, obtain advanced degrees at universities in the United States and in Western Europe.

The social importance of education is one of the major continuities between traditional and contemporary Korea. People at the top require blue-ribbon educational backgrounds, not only because education gives them the cultural sophistication and technical expertise needed to manage large, complex organizations, but also because subordinates will not work diligently for an uneducated person—especially if subordinates are educated themselves. "Old school ties" are also increasingly necessary for advancement in a highly competitive society. At the bottom of the steep higher-education pyramid are low-prestige "diploma mills" whose graduates have little chance of breaking into elite circles. Yet graduation even from these institutions confers a sort of middle-class status.

Despite impressive increases in university enrollments, the central importance of education credentials for social advancement has tended to widen the gap between the middle and lower classes. Income distribution is more unequal than in Japan or Taiwan, with pronounced disparities between college and secondary-school graduates. Many workers know that their comparatively low wages make it virtually impossible for them to give their children a college education, a heavy financial burden even for middle-class families.

In the workplace, men and women with a middle-school or secondary-school education are often treated with open contempt by university graduate managers. The latter address them with rude or abrupt words whose impact is amplified by the status-sensitive nature of the Korean language (see The Korean Language, this ch.). The result has been bitter resentment and increasing labor militancy bordering on political opposition to the status quo.

During the 1980s, the concept of *minjung* (the masses) became prominent in the thinking and rhetoric of radical students, militant labor unionists, activists identified with the Christian churches, and progressive but generally non-Marxist intellectuals. Although its meaning is vague, *minjung* encompasses not only the urban proletariat in the Marxist sense but also the groups, including farmers, small bourgeoisie, students, and skilled craftsmen, who allegedly have been exploited by the country's numerically small ruling class (the military elite, top bureaucrats, and big business). National elites were viewed as collaborating with foreign (particularly United States and Japanese) capitalists in order to create a situation of permanent dependence on foreign capital. The emphasis on neo-colonialist themes by *minjung* spokespeople drew deeply on South Korean populist, nationalist, and xenophobic sentiments to place the origin of social evils outside the Korean race.

Traditional Family Life

Filial piety (*hyo* in Korean; *xiao* in Chinese), the second of the Five Relationships, defined by Mencius as affection between father and son, traditionally has been the normative foundation of Korean family life. Though its influence has diminished over time, this relationship remains vitally important in contemporary South Korea. Entailing a large number of reciprocal duties and responsibilities between the generations of a single family, it generally has been viewed as an unequal relationship in which the son owed the father unquestioning obedience. Neo-Confucianists thought that the subordination of son to father was the expression, on the human level, of an immutable law of the cosmos. This law also imposed a rigidity on family life.

Family and lineage continuity traditionally was, and to a great extent remains, a supremely important principle. This principle reflects Mencius's view that of all possible unfilial acts, to deprive one's parents of posterity is the worst. Historically, the Korean family has been patrilineal. The most important concern for the family group was producing a male heir to carry on the family line and to perform ancestor rituals in the household and at the family gravesite. The first son customarily assumed leadership of the family after his father's death and inherited his father's house and a greater portion of land than his younger brothers. This inheritance enabled him to carry out the ritually prescribed obligations to his ancestors.

Ancestor worship was, simultaneously, a social ethic and a religion. In some ways, it was the most optimistic of faiths. It taught that deceased family members do not pass into oblivion, to an afterlife, or, as the Buddhists believe, to rebirth as humans or animals in some remote place, but remain, in spiritual form, securely within the family circle. For traditionally minded Koreans, the presence of the deceased could be an intensely real and personal one. Fear of death was blunted by the consoling thought that even in the grave one would be cared for by one's own people. Succeeding generations had the obligation of remembering the deceased in a yearly cycle of rituals and ceremonies.

Traditionally, the purpose of marriage was to produce a male heir to carry on the family line rather than to provide mutual companionship and support for husband and wife. Marriages were arranged. A go-between or matchmaker, usually a middle-aged woman, carried on the negotiations between the two families involved who, because of a very strict law of exogamy, sometimes did not know each other and often lived in different communities. The bride and groom met for the first time at the marriage ceremony, a practice that ended in the cities by the 1930s.

The traditional Korean kinship system, defined by different obligations in relation to ancestor worship, was complex. Anthropologists generally view it in terms of four separate levels, beginning with the household on the lowest level and reaching to the clan, which included a large number of persons often spread over an extensive geographical area. The household, *chip* or *jip* (see Glossary) in Korean, consisted of husband and wife, their children, and if the husband were the eldest son, his parents as well. The eldest son's household, the stem family, was known as the "big house" (*k'ŭnjip*), whereas that of each of the younger sons, a branch family containing husband, wife and children only, was known as the "little house" (*chagŭnjip*). It was through the stem family of the eldest son

"Spring Time," a traditional dance performance
Courtesy Robert L. Worden

that the main line of descent was traced from generation to generation. The eldest son was responsible for rituals in honor of the ancestors, and his wife was responsible for producing the all-important male heir.

The second level of kinship was the "mourning group" (*tangnae*), which consisted of all those descendants of a common patrilineal forbearer up to four generations back. Its role was to organize ceremonies at the grave site. These rites included the reading of a formal message by the eldest male descendant of the *tangnae* progenitor and the offering of elaborate and attractive dishes to the ancestral spirits.

Similar rituals were carried out at the third level of kinship organization, the lineage (*p'a*—see Glossary). A lineage might comprise only a handful of households, but in some cases included hundreds and even thousands of households. The lineage was responsible for the rites honoring ancestors of the fifth generation or above, performed at a common grave site. During the Chosŏn Dynasty, the lineage commonly possessed land, grave sites, and buildings. Croplands were allocated to support the ancestral ceremonies. The lineage also performed other functions: the aid of poor or distressed lineage members, the education of children at schools maintained by the *p'a,* and the supervision of the behavior of younger lineage members. Because most villagers were members of a common lineage during the Chosŏn Dynasty, the *p'a* performed

101

many of the social services on the local level that are now provided by public schools, police, and social welfare agencies.

The fourth and most inclusive kinship organization was the clan, or, more accurately, the *tongjok* (surname origin group). Among ordinary South Koreans, this group was commonly known as the *pongwan,* or "clan seat." Members of the same *tongjok* shared both a surname and origins in the generally remote past. Unlike members of the smaller kinship groups, however, they often lacked strong feelings of solidarity. Important *tongjok* include the Chŏnju Yi, whose lineage seat was in Chŏnju in North Chŏlla Province and who claimed as their progenitor the founder of the Chosŏn Dynasty, Yi Sŏng-gye; and the Kimhae Kim, whose lineage seat was in Kimhae in South Kyŏngsang Province and who claimed as their common ancestor either the founder of the ancient kingdom of Kaya or one of the kings of the Silla Dynasty (A.D. 668–935).

Approximately 249 surnames were used by South Koreans in the late 1980s. The most common were Kim (about 22 percent of the population), Li or Yi (15 percent of the population), Pak or Park (8.5 percent), Ch'oe (4.8 percent), and Chŏng (4.2 percent). There are, however, about 150 surname origin groups bearing the name Kim, 95 with the name Yi, 35 with the name Pak, 40 with the name Ch'oe, and 27 with the name Chŏng.

In many if not most cases, the real function of the *tongjok* was to define groups of permissible marriage partners. Because of the strict rule of exogamy, people from the same *tongjok* were not permitted to marry, even though their closest common ancestors in many cases might have lived centuries ago. This prohibition, which originated during the Chosŏn Dynasty, had legal sanction in present-day South Korea. An amendment to the marriage law proposed by women's and other groups in early 1990 would have changed this situation by prohibiting marriages only between persons who had a common ancestor five generations or less back. However, the amendment was strongly opposed by conservative Confucian groups, which viewed the exogamy law as a crystallization of traditional Korean values. Among older South Koreans, it is still commonly thought that only uncivilized people marry within their clan group.

Family and Social Life in the Cities

Contemporary urban family and social life in South Korea at the start of the 1990s exhibits a number of departures from traditional family and kinship institutions. One example is the tendency for complex kinship and family structures to weaken or break down and be replaced by structurally simpler two-generation, nuclear families. Another closely related trend is the movement toward equality in family relations and the resulting improvement in the status of women. Thirdly, there is a movement away from lineage- and neighborhood-based social relations toward functionally based relations. People in the cities no longer work among their relatives or neighbors in the fields or on fishing boats, but among unrelated people in factories, shops, and offices. Finally, there is an increasing tendency for an individual's location and personal associations to be transitory and temporary rather than permanent and lifelong, although the importance of school ties is pivotal. There is greater physical mobility as improved transportation facilities, superhighways, and rapid express trains make it possible to travel between cities in a few hours. Subsidiary transportation networks have broken down barriers between once-isolated villages and the urban areas (see Transportation and Telecommunications, ch. 3). Mobility in human relations also is becoming more apparent as people change their residences more frequently, often because of employment, and an increasing proportion of the urban population lives in large, impersonal apartment complexes.

Matchmaking was a big business in Seoul and other cities in contemporary society; coffee shops and lounges often were crowded on weekends. In a change from traditional society, prospective brides and grooms held scores of interviews, *sŏn pogi,* before deciding on the companion they would like to date-for-marriage. Many of these young men and women changed their minds after these dates, and the process began again. *Yŏnae,* or "love match" marriages, occurred with increasing frequency.

Contrary to the Confucian ideal, the nuclear family consisting of a husband, wife, and children is becoming predominant in contemporary South Korea. It differs from the traditional "branch family," or "little house" (*chagŭnjip*), for two reasons: the conjugal relationship between husband and wife tends to take precedence over the relationship between the son and his parents, and the nuclear family unit is becoming increasingly independent, both economically and psychologically, of larger kinship groups. These developments have led to greater equality among the family units established by the eldest and younger sons. Whereas the isolated nuclear family was perceived in the past as a sign of poverty and misfortune, the contemporary nuclear family is often viewed as the result of a conscious choice made by those who do not wish their privacy invaded by intrusive relatives.

Economic relations between the generations of a single family changed radically in the transition from traditional rural to modern urban society. In the past, the male head of the patrilineal family controlled all the property, usually in the form of land, and was generally the sole provider of economic support. With the development of modern industry and services, however, each adult generation and nuclear family unit has become more or less economically independent, although sons might depend upon their parents or even their wife's parents for occasional economic assistance—for example, in purchasing a house. Because urban families usually live apart from their paternal in-laws, even when the householder is the eldest son, the wife no longer has to endure the domination of her mother-in-law and sister-in-law. In many cases, the family is closer to the wife's parents than to the husband's. The modern husband and wife often are closer emotionally than in the old family system. They spend more time together and even go out socially, a formerly unheard-of practice. Yet the expectation still remains that elderly parents will live with one of their children, preferably a son, rather than on their own or in nursing homes. This expectation could change in the last decade of the century, however, with the expansion of health care and social welfare facilities.

Outside the nuclear family, blood relationships still are important, particularly among close relatives, such as members of the same *tangnae,* or mourning group. Relations with more distant relatives, such as members of the same lineage, tend to be weak, especially if the lineage has its roots in a distant rural village, as most do. Ancestor rites are practiced in urban homes, although for fewer generations than formerly: the majority of urban dwellers seem to conduct rites only in honor of the father and mother of the family head. As a result, there are far fewer ancestors to venerate and far fewer occasions on which to hold the household ceremonies. In some ways, however, increased geographical mobility has helped to preserve family solidarity. In the late 1980s, during New Year's, Hansik (Cold Food Day in mid-April), and Ch'usŏk (the Autumn Harvest Festival in mid-September), the airplanes, trains, and highways were jammed with people traveling to visit both living relatives and grave sites in their ancestral communities.

Changing Role of Women

During the Koryŏ and early Chosŏn Dynasties, it was customary for the married couple to live in the wife's parents' household. This arrangement suggests that the status of women was then higher than it was later during most of the Chosŏn Dynasty. Neo-Confucian orthodoxy dictated that the woman, separated from her parents, had a primary duty of providing a male heir for her husband's family. According to Confucian custom, once married, a woman had to leave her parents' household permanently and then occupy the lowest position in her husband's family. She was often abused and mistreated by both her mother-in-law and sisters-in-law—at least until the birth of a son gave her some status in her husband's family. The relationship between wife and husband was often, if not usually, distant, aptly described by the Korean proverb: ''By day, like seeing a stranger; by night, like seeing a lover.'' Chosŏn Dynasty law prohibited widows from remarrying, although a similar prohibition was not extended to widowers. Further, the sons and grandsons of widows who defied the ban, like children of secondary wives, were not allowed to take the civil service examinations and become scholar-officials.

The duty of a woman to her husband, or rather to her husband's family, was absolute and unquestionable. In the traditional society, only men could obtain a divorce. A husband could divorce his spouse if she were barren—barrenness being defined simply as the inability to bear sons. Even if a husband did not divorce his wife, he had the right to take a second wife, although the preferred solution for a man without a son during the Chosŏn Dynasty was to adopt a son of one of his brothers, if available. The incompatibility of a wife and her in-laws was also grounds for divorce.

In contemporary society, both men and women have the right to obtain a divorce. Social and economic discrimination, however, makes the lot of divorced women more difficult. The husband may still demand custody of the children, although a revision of the Family Law in 1977 made it more difficult for him to coerce or to deceive his wife into agreeing to an unfair settlement. The rate of divorce in South Korea is increasing rapidly. In 1975 the number of divorces was 17,000. In the mid-1980s, the annual number of divorces was between 23,000 and 26,000, and in 1987 there were 45,000 divorces.

The tradition of total female submission persisted in Korean villages until relatively recent times. One Korean scholar who came from the conservative Ch'ungch'ŏng region south of Seoul recalled that when a high school friend died of sickness during the 1940s, his young bride committed suicide. Her act was commemorated in her own and the surrounding communities as an outstanding example of devotion to duty.

Traditionally, men and women were strictly segregated, both inside and outside the house. *Yangban* women spent most of their lives in seclusion in the women's chamber. It is said that the traditional pastime of *nolttwigi*, a game of jumping up and down on a seesaw-like contraption, originated among bored women who wanted to peek over the high walls of their family compounds to see what the outside world was like. Economic necessity gave women of the lower classes some freedom as they participated in farm work and sometimes earned supplemental income through making and selling things.

A small minority of women played an active role in society and even wielded political influence. These people included female shamans (*mudang*), who were called upon to cure illnesses, tell fortunes, or in other ways enlist the help of spirits in realizing the wishes of their clients. Despite its sponsorship of neo-Confucianism, the Chosŏn Dynasty had an office of shamanism, and female shamans often were quite influential in the royal palace. The female physicians who treated female patients (because male physicians were forbidden to examine them) constituted another important group of women. Sometimes they acted as spies or policewomen because they could get into the female quarters of a house. Still another group of women were the *kisaeng.* Some *kisaeng,* or entertainers, were merely prostitutes; but others, like their Japanese counterparts the geisha, were talented musicians, dancers, painters, and poets and interacted on nearly equal terms with their male patrons. The *kisaeng* tradition perpetuated one of the more dubious legacies of the Confucian past: an extreme double standard concerning the sexual behavior of married men and women that still persists. In the cities, however, many middle class women have begun to break with these traditions.

An interesting regional variation on traditional female roles continued in the late 1980s. In the coastal villages of Cheju Island, women divers swam in search of seaweed, oysters, and other marine products and were economically self-sufficient. Often they provided the main economic support for the family while the husband did subsidiary work—took care of the children and did household chores—in sharp contrast to the Confucian norm. The number of women divers was dwindling, however, and men were increasingly performing jobs in service industries. Confucian ancestor worship was rarely practiced; female-centered shamanistic rites, however, were widespread.

The factories of South Korea employ hundreds of thousands of young women on shop floors and assembly lines making, among other things, textiles and clothes, shoes, and electronic components. South Korea's economic success was bought in large measure with the sweat of these generally overworked and poorly paid female laborers. In the offices of banks and other service enterprises, young women working as clerks and secretaries are indispensable. Unlike their sisters on Cheju Island, however, the majority of these women work only until marriage.

Although increasing numbers of women work outside the home, the dominant conception, particularly for the college-educated middle class, is that the husband is the "outside person," the one whose employment provides the main source of economic support; the wife is the "inside person," whose chief responsibility is maintenance of the household. Women tend to leave the labor force when they get married. Many women manage the family finances, and a large number join *kye,* informal private short-term credit associations that give them access to funds that might not be obtainable from a conventional bank. Probably the most important responsibility of married women is the management of their children's education.

On the surface, Korean women often appear docile, submissive, and deferential to the wishes of their husbands and in-laws. Yet behind the scenes, there is often considerable "hidden" female power, particularly within the private sphere of the household. In areas such as household finances, South Korean husbands usually defer to their wives' judgment. Public assertion of a woman's power, however, is socially disapproved, and a traditional wife maintained the image, if not the reality of submissiveness. And, as in other male-dominated societies, Korean men often jokingly complain that they are henpecked.

In traditional Korean society, women received little formal education. Christian missionaries began establishing schools for girls during the late nineteenth and early twentieth centuries. Ehwa Woman's University, the most prestigious women's institution, began as a primary school established by Methodist missionaries in 1886 and achieved university status after 1945. Chǒngsin Girls' School and Paehwa Girls' School were founded in 1890 and 1898, respectively, in Seoul. Sǒngǔi Girls' School was established in 1903 in P'yǒngyang. By 1987 there were ten institutions of higher education for women, including universities, colleges, and junior colleges; women accounted for approximately 28 percent of total enrollment in higher education. There were approximately 262,500 women students in colleges and universities in 1987. However, only about 16 percent of college and university teachers were women in 1987.

The growing number of women receiving a college education has meant that their sex role differs from that of their mothers and grandmothers. Many college-educated women plan independent careers and challenge the right of parents to choose a marriage partner. The often fierce battles between university students and police during the late 1980s included female participants. A correspondent for the *Far Eastern Economic Review* quoted a male student leader as saying that "short girls make great demonstrators, as they're very tough and very hard to catch." Whether politically active South Korean university women will follow their Japanese counterparts, who demonstrated during the 1960s and 1970s, into a world of child-raising and placid consumerism remains to be seen. The number of employed married women, however, increased by approximately 12.6 percent annually in the years since 1977.

In 1983, 51.8 percent of women living in rural areas were employed as compared with 37.8 percent of women living in urban areas. Most of the women working in rural areas were over the age of thirty, as young females (and males) tended to move to, and seek employment in, cities and industrial areas.

Official South Korean statistics indicated that 43.6 percent of women were in the work force by 1988. Prospects for lower class women, however, were frequently grim. In some cases, they were obliged to become part of the "entertainment industry" in order to survive economically. According to one estimate, brothels, bars, massage parlors, discos, and what are known as "Taiwan style" barbershops (that is, those often employing a greater number of masseuses than barbers) employed as many as 1 million women, though not all were prostitutes. This underworld of abuse, exploitation, and bitter shame had begun to be criticized and exposed by women's activists.

Cultural Identity

South Korea's homogeneous population shares a common ethnic, cultural, and linguistic heritage. National self-image is, on one level, unambiguously defined by the convergence of territorial, ethnic, linguistic, and cultural identities (see Population, this ch.). Yet intense feelings of nationalism, so evident in athletic events like the 1986 Asian Games and the 1988 Olympic Games held in Seoul, revealed anxiety as well as pride concerning South Korea's place in the world. More than Western peoples and even more than the Japanese, South Korean individuals are inclined to view themselves as a tightly knit national community with a common destiny. In a rapidly changing world, however, it is often difficult for them to define exactly what being a South Korean is. To outsiders, the intense concern with identity is perhaps difficult to understand; it reflects a history of subordinate relations to powerful foreign states and the tragedy of national division after World War II.

Many modernized, urban-dwelling South Koreans embark on a search for the "essence" of their culture, which commonly expresses itself as hostility to foreign influences. For example, the poet Kim Chi-ha, whose opposition to the Park regime in the 1970s was a model for a younger generation of dissidents, attacked the government as much for its neglect of traditional values as for its antidemocratic tendencies.

Seoul has not been slow to employ traditionalism for its own ends. In 1987 the government adopted guidelines for the revision of history textbooks, instructing publishers to describe the foundation of the Korean nation by Tan'gun in 2333 B.C. as "a reflection of historical facts" rather than simply a myth. The legendary Tangun was, according to the myth, the son of god and a bear-woman. According to a *Far Eastern Economic Review* commentator, ". . . people ranging from reputable university scholars to chauvinist mystics regard Tan'gun as the personification of ethics and values that emphasize a native Korean identity against the foreign religions and philosophies of Buddhism, neo-Confucianism, Christianity and Marxism that have otherwise dominated Korean history and thought." Tan'gun's legendary kingdom is older than China's first legendary dynasty, the Xia (2205–1766 B.C.), and its antiquity asserts Korea's cultural autonomy in relation to its largest neighbor. There have been proposals that the government subsidize the rites of the numerically small community of believers in Taejonggyo and other cults that worship Tan'gun.

Problems of cultural identity are closely connected to the tragedy of Korea's division into two hostile states. Many members of the younger generation of South Koreans born after the Korean War fervently embrace the cause of *t'ongil,* or reunification, and believe that it is the superpowers, the United States and the Soviet Union, who are to blame for Korea's national division. The South Korean government's dependence on the United States has been cited as one of the principal reasons for the lack of improvement in north-south ties. While a majority of South Koreans remain suspicious of the North Koreans, many South Koreans also share the sentiments expressed by Kim Chi-ha: "Our name is division, and this soiled name, like an immovable destiny, oppresses all of us." When parts of the wall dividing East Berlin and West Berlin were knocked down in November 1989, Koreans reflected sadly that breaching the DMZ would not be such a simple task.

Korea and Japan

National or ethnic groups often need an "other," a group of outsiders against whom they can define themselves. While Western countries with their individualistic and, from a Confucian perspective, self-centered ways of life provide important images of "otherness" for South Koreans, the principal source of such images for many years has been Japan. Attitudes toward Japan as an "other"

109

are complex. On the most basic level, there is hostility fed by memories of invasion and colonial oppression, present-day economic frictions, and the Japanese government's inability or unwillingness to do anything about discriminatory treatment of the large Korean minority in Japan. The two countries have a long history of hostility. Admiral Yi Sun-sin, whose armor-plated boats eventually defeated the Japanese navy's damaging attacks in the 1590s, is South Korea's most revered national hero.

The Japanese Ministry of Education, Science, and Culture's adoption in the 1980s of revised textbook guidelines, softening the language used to describe Japan's aggression during World War II, inspired outrage in South Korea as well as in other Asian countries. The textbook controversy was a major impetus for a national campaign to build an Independence Hall, located about 100 kilometers south of Seoul, to keep alive memories of Japanese colonial exploitation. Opened on August 15, 1987, the anniversary of Korea's liberation from Japan, the building houses grim exhibits depicting the atrocities of the Japanese military against Korean nationalists during the colonial period.

During the colonial period, and particularly during World War II, the Japanese initiated assimilation policies designed to turn Koreans into obedient subjects of the Japanese emperor. Under the slogan ''Nissen ittai'' (Japan and Korea as One), newspapers and magazines published in the Korean language were closed, the Korean Language Society was disbanded, and Korean writers were forced to publish only in Japanese. Students who spoke Korean in school were punished. There was pressure to speak Japanese at home, adopt Japanese family and given names, and worship at Shinto shrines, the religious basis for which had been transplanted from the home islands. Korean Christians who refused to show reverence to the emperor as a divinity were imprisoned or ostracized. In the words of historian Ki-baik Lee (called Yi Ki-baek in Korean), ''Japan's aim was to eradicate consciousness of Korean national identity, roots and all, and thus to obliterate the very existence of the Korean people from the face of the earth.''

This shared historical experience has provoked not only hostility but also a desire to purge Korean culture of lingering Japanese influences. In the late 1980s, the government continued to prohibit the distribution of Japanese-made movies and popular music within the country in order to prevent unwanted contemporary influences from crossing the Korea Strait.

On a more polite level, depiction of Japan as the ''other'' involves contrasting the ''essences'' of the two countries' cultures. This process has spawned a popular literature that compares, among other things, the naturalness and ''resonance'' of Korean art and music and the alleged imitativeness and constriction of their Japanese counterparts; the ''individualism'' (of a non-Western sort) of Koreans and the ''collectivism'' or group consciousness of the Japanese; and the lyric contrast between the rose of Sharon, Korea's national flower, which blooms robustly all summer long, and the Japanese cherry blossom, which has the ''beauty of frailty'' in springtime.

The search for a cultural ''essence'' involves serious contradictions. The literature of Korean cultural distinction is strikingly similar to Japanese attempts to prove the ''uniqueness'' of their own cultural heritage, although ''proof'' of Japan's uniqueness is usually drawn from examples of Western countries (the significant ''other'' for modernized Japanese). Ironically, official and unofficial sponsorship of the Tan'gun myth, although a minor theme, bears an uncanny resemblance to pre-World War II Japanese policies promoting historical interpretations of the nation's founding based on Shinto mythology.

Mixed in with feelings of hostility and competition, however, is genuine admiration for Japanese economic, technological, and social achievements. Japan has become an important market for South Korean manufactured products. Both countries have been targets of criticism by Western governments accusing them of unfair trading practices. Friendly interest in South Korea is growing among the Japanese public despite old prejudices, and large numbers of young Japanese and South Koreans visit each others' countries on school and college excursions. Like South Koreans, Japanese liberals have been disturbed by official attempts to revise wartime history.

The Korean Language

Modern Korean language is descended from the language of the Silla Kingdom, which unified the peninsula in the seventh century. As Korean linguist Yi Ki-mun notes, the more remote origins of the Korean language are disputed, although many Korean linguists, together with a few western scholars, continue to favor the now widely-contested nineteenth-century theory of an Altaic family of languages supposed to include Korean, Japanese, and Mongolian, among other languages. Although a historical relationship between Korean and Japanese has not been established, modern Korean and Japanese have many similar grammatical features, no doubt in part because of close contacts between the two during the past century. These similarities have given rise to considerable speculation in the popular press. The linguist Kim Chin-wu, for example, has hypothesized that Korea and Japan stood at the end of two routes of large-scale migration in ancient times: a northern route from Inner Asia and a southern route from southern China or Southeast Asia. In a variant on the "southern origins" theory of some Japanese scholars, he views the two languages as reflecting disparate "northern" and "southern" influences, with Korean showing more influence from the northern, Inner Asian strain.

Both Korean and Japanese possess what is sometimes called "polite" or "honorific" language, the use of different levels of speech in addressing persons of superior, inferior, or equal rank. These distinctions depend both on the use of different vocabulary and upon basic structural differences in the words employed. For example, in Korean the imperative "go" can be rendered *kara* when speaking to an inferior or a child, *kage* when speaking to an adult inferior, *kaseyo* when speaking to a superior, and *kasipsio* when speaking to a person of still higher rank. The proper use of polite language, or levels of polite speech, is an extremely complex and subtle matter. The Korean language, like Japanese, is extremely sensitive to the nuances of hierarchical human relationships. Two persons who meet for the first time are expected to use the more distant or formal terms, but they will shift to more informal or "equal" terms if they become friends. Younger people invariably use formal language in addressing elders; the latter will use "inferior" terms in "talking down" to those who are younger.

The Korean language may be written using a mixture of Chinese ideograms (*hancha*) and a native Korean alphabet known as *han'gŭl*, or in *han'gŭl* alone, much as in a more limited way Indo-European languages sometimes write numbers using Arabic symbols and at other times spell numbers out in their own alphabets or in some combination of the two forms. *Han'gŭl* was invented by scholars at the court of King Sejong (1418–50), not solely to promote literacy among the common people as is sometimes claimed, but also, as Professor Gari K. Ledyard has noted, to assist in studies of Chinese historical phonology. According to a perhaps apocryphal decree of the king, an intelligent man could learn *han'gŭl* in a morning's time, and even a fool could master it in ten days. As a result, it was scorned by scholars and relegated to women and merchants. The script, which in its modern form contains forty symbols, is considered by linguists to be one of the most scientific ever devised; it reflects quite consistently the phonemes of the spoken Korean language.

Because of its greater variety of sounds, Korean does not have the problem of the Japanese written language, which some experts have argued needs to retain a sizable inventory of Chinese characters to distinguish a large number of potentially ambiguous homophones. Since 1948 the continued use of Chinese characters in South Korea has been criticized by linguistic nationalists and some educators and defended by cultural conservatives, who fear that the loss of character literacy could cut younger generations off from a major part of their cultural heritage. Since the early 1970s, Seoul's policy governing the teaching and use of Chinese characters has shifted several times, although the trend clearly has been toward writing in *han'gŭl* alone. By early 1990, all but academic writing used far fewer Chinese characters than was the case in the 1960s. In 1989 the Korean Language and Education Research Association, citing the need for Chinese character literacy "at a time when the nation is entering into keen competition with Japan and China" and noting that Japanese educators were increasing the number of Chinese characters taught in elementary schools, recommended to the Ministry of Education that instruction in Chinese characters be reintroduced at the primary-school level.

Although the Korean and Chinese languages are not related in terms of grammatical structure, more than 50 percent of all Korean vocabulary is derived from Chinese loanwords, a reflection of the cultural dominance of China over 2 millennia. In many cases there are two words—a Chinese loanword and an indigenous Korean word—meaning the same thing. The Chinese-based word in Korean sometimes has a bookish or formal flavor. Koreans select one or the other variant to achieve the proper register in speech, or in writing, and to make subtle distinctions of meaning in accordance with established usage.

Large numbers of Chinese character compounds coined in Japan in the nineteenth or twentieth centuries to translate modern Western scientific, technical, and political vocabulary came into use in Korea during the colonial period. Post-1945 United States influence has been reflected in a number of English words that have been absorbed into Korean.

Unlike Chinese, Korean does not encompass dialects that are mutually unintelligible, with the possible exception of the variant spoken on Cheju Island. There are, however, regional variations both in vocabulary and pronunciation, the range being comparable to the differences that might be found between Maine and Alabama in the United States. Despite several decades of universal education, similar variations also have been heard between highly educated and professional speakers and Koreans of working class or rural backgrounds. Standard Korean is derived from the language spoken in and around Seoul. More than forty years of division has meant that there are also some divergences in the development of the Korean language north and south of the DMZ.

Education

Like other East Asian countries with a Confucian heritage, South Korea has had a long history of providing formal education. Although there was no state-supported system of primary education, the central government established a system of secondary schools in Seoul and the provinces during the Chosŏn Dynasty. State schools suffered a decline in quality, however, and came to be supplanted in importance by the *sŏwŏn,* private academies that were the centers of a neo-Confucian revival in the sixteenth century. Students at both private and state-supported secondary schools were exempt from military service and had much the same social prestige as university students enjoy today in South Korea. Like modern students, they were frequently involved in politics. Higher education was provided by the Confucian national university in the capital, the Sŏnggyungwan. Its enrollment was limited to 200 students who had passed the lower civil service examinations and were preparing for the higher examinations.

During the late nineteenth and early twentieth centuries, modern private schools were established both by Koreans and by foreign Christian missionaries. The latter were particularly important because they promoted the education of women and the diffusion of Western social and political ideas. Japanese educational policy after 1910 was designed to turn Koreans into obedient colonial subjects and to teach them limited technical skills. A state university modeled on Tokyo Imperial University was established in Seoul in 1923, but the number of Koreans allowed to study there never exceeded 40 percent of its enrollment; 60 percent of its students were Japanese expatriates.

When United States military forces occupied the southern half of the Korean Peninsula in 1945, they established a school system based on the American model: six years of primary school, six years of secondary school (divided into junior and senior levels), and four years of higher education. Other occupation period reforms included coeducation at all levels, popularly elected school boards in local areas, and compulsory education up to the ninth grade. The government of Syngman Rhee reversed many of these reforms after 1948: in most cases only primary schools remained coeducational and education was compulsory only up to the sixth grade because of a lack of resources. The school system in 1990, however, reflects the system established under the United States occupation.

During the years when Rhee and Park Chung Hee were in power, the control of education was gradually taken out of the hands of local school boards and concentrated in a centralized Ministry of Education. In the late 1980s, the ministry was responsible for administration of schools, allocation of resources, setting of enrollment quotas, certification of schools and teachers, curriculum development (including the issuance of textbook guidelines), and other basic policy decisions. Provincial and special city boards of education still existed. Although each board was composed of seven members who were supposed to be selected by popularly elected legislative bodies, this arrangement ceased to function after 1973. Subsequently, school board members were approved by the minister of education.

Most observers agree that South Korea's spectacular progress in modernization and economic growth since the Korean War is largely attributable to the willingness of individuals to invest a large amount of resources in education: the improvement of "human capital." The traditional esteem for the educated man, originally confined to the Confucian scholar as a cultured generalist, now extends to scientists, technicians, and others working with specialized knowledge. Highly educated technocrats and economic planners could claim much of the credit for their country's economic successes since the 1960s. Scientific professions were generally regarded as the most prestigious by South Koreans in the 1980s.

Statistics demonstrate the success of South Korea's national education programs. In 1945 the adult literacy rate was estimated at 22 percent; by 1970 adult literacy was 87.6 percent, and by the late 1980s various sources estimated it at around 93 percent. South Korean students have performed exceedingly well in international competitions in mathematics and science. Although only primary school (grades one through six) was compulsory, percentages of age-groups of children and young people enrolled in primary, secondary, and tertiary level schools were equivalent to those found in industrialized countries, including Japan. Approximately 4.8 million students in the eligible age-group were attending primary school in 1985. The percentage of students going on to optional middle school the same year was more than 99 percent. Approximately 34 percent, one of the world's highest rates of secondary-school graduates, attended institutions of higher education in 1987, a rate similar to Japan's (about 30 percent) and exceeding Britain's (20 percent).

Government expenditure on education has been generous. In 1975 it was W220 billion (for value of the wŏn—see Glossary), the equivalent of 2.2 percent of the gross national product (GNP—see

Glossary), or 13.9 percent of total government expenditures. By 1986 education expenditure had reached wŏn 3.76 trillion, or 4.5 percent of the GNP, and 27.3 percent of government budget allocations.

Social emphasis on education was not, however, without its problems, as it tended to accentuate class differences. In the late 1980s, possession of a college degree was considered necessary for entering the middle class; there were no alternative pathways of social advancement, with the possible exception of a military career. People without a college education, including skilled workers with vocational school backgrounds, often were treated as second-class citizens by their white-collar, college-educated managers, despite the importance of their skills for economic development. Intense competition for places at the most prestigious universities—the sole gateway into elite circles—promoted, like the old Confucian system, a sterile emphasis on rote memorization in order to pass secondary school and college entrance examinations. Particularly after a dramatic expansion of college enrollments in the early 1980s, South Korea faced the problem of what to do about a large number of young people kept in school for a long time, usually at great sacrifice to themselves and their families, and then faced with limited job opportunities because their skills were not marketable.

Primary and Secondary Schools

In the late 1980s, primary schools were coeducational, although coeducation was quite rare at the middle-school and high-school levels. Enrollment figures for 1987 on the primary-school level were 4,771,722 pupils in 6,531 schools, with 130,142 teachers. A decline from the 1980 figure of 5,658,002 pupils was caused by population trends. Some 54 percent of primary school teachers were male.

In 1987 there were approximately 4,895,354 students enrolled in middle schools and high schools, with approximately 150,873 teachers. About 69 percent of these teachers were male. The secondary-school enrollment figure also reflected changing population trends; there were 3,959,975 students in secondary schools in 1979. Given the importance of entry into higher education, the majority of students attended general or academic high schools in 1987: 1,397,359 students, or 60 percent of the total, attended general or academic high schools, as compared with 840,265 students in vocational secondary schools. Vocational schools specialized in a number of fields: primarily agriculture, fishery, commerce, trades, merchant marine, engineering, and the arts.

Enrollment in kindergartens or preschools expanded impressively during the 1980s. In 1980 there were 66,433 children attending

901 kindergartens or preschools. By 1987 there were 397,020 children in 7,792 institutions. The number of kindergarten and preschool teachers rose from 3,339 to 11,920 during the same period. The overwhelming majority of these teachers—approximately 92 percent—were women. This growth was attributable to several factors: Ministry of Education encouragement of preschool education, the greater number of women entering the work force, growth in the number of nuclear families without a grandparent available to take care of children, and the feeling that kindergarten might give children an ''edge'' in later educational competition. Kindergartens often paid homage to the expectations of parents with impressive graduation ceremonies, complete with diplomas, academic caps, and gowns.

Competitive entrance examinations at the middle-school level were abolished in 1968. Although as of the late 1980s, students still had to pass noncompetitive qualifying examinations, they were assigned to secondary institutions by lottery, or else by location within the boundary of the school district. Secondary schools, formerly ranked according to the quality of their students, have been equalized, with a portion of good, mediocre, and poor students being assigned to each one. The reform, however, did not equalize secondary schools completely. In Seoul, students who performed well in qualifying examinations were allowed to attend better quality schools in a ''common'' district, whereas other students attended schools in one of five geographical districts. The reforms applied equally to public and private schools, both of whose enrollments were strictly controlled by the Ministry of Education.

Although primary- and secondary-school teachers traditionally enjoyed high status, they often were overworked and underpaid during the late 1980s. Salaries were less than those for many other white-collar professions and even some blue-collar jobs. High school teachers, particularly those in the cities, did however, receive sizable gifts from parents seeking attention for their children, but teaching hours were long and classes crowded (the average class contained around fifty to sixty students).

In May 1989, teachers established an independent union, the National Teachers Union (NTU—Chŏn'gyojo). Their aims included improving working conditions and reforming a school system that they regarded as overly controlled by the Ministry of Education. Although the government promised large increases in allocations for teachers' salaries and facilities, it refused to give the union legal status. Because teachers were civil servants, the government claimed they did not have the right to strike and, even if they did have the right to strike, unionization would undermine the status

117

of teachers as "role models" for young Koreans. The government also accused the union of spreading subversive, leftist propaganda that was sympathetic to the communist regime in North Korea. According to a report in the *Asian Wall Street Journal*, the union claimed support from 82 percent of all teachers. The controversy was viewed as representing a major crisis for South Korean education because a large number of teachers (1,500 by November 1989) had been dismissed; violence among union supporters, opponents, and police had occurred at several locations; and class disruptions had caused anxieties for families of students preparing for the college entrance examinations. The union's challenge to the Ministry of Education's control of the system and the charges of subversion had made compromise seem a very remote possibility at the start of 1990.

Higher Education

In the late 1980s, the university a South Korean high school graduate attended was perhaps the single most important factor in determining his or her life chances. Thus, entrance into a prestigious institution was the focus of intense energy, dedication, and self-sacrifice. Prestigious institutions included the state-run Seoul National University, originally established by the Japanese as Seoul Imperial University in 1923, and a handful of private institutions such as Yŏnse University, Koryŏ University, and Ehwa Woman's University.

Because college entrance depends upon ranking high in objectively graded examinations, high school students face an "examination hell," a harsh regimen of endless cramming and rote memorization of facts that is probably even more severe than the one faced by their counterparts in Japan. Unlike the Confucian civil service examinations of the Chosŏn Dynasty, their modern reincarnation is a matter of importance not for an elite, but for the substantial portion of the population with middle-class aspirations. In the late 1980s, over one-third of college-age men and women (35.2 percent in 1989) succeeded in entering and attending institutions of higher education; those who failed faced dramatically reduced prospects for social and economic advancement.

The number of students in higher education had risen from 100,000 in 1960 to 1.3 million in 1987, and the proportion of college-age students in higher-education institutions was second only to the United States. The institutions of higher education included regular four-year colleges and universities, two-year junior vocational colleges, four-year teachers' colleges, and graduate schools. The main drawback was that college graduates wanted careers that

University chemistry laboratory
Courtesy Embassy of the Republic of Korea, Washington

would bring them positions of leadership in society, but there simply were not enough positions to accommodate all graduates each year and many graduates were forced to accept lesser positions. Ambitious women, especially, were frustrated by traditional barriers of sex discrimination as well as by the lack of positions.

A college-bound high school student, in the late 1980s, typically rose at dawn, did a bit of studying before school began at 7:30 or 8:00 A.M., attended school until 5:00 P.M., had a quick dinner (often away from home), and then attended evening cramming classes that could last until 10:00 or 11:00 P.M. Sundays and holidays were devoted to more cramming. Because tests given in high school (generally once every two or four weeks) were almost as important in determining college entrance as the final entrance examinations, students had no opportunity to relax from the study routine. According to one contemporary account, a student had to memorize 60 to 100 pages of facts to do well on these periodic tests. Family and social life generally were sacrificed to the supreme end of getting into the best university possible.

The costs of the "examination hell" have been evident not only in a grim and joyless adolescence for many, if not most, young South Koreans, but also in the number of suicides caused by the constant pressure of tests. Often suicides have been top achievers who despaired after experiencing a slump in test performance. In addition, the multiple choice format of periodic high school tests and university entrance examinations has left students little opportunity to develop their creative talents. A "facts only" orientation has promoted a cramped and unspontaneous view of the world that has tended to spill over into areas of life other than academic work.

The prospects for basic change in the system—a deemphasis on tests—were unlikely in the late 1980s. The great virtue of facts-based testing is its objectivity. Although harsh, the system is believed to be fair and impartial. The use of nonobjective criteria such as essays, personal recommendations, and the recognition of success in extracurricular activities or personal recommendations from teachers and others could open up all sorts of opportunities for corruption. In a society where social connections are extremely important, connections rather than merit might determine entry into a good university. Students who survive the numbing regimen of examinations under the modern system are at least universally acknowledged to have deserved their educational success. Top graduates who have assumed positions of responsibility in government and business have lent, through their talents, legitimacy to the whole system.

Following the assumption of power by General Chun Doo Hwan in 1980, the Ministry of Education implemented a number of reforms designed to make the system fairer and to increase higher education opportunities for the population at large. In a very popular move, the ministry dramatically increased enrollment at large. The number of high school graduates accepted into colleges and universities was increased from almost 403,000 students in 1980 to more than 1.4 million in 1989. This reform decreased, temporarily, the acceptance ratio from one college place for every four applicants in 1980 to one for every three applicants in 1981. In 1980 the number of students attending all kinds of higher educational institutions was almost 600,000; that number grew almost 100 percent to 1,061,403 students by 1983. By 1987 there were 1,340,381 students attending higher educational institutions. By 1987 junior colleges had an enrollment of almost 260,000 students, and colleges and universities had an enrollment of almost 990,000 students. Other higher education institutions enrolled the balance.

A second reform was the prohibition of private, after-school tutoring. Formerly, private tutors could charge exorbitant rates if they had a good "track record" of getting students into the right schools through intensive coaching, especially in English and in mathematics. This situation gave wealthy families an unfair advantage in the competition. Under the new rules, students receiving tutoring could be suspended from school and their tutors dismissed from their jobs. There was ample evidence in the mid-1980s, however, that the law had simply driven the private tutoring system underground and made the fees more expensive. Some underpaid teachers and cash-starved students at prestigious institutions were willing to run the risk of punishment in order to earn as much as W300,000 to W500,000 a month. Students and their parents took the risk of being caught, believing that coaching in weak subject areas could give students the edge needed to get into a better university. By the late 1980s, however, the tutorial system seemed largely to have disappeared.

A third reform was much less popular. The ministry established a graduation quota system, in which increased freshman enrollments were counterbalanced by the requirement that each four-year college or university fail the lowest 30 percent of its students; junior colleges were required to fail the lowest 15 percent. These quotas were required no matter how well the lowest 30 or 15 percent of the students did in terms of objective standards. Ostensibly designed to ensure the quality of the increased number of college graduates, the system also served, for a while to discourage students from devoting their time to political movements. Resentment of the quotas was widespread, and family counterpressures were intense. The government abolished the quotas in 1984.

College Student Activism

Student activism has a long and honorable history in Korea. Students in Chosŏn Dynasty secondary schools often became involved in the intense factional struggles of the scholar-official class. Students played a major role in Korea's independence movement, particularly the March 1, 1919, country-wide demonstrations that were harshly suppressed by the Japanese military police. Students protested against the Rhee and Park regimes during the 1950s, 1960s, and 1970s. Observers noted, however, that while student activists in the past generally embraced liberal and democratic values, the new generation of militants in the 1980s was far more radical. Most participants have adopted some version of the *minjung* ideology that was heavily influenced by Marxism, Western "dependence theory," and Christian "liberation theology," but was also animated by strong feelings of popular nationalism and xenophobia.

The most militant university students, perhaps about 5 percent of the total enrollment at Seoul National University and comparable numbers at other institutions in the capital during the late 1980s, were organized into small circles or cells rarely containing more than fifty members. Police estimated that there were seventy-two such organizations of varying orientation (see Political Extremism and Political Violence, ch. 4).

Religion

Religious Traditions

Shamanism

Koreans, like other East Asians, have traditionally been eclectic rather than exclusive in their religious commitments. Their religious outlook has not been conditioned by a single, exclusive faith but by a combination of indigenous beliefs and creeds imported into Korea. Belief in a world inhabited by spirits is probably the oldest form of Korean religious life, dating back to prehistoric times. There is a rather unorganized pantheon of literally millions of gods, spirits, and ghosts, ranging from the "god generals" who rule the different quarters of heaven to mountain spirits (*sansin*). This pantheon also includes gods who inhabit trees, sacred caves, and piles of stones, as well as earth spirits, the tutelary gods of households and villages, mischievous goblins, and the ghosts of persons who in many cases met violent or tragic ends. These spirits are said to have the power to influence or to change the fortunes of living men and women.

Korean shamans are similar in many ways to those found in Siberia, Mongolia, and Manchuria. They also resemble the *yuta* found on the Ryūkyū Islands, in Okinawa Prefecture, Japan. Cheju Island is also a center of shamanism.

Shamans, most of whom are women, are enlisted by those who want the help of the spirit world. Female shamans hold *kut,* or services, in order to gain good fortune for clients, cure illnesses by exorcising evil spirits, or propitiate local or village gods. Such services are also held to guide the spirit of a deceased person to heaven.

Often a woman will become a shaman very reluctantly—after experiencing a severe physical or mental illness that indicates "possession" by a spirit. Such possession allegedly can be cured only through performance of a *kut.* Once a shaman is established in her profession, she usually can make a good living.

Many scholars regard Korean shamanism as less a religion than a "medicine" in which the spirits are manipulated in order to achieve human ends. There is no notion of salvation or moral and spiritual perfection, at least for the ordinary believers in spirits. The shaman is a professional who is consulted by clients whenever the need is felt. Traditionally, shamans had low social status and were members of the *ch'ŏmmin* class. This discrimination has continued into modern times.

Animistic beliefs are strongly associated with the culture of fishing villages and are primarily a phenomenon found in rural communities. Shamans also treat the ills of city people, however, especially recent migrants from the countryside who find adjustment to an impersonal urban life stressful. The government has discouraged belief in shamanism as superstition and for many years minimized its persistence in Korean life. Yet in a climate of growing nationalism and cultural self-confidence, the dances, songs, and incantations that compose the *kut* have come to be recognized as an important aspect of Korean culture. Beginning in the 1970s, rituals that formerly had been kept out of foreign view began to resurface, and occasionally a Western hotel manager or other executive could even be seen attending a shamanistic exorcism ritual in the course of opening a new branch in Seoul. Some of these aspects of *kut* have been designated valuable cultural properties that should be preserved and passed on to future generations.

The future of shamanism itself was uncertain in the late 1980s. Observers believed that many of its functions in the future probably will be performed by the psychiatric profession as the government expands mental health treatment facilities. Given the uncertainty of social, economic, and political conditions, however, it appears certain that shamans will find large numbers of clients for some time to come.

Taoism and Buddhism

Taoism, which focuses on the individual in nature rather than the individual in society, and Buddhism entered Korea from China during the Three Kingdoms period (fourth to seventh centuries A.D.). Taoist motifs are seen in the paintings on the walls of Koguryŏ tombs. Buddhism was the dominant religious and cultural influence during the Silla (A.D. 668-935) and Koryŏ (918-1392) dynasties. Confucianism also was brought to Korea from China in early centuries, but it occupied a subordinate position until the establishment of the Chosŏn Dynasty and the persecution of Buddhism carried out by the early Chosŏn Dynasty kings (see Social Structures and Values, this ch.).

Christianity

Roman Catholic missionaries did not arrive in Korea until 1794, a decade after the return of the first baptized Korean from a visit to Beijing. However, the writings of the Jesuit missionary, Matteo Ricci, who was resident at the imperial court in Beijing, had been brought to Korea from China in the seventeenth century. It appears that scholars of the Sirhak, or practical learning, school were interested in these writings. Largely because converts refused to perform Confucian ancestor rites, the government prohibited the proselytization of Christianity. Some Catholics were executed during the early nineteenth century, but the anti-Christian law was not strictly enforced. By the 1860s, there were some 17,500 Roman Catholics in the country. There followed a more rigorous persecution, in which thousands of Christians died, that continued until 1884.

Protestant missionaries entered Korea during the 1880s and, along with Catholic priests, converted a remarkable number of Koreans. Methodist and Presbyterian missionaries were especially successful. They established schools, universities, hospitals, and orphanages and played a significant role in the modernization of the country. During the Japanese colonial occupation, Christians were in the front ranks of the struggle for independence. Factors contributing to the growth of Protestantism included the degenerate state of Korean Buddhism, the efforts made by educated Christians to reconcile Christian and Confucian values (the latter being viewed as purely a social ethic rather than a religion), the encouragement of self-support and self-government among members of the Korean church, and the identification of Christianity with Korean nationalism.

A large number of Christians lived in the northern part of the peninsula where Confucian influence was not as strong as in the south. Before 1948 P'yŏngyang was an important Christian center: one-sixth of its population of about 300,000 people were converts. Following the establishment of a communist regime in the north, however, most Christians had to flee to South Korea or face persecution.

New Religions

Ch'ŏndogyo, generally regarded as the first of Korea's "new religions," is another important religious tradition. It is a synthesis of Confucian, Buddhist, shamanistic, Taoist, and Catholic influences. Ch'ŏndogyo grew out of the Tonghak Movement (also called Eastern Learning Movement) established by Ch'oe Che-u, a man of *yangban* background who claimed to have experienced a mystic encounter with God, who told him to preach to all the world. Ch'oe was executed by the government as a heretic in 1863, but not before he had acquired a number of followers and had committed his ideas to writing. Tonghak spread among the poor people of Korea's villages, especially in the Chŏlla region, and was the cause of a revolt against the royal government in 1894. While some members of the Tonghak Movement—renamed Ch'ŏndogyo

Eighth-century granite Buddha, Sŏkkuram Grotto, near Kyŏngju
Courtesy Embassy of the Republic of Korea, Washington

(Teachings of the Heavenly Way)—supported the Japanese annexation in 1910, others opposed it. This group played a major role, along with Christians and some Confucians, in the Korean nationalist movement. In the 1920s, Ch'ŏndogyo sponsored *Kaebyŏk* (Creation), one of Korea's major intellectual journals during the colonial period (see The Media, ch. 4).

Ch'ŏndogyo's basic beliefs include the essential equality of all human beings. Each person must be treated with respect because all persons "contain divinity;" there is "God in man." Moreover, men and women must sincerely cultivate themselves in order to bring forth and express this divinity in their lives. Self-perfection, not ritual and ceremony, is the way to salvation. Although Ch'oe and his followers did not attempt to overthrow the social order and establish a radical egalitarianism, the revolutionary potential of Ch'ŏndogyo is evident in these basic ideas, which appealed especially to poor people who were told that they, along with scholars and high officials, could achieve salvation through effort. There is reason to believe that Ch'ŏndogyo had an important role in the development of democratic and anti-authoritarian thought in Korea. In the 1970s and 1980s, Ch'ŏndogyo's antecedent, the Tonghak Movement, received renewed interest among many Korean intellectuals.

Apart from Ch'ŏndogyo, major new religions included Taejonggyo, which has as its central creed the worship of Tan'gun, legendary founder of the Korean nation. Chungsanggyo, founded in the early twentieth century, emphasizes magical practices and the creation of a paradise on earth. It is divided into a great number of competing branches. Wŏnbulgyo, or Wŏn Buddhism, attempts to combine traditional Buddhist doctrine with a modern concern for social reform and revitalization. There are also a number of small sects which have sprung up around Mount Kyeryong in South Ch'ungch'ŏng Province, the supposed future site of the founding of a new dynasty originally prophesied in the eighteenth century.

Several new religions derive their inspiration from Christianity. The Chŏndogwan, or Evangelical Church, was founded by Pak T'ae-sŏn. Pak originally was a Presbyterian, but was expelled from the church for heresy in the 1950s after claiming for himself unique spiritual power. By 1972 his followers numbered as many as 700,000 people, and he built several "Christian towns," established a large church network, and managed several industrial enterprises.

Because of its overseas evangelism, the Hold Spirit Association for the Unification of the World Christianity, or Unification Church (T'ongilgyo), founded in 1954 by Reverend Sun Myong Moon (Mun Sŏn-myŏng), also a former Christian, is the most famous

Korean new religion. During its period of rigorous expansion during the 1970s, the Unification Church had several hundred thousand members in South Korea and Japan and a substantial (although generally overestimated) number of members in North America and Western Europe. Moon claimed that he was the "messiah" designated by God to unify all the peoples of the world into one "family," governed theocratically by himself.

Like Pak's Evangelical Church, the Unification Church has been highly authoritarian, demanding absolute obedience from church members. Moon, for example, has arranged marriages for his younger followers; United States television audiences were treated some years ago to a mass ceremony at which several hundred young "Moonies" were married. Also like Pak, Moon has coupled the church's fortunes to economic expansion. Factories in South Korea and abroad manufacture arms and process ginseng and seafood, artistic bric-a-brac, and other items. Moon's labor force has worked long hours and been paid minimal wages in order to channel profits into church coffers. Virulently anticommunist, Moon has sought to influence public opinion at home and abroad by establishing generally unprofitable newspapers such as the *Segye ilbo* in Seoul, the *Sekai nippo* in Tokyo, and the *Washington Times* in the United States capital and by inviting academics to lavish international conferences, often held in South Korea. At home, the Unification Church was viewed with suspicion by the authorities because of its scandals and Moon's evident desire to create a "state within a state." His influence, however, had declined by the late 1980s.

Religion in Contemporary South Korea

According to government statistics, 42.6 percent or more than 17 million of South Korea's 1985 population professed adherence to an organized religious community. There were at least 8 million Buddhists (about 20 percent of the total population), about 6.5 million Protestants (16 percent of the population), some 1.9 million Roman Catholics (5 percent), nearly 500,000 people who belonged to Confucian groups (1 percent), and more than 300,000 others (0.7 percent). Significantly, large metropolitan areas had the highest proportions of people belonging to formal religious groups: 49.9 percent in Seoul, 46.1 percent in Pusan, and 45.8 percent in Taegu. The figures for Christians revealed that South Korea had the highest percentage of Christians of any country in East Asia or Southeast Asia, with the exception of the Philippines.

Except for the Christian groups, which maintain a fairly clear-cut distinction between believers and nonbelievers, there is some ambiguity in these statistics. As has been pointed out, there is no exact or exclusive criterion by which Buddhists or Confucianists can be identified. Many people outside of formal groups have been deeply influenced by these traditions. Moreover, there is nothing contradictory in one person's visiting and praying at Buddhist temples, participating in Confucian ancestor rites, and even consulting a shaman and sponsoring a *kut*. Furthermore, the statistics may underrepresent the numbers of people belonging to new religions. Some sources have given the number of adherents of Ch'ŏndogyo as over 1 million.

Given the great diversity of religious expression, the role of religion in South Korea's social development has been a complex one. Some traditions, especially Buddhism, are identified primarily with the past. Buddhist sites such as the Pulguksa Temple and the Sŏkkuram Grotto in Kyŏngju and the Haeinsa Temple near Taegu are regarded by most South Koreans as important cultural properties rather than as places of worship. Confucianism remains important as a social ethic; its influence is evident in the immense importance Koreans ascribe to education. Christianity is identified with modernization and social reform. Many Christians in contemporary South Korea, such as veteran political opposition leader Kim Dae Jung, a Catholic, have been outspoken advocates of human rights and critics of the government. Christian-sponsored organizations such as the Urban Industrial Mission promote labor organizations and the union movement. New religions draw on both traditional beliefs and on Christianity, achieving a baffling variety and diversity of views. It has been estimated that there were as many as 300 new religions in South Korea in the late 1980s, although many were small and transient phenomena.

Public Health and Welfare

Health conditions have improved dramatically since the end of the Korean War. Between 1955 and 1960, life expectancy was estimated at 51.1 years for men and 54.2 years for women. In 1990 life expectancy was sixty-six years for men and seventy-three years for women. The death rate declined significantly, from 13.8 deaths per 1,000 in 1955–60 to 6 deaths per 1,000 in 1989—one of the lowest rates among East Asian and Southeast Asian countries.

Nevertheless, serious health problems remained in 1990. South Korea's infant mortality rate was significantly higher than the rates of other Asian countries and territories such as Japan, Taiwan, Hong Kong, Singapore, and peninsular Malaysia. Although practically all the inhabitants of Seoul and other large cities had access to running water and sewage disposal in the late 1980s, environmental pollution and poor sanitation still posed serious threats to public health in both rural and urban areas.

Health Conditions

The main causes of death traditionally have been respiratory diseases—tuberculosis, bronchitis, and pneumonia—followed by gastrointestinal illnesses. However, the incidence and fatality of both types of illness declined during the 1970s and 1980s. Diseases typical of developed, industrialized countries—cancer, heart, liver and kidney ailments, diabetes, and strokes—were rapidly becoming the primary causes of death. The incidence of parasitism, once a major health problem in farming communities because of the widespread use of night soil as fertilizer, was reported in the late 1980s to be only 4 percent of what it had been in 1970. Encephalitis, a viral disease that can be transmitted to humans by mosquitoes, caused ninety-four deaths in 1982. To reduce fatalities, the Ministry of Health and Social Affairs planned to vaccinate 17.2 million persons against the disease by 1988.

The tensions and social dislocations caused by rapid urbanization apparently increased the incidence of mental illness. In 1985 the Ministry of Health and Social Affairs began a large-scale program to expand mental health treatment facilities by opening mental institutions and requiring that new hospitals have wards set aside for psychiatric treatment. The ministry estimated the number of persons suffering from mental ailments at around 400,000.

South Korea has not been entirely immune from the health and social problems generally associated with the West, such as acquired immune deficiency syndrome (AIDS) and addictive drugs. A handful of AIDS cases was reported during the late 1980s. Seoul responded by increasing the budget for education programs and instituting mandatory AIDS testing of prostitutes and employees of entertainment establishments. An AIDS Prevention Law was promulgated in November 1987. In late 1989, the government drafted a law requiring AIDS testing of foreign athletes and entertainers intending to reside in South Korea without their spouses for more than three months. Previously, the majority of those infected with AIDS had been prostitutes working near United States military bases, ocean-going seamen, and South Koreans working abroad. In the late 1980s, however, homosexuals began to account for an increasing number of those infected with the AIDS virus. The traditional Korean attitude toward homosexuality, which was to deny its existence, made it extremely difficult to treat this part of the population. The 200-percent annual increase in the number of AIDS-infected persons (from one reported case in 1985 to twenty-two cases in 1988) worried health officials.

While the use of heroin and other opiates was rare in South Korea and the use of cocaine limited, the use of crystalline methamphetamine, or "ice," known in South Korea as *hiroppon,* had become a serious problem by the late 1980s. Estimates of the number of South Korean abusers of this illegal drug (known in the United States as speed) ranged from 100,000 to 300,000 people in the late 1980s. Because use of the drug was believed to involve just low-status members of society, such as prostitutes and gangsters, the problem of *hiroppon* abuse had long been ignored in South Korea. The problem received greater attention from police and other government agencies during the late 1980s as the drug increased in popularity among professionals, students, office workers, house-wives, entertainers, farmers, and laborers. Some observers suggested the drug's popularity was caused in part by a high-pressure work environment, in which people used *hiroppon* to cope with long working hours. It also has been suggested that the tighter border controls imposed by Seoul have resulted in diverting the product to the domestic market and contributing to greater domestic consumption.

An estimated 2,000 to 4,000 kilograms of methamphetamine were produced within South Korea annually, much of this total destined for shipment to Taiwan, Japan, and the United States by South Korean and Japanese *yakuza,* or gangsters. Since the majority of users injected the drug intravenously (although smoking and snorting it were becoming popular), South Korean health officials were concerned that the drug could contribute to the spread of AIDS. In 1989 Seoul established a new antinarcotics division attached to the prosecutor general's office and increased almost fourfold the number of drug agents.

Health Care and Social Welfare

The traditional practice of medicine in Korea was influenced primarily, although not exclusively, by China. Over the centuries, Koreans had used acupuncture and herbal remedies to treat a wide variety of illnesses. Large compilations of herbal and other prescriptions were published during the Chosŏn Dynasty: the 85-volume *Hyangyak chipsŏngbang* (Great Collection of Korean Prescriptions) published in 1433 and the 365-volume *Ŭibang yuch'wi* (Great Collection of Medicines and Prescriptions) published in 1445. Shops selling traditional medicines, including ginseng, a root plant believed to have strong medicinal and aphrodisiac qualities, still were common in the 1980s. Because of the expense of modern medical care, people still had to rely largely on such remedies to treat serious illnesses until the 1980s, particularly in rural areas.

The number of physicians, nurses, dentists, pharmacists, and other health personnel and the number of hospitals and clinics have increased dramatically since the Korean War (see fig. 8). In 1974 the population per physician was 2,207; by 1983 this number had declined to 1,509. During the same period, the number of general hospitals grew from 36 to 156 and the number of hospital beds tripled from 19,062 to 59,099. Most facilities, however, tended to be concentrated in urban areas, particularly in Seoul and Pusan. Rural areas had limited medical facilities because in the past there had been little incentive for physicians to work in areas outside the cities, where the major of the people could not pay for treatment. Several private rural hospitals had been established with government encouragement but had gone bankrupt in the late 1980s. The extension of medical insurance programs to the rural populace, however, was expected to alleviate this problem to some extent during the 1990s.

The South Korean government committed itself to making medical security (medical insurance and medical aid) available to virtually the entire population by 1991. There was no unified national health insurance system, but the Ministry of Health and Social Affairs coordinated its efforts with those of employers and private insurance firms to achieve this goal. Two programs were established in 1977: the Free and Subsidized Medical Aid Program for people whose income was below a certain level and a medical insurance program that provided coverage for individuals and their immediate families working in enterprises of 500 people or more. Expenses were shared equally by employers and workers. In 1979 coverage was expanded to enterprises comprising 300 or more people, as well as to civil servants and teachers in private schools. In 1981 coverage was extended to enterprises employing 100 or more people and in 1984 to firms with as few as 16 employees. In that year, 16.7 million persons, or 41.3 percent of the population, had medical insurance. By 1988 the government had expanded medical insurance coverage in rural areas to almost 7.5 million people. As of the end of 1988, approximately 33.1 million people, or almost 79 percent of the population, received medical insurance benefits. At that time, the number of those not receiving medical insurance benefits totaled almost 9 million people, mostly independent small business owners in urban areas. In July 1989, however, Seoul extended medical insurance to cover these self-employed urbanites, so that the medical insurance system extended to almost all South Koreans. Differences in insurance premiums among small business

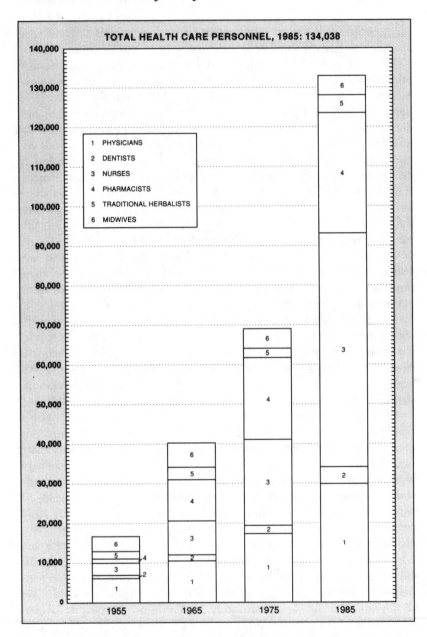

Source: Based on information from Edward S. Mason et al., *The Economic and Social Modernization of the Republic of Korea,* Cambridge, 1980, 402, 404; and *The Statesman's Yearbook, 1988–89,* New York, 1988, 775.

Figure 8. Increase in Licensed Health Care Personnel, Selected Years, 1955–85

owners, government officials and teachers, people in farming and fishing areas, and those employed by business firms remained a divisive and unresolved issue.

Medical insurance programs for farming and fishing communities, where the majority of people were self-employed or worked for very small enterprises, also were initiated by the government. In 1981 three rural communities were selected as experimental sites for implementation of a comprehensive medical insurance program. Three more areas, including Mokp'o in South Chŏlla Province, were added in 1982. Industrial injury compensation schemes were begun in the early 1960s and by 1982 covered 3.5 million workers in most major industries.

During the 1980s, government pension or social security insurance programs covered designated groups, such as civil servants, military personnel, and teachers. Private employers had their own schemes to which they and workers both contributed. Government planners envisioned a public and private system of pensions covering the entire population by the early 1990s. In the wake of rapid economic growth, large sums have been allocated for social development programs in the national budget. In FY (fiscal year—see Glossary) 1990, total spending in this area increased 40 percent over the previous year. Observers noted, however, that serious deficiencies existed in programs for the handicapped, single-parent families, and the unemployed.

* * *

A New History of Korea by Ki-baik Lee provides ample coverage of social developments during the Three Kingdoms, Silla, Koryŏ, and Chosŏn Dynasty periods and during the Japanese colonial occupation. James B. Palais's *Politics and Policy in Traditional Korea* gives a succinct overview of Chosŏn Dynasty social structure. Michael C. Kalton's translation and commentary on Yi T'oe-gye's *The Ten Diagrams on Sage Learning* contains a valuable discussion not only of the career of Korea's most noted Confucian scholar, but also of the philosophical and ethical fundamentals of neo-Confucian orthodoxy. Donald N. Clark's *Christianity in Modern Korea* provides excellent coverage of Christianity in contemporary Korea.

Vincent S.R. Brandt's *A Korean Village* and Han Sang-Bok's *Korean Fishermen* remain among the best descriptions of rural Korean life during the mid-1960s. Although published in 1971, Lee Hyojae et al.'s "Life in Urban Korea" remains informative. Korean family and kinship organizations are described exhaustively by Lee Kwang-Kyu in his two-volume *Kinship System in Korea.*

Virtues in Conflict, a collection of essays edited by Sandra Matielli, and Kim Yung-chung's *Women of Korea* discuss women's roles in Korean society. Female shamans are discussed in Kim Harvey Youngsook's *Six Korean Women* and Laurel Kendall's *The Life and Hard Times of a Korean Shaman.* Kim Chin-wu's *The Making of the Korean Language* provides an informative account of that subject.

Interesting discussions of South Korea's changing social classes are contained in David I. Steinberg's *The Republic of Korea* and in Kim Kyong-Dong's "Social Change and Societal Developments in Korea since 1945." Although its 1980 publication date precludes discussion of the major changes that have occurred since that year, *Education and Development in Korea* by Noel F. McGinn et al. provides excellent background on this important subject. Recent developments are covered in some depth by publications such as the *Far Eastern Economic Review,* whose weekly "Arts and Society" section deals extensively with education and other social matters. Other periodicals containing discussions of South Korean society, education, and cultural expression include *Korea Journal,* the *Social Science Journal,* and *Korean Studies.* (For further information and complete citations, see Bibliography.)

Chapter 3. The Economy

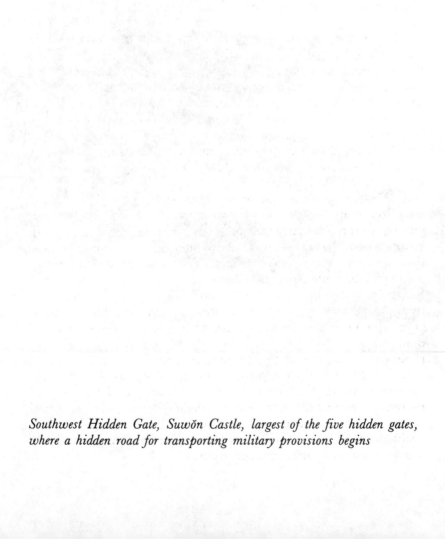

Southwest Hidden Gate, Suwŏn Castle, largest of the five hidden gates, where a hidden road for transporting military provisions begins

IN THE FIRST THREE decades after the Park Chung Hee government launched the First Five-Year Economic Development Plan in 1962, the South Korean economy grew enormously and the economic structure was radically transformed. South Korea's real gross national product (GNP—see Glossary) expanded by an average of more than 8 percent per year, from US$2.3 billion in 1962 to US$204 billion in 1989. Per capita annual income grew from US$87 in 1962 to US$4,830 in 1989. The manufacturing sector grew from 14.3 percent of the GNP in 1962 to 30.3 percent in 1987. Commodity trade volume rose from US$480 million in 1962 to a projected US$127.9 billion in 1990. The ratio of domestic savings to GNP grew from 3.3 percent in 1962 to 35.8 percent in 1989.

The rapid economic growth of the late 1980s, however, slowed considerably in 1989. The growth rate was cut almost in half from the previous year (to a still-robust approximate 6.5 percent), the inflation rate increased as wages soared even higher, and there was speculation concerning a small trade deficit in the early 1990s. These developments all pointed to a gradual slowing of the expansion of the rapidly maturing economy. Nevertheless, it also was clear that rapidly rising domestic demand would keep the economy healthy (even with a slight drop-off of exports), unless a major political crisis were to shock the country.

The most significant factor in rapid industrialization was the adoption of an outward-looking strategy in the early 1960s. This strategy was particularly well suited to that time because of South Korea's poor natural resource endowment, low savings rate, and tiny domestic market. The strategy promoted economic growth through labor-intensive manufactured exports, in which South Korea could develop a competitive advantage. Government initiatives played an important role in this process. The inflow of foreign capital was greatly encouraged to supplement the shortage of domestic savings. These efforts enabled South Korea to achieve rapid growth in exports and subsequent increases in income.

By emphasizing the industrial sector, Seoul's export-oriented development strategy left the rural sector relatively underdeveloped. Increasing income disparity between the industrial and agricultural sectors became a serious problem by the 1970s and remained a problem, despite government efforts to raise farm income and improve living standards in rural areas.

By the early 1970s, however, the industrial sector had begun to face problems of its own. Up to that time, the industrial structure had been based on low value-added and labor-intensive products, which faced increasing competition and protectionism from other developing countries. The government responded to this problem in the mid-1970s by emphasizing the development of heavy and chemical industries and by promoting investment in high value-added, capital-intensive industries.

The structural transition to high value-added, capital-intensive industries was difficult. Moreover, it occurred at the end of the 1970s, a time when the industrial world was experiencing a prolonged recession following the second oil price shock of the decade and protectionism was resulting in a reduction of South Korean exports. By 1980 the South Korean economy had entered a period of temporary decline: negative growth was recorded for the first time since 1962, inflation had soared, and the balance-of-payments position had deteriorated significantly.

In the early 1980s, Seoul instituted wide-ranging structural reforms. In order to control inflation, a conservative monetary policy and tight fiscal measures were adopted. Growth of the money supply was reduced from the 30 percent level of the 1970s to 15 percent. Seoul even froze its budget for a short while. Government intervention in the economy was greatly reduced and policies on imports and foreign investment were liberalized to promote competition. To reduce the imbalance between rural and urban sectors, Seoul expanded investments in public projects, such as roads and communications facilities, while further promoting farm mechanization.

These measures, coupled with significant improvements in the world economy, helped the South Korean economy regain its lost momentum in the late 1980s. South Korea achieved an average of 9.2 percent real growth between 1982 and 1987 and 12.5 percent between 1986 and 1988. The double digit inflation of the 1970s was brought under control. Wholesale price inflation averaged 2.1 percent per year from 1980 through 1988; consumer prices increased by an average of 4.7 percent annually. Seoul achieved its first significant surplus in its balance of payments in 1986 and recorded a US$7.7 billion and a US$11.4 billion surplus in 1987 and 1988 respectively. This development permitted South Korea to begin reducing its level of foreign debt. The trade surplus for 1989, however, was only US$4.6 billion dollars, and a small negative balance was projected for 1990 (see table 2, Appendix).

In the late 1980s, the domestic market became an increasing source of economic growth. Domestic demand for automobiles and other indigenously manufactured goods soared because South

Korean consumers, whose savings had been buoyed by double-digit wage increases each year since 1987 and whose average wages in 1990 were about 50 percent above what they had been at the end of 1986, had the wherewithal to purchase luxury items for the first time. The result was a gradual reorientation of the economy from a heavy reliance on exports toward greater emphasis on meeting the needs of the country's nearly 43 million people. The shifts in demand and supply indicated that economic restructuring was underway, that is, domestic consumption was rising as net foreign demand was falling. On the supply side, the greater growth in services mirrored what the people wanted—more goods, especially imports, and many more services.

By 1990 there was evidence that the high growth rates of the late 1980s would slow during the early 1990s. In 1989 real growth was only 6.5 percent. One reason for this development was the economic restructuring that began in the late 1980s—including the slower growth of major export industries that were no longer competitive on the world market (for example, footwear) and the expansion of those industries that were competitive, such as electronics.

The Japanese Role in Korea's Economic Development

The Japanese, who dominated Korea from the late 1890s to 1945 and who governed Korea as a colony from 1910 to 1945, were responsible for the initial economic modernization of Korea. Before 1900 Korea had a relatively backward agricultural economy. According to scholar Donald S. Macdonald, for centuries most Koreans lived as subsistence farmers of rice and other grains and satisfied most of their basic needs through their own labor or through barter. The manufactures of traditional Korea—principally cloth, cooking and eating utensils, furniture, jewelry, and paper—were produced by artisans in a few population centers.

Following the annexation of Korea in 1910, Japan thrust a modern blend of industrial capitalism onto a feudal agrarian society. By the end of the colonial period, Japan had built an extensive infrastructure of roads, railroads, ports, electrical power, and government buildings that facilitated both the modernization of Korea's economy and Japan's control over the modernization process. The Japanese located various heavy industries—steel, chemicals, and hydroelectric power—across Korea, but mainly in the north.

The Japanese government played an even more active role in developing Korea than it had played in developing the Japanese economy in the late nineteenth century. Many programs drafted

139

in Korea in the 1920s and 1930s originated in policies drafted in Japan during the Meiji period (1868–1912). The Japanese government helped to mobilize resources for development and provided entrepreneurial leadership for these new enterprises. Colonial economic growth was initiated through powerful government efforts to expand the economic infrastructure, to increase investment in human capital through health and education, and to raise productivity.

In some respects, South Korean patterns of development after the early 1960s closely followed the methodology introduced by the Japanese fifty years earlier—industrialization from above using a strong bureaucracy that formulated and implemented economic policies. Many of the developments that took place in Chōsen, the Japanese name for Korea during the period of colonization, had also occurred in pre-World War II Japan; they were implementation of a strong education system and the spread of literacy; the rise of a strong, authoritarian government that combined civilian and military administration to govern the state with strict discipline; the fostering and implementation of comprehensive economic programs by the state through its control of the huge national bureaucracy; the close collaboration between government and business leaders; and the development of industries by the major Japanese *zaibatsu* (commercial conglomerates).

Some political analysts, for example, Bruce Cumings and Gavan McCormick, have been impressed with the common elements in prewar and postwar economic growth in South Korea and especially with top-down government management of the economy. Economists, such as Paul W. Kuznets, however, also draw attention to the dysfunctional aspects of the colonial legacy and find some of the discontinuities important.

Between the end of World War II and Park Chung Hee's ascension to power in 1961, South Korea's political and economic links to the Japanese colonial period were ruptured. There was considerable disruption after 1945 because of plant exhaustion; the loss of linkages with Japanese capital and with upstream and downstream industrial facilities; the loss of technical expertise, distribution systems, and markets; and the subsequent obliteration of the industrial plant during the Korean War (1950–53).

The Government Role in Economic Development

In 1961 General Park Chung Hee overthrew the popularly elected regime of Prime Minister Chang Myŏn. A nationalist, Park wanted to transform South Korea from a backward agricultural nation into a modern industrial nation that would provide a decent way of life for its citizens while at the same time defending itself from outside aggression. Lacking the anti-Japanese nationalist credentials of Syngman Rhee, for example, Park sought both legitimacy for his regime and greater independence for South Korea in a vigorous program of economic development that would transform the country from an agricultural backwater into a modern industrial nation.

Park's government was the beneficiary of the Syngman Rhee administration's decision to use foreign aid from the United States during the 1950s to build an infrastructure that included a nationwide network of primary and secondary schools, modern roads, and a modern communications network. The result was that by 1961, South Korea had a well-educated young work force and a modern infrastructure that provided Park with a solid foundation for economic growth.

The Park administration decided that the central government must play the key role in economic development because no other South Korean institution had the capacity or resources to direct such drastic change in a short time. The resulting economic system incorporated elements of both state capitalism and free enterprise. The economy was dominated by a group of *chaebŏl* (see Glossary), large private conglomerates, and also was supported by a significant number of public corporations in such areas as iron and steel, utilities, communications, fertilizers, chemicals, and other heavy industries. The government guided private industry through a series of export and production targets utilizing the control of credit, informal means of pressure and persuasion, and traditional monetary and fiscal policies (see The Origins and Development of Chaebŏl, this ch.).

The government hoped to take advantage of existing technology to become competitive in areas where other advanced industrial nations had already achieved success. Seoul presumed that the well-educated and highly motivated work force would produce low-cost, high-quality goods that would find ready markets in the United States and the rest of the industrial world. Profits generated from the sale of exports would be used to further expand capital, provide new jobs, and eventually pay off loans.

In 1961 Park extended government control over business by nationalizing the banks and merging the agricultural cooperative movement with the agricultural bank. The government's direct control over all institutional credit further extended Park's command over the business community. The Economic Planning Board was created in 1961 and became the nerve center of Park's plan to

141

promote economic development. It was headed by a deputy prime minister and staffed by bureaucrats known for their high intellectual capability and educational background in business and economics. Beginning in the 1960s, the board allocated resources, directed the flow of credit, and formulated all of South Korea's economic plans. In the late 1980s, the power to allocate resources and credit was restored to the functional ministries. In 1990 the Economic Planning Board primarily was charged with economic planning; it also coordinated and often directed the economic functions of other government ministries, including the Ministry of Finance. The board was complemented by the Korea Development Institute, an independent economic research organization funded by the government. Other government bodies directing the economy included the Office of the President, which included a senior secretary for economic affairs; the Ministry of Finance; the Ministry of Trade and Industry; the Ministry of Labor; and the Bank of Korea, which was controlled by the Ministry of Finance.

Park's first major goal, which was immediately successful, was to establish a self-reliant industrial economy independent of the massive waves of United States aid that had kept South Korea afloat during the Rhee years. Modernizing the economy and maintaining overall sustained growth were additional goals in the 1970s. Significant economic policies included strengthening key industries, increasing employment, and developing more effective management systems. Because South Korea was dependent on imports of raw materials, such as oil, a major government objective was to significantly increase the level of exports, which meant stressing greater international competitiveness and higher productivity. The early economic plans emphasized agriculture and infrastructure, the latter were closely tied to construction. Later, the emphasis shifted consecutively to light industry, electronics, and heavy and chemical industries. Using these strategies, an export-driven economy developed.

The government combined a policy of import substitution with the export-led approach. Policy planners selected a group of strategic industries to back, including electronics, shipbuilding, and automobiles. New industries were nurtured by making the importation of such goods difficult. When the new industry was on its feet, the government worked to create good conditions for its export. Incentives for exports included a reduction of corporate and private income taxes for exporters, tariff exemptions for raw materials imported for export production, business tax exemptions, and accelerated depreciation allowances.

The export-led program took off in the 1960s; during the 1970s, some estimates indicate, Seoul had the world's most productive

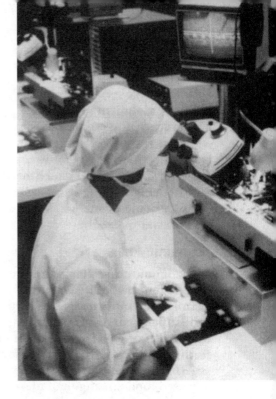

Woman worker,
Hyundai Corporation
Courtesy Embassy of the
Republic of Korea, Washington

economy. The annual industrial production growth rate was about 25 percent; there was a fivefold increase in the GNP from 1965 to 1978. In the mid-1970s, exports increased by an average of 45 percent a year.

Industrial Policies

The major issue facing the Park regime in the early 1960s was the grinding poverty of the nation and the need for economic policies to overcome this poverty. A critical problem was raising funds to foster needed industrial development. Domestic savings were very low, and there was little available domestic capital. This obstacle was overcome by introducing foreign loans and inaugurating attractive domestic interest rates that enticed local capital into production. Of South Korea, Taiwan, Hong Kong, and Singapore, only South Korea financed its economic development with a dramatic build-up of foreign debt, debt that totaled US$46.8 billion in 1985, making it the fourth largest Third World debtor. Foreign corporate investments were primarily of Japanese origin.

As noted by consultant David I. Steinberg, Seoul administered a series of economic development plans. The government mobilized domestic capital by encouraging savings, determined what kinds of plants could be constructed with these funds, and reviewed the potential of the products for export. In this sense, the will of the government to undertake economic development played a crucial role; the

143

role of the government, however, was not limited to such measures as mobilizing capital and allocating investments.

Steinberg also pointed out that Park's government restructured industries, such as defense and construction, sometimes to stimulate competition and other times to reduce or eliminate it. The Economic Planning Board established export targets that, if met, yielded additional government-subsidized credit and further access to the growing domestic market. Failure to meet such targets led to Seoul's withdrawal of credit.

Economic Plans

Economic programs were based on a series of five-year plans that began in 1962. The First Five-Year Economic Development Plan (1962–66) consisted of initial steps toward the building of a self-sufficient industrial structure that was neither consumption oriented nor overdependent on oil. Such areas as electrification, fertilizers, oil refining, synthetic fibers, and cement were emphasized. The Second Five-Year Economic Development Plan (1967–71) stressed modernizing the industrial structure and rapidly building import-substitution industries, including steel, machinery, and chemical industries. The Third Five-Year Economic Development Plan (1972–76) achieved rapid progress in building an export-oriented structure by promoting heavy and chemical industries. Industries receiving particular attention included iron and steel, transport machinery, household electronics, shipbuilding, and petrochemicals. The developers of heavy and chemical industries sought to supply new industries with raw materials and capital goods and to reduce or even eliminate dependence on foreign capital. New (and critical) industries were to be constructed in the southern part of the peninsula, far from the border with North Korea, thus encouraging economic development and industrialization outside the Seoul area and providing new employment opportunities for residents of the less developed areas.

The Fourth Five-Year Economic Development Plan (1977–81) fostered the development of industries designed to compete effectively in the world's industrial export markets. These major strategic industries consisted of technology-intensive and skilled labor-intensive industries such as machinery, electronics, and shipbuilding. The plan stressed large heavy and chemical industries, such as iron and steel, petrochemicals, and nonferrous metal. As a result, heavy and chemical industries grew by an impressive 51.8 percent in 1981; their exports increased to 45.3 percent of total output. These developments can be ascribed to a favorable turn in the export performance of iron, steel, and shipbuilding, which occurred because high-quality, low-cost products could be produced in South Korea. By contrast, the heavy and chemical industries of advanced countries slumped during the late 1970s. In the machinery industries, investments were doubled in electric power generation, integrated machinery, diesel engines, and heavy construction equipment; the increase clearly showed that the industries benefited from the government's generous financial assistance program.

The late 1970s, however, witnessed worldwide recession, rising fuel costs, and growing inflation. South Korea's industrial structure became somewhat imbalanced, and the economy suffered from acute inflation because of an overemphasis on investment in heavy industry at a time when many potential customers were not in a position to buy heavy industrial goods.

The Fifth Five-Year Economic and Social Development Plan (1982–86) sought to shift the emphasis away from heavy and chemical industries, to technology-intensive industries, such as precision machinery, electronics (televisions, videocassette recorders, and semiconductor-related products), and information. More attention was to be devoted to building high-technology products in greater demand on the world market.

The Sixth Five-Year Economic and Social Development Plan (1987–91) to a large extent continued to emphasize the goals of the previous plan. The government intended to accelerate import liberalization and to remove various types of restrictions and nontariff barriers on imports. These moves were designed to mitigate adverse effects, such as monetary expansion and delays in industrial structural adjustment, which can arise because of a large surplus of funds. Seoul pledged to continue phasing out direct assistance to specific industries and instead to expand manpower training and research and development in all industries, especially the small and medium-sized firms that had not received much government attention previously. Seoul hoped to accelerate the development of science and technology by raising the ratio of research and development investment from 2.4 percent of the GNP to over 3 percent by 1991.

The goal of the Seventh Five-Year Economic and Social Development Plan (1992–96), formulated in 1989, was to develop high-technology fields, such as microelectronics, new materials, fine chemicals, bioengineering, optics, and aerospace. Government and industry would work together to build high-technology facilities in seven provincial cities to better balance the geographic distribution of industry throughout South Korea.

Revenues and Expenditures

The central government budget has generally expanded, both

in real terms and as a proportion of real GNP, since the end of
the Korean War, stabilizing at between 20 and 21 percent of GNP
during most of the 1980s. Government spending in South Korea
has been less than that for most countries in the world (excepting
the other rapidly growing Asian economies of Japan, Taiwan, and
Singapore). The share of government spending devoted to investment and other capital formation activities increased steadily through
the periods of the first and second five-year plans (1962–71), peaking
at more than 41 percent of the budget in 1969. Since 1971 investment expenditures have remained at less than 30 percent of the
budget, while the share of the budget occupied by direct government consumption and transfer payments has continued to increase,
averaging more than 70 percent during the 1980s.

During the 1980s, the largest areas of government expenditure
were economic services (including infrastructural projects and
research and development), national defense, and education. Economic expenditures averaged several percentage points higher than
defense expenditures, which remained stable at about 22 to 23 percent of the budget (about 6 percent of GNP) during the decade.
In 1990 the government was studying plans to lower defense expenditures to 5 percent of GNP. Some observers noted a trend
toward a slight increase in the portion of the budget devoted to
social spending during the 1980s. In 1987 expenditures for social
services—including health, housing, and welfare—were 16.4 percent of the budget, up from 13.9 percent in 1980, and slightly higher
than 1987 government outlays for education (see table 3, Appendix).

The government revenue structure was virtually totally dependent on taxes (see table 4, Appendix). By the early 1980s, nearly
two-thirds of tax money was collected in the form of indirect taxes.
Revenues collected by the central government in 1987 rose to
19,270.3 billion wŏn (for value of the wŏn—see Glossary), up from
13.197.5 billion wŏn in 1984.

The Government and Public and Private Corporations

Following the Korean War, foreign aid became the most important source of funds for the reconstruction and rehabilitation
of the economy. What was left of the Japanese-built industrial plant,
most of which by the 1950s either was obsolete or had been destroyed by warfare), generally was turned over to private owners,
who were chosen more often for their political loyalty than for their
economic acumen. Moreover, Rhee favored certain businessmen
and companies with government contracts in exchange for financial support of his political endeavors. It was during this period
that a group of entrepreneurs began companies that later became

the *chaebŏl,* or business conglomerates. The *chaebŏl* were groups of specialized companies with interrelated management. These groupings of affiliated companies dominated South Korea's economy in the late 1980s and often included businesses involved in heavy and consumer industries and electric and electronic goods, as well as trading companies and real estate and insurance concerns.

The *chaebŏl* were responsible for the successful expansion of South Korea's export capacity. According to Steinberg, in 1987 the revenues of the four largest *chaebŏl* were US$80.7 billion, a figure equivalent to two-thirds of Seoul's total GNP. In that year, the Samsung Group had revenues of US$24 billion; Hyundai, US$22.7 billion; Daewoo, US$16 billion; and Lucky-Goldstar, US$18 billion. The revenues of the next largest *chaebŏl,* Sunkyong, totaled US$7.3 billion in 1987. The top ten *chaebŏl* represented 40 percent of all bank credit in South Korea, 30 percent of value added in manufacturing, and approximately 66 percent of the value of all South Korean exports in 1987. The five largest *chaebŏl* employed 8.5 percent of the manufacturing work force and produced 22.3 percent of all manufacturing shipments. Despite a rash of strikes against the *chaebŏl* beginning in 1987, the *chaebŏl* generally had higher compensation and better working conditions than their lesser South Korean competitors.

The Origins and Development of Chaebŏl

Although South Korea's major industrial programs did not begin until the early 1960s, the origins of the country's entrepreneurial elite were found in the political economy of the 1950s. Very few Koreans had owned or managed larger corporations during the Japanese colonial period. After the departure of the Japanese in 1945, some Korean businessmen obtained the assets of some of the Japanese firms, a number of which grew into the *chaebŏl* of the 1990s. These companies, as well as certain other firms that were formed in the late 1940s and early 1950s, had close links with Syngman Rhee's First Republic, which lasted from 1948 to 1960 (see The Syngman Rhee Era, 1948–60, ch. 1). It was alleged that many of these companies received special favors from the government in return for kickbacks and other payments.

When the military took over the government in 1961, military leaders announced that they would eradicate the corruption that had plagued the Rhee administration and eliminate injustice from society. Some leading industrialists were arrested and charged with corruption, but the new government realized that it would need the help of the entrepreneurs if the government's ambitious plans to modernize the economy were to be fulfilled. A compromise was reached, under which many of the accused corporate leaders paid fines to the government. Subsequently, there was increased cooperation between corporate and government leaders in modernizing the economy.

Government-*chaebŏl* cooperation was essential to the subsequent economic growth and astounding successes that began in the early 1960s. Driven by the urgent need to turn the economy away from consumer goods and light industries toward heavy, chemical, and import-substitution industries, political leaders and government planners relied on the ideas and cooperation of the *chaebŏl* leaders. The government provided the blueprints for industrial expansion; the *chaebŏl* realized the plans. However, the *chaebŏl*-led industrialization accelerated the monopolistic and oligopolistic concentration of capital and economically profitable activities in the hands of a limited number of conglomerates.

Park used the *chaebŏl* as a means towards economic growth. Exports were encouraged, reversing Rhee's policy of reliance on imports. Performance quotas were established.

The *chaebŏl* were able to grow because of two factors—foreign loans and special favors. Access to foreign technology also was critical to the growth of the *chaebŏl* through the 1980s. Under the guise of "guided capitalism," the government selected companies to undertake projects and channeled funds from foreign loans. The government guaranteed repayment should a company be unable to repay its foreign creditors. Additional loans were made available from domestic banks. In the late 1980s, the *chaebŏl* dominated the industrial sector and were especially prevalent in manufacturing, trading, and heavy industries.

The *chaebŏl* were often compared with Japanese *keiretsu* (the successor of the *zaibatsu*), but as David I. Steinberg has noted, there were at least three major differences. First, the *chaebŏl* were family dominated. In 1990, for example, in most cases the family that founded the major business in the *chaebŏl* remained in control, while in Japan the *keiretsu* were controlled by professional corporate management. Second, individual *chaebŏl* were prevented from buying controlling shares of banks, and in 1990 government regulations made it difficult for a *chaebŏl* to develop an exclusive banking relationship. The *keiretsu* usually worked with an affiliated bank and had almost unlimited access to credit. Third, the *chaebŏl* often formed subsidiaries to produce components for exports, while large Japanese corporations often employed outside contractors.

The tremendous growth that the *chaebŏl* experienced, beginning in the early 1960s, was closely tied to the expansion of South Korean exports. Growth resulted from the production of a diversity of goods rather than just one or two products. Innovation and the willingness to develop new product lines were critical. In the 1950s and early 1960s, *chaebŏl* concentrated on wigs and textiles; by the mid-1970s and 1980s, heavy, defense, and chemical industries had become predominant. While these activities were important in the early 1990s, real growth was occurring in the electronics and high-technology industries. The *chaebŏl* also were responsible for turning the trade deficit in 1985 to a trade surplus in 1986. The current account balance, however, fell from more than US$14 billion in 1988 to US$5 billion in 1989.

The *chaebŏl* continued their explosive growth in export markets in the 1980s. By the late 1980s, the *chaebŏl* had become financially independent and secure—thereby eliminating the need for further government-sponsored credit and assistance. By 1990 the *chaebŏl* also had begun to produce for a growing domestic market.

The *chaebŏl* were powerful independent entities acting in the economy and politics, but sometimes they cooperated with the government in the areas of planning and innovation. The government worked hard to encourage competition among the *chaebŏl* in certain areas and to avoid total monopolies.

Another reason for the success of the *chaebŏl* was their access to foreign technology. Rather than having to develop new areas through research and technology, South Korean firms could purchase foreign patents and technology and produce the same goods made elsewhere at lower costs. Hyundai cars, for example, used an engine developed by the Mitsubishi Corporation of Japan.

The role of big business extended to the political arena. In 1988 a member of a *chaebŏl* family, Chŏng Mong-jun, president of Hyundai Heavy Industries, successfully ran for the National Assembly. Other business leaders also were chosen to be members of the National Assembly through the proportional representation system.

The Role of Public Enterprise

A government-led economic development policy during the 1960s was necessary because the less experienced and capital-poor private entrepreneurs lacked the wherewithal to develop several critical industries that were necessary to the nation's economic growth. The government determined that establishing public corporations to develop and manage these highly strategic industries was the fastest and most efficient way to foster growth in a variety of key areas.

During the 1960s, public enterprises were concentrated in such areas as electrification, banking, communications, and manufacturing. In 1990 these enterprises were, in many cases, efficient revenue-producing concerns that produced essential goods and services at low costs, but which also produced profits that were used for new capital investments or to produce funds for public use elsewhere. In the 1980s, Seoul was slowly privatizing a number of these firms by selling stocks, but the government remained the principal stockholder in each company. In the 1980s, an important function of public enterprises was the introduction of new and expensive technology ventures.

In 1985 the public enterprise sector consisted of about 90 enterprises employing 305,000 workers, or 2.7 percent of total employment in the nonagricultural sector. There were four categories of public enterprises: government enterprises (staffed and run by government officials), government-invested enterprises (with at least 50 percent government ownership), subsidiaries of government-invested enterprises (usually having indirect government funding), and other government-backed enterprises. Government-invested public enterprises, such as the Korea Electric Power Corporation (KEPCO) and the Pohang Iron and Steel Company (POSCO), represented the core of the new enterprises established during Park's regime. In the late 1980s, roughly 30 percent of the revenues produced by public enterprises came from the manufacturing sector and the other 70 percent from such service sectors as the electrical, communications, and financial industries.

Pohang Iron and Steel Company

In the 1960s, the Park government concluded that self-sufficiency in steel and the construction of an integrated steelworks were essential to economic development. Because South Korea had not had a modern steel plant before 1968, many foreign and domestic businesses were skeptical of Seoul's decision to invest heavily in constructing a steel plant. Despite the skepticism, however, POSCO began production in 1972, just four years after the company's inauguration in April 1968 with only thirty-nine employees.

Japan provided the money for the construction of the initial plant, following an agreement made at the Third South Korea-Japan Ministerial Meeting in 1969. Financing included US$73.7 million in government grants and loans, US$50 million in credit from the Japan Export-Import Bank, and technical assistance from Nippon Steel and other corporations. This cooperation was one consequence of the normalization of relations with Japan in 1965 and reflected the view of the government of Japan as noted in the Nixon-Sato communiqué of November 21, 1969, that "the security of the Republic of Korea is essential to the security of Japan."

Fresh produce at the market, Seoul
Courtesy Oren Hadar

It'aewŏn shopping district
and entertainment center, Seoul
Courtesy Oren Hadar

151

POSCO is located in the southeastern port city of P'ohang. Previously a fishing port whose major industry was processing fish and marine products, P'ohang is now a major industrial center with almost 250,000 people. In addition to the huge integrated steel mill, P'ohang has an industrial complex housing companies that manufacture finished steel products of raw materials provided by POSCO.

POSCO first began to sell plate products in 1972 and focused its sales policies on the domestic market to improve steel self-sufficiency at home. Special efforts were made to supply quality iron and steel to related domestic companies at below export price to strengthen their international competitiveness.

POSCO's growth has been immense. By the late 1980s, POSCO was the fifth biggest steel company in the noncommunist world, with an annual production approaching 12 million tons worth 3 trillion wŏn. The further expansion of POSCO's productivity and size, however, was sought at a time when the steel industries of the United States and Japan were declining. POSCO's second-phase mill at Kwangyang was completed in August 1988. A third-phase mill was expected, by the early 1990s, to further increase crude steel production to a total output of approximately 17.2 million tons a year. In terms of productivity, POSCO was rated the world's best steel manufacturer throughout the late 1980s and also was rated at the top in terms of facilities.

In 1987 Seoul announced that it was going to transform POSCO into a private company in line with the government's new policy of privatizing state-run corporations. The government planned to retain a majority share of the stock; initial reports in the South Korean press in 1988 indicated that the sale of public shares was going slower than anticipated.

Korea Electric Power Corporation

KEPCO is a government agency whose goal is to provide abundant electric power and to develop reliable power resources. The south of Korea traditionally had received its electric power from power stations in present-day North Korea, but the Pyŏngyang government cut off power to South Korea in 1948. The catastrophes of the Korean War also posed electrical supply problems. The situation had not improved greatly by 1961 when the new military junta merged three smaller electric companies to form the Korea Electric Company (KECO). Seoul invested heavily in KECO, realizing that adequate sources of power were a basic prerequisite to industrialization. In 1982 KECO was reorganized as a public corporation and became known as KEPCO. All shares were owned by the government. In 1988 Seoul decided to sell 30 percent of all shares to the public.

KEPCO, one of the largest public corporations in South Korea, with 30,289 employees, serviced about 99.8 percent of the populace in 1988. It derived about 12 percent of its electricity from hydroelectric sources, 50 percent from thermal sources (coal, oil, and gas-fired), and the rest from a growing number of nuclear power plants. It was hoped that nuclear power would be developed further to lower reliance on oil, gas, and coal imports. KEPCO officials pronounced their nuclear power plants safe from any potential nonmilitary accidents and said that extraordinary measures had been taken to protect the plants in case of a North Korean attack.

Financing Development

Financing South Korea's economic development in the 1990s was expected to differ from previous decades in two main respects: greater reliance on domestic sources and more emphasis on equity relative to debt. Beginning in the 1960s, foreign credit was used to finance development, but the amount of foreign debt had decreased since the mid-1980s. According to the Sixth Five-Year Economic and Social Development Plan (1987–91), an average annual growth rate of 8 percent was expected, together with account surpluses of about US$5 billion a year through 1991.

To realize these growth targets, South Koreans needed the gross domestic savings rate to exceed the domestic investment rate; additionally, they needed the financing of future economic growth to come entirely from domestic sources. Such a situation would involve reducing foreign debt by US$2 billion a year; and South Korea would become a net creditor nation in the mid-1990s. Through the promotion and reform of the securities markets, especially the stock market, and increased foreign investment, the sixth plan encouraged the diversification of sources and types of corporate finance, especially equity finance.

Domestic savings were very low before the mid-1960s, equivalent to less than 2 percent of GNP in the 1960 to 1962 period. The savings rate jumped to 10 percent between 1970 and 1972 when banks began offering depositors rates of 20 percent or more on savings accounts. This situation allowed banks to compete effectively for deposits with unorganized money markets that had previously offered higher rates than the banks. The savings rate increased to 16.8 percent of GNP in 1975 and 28 percent in 1979, but temporarily plunged to 20.8 percent in 1980 because of the oil price rise. After 1980, as incomes rose, so did the savings rate. The surge of the savings rate to 36.3 percent in 1987 and 35.8 percent in

1989 reflected the sharp growth of GNP in the 1980s. The prospects for continued high rates of saving were associated with continued high GNP growth, which nevertheless declined to 6.5 percent in 1989.

According to Donald S. Macdonald, through the early 1980s funds for investment came primarily from bilateral government loans (mainly from the United States and Japan), international lending organizations, and commercial banks. In the late 1980s, however, domestic savings accounted for two-thirds or more of total investment.

Throughout the 1980s, the financial sector underwent significant expansion, diversification of products and services, and structural changes brought about by economic liberalization policies. As noted by Park Yung-chul, financial liberalization eased interest ceilings. Deregulation increased competition in financial markets, which in turn accelerated product diversification. In the early 1980s, securities companies were permitted to sell securities through a repurchase agreement. By 1985 banks also were allowed to engage in the repurchase agreements of government and public bonds. In 1981 finance and investment corporations started dealing in large-denomination commercial paper. The new form of commercial paper was issued in minimum denominations of 10 million wŏn, compared to the previous minimum value for commercial paper of 1 million wŏn.

In order to extend their ability to raise cash, investment and finance companies introduced a new cash-management account with a 4 million wŏn minimum deposit in 1983. Investment and finance corporations managed client funds by investing them in commercial paper corporate bonds and certificates of deposit. Money-deposit banks in the mid-1980s began offering similar accounts, known as household money-in-trust. Trust business formerly had been the exclusive domain of the Bank of Seoul and Trust Company; however, after 1983 all money-deposit banks were authorized to offer trust services.

The financial system underwent two major structural changes in the late 1970s and 1980s. First, money-deposit banks saw a sustained erosion of their once-dominant market position (from 80 percent in the 1970 to 1974 period to 55 percent by 1984). One reason for this decline was that in the 1970s nonbank financial intermediaries, such as investment trust corporations, finance companies, and merchant banking corporations, were given preferential treatment. Further, because the costs of intermediation at these nonbank financial institutions were lower than at banks (with their many branches nationwide and their multitudes of small savers and borrowers), their cost advantages and higher lending rates allowed them a larger market share.

The second structural change was the rapid increase of commercial paper and corporate debenture markets. Another development was the steady growth of investment trust corporations in the 1980s.

Because of the introduction of tax and financing incentives by the government that encouraged companies to list their shares on the stock market, the Korean Stock Exchange grew rapidly in the late 1980s. In 1987 more than 350 companies were listed on the exchange. There was an average daily trading volume of 10 million shares, with a turnover ratio of 80 percent. In 1989 the stock market was tarnished by accusations of insider trading among the five major South Korean securities firms. The Securities and Exchange Commission launched an investigation in late 1989. The popular index of the market soared to a high of 1,007.77 points on April 1, 1989, but plunged back to the 800s in late 1989 and early 1990.

Business financing was obtained primarily through bank loans or borrowing on the informal and high-interest "curb market" of private lenders. The curb market served individuals who needed cash urgently, less reputable businesspeople who engaged in speculation, and the multitudes of smaller companies that needed operating funds but could not procure bank financing. The loans they received, often in exchange for weak collateral, had very high interest rates. The curb market played a critical role in the 1960s and 1970s in pumping money into the economy and in assisting the growth of smaller corporations. The curb market continued to exist, along with the formal banking system, through the 1980s.

Industry

The growth of the industrial sector was the principal stimulus to economic development. In 1987 manufacturing industries accounted for approximately 30 percent of the gross domestic product (GDP—see Glossary) and 25 percent of the work force. Benefiting from strong domestic encouragement and foreign aid, Seoul's industrialists introduced modern technologies into outmoded or newly built facilities at a rapid pace, increased the production of commodities—especially those for sale in foreign markets—and plowed the proceeds back into further industrial expansion. As a result, industry altered the country's landscape, drawing millions of laborers to urban manufacturing centers.

A downturn in the South Korean economy in 1989 spurred by a sharp decrease in exports and foreign orders caused deep concern in the industrial sector. Ministry of Trade and Industry analysts stated that poor export performance resulted from structural problems embedded in the nation's economy, including an overly strong wŏn, increased wages and high labor costs, frequent strikes, and high interest rates. The result was an increase in inventories and severe cutbacks in production at a number of electronics, automobile, and textile manufacturers, as well as at the smaller firms that supplied the parts. Factory automation systems were introduced to reduce dependence on labor, to boost productivity with a much smaller work force, and to improve competitiveness. It was estimated that over two-thirds of South Korea's manufacturers spent over half of the funds available for facility investments on automation.

In 1990 South Korean manufacturers planned a significant shift in future production plans toward high-technology industries. In June 1989, panels of government officials, scholars, and business leaders held planning sessions on the production of such goods as new materials, mechatronics—including industrial robotics, bioengineering, microelectronics, fine chemistry, and aerospace. This shift in emphasis, however, did not mean an immediate decline in heavy industries such as automobile and ship production, which had dominated the economy in the 1980s.

Except for mining, most industries were located in the urban areas of the northwest and southeast. Heavy industries generally were located in the south of the country. Factories in Seoul contributed over 25 percent of all manufacturing value-added in 1978; taken together with factories in surrounding Kyŏnggi Province, factories in the Seoul area produced 46 percent of all manufacturing that year. Factories in Seoul and Kyŏnggi Province employed 48 percent of the nation's 2.1 million factory workers.

Steel

In 1989 South Korea was the world's tenth largest steel producer, accounting for 2.3 percent of world steel production. South Korea continued to expand crude steel production—19.3 million tons for 1988, up 14.9 percent over 1987. Domestic demand for steel products increased 8.5 percent from 15 million tons to 16.3 million tons over the same period because of the growing demands of South Korean industry. Domestic demand accounted for 70 percent of the total, mostly because of the increased needs of such steel-consuming industries as automobiles, shipbuilding, and electronics.

The steel industry grew in the 1970s after the government constructed the POSCO mill to service Seoul's rapidly growing automobile, shipbuilding, and construction industries. In 1988 South Korea's steel industry included 200 steel companies. Iron and steel production was expected to increase in the early 1990s, given the output increases in domestic user industries. Exports were likely to be flat or to decline because of decreased international demand.

Electronics

In 1989 South Korea was a major producer of electronics, producing color televisions, videocassette recorders, microwave ovens, radios, watches, personal computers, and videotapes. In 1988 the electronics industry produced US$23 billion worth of goods (up 35 percent from 1987), to become the world's sixth largest manufacturer. The total value of parts and components (including semiconductors) produced in 1988 totaled US$9.7 billion, overtaking consumer electronics production (US$9.2 billion) for the first time. Manufacture of industrial electronics also grew significantly in 1988 and totaled US$4.6 billion (20 percent of total production). Electronics exports grew rapidly in the late 1980s to more than US$15 billion in 1988, up 40 percent from 1987—to become Seoul's leading export industry. Although South Korean electronic goods enjoyed substantial price competitiveness over Japanese products, the electronics industry continued to be heavily dependent on Japanese components, an important factor in South Korea's chronic trade deficit with Japan. Some South Korean firms formed joint ventures with foreign concerns to acquire advanced technology. In the late 1980s, South Korea's leading electronics firms (Samsung, Lucky-Goldstar, and Hyundai) began establishing overseas plants in such markets as the Federal Republic of Germany (West Germany), Britain, Turkey, and Ireland.

By 1990 significant shifts were occurring within the electronics industry. In 1989 South Korea had lost some of its cost advantage to newer consumer electronics producers in Southeast Asia. At the same time, production of electronic components and of industrial electronics, particularly computers and telecommunications equipment, continued to expand to such an extent that overall demand for South Korean electronics products was expected to increase modestly in the early 1990s. In 1990 Seoul projected that the microelectronics industry would grow at an annual rate of 17.2 percent in the early 1990s.

Shipbuilding

During the 1970s and 1980s, South Korea became a leading producer of ships, including oil supertankers, and oil-drilling platforms. The country's major shipbuilder was Hyundai, which built a 1-million-ton capacity drydock at Ulsan in the mid-1970s. Daewoo

157

joined the shipbuilding industry in 1980 and finished a 1.2-million-ton facility at Okp'o on Kŏje Island, south of Pusan, in mid-1981. The industry declined in the mid-1980s because of the oil glut and because of a worldwide recession. There was a sharp decrease in new orders in the late 1980s; new orders for 1988 totaled 3 million gross tons valued at US$1.9 billion, decreases from the previous year of 17.8 percent and 4.4 percent, respectively. These declines were caused by labor unrest, Seoul's unwillingness to provide financial assistance, and Tokyo's new low-interest export financing in support of Japanese shipbuilders. However, the South Korean shipping industry was expected to expand in the early 1990s because older ships in world fleets needed replacing.

Automobiles and Automotive Parts

The automobile industry was one of South Korea's major growth and export industries in the 1980s. By the late 1980s, the capacity of the South Korean motor industry had increased more than fivefold since 1984; it exceeded 1 million units in 1988. Total investment in car and car-component manufacturing was over US$3 billion in 1989. Total production (including buses and trucks) for 1988 totaled 1.1 million units, a 10.6 percent increase over 1987, and grew to an estimated 1.3 million vehicles (predominantly passenger cars) in 1989. Almost 263,000 passenger cars were produced in 1985—a figure that grew to approximately 846,000 units in 1989. In 1988 automobile exports totaled 576,134 units, of which 480,119 units (83.3 percent) were sent to the United States. Throughout most of the late 1980s, much of the growth of South Korea's automobile industry was the result of a surge in exports; 1989 exports, however, declined 28.5 percent from 1988. This decline reflected sluggish car sales to the United States, especially at the less expensive end of the market, and labor strife at home.

The industry continued to grow, however, because of a surge in domestic demand, up 47 percent during the first half of 1989. In 1989, for the first time since car exports had doubled in 1985, domestic sales surpassed exports; two-thirds of the cars manufactured were sold domestically. Most of the domestic demand came from first-time car buyers whose savings had been buoyed by double-digit wage increases each year since 1987. Other factors leading to the growing domestic demand for motor vehicles included stable or slightly decreased new car prices because of cuts in special consumption taxes, reduced fuel taxes, and growing economies of scale by manufacturers.

Throughout the 1970s and 1980s, the automobile industry was subject to a series of government controls and directives designed

Ulsan shipyard, one of the world's largest
Courtesy Hyundai Corporation

to nurture the industry and prevent excess competition. For most of the 1980s, Hyundai was the only company permitted to manufacture passenger cars, but in 1989 Kia Motors and Daewoo were allowed to reenter the passenger car business. In 1989 Ssangyong Motors became South Korea's fourth car manufacturer.

South Korea's auto parts industry grew rapidly in the late 1980s, from US$3.8 billion in 1987 to US$4.6 billion in 1988 (US$4 billion produced locally). Automotive parts imports, most of which came from Japan, totaled US$610 million in 1988 (down from US$700 million in 1987). In 1989 South Korean automobile and parts manufacturers planned to spend more than 2 trillion wŏn (US$2.8 billion) on facility expansion, research, and development.

Armaments

South Korea is an important manufacturer of armaments, both for domestic use and for export (see Military Production, ch. 5). During the 1960s, South Korea was largely dependent on the United States to supply its armed forces, but after the elaboration of President Richard M. Nixon's policy of Vietnamization in the early 1970s, South Korea began to manufacture many of its own weapons. These included M-16 rifles, artillery, ammunition, tanks, other military vehicles, and ships. Aircraft were assembled under coproduction arrangements with United States firms. Arms exports, including quartermaster goods, vehicles, and weaponry, reached nearly US$975 million in 1982 but declined during the rest of the decade, reaching only US$50 million in 1988. In 1989 Seoul announced that its fledgling aerospace industry was planning to produce an indigenously designed high-performance jetfighter for its air force within two decades. The South Korean aerospace industry also developed a Korean Fighters Program in cooperation with McDonnell Douglas of the United States, with the goal of "acquiring the capacity to design and manufacture supersonic jet-fighters."

Construction

Construction has been an important South Korean export industry since the early 1960s and remains a critical source of foreign currency and "invisible" export earnings. By 1981 overseas construction projects, most of them in the Middle East, accounted for 60 percent of the work undertaken by South Korean construction companies. Contracts that year were valued at US$13.7 billion. In 1988, however, overseas construction contracts totaled only US$1.6 billion (orders from the Middle East were US$1.2 billion), a 1 percent increase over the previous year, while new orders for domestic construction projects totaled US$13.8 billion, an 8.8 percent increase over 1987. The result was that South Korean construction companies concentrated on the rapidly growing domestic market in the late 1980s. By 1989 there were signs of a revival of the overseas construction market—the Dong Ah Construction Company signed a US$5.3 billion contract with Libya for the second phase of Libya's Great Man-Made River Project, which, when all five phases were completed, was projected to cost US$27 billion. South Korean construction companies signed over US$7 billion of overseas contracts in 1989.

Textiles and Footwear

Textiles, clothing, and leather products made up about 24 percent of South Korea's manufacturing output in 1980. Over 10,000 textile and footwear enterprises employed more than four workers each, and 34,000 smaller shops manufactured such products in 1978. Throughout the 1980s, textiles played a critical role in Seoul's exports, accounting for US$11.9 billion, or 19.6 percent of total export earnings. In 1989 the export of textiles (valued at US$15,340 million) grew 8.5 percent over the 1988 level. Textile manufacturers, concerned about diminishing export competitiveness because of wage increases and wŏn revaluation, expanded their overseas investments in 1987 and 1988. Seoul approved sixty-six investment projects totaling US$38.4 million from January 1, 1978, through the end of September 1988. Most of these investments were located in the Caribbean Basin region and Southeast Asia. Upgrading product lines—particularly towards high fashion—and further shifting to the expanding domestic market were expected to cause slow growth in the industry in the early 1990s.

South Korea's footwear industry also expanded in the late 1980s. Footwear exports in 1988 totaled US$3.8 billion, a 34.7 percent increase over 1987, 6.3 percent of Seoul's total exports by value. Economic forecasters, however, predicted that the industry would decline in the 1990s despite the surge of orders in 1989; they attributed the 1989 surge to political unrest in China, normally a major producer of footwear.

Chemicals

The chemical industry began full production in the 1970s. Although dependent on imports of raw materials and certain high-technology commodities, the chemical industry supplied many of the intermediate inputs for textile, plastic, synthetic rubber, rubber shoe, and paint factories, and had made South Korea virtually self-sufficient in fertilizers. The chemical fertilizer industry, a

161

large part of the chemical industry, met most of South Korea's domestic consumption demands.

In 1987 chemical and pharmaceutical exports increased by 27 percent over the previous year, but accounted for only 2.8 percent of total exports; imports in that category comprised 11.2 percent of total imports. The chemical industry was expected to expand in the early 1990s, with new capacity coming online and Seoul committed to spending money for research and development and constructing new production facilities. Pharmaceuticals, agricultural chemicals, dyes, pigments, paint, perfumes, surface active agents (surfactants) including synthetic detergents, and catalysts were targeted as major areas for investment.

In the late 1980s, petrochemical production facilities included twenty-five companies, thirty-six plants, two naphtha crackers, and three aromatics extraction plants, with an aggregate total production capacity of 505,000 tons of ethylene per annum. There were two large petrochemical complexes, one in Ulsan, the other in Yŏsu. South Korea was an important producer of chemical fertilizers in the late 1970s (671,000 nutrient tons exported in 1980), but both exports and production declined in the 1980s.

Energy

The Korean Peninsula is only modestly endowed with natural resources, and North Korea has far more natural resources than South Korea. During the Japanese colonial period (1910–45), the north served as the center for mining and industry whereas the south, with somewhat greater rainfall, a warmer climate, and slightly greater arable terrain, served as the center for rice production. (see Physical Environment, ch. 2).

South Korea's mineral production is not adequate to supply its manufacturing output. Energy needs are also met by importing bituminous and anthracite coal and crude petroleum. In 1987 approximately 23.4 million tons of anthracite coal, approximately 4,000 tons of tungsten, 565,000 tons of iron ore, and 47,000 tons of zinc ore were mined. Lesser amounts of copper, lead, molybdenum, gold, silver, kaolin, and fluorite also were mined (see fig. 9).

Energy producers were dominated by government enterprises, although privately operated coal mines and oil refineries also existed. In 1990 South Korea still had no proven oil reserves. Offshore oil possibilities in the Yellow Sea and on the continental shelf between Korea and Japan yielded nothing through the 1980s, but exploration continued. South Korea's coal supply was both insufficient and of low quality. The potential for hydroelectric power was very limited because of tremendous seasonal variations in the weather and the concentration of most of the rainfall in the summer months. Accordingly, Seoul placed an increasingly heavy emphasis on developing nuclear power generation.

Electric power in South Korea was provided by the Korea Electric Power Corporation (KEPCO). When KEPCO's predecessor, KECO, was founded in 1961, annual power production was 1,770 million kilowatt-hours (kwhr); production reached 73,992 million kwhr in 1987. The ratio of usage during 1987 was 17.9 percent for residential customers, 16.2 percent for public and service businesses, and 65.9 percent for the industrial sector. Energy used in electric power generation consisted primarily of nuclear, coal, oil, and liquified natural gas (LNG). Of the 54,885 million kwhr of electricity generated in 1985, 22 percent came from nuclear plants then in operation, 74 percent from thermal plants (oil and coal), and 4 percent from hydroelectric sites. It was predicted in 1988 that the generation structure by the year 2000 would be 10.2 percent hydroelectric, 12.2 percent oil, 22.9 percent coal, 10.2 percent LNG, and 44.5 percent nuclear.

South Korea placed a heavy emphasis on nuclear power generation. The country's first nuclear power plant, the Kori Number One located near Pusan, opened in 1977. Eight plants were operational in 1987 when atomic power generation was an estimated 71,158 million kilowatts, or 53.1 percent of total electric power.

South Korea's first antinuclear protests occurred in December 1988 when residents near the Kori complex demonstrated against low-level waste that had been secretly buried just outside the plant. In 1989 residents near other nuclear reactors protested the environmental damage they said was caused by the units. Sixteen antinuclear groups joined together to form the Movement for the Eradication of Nuclear Power Plants. The government, however, asserted that the South Korean nuclear program was well run and that none of the 193 antinuclear protests reported since 1977 was serious.

Agriculture

At the start of the economic boom in 1963, the majority of South Koreans were farmers. Sixty-three percent of the population lived in rural areas. In the next twenty-five years, South Korea grew from a predominantly rural, agricultural nation into an urban, newly industrialized country and the agricultural workforce shrunk to only 21 percent in 1989 (see fig. 10). Government officials expected that urbanization and industrialization would further reduce the number of agricultural workers to well under 20 percent by 2000.

South Korea's agriculture had many inherent problems. South Korea is a mountainous country with only 22 percent arable land

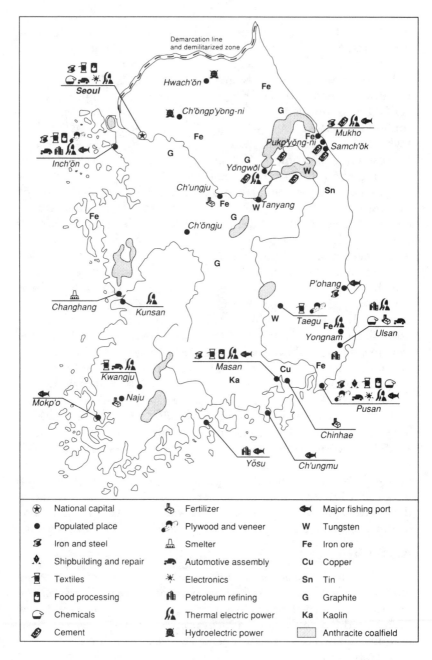

Source: Based on information from K.P. Wang et al., *Mineral Industries of the Far East and South Asia,* Washington, 1988, 74–75.

Figure 9. Selected Industrial and Mining Activity, 1988

and less rainfall than most other neighboring rice-growing countries (see Land Area and Borders; Climate, ch. 2). A major land reform in the late 1940s and early 1950s spread ownership of land to the rural peasantry. Individual holdings, however, were too small (averaging one hectare, which made cultivation inefficient and discouraged mechanization) or too spread out to provide families with much chance to produce a significant quantity of food. The enormous growth of urban areas led to a rapid decrease of available farmland, while at the same time population increases and bigger incomes meant that the demand for food greatly outstripped supply. The result of these developments was that by the late 1980s roughly half of South Korea's needs, mainly wheat and animal feed corn, was imported.

Compared with the industrial and service sectors, agriculture remained the most sluggish sector of the economy. In 1988 the contribution of agriculture to overall GDP was only about 10.8 percent, down from approximately 12.3 percent the previous year. Most economists agreed that the country's rural areas had gained more than they had contributed in the course of industrialization. Still, the growth of agricultural output, which averaged 3.4 percent per year between 1945 and 1974, 6.8 percent annually during the 1974–79 period, and 5.6 percent between 1980 and 1986, was credible. The gains were even more impressive because they added to a traditionally high level of productivity. On the other hand, the overall growth of the agriculture, forestry, and fishing sector was only 0.6 percent in 1987 as compared with the manufacturing sector, which grew 16 percent during 1986 and 1987. During the first half of 1989, the agriculture, forestry, and fisheries sector grew 5.9 percent, as opposed to manufacturing's 2.9 percent.

Major Crops

Rice was the most important crop and yields were impressive. As noted by Donald S. Macdonald, however, rising wage levels and land values have made it expensive to produce. Rice represented about 90 percent of total grain production and over 40 percent of farm income; the 1988 rice crop was 6.5 million tons. Rice was imported in the 1980s, but the amount depended on the success of domestic harvests. The government's rice support program reached a record US$1.9 billion in 1986, as compared with US$890 million in 1985. By raising procurement prices by 14 percent over the 1986 level, Seoul achieved a rice price structure that was about five times that of the world market in 1987.

Barley was the second most important crop. Its production declined from about 1.5 million tons in 1970 to about 561,500 tons

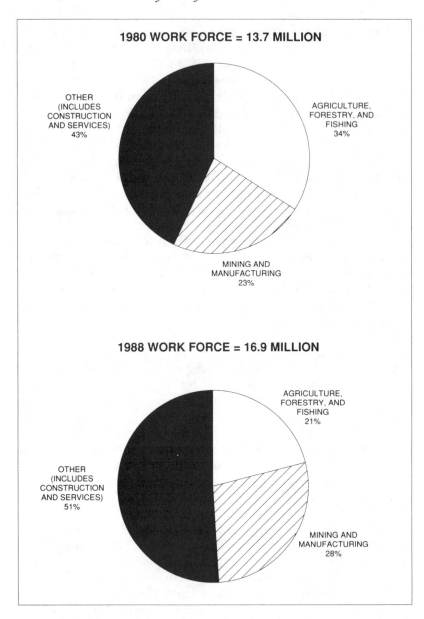

1980 WORK FORCE = 13.7 MILLION

OTHER
(INCLUDES
CONSTRUCTION
AND SERVICES)
43%

AGRICULTURE,
FORESTRY, AND
FISHING
34%

MINING AND
MANUFACTURING
23%

1988 WORK FORCE = 16.9 MILLION

AGRICULTURE,
FORESTRY, AND
FISHING
21%

OTHER
(INCLUDES
CONSTRUCTION
AND SERVICES)
51%

MINING AND
MANUFACTURING
28%

Source: Based on information from Republic of Korea, Ministry of Culture and Information, Korean Overseas Information Service, *A Handbook of Korea,* Seoul, 1982, 489; Byung-Nak Song, *The Rise of the Korean Economy,* Hong Kong, 1990, 109; and *Europa World Yearbook, 1990,* 2, London, 1990, 1556.

Figure 10. Employment by Sector, 1980 and 1988

in 1988. Other crops included such grains as millet, corn, sorghum, buckwheat, soybeans, and potatoes. Fruits and vegetables included pears, grapes, mandarin oranges, apples, peaches, Welsh onions, Chinese cabbage, red peppers, persimmons, cabbage, peaches, and radishes. Other important cash crops included cotton, hemp, sesame, tobacco, and ginseng. In 1988, livestock heads included native Korean cattle (2 million), hogs (4.9 million), and poultry (almost 59 million).

Forestry and Fishing

South Korean farmers have always used the nation's forests for fuel and household products, but centuries of overutilization and poor resource management had practically denuded the countryside by the end of the Chosŏn Dynasty (1392–1910). World War II interrupted Japanese efforts to replace the ravaged forest stock and the Korean War brought to a peak the destruction of Korea's forests. After the 1950s, Seoul slowly developed the organizational and technical expertise to save the nation's trees. Despite frequent setbacks, reforestation had proceeded fairly successfully by the 1970s; the total volume of timber had grown from a low of 30.8 million cubic meters in 1954 to over 164.4 million cubic meters in 1984. The density of the woodlands expanded from an average of 4.8 to 17.8 cubic meters per hectare of forest during the same period.

By 1984 over 20 percent of the nation's 6.5 million hectares of forest belonged to the government; most was managed by the Office of Forestry, a branch of the Ministry of Home Affairs. Another 8 percent was owned by local public authorities; 72 percent was privately owned. In 1985 about two-thirds of South Korea was covered by forests. Until the 1970s, reforestation had taken place primarily in national forests; as a result of this situation, the density of government-owned forests was about three times greater than that of private forests. Most forest owners were smallholders with inadequate financial resources to purchase and maintain seedlings. However, upon the introduction of the Saemaŭl Movement, an ambitious rural development program launched by Park in 1971, the performance of the Village Forestry Associations—similar to and often overlapping with the agricultural cooperatives—improved significantly. Between 1972 and 1979, forestry agents and village associations planted 1.4 million hectares with 3.4 million seedlings.

Although the fuel needs of most farmers were met by wood from local forests or coal briquettes, the growing industrial demand for timber was not adequately supplied by domestic production. In 1977 South Korea imported 88 percent of its timber, mostly from

Malaysia and Indonesia. In 1985 South Korea imported US$538 million worth of wood, lumber, and cork; imports were US$549 million in 1986.

South Korea's fishing industry contributed both to the welfare of the consumer and to export earnings. Although the value-added income from fishing contributed less than 1 percent of GNP and the fishing population decreased by over 18 percent during the 1970s (to 745,000 persons), fishery products contributed 5 percent of the value of commodity exports. Fishery production totaled 470,000 tons in 1962, 1.3 million tons in 1972, 2.6 million tons in 1982, and 3.3 million tons in 1987. In 1988 South Korean fishing households earned about US$10,000 on average.

Most of the expansion of production in the 1970s and 1980s was the result of deep-sea fishing operations. The major fishing ports were Ulsan and Masan. In the late 1980s, the production of sea-weed, oyster, and other products of coastal and offshore breeding farms declined, but the catch of tuna and squid in deep-sea fishing rose. Fishing trawlers brought in about 250,000 tons of pollock off the coast of Alaska in 1985, a catch that both contributed to the South Korean diet and was exported to United States food processors.

In 1985 there were 90,970 fishing vessels harvesting a total catch of 858,471 tons. Of these vessels, 71,836 were motorized (836,633 tons) and 19,134 (21,838 tons) were nonmotorized. These numbers reflected a major change from 1962, when only 6,085 vessels out of 45,504 were motorized.

The Agricultural Crisis of the Late 1980s

Agricultural labor costs rose as young people left rural areas for urban jobs, and farm work mainly was done by women and old men. Farmers' relative earnings improved during the 1970s, but fell in the 1980s. The gap between incomes of urbanites and people in rural areas widened considerably in the late 1980s. In 1988 the average income of people in *gun* (counties) amounted to 79.1 percent of that of people in cities, as compared with 84.7 percent in 1985. South Korean farming households earned about US$12,000 in 1988, up 24.4 percent from 1987. In comparison, the average income for an urban family in 1989 was about US$15,000. Nonfarm income in 1989 comprised 39.5 percent of average farm household earnings, as compared with more than 50 percent in Japan and approximately 70 percent in Taiwan.

Farm families accumulated debts averaging about US$4,620 per household in 1988 and had average assets of about US$66,057. The purchase of modern farm machinery as well as of many new consumer goods contributed to higher debts. The 35 percent rise in assets between 1987 and 1988 mainly was because of a 41 percent increase in the price of land. Budgetary pressures from the government on agricultural price supports also reduced farm income.

There was increased rental of farmland in the 1980s. The percentage of rented farmland among total farmland rose from 21 percent in 1980 to 30.5 percent in 1985. The percentage of farm households renting some of their land among total farm households expanded rapidly from 37.1 percent in 1980 to 64.7 percent in 1985. Nonfarmer ownership of tenant farmland also increased to 63 percent in 1985.

The farmers who rented land were mainly the small-landed farmers adversely affected by Seoul's agricultural open-door policy of the 1980s. Under this policy, the government sought cheap cereal prices by increasing cheap imports and promoted large-scale farming where crops could be produced more cheaply and efficiently. In the early 1970s, a farm family could meet almost 100 percent of household expenses by farming 0.5 to 1 hectare, but by 1985 such small plots of land only met 59.8 percent of expenses. Many farmers had to rent extra land to augment their incomes.

Poor prospects on the farm depleted farm villages as the young left and the old died. Parents sent their children to the towns and cities for a better education. Young farmers who could not find wives also left for the cities.

The government initiated various programs to improve rural conditions. The most extensive of these was the New Community Movement (Saemaŭl undong, known as the Saemaŭl Movement). Its goal was to mobilize villagers in their own service. At first Saemaŭl projects were aimed at improving household living conditions. Later, projects were directed more to the village as a whole and included the construction of roads, bridges, irrigation ditches, and common compost plots. Next, the program focused on more economic concerns—group farming, common seed beds, livestock production, forestation, and even joint marketing and factories. Better health and sanitation as well as beautification of the environment also became program goals. The government provided the materials and small amounts of money to the villagers, who supplied the labor. In the early 1980s, President Chun removed control over the Saemaŭl Movement from the Ministry of Home Affairs and left most decisionmaking to the Saemaŭl leaders and bureaucrats, headed by the president's younger brother, Chŏn Kyŏng-hwan. The Saemaŭl Movement initially was quite successful but deteriorated in the early 1980s. Chŏn Kyŏng-hwan, arrested on a variety of corruption charges in 1988, was accused of large-scale extortion and embezzlement while he was chairman of the movement between 1981 and 1987.

South Korea, a high-cost agricultural producer, prohibited unrestricted beef and rice imports and severely limited many other agricultural imports. Foreign trading partners such as the United States pressured South Korea to open up the agricultural market, but Seoul said that its farmers would be hurt badly by the importation of inexpensive beef, rice, tobacco, and other products. In April 1989, Seoul released a list of 243 agricultural products scheduled for import liberalization by 1991, but the list did not include beef. In the late 1980s, many farmers, already deeply in debt, were told by the government that they might have to compete in the world market and took to the streets to protest against foreign demands and to demand further protection from the government.

In the late 1980s, farmers gained political strength through the increased activities of various farm associations and the formation of new organizations, such as the National Association of Farmers (Chŏn'guk-nongmin hyŏphoe) established in 1987. The Korean Catholic Farmers Association and Protestant Farmers Association became active in 1987. These and other independent farm groups applied strong pressure on the government to alleviate their problems. Rural residents made up less than one quarter of South Korea's voters, but they elected almost half of the National Assembly; thus, they exercised virtual veto power over farming legislation.

Prospects

The long-term prospects for agriculture were not encouraging. Traditionally the peninsula's rice basket, South Korea had not been self-sufficient agriculturally for many years. In the late 1980s, almost half the nation's foodstuff needs were imports, mostly wheat and animal feed corn. Natural disasters compounded the problems of farmers in the 1980s. As a result of these factors, the share of the GNP provided by the agriculture, forestry, and fishing sector share of the GNP shrank 5.2 percent in 1987.

However, the situation was not totally bleak in the early 1990s. Although the purchasing power of the agricultural sector had been declining since the early 1960s relative to other sectors of the economy, the rate of agricultural productivity increased in the 1980s. Livestock raising and rice cultivation had come to dominate the agricultural sector over a variety of traditional agricultural pursuits.

Service Industries

Service industries included insurance, restaurants, hotels, laundries, public bath houses, health-related services, and entertainment establishments. There were thousands of small shops marketing specialized items, large traditional marketplaces, and streamlined buildings housing corporate and professional offices. Game rooms featuring Ping-Pong tables, or billiards, and tearooms serving a variety of beverages were located on almost every downtown city corner.

South Korea's hosting of the 1988 Seoul Olympics from September 18 to October 2, 1988, made 1988 a boom year for tourism. More than 2 million tourists spent US$3.3 billion, an increase in the number of tourists and the dollars spent, respectively, of 24.9 percent and 42.2 percent over 1987. Japanese visitors accounted for 48 percent of the total; tourists from the United States made up 14.9 percent. The Korean National Tourist Corporation predicted that in 1990 almost 3 million tourists would visit the country.

An improved transportation and communications infrastructure, increasing incomes, enhanced consumer sophistication, and government tax incentives encouraged the development of a modern distribution network of chain stores, supermarkets, and department stores (see Transportation and Telecommunications, this ch.).

In the mid-1980s, the largest employer of South Korea's service sector was retail trade. A growing number of workers were employed by the mostly department stores (most of which were owned by *chaebŏl*) that were opening rapidly in the downtown areas of major urban centers. The vast majority of retailers were small merchants in cities, towns, and villages, each with a modest storefront, or stand, limited stock, and poor access to capital, but the great majority of South Koreans made their purchases from these small retailers. In 1986 there were approximately 26,054 wholesale and 542,548 retail establishments and 233,834 hotels and restaurants that employed about 1.7 million people (these figures probably do not include family members working in small stores).

The distribution system was far from perfect, and managers recognized the need for better organization and management. Most of the nation's wholesalers were located in Seoul and accounted for most of the turnover of goods. Most of the sales outlets were located in the heart of urban centers. Cargo truck terminals and warehouse facilities were spread irregularly through city neighborhoods.

Money and Banking

When Park Chung Hee became president in 1961, he organized a highly centralized government with the power to direct the economy. Park quickly nationalized all banks, took control of foreign borrowing, and merged the agricultural cooperative movement with the agricultural bank. The government also took control of all forms of institutional credit, giving Park great control over the business community.

The government began to liberalize the banking system in the mid-1980s by denationalizing several banks, but refused to allow individual *chaebŏl* to acquire controlling shares in these banks. The government still maintained strong managerial controls over these banks through the Bank of Korea's Office of Bank Supervision and Examination, which, under the guidance of the Monetary Board, supervised and regularly examined banking institutions. Most of the credit provided by these banks went to the *chaebŏl,* but the banks also were required by law to make at least one-third of their business loans to small and medium-sized firms.

South Korea's financial sector in the late 1980s included a diversified commercial banking system, a securities market, and a wide range of secondary financial institutions. The banks kept pace with the rest of the economy, particularly after the liberalization and modernization of financial institutions in the mid-1980s and the establishment of the capital market system based on the Fifth Five-Year Economic and Social Development Plan.

The Bank of Korea was established as the central bank on June 12, 1950. Its major functions included the issuance of all currency; the formulation and execution of monetary and credit policies; the conduct of the bulk of foreign exchange control business; the research, collection, and preparation of statistics on many aspects of South Korea's financial system; and the supervision and regulation of the activities of private banks. The Bank of Korea engaged in loan and deposit transactions for the government; additionally, the bank transacted various government business activities. It also made loans to and received deposits from other banking institutions; all banks maintained their solvency through balances at the Bank of Korea.

South Korea's five major commercial banks (Chohung, Commercial, First, Hanil, and Seoul) were privately held. Together with two city bank joint ventures—the Kor-Am Bank and the Shin-Han (co-owned with the United States and Japan respectively)—there were 961 commercial bank branches across South Korea at the end of 1987. Local banks were found in every province.

The Bank of Korea regulated all commercial banking activities under the provisions of the General Banking Act passed in 1954. Commercial banks got their money through deposits from the general public, international loans, and funds borrowed from the Bank of Korea. The lending activities of commercial banks focused on short-term loans or discounts because long-term lending was

Urban freeway, Seoul
Courtesy Oren Hadar

A bus in the It'aewŏn area
of Seoul
Courtesy Oren Hadar

still the prerogative of such specialized banks as the Korea Exchange Bank, Korea Housing Bank, and National Agricultural Cooperatives Federation. In the late 1980s, the banking industry operated according to a "prime" bank system whereby each major South Korean bank was assigned one domestic commercial bank. Under specific legislation designed to achieve certain functions or to assist special markets, six special banks received funds from the government and from the sales of debentures.

Three other financial development institutions supplied credit for business and government projects. The Export-Import Bank of Korea extended medium- and long-term credit to both suppliers and buyers to facilitate exports of capital goods and services, major resources development, and overseas investment. The Korea Development Bank, which was the government's shareholder in state-run enterprises, raised funds from the government as well as from international financial institutions and foreign banks to fund key industries and infrastructure projects. The Korea Long-Term Credit Bank financed equipment investment.

Small and Medium-Sized Businesses

Small and medium-sized businesses—generally those with less than 400 employees—accounted for US$11 billion, or 32 percent, of South Korea's exports in 1986. By 1987 these businesses generated an estimated US$14 billion, but the export percentage dropped to 30 percent as large automobile and electronics groups led export growth. Small and medium-sized businesses contributed 38.9 percent to the GNP in 1986 when calculated on a value-added basis.

Many of South Korea's smaller firms manufacture specialized parts or equipment for the larger *chaebŏl*. As is the case with *keiretsu* in Japan, many of the *chaebŏl* in South Korea assemble and market goods under their own brandnames, but rely on smaller support firms to manufacture most of the individual parts. Wages are often lower in the smaller firms than at the *chaebŏl,* and working conditions often are worse.

Starting in 1983, Seoul selected a number of the more promising smaller firms to receive special government assistance. These businesses were eligible for a number of tax breaks, help in securing financing, and consultations and technical education from the Ministry of Trade and Industry. Small businesses were central to the government's policy of producing more sophisticated technology locally; additionally, they were critical to the government's strategy of encouraging regional development away from the overcrowded area around Seoul. In 1989 the government announced a plan to spend billions of wŏn to help small and medium-sized industries seek structural improvements so that they could move away from labor-intensive production in favor of technology-intensive production.

The Labor Force

Despite significant increases in wages in the 1980s, labor unions in the late 1980s continued their wave of strikes demanding better working conditions and wages. The ferocity and sheer size of the labor movement caught management and the government by surprise. During his first year or so in office, President Roh Tae Woo was confronted with considerable labor unrest; there were more than 300 strikes in the first three months of 1989 (see Interest Groups, ch. 4). Emboldened by the political reforms of 1987 and by reports that the rate of South Korea's economic growth was greater than the improvements in their own incomes and life-styles, many workers agitated for a greater share of the nation's prosperity and sought more freedom and responsibility at the workplace and an end to the traditional paternalism of management. Lost production was estimated to have climbed to US$6 billion in 1989 from US$4.4 billion in 1988.

Workers were caught in a revolution of rising expectations, as a wave of rising urban land values and housing costs outpaced average real wage increases of more than 70 percent during the 1980s. Moreover, wages for manual workers, who were responsible for much of the production and export that fueled the economy, were much lower than the national average. In the late 1980s, working families still found themselves struggling to meet minimum standards of living. Employees also were expected to work long and often erratic hours in exchange for steady employment and were frustrated over a lack of benefits and individual say. One labor activist noted in 1989 that the labor movement ''is not a class struggle. We just want better working conditions and better status for workers. We have been looked down on in Korea for a very long time.''

Worker complaints were focused on three areas: low wages, long working hours, and a high number of industrial accidents. In 1986 the average wage of a South Korean worker was US$381 a month (339,474 wŏn), including overtime and all allowances. The basic wage was US$287, or 255,408 wŏn, but, according to the government, the basic wage necessary to sustain a ''decent'' way of life was US$588 (524,113 wŏn). Thus, the average worker only earned two-thirds of what the government thought necessary to sustain a family of four. In 1987 semiskilled workers typically received US$1.50 to US$2.00 per hour and worked fifty-five to sixty hours a week; unskilled workers worked twelve-hour days seven days a week, earning US$125 a month.

There were, however, dramatic increases in wages in 1988 and 1989. Labor stoppages in the manufacturing sector, coupled with a scarcity of labor, led to 20-percent salary increases for workers in the manufacturing sector in 1988 and 25-percent salary increases in that sector in 1989. These raises later spread, increasing wages across the entire economy 18.7 percent in 1989. By 1989 some South Korean economists were worrying about the effect that skyrocketing wages would have on the cost of domestic-made goods and the consequent impact on export prices. The situation was especially worrisome because the wages paid to workers in South Korea's major competitors were growing far more slowly.

South Korea was known for having the world's longest working hours. In 1986 the Korean worker averaged about 54.7 hours a week. This situation was the natural consequence of the low wage system that necessitated extended hours and extra work to earn minimum living expenses.

Wages and Living Conditions

The economic expansion of the 1980s caused rapid improvements in the living conditions of many South Koreans, which does not mean, however, that all lived comfortably. Indeed, one had only to wander the narrow alleys of Seoul, Inch'ŏn, or other South Korean cities to see poor living conditions. In 1990 families in slum areas of Seoul usually had electricity and running water, as well as a small range for cooking, a television, and a radio or two. But living space was crowded, furniture was shabby, and buildings were badly built and gloomy. People in poorer families seemed to be fairly healthy and had adequate diets. The level of starvation, as well as the cost of some foodstuffs, seemed low. Beggars and the homeless who wandered the streets were infrequent. Although there were some noticeable exceptions, farming families generally lived in small houses, with few of the basic luxuries of middle-class urban families.

Living conditions in South Korea's cities, however, were improving in the late 1980s. According to the Economic Planning Board, in April 1988, the average monthly income in Seoul and other major cities was 612,400 wŏn (US$868) a rise of 16.1 percent over the previous year.

A composite portrait of average middle-class families in Seoul would show the following: a husband in his early forties, a wife about six years younger, and two children, aged thirteen and ten. The family would live in a fairly small apartment, consisting of a hallway, one small bedroom with bunk beds for the children, a small room with several bureaus and with mats as floor coverings, a television set and a videocassette recorder, and a hi-fi stereo. This room would serve as an eating area and family room during the day and as the parents' sleeping area at night. There also would be a larger room partitioned off into three sections: a living room with three elaborate easy chairs, a more formal dining area, and a small kitchen with an oven-range, sink, washing machine, shelves, and cabinets. The mother would stay at home; the father would work from 9:00 A.M. to 10:00 P.M. six days a week. There would be a fairly new car, probably a Hyundai, which the father would use to drive to work.

A survey of income distribution in South Korea in 1985 and 1988 showed that average household income had risen on average 14.8 percent per year, from 5,857,000 wŏn (US$8,645 based on the 1989 exchange rate of US$1 = 677.5 wŏn) to 8,863,000 wŏn (US$13,081). The Gini coefficient, a commonly used measure of income distribution, dropped slightly from 0.3449 in 1985 to 0.3355 in 1988. The comparable figure stood at 0.285 in Japan in 1985 and at 0.364 in the United States in 1978.

As noted by David I. Steinberg, economic growth translated into fairly equitable income distribution when compared with other nations experiencing similar development and its attendant problems. When Park took office, approximately 40 percent of the population lived below the poverty line; by the late 1980s, less than 10 percent of the population lived under the poverty line, although incomes at the top of the scale had increased faster than those at the bottom. Salary increases had not been constant under Park's regime because Park did not want high labor costs to detract from the competitiveness of South Korean goods on the international market. By the late 1980s, capital-intensive higher technology was more important. Further, although wages had increased substantially in the late 1980s, this increase was not because of the good will of the *chaebŏl* or the government, but was the result of a great many strikes and a shortage of skilled workers as industry expanded and large numbers of workers moved to the Middle East to work on construction projects.

The purchasing power of the average citizen rose rapidly in the 1980s. Real per capita GNP more than doubled between 1983 and 1988 (from US$1,914 to US$4,040) and was expected to reach US$5,100 by 1991. South Korea was already transforming itself into a durable consumer society. By the late 1980s, television sets and refrigerators had become a standard part of the average household, and ownership of an automobile was not unusual. Families tended to consume more meat, fresh vegetables and fruit, canned or processed foods, and to eat less rice than in previous decades. They also dressed in modern fashions made from quality fabrics.

Higher incomes led to significant shifts in consumption patterns. For example, in 1963 the average family spent 57.4 percent of its budget on food. Twenty years later, the share going to food had fallen to 40 percent and was expected to continue to fall (but not as rapidly as in the past). Despite the decreasing share of food in the consumer budget, the absolute value of food consumed grew regularly in the 1970s and 1980s and was expected to continue to do so in the 1990s. Rising incomes, the increased mobility of the average person, and a high literacy rate demonstrated evident socioeconomic progress.

Industrial Safety

Of the almost 5 million workers employed in 70,865 South Korean factories in 1986, some 142,000 (nearly 3 percent) were so badly injured that they had to be hospitalized for more than four days. There were 1,660 workers killed in industrial accidents, meaning an average of just over four workers died each day. Long working hours and bad working conditions contributed to high rates of injury and death.

Transporation and Telecommunications

Roads

Domestic transportation improved greatly during the 1980s, and growth was evident in all sectors. The rapid improvement and extension of public roads and the increasing availability of motor vehicles contributed enormously to the mobility of the population. Approximately 51,000 kilometers of roadways spanned the country in 1988, 46.3 percent of which were paved. Express highways facilitated travel between major cities and reached a combined length of 1,539 kilometers in 1988, as compared to 86.8 kilometers in 1967 (see fig. 11). The 1980s saw the increased paving of roads and the building of ultramodern highways around Seoul (especially in the vicinity of the Olympic stadiums) and between Seoul and such major cities as Pusan and Taegu. In 1989 the government announced that it would start construction on nine new expressways with a combined length of 1,243 kilometers. In 1996, when the expressways and two additional projects were expected to be completed, South Korea was expected to have twenty-one expressways with a combined length of 2,840 kilometers.

The total number of motor vehicles climbed rapidly in the 1980s.

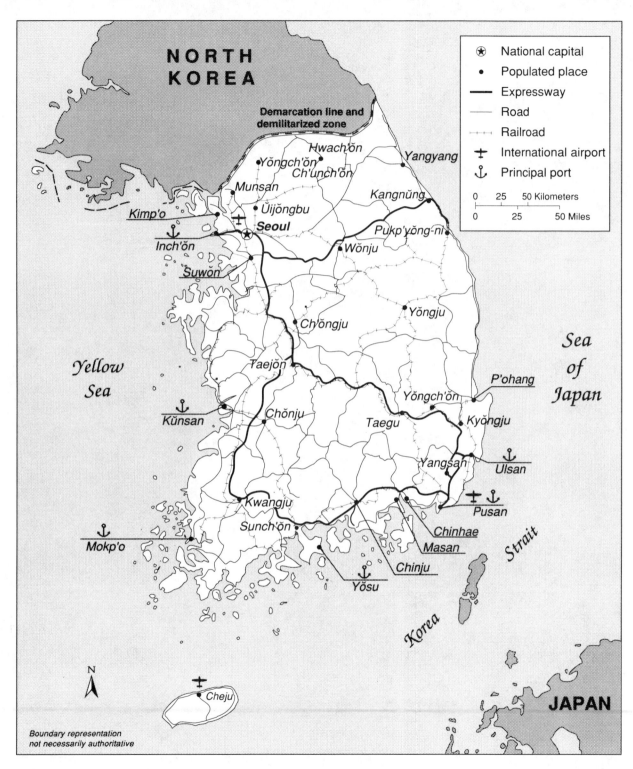

Figure 11. Transportation System, 1988

By 1987 there were approximately 845,000 passenger cars and 748,000 commercial vehicles, up from a combined total of about 744,000 in 1980. In 1988 South Korean automakers produced 504,000 vehicles for domestic sale and 576,134 vehicles for export. In the first nine months of 1989, domestic sales reached nearly 800,000 vehicles.

The expansion and rapid improvement of South Korea's long-distance highway system led to the growth of an excellent intercity bus system in the 1980s. In 1988 there were ten express bus companies operating a fleet of some 900 buses connecting all of the major cities of Korea.

Subways and Railroads

In 1990 subways were gradually replacing buses as the main means of transportation in Seoul. The Seoul subway, the first part of which opened in 1974, was operated by the Seoul Metropolitan Rapid Transit Company. In 1985 the system carried approximately 3 million passengers daily. In 1990 the subway had more than 200 kilometers of track, enabling commuters to reach any station within the 45-kilometer radius of the capital city within an hour. One line connected Seoul with Inch'ŏn. Four subway lines served Seoul, in addition to the lines of the Korean National Railroad.

South Korea has an excellent railroad network. The first railroad, which linked Seoul and Inch'ŏn, was opened in September 1899. Other major lines were laid by the Japanese during the colonial period; these included lines originating in Mokp'o, Masan, and Pusan. These lines connected to Seoul and to Sinŭiju in North Korea, where they were linked with the Trans-Siberian Railway. The railroad network was badly damaged during the Korean War, but it was later rebuilt and improved.

Throughout the 1970s and 1980s, the Korean National Railroad, a state-run corporation under the Ministry of Transportation, was in charge of all rails and continued electrifying heavily used tracks and laying additional tracks. As of 1987, the combined length of the country's railroad network was approximately 6,340 kilometers, including approximately 761.8 kilometers of double-track railroads and 1,023 kilometers of electric railroads. Suburban lines were electrified and connected to the Seoul subway system. Rolling stock included 459 diesel locomotives, 90 electric locomotives, 133 motor coaches, and 370 electric motor cars. In 1989 Seoul announced that it was studying the possibility of constructing high-speed railway systems similar to those in Japan and France.

Railroads in the 1980s were useful primarily in the transportation of freight, but they also were important for passenger traffic around Seoul and in the heavily-traveled corridor linking the capital with the southern port of Pusan. Although the railroad system grew little during the 1980s (there were already 5,600 kilometers of tracks in 1980), rail improvements—the increased electrification of tracks, replacement of older tracks, and the addition of rolling stock—allowed rail traffic to boom. Some of the busiest lines south of Seoul linking the capital with Pusan and Mokp'o had three or four tracks. The 1980s also saw the introduction of high-speed trains connecting Seoul with Pusan, Chŏnju, Mokp'o, and Kyŏngju. The famous "Blue Train" between Seoul and Pusan (via Taejŏn and Taegu) took only four hours and fifty minutes and offered two classes of service, first class and special. In 1987 approximately 525 million passengers and 59.28 million metric tons were transported by the railroad system.

Civil Aviation

Although most interurban travel was either by express bus or by train, air service between major cities was increasingly available and popular, especially among business travelers. Korean Air, founded by the government in 1962 and privately owned since 1969, was South Korea's sole airline until 1988. Korean Air served nine major domestic routes in 1988 and also offered international service to Japan, the United States, Canada, West Germany, France, Hong Kong, Iraq, Libya, Malaysia, the Philippines, Saudi Arabia, Singapore, Switzerland, Taiwan, Thailand, and the United Arab Emirates. A second carrier, Asiana Airlines, was established in 1988 to serve three domestic cities. Seoul's Kimp'o International Airport nearly doubled in size by 1989 (largely because of the Seoul Olympics) to accommodate the rapidly growing number of air travelers. There also were international airports at Pusan and Cheju; another was planned for Ch'ŏngju.

Telecommunications

Communications services improved dramatically in the 1980s with the assistance of foreign partners and as a result of the development of the electronics industry. The number of telephones in use in 1987 reached 9.2 million, a considerable increase from 1980, when there were 2.8 million subscribers (which, in turn, was four times the number of subscribers in 1972).

Radio, and in more recent years television, reached virtually every resident (see The Media, ch. 4). The Japanese established a radio station in Seoul in 1927; by 1945 there were about 60,000 radio sets in the country. By 1987 there were approximately 42 million radio receivers in use, and more than 100 radio stations were broadcasting. Transistor radios and television sets have made their way to the most remote rural areas. Television sets, now mass-produced in South Korea, became far less expensive; most city people and a significant number of rural families owned or had access to a television. Ownership of television sets grew from 25,000 sets when broadcasting was initiated in 1961 to an estimated 8.6 million sets in 1987, and more than 250 television stations were broadcasting.

Foreign Economic Relations

Exports were the key to South Korea's industrial expansion. Until 1986 the value of imports was greater than exports. This situation was reversed, however, in 1986 when South Korea registered a favorable balance of trade of US$4.2 billion. By 1988 the favorable balance had grown to US$11.4 billion. Financing this persistent, although not unexpected, gap between domestic and imported resources was a principal concern for economic planners. In the 1950s and 1960s, much of the trade deficit was financed by foreign aid funds, but in the last two decades, borrowing from and investment in international capital markets have almost completely substituted for economic aid.

Aid, Loans, and Investment

Foreign economic assistance was essential to the country's recovery from the Korean War in the 1950s and to economic growth in the 1960s because it saved Seoul from having to devote scarce foreign exchange to the import of food and other necessary goods, such as cement. It also freed South Korea from the burden of heavy international debts during the initial phase of growth and enabled the government to allocate credit in accordance with planning goals (see The Post-War Economy, ch. 1). From 1953 to 1974, when grant assistance dwindled to a negligible amount, the nation received some US$4 billion of grant aid. About US$3 billion was received before 1968, forming an average of 60 percent of all investment in South Korea. As Park's policies took effect, however, the dependence on foreign grant assistance lessened. During the 1966–74 period, foreign assistance constituted about 4.5 percent of GNP and less than 20 percent of all investment. Before 1965 the United States was the largest single aid contributor, but thereafter Japan and other international sponsors played an increasingly important role.

Apart from grant assistance, other forms of aid were offered; after 1963 South Korea received foreign capital mainly in the form of loans at concessionary rates of interest. According to government sources, between 1964 and 1974 such loans averaged about 6.5 percent of all foreign borrowing. Other data suggested a much higher figure; it seemed that most loans to the government were concessional, at least through the early 1970s. International Monetary Fund (IMF—see Glossary) data showed that imports financed through such means as foreign export-import loans with reduced rates of interest totaled 11.6 percent of all imports from 1975 to 1979. The aid component of these loans was only a fraction of their total value.

During the mid-1960s, South Korea's economy grew so rapidly that the United States decided to phase out its aid program to Seoul. South Korea became increasingly integrated into the international capital market; from the late 1960s to the mid-1980s, development was financed with a series of foreign loans, two-thirds of which came from private banks and suppliers' credits. Total external debt grew to a high of US$46.7 billion in 1985. Positive trade balances in the late 1980s led to a rapid decline in foreign debt—from US$35.6 billion in 1987 to an expected US$23 billion by 1991. Account surpluses in 1990 were expected to enable Seoul to reduce its foreign debt from its 1987 level of about 28 percent of GNP to about 10 percent by 1991.

United States assistance ended in the early 1970s, from which time South Korea had to meet its need for capital investment on the competitive international market and, increasingly, from domestic accounts. The government and private industry received funds through commercial banks, the World Bank (see Glossary), and other foreign government agencies. In the mid-1980s, total direct foreign equity investment in South Korea was well over US$1 billion.

The fact that South Korea was so dependent on foreign trade made it very vulnerable to international market fluctuations. The rapid growth of South Korea's domestic market in the late 1980s, however, began to reduce that dependence. For example, a dramatic rise in domestic demand for automobiles in 1989 more than compensated for a sharp drop in exports. Furthermore, while Seoul's huge foreign debt left it vulnerable to changes in the availability of foreign funds and in international interest rates, Seoul's economic and debt management strategy was very effective.

South Korea's philosophy concerning direct foreign investment had undergone several major changes tied to the changing political environment. Foreign investment was not allowed through the 1950s. In 1962 the Foreign Capital Inducement Act established tax holidays, equal treatment with domestic firms, and guarantees of profit remittances and withdrawal of principal. Despite the provisions of the act, there was little foreign investment activity until after the establishment of diplomatic relations between South Korea and Japan in 1965.

Seoul had to mobilize both external and internal sources when it launched its First Five-Year Economic Development Plan in 1962. The Foreign Capital Inducement Act was amended in 1966 to encourage a greater inflow of foreign capital to make up for insufficient domestic savings. A rapid inflow of investment followed until 1973, when the act was changed to restrict the flow of investments. Beginning in the late 1970s, however, the government gradually began to remove restrictions as domestic industries began to grow and needed to be strengthened to cope with international competition. But until the early 1980s, South Korea relied heavily on borrowing and maintained a somewhat restrictive policy towards foreign direct investment.

Donald S. Macdonald has pointed out that under the liberalization policy, restrictions on foreign direct investment were eased in 1984 and 1985. Seoul changed its control policy on foreign investment from a "positive list" to a "negative list" basis, which meant that any activity not specifically restricted or prohibited was open to investment. An automatic approval system was introduced under which all projects meeting certain requirements were to be immediately and automatically approved by the Ministry of Finance.

Seoul twice revised the negative list system after its initial introduction—first in September 1985 and again in April 1987—to open more industrial sectors to foreign investors. In 1984 there were 339 items, or 34 percent of the 999 items on the Korean Standard Industrial Classification, on the negative list. As of July 1987, there were 788 industrial sectors open to foreign investment. In the manufacturing sector, 97.5 percent of all industries (509 out of 522) were open to foreign investment.

In December 1987, Seoul announced a policy to liberalize the domestic capital market by 1992. The program called for liberalizing foreigners' investment funds, offering domestic enterprises rights on overseas stock markets, and consolidating fair transaction orders. Seoul planned to allow direct foreign investment in its stock market in 1992.

Of the total direct investment in South Korea from 1962 to 1986, which amounted to US$3.631 billion, Japan accounted for 52.2 percent and the United States for 29.6 percent. In 1987 Japan invested US$494 million, or 44.9 percent of the total foreign investment of US$1.1 billion. Japan invested mainly in hotels and tourism, followed by the electric and electronics sector. Direct investment from the United States showed a remarkable increase since the early 1980s, accounting for 54.4 percent of the 1982–86 total investment. The United States invested a total of about US$255 million, or approximately 24 percent of the 1987 investment. Cumulative United States investment was about US$1.4 billion by 1988.

There was a dramatic rise in foreign investment in the late 1980s. Approvals of foreign equity investments reached an all-time high of US$1.283 billion in 1988, a 16.6 percent increase over 1987. As in previous years, approvals for Japanese investments were the dominant factor; they totaled US$696 million (up 41 percent from 1987), followed by United States investors with US$284 million (up 11 percent), and West European sources, US$240 million (up 14 percent). Investment approvals in the service sector doubled in 1988 to US$561 million, which included two large Japanese hotel projects totaling US$344 million. Investment approvals in the manufacturing sector, however, declined from US$775 million in 1987 to US$710 million in 1988.

South Koreans began investing abroad in the 1980s. Before 1967 there was virtually no South Korean investment overseas, but thereafter there was a slow growth because of Seoul's need to develop export markets and procure natural resources abroad. In the 1970s, South Koreans invested in trading, manufacturing, forestry, and construction industries. By the early 1980s, a sharp reduction in development projects in the Middle East led to a decline in South Korean investment there. Mining and manufacturing investments continued to grow throughout the decade. In 1987, out of a total South Korean overseas investment of US$1,195 million (745 projects), US$574 million was invested in developed countries and the remaining US$621 million was invested in developing countries.

One of the most noticeable economic achievements in the 1980s was Seoul's reversal of the balance of payments deficit to a surplus. This improvement was largely attributable to strong overseas demand for South Korean products and to the reduction in expenditures for oil imports. In addition, the "invisible" trade account (monies from tourism and funds sent home by nationals) had improved considerably in the late 1980s because of temporary increases in revenue from tourism, receipts from overseas construction, and structural decreases in interest payments (see table 5, Appendix).

South Korea's success in achieving a balance of payments surplus, however, was not without some drawbacks. It led to harsh trade disputes with the United States and other developed nations, as well as to inflationary pressures. To cope with these problems, Seoul had to modify its enthusiastic promotion of exports in favor of a policy restraining trade surpluses within reasonable limits.

*Sixty-three-story Daehan Life Insurance Building, a popular
tourist attraction and one of the tallest buildings in Asia
Courtesy Oren Hadar*

An important measure restraining the growing foreign trade imbalance between South Korea and the United States was Seoul's decision to revalue the wŏn against the United States dollar. A stronger wŏn made American imports cheaper, increased the cost of South Korean exports to the United States, and slowed, but did not reverse, the growth in the South Korea-United States trade deficit as of 1989. The United States pressed for further appreciation of the wŏn in 1989. In April 1989, the United States Department of the Treasury accused South Korea of continued "manipulation" of the South Korean currency to retain an artificial trade advantage. South Korean officials and businesspeople, however, complained that the already rapid appreciation of the wŏn was slowing economic growth and threatening exports. In May 1989, South Korea avoided being called an unfair trader by the United States and forestalled possible United States trade sanctions, but the nation paid a high price by promising to open up its agricultural market, ease investment by foreigners, and remove many import restrictions (see table 6, Appendix).

Foreign Trade Policy

Seoul stated in 1987 that its foreign trade policy was structured for further expansion, liberalization, and diversification. Because of the paucity of natural resources and traditionally small domestic market, South Korea has had to rely heavily on international trade as a major source of development. Seoul also sought to diversify trading partners to ease dependence on a few specific markets and to remedy imbalances in the present tendency to bilateral trade.

Exports and Imports

The rapid growth of South Korea's economy in the late 1980s led to significant increases in exports and imports (see table 7, Appendix). In the wake of the 1988 Seoul Olympics, South Korea's trade surplus exceeded US$11 billion and foreign exchange revenue had increased sharply. Seoul's trade with communist countries surged in 1988. Trade with Eastern Europe was US$215 million, trade with China almost US$1.8 billion, and trade with the Soviet Union US$204 million.

In 1989 total exports grew to US$74.29 billion, and imports totaled US$67.21 billion. South Korea's annual trade exceeded US$100 billion for the first time in 1988, making it the world's tenth largest trading nation.

During the 1960s and early 1970s, the commodity structure of Seoul's principal exports changed from the production of primary goods to the production of light industrial goods. After 1974 there was a rapid expansion in the production and export of heavy industrial and chemical products. By 1986 the share of heavy industrial and chemical products in total exports had expanded to 55.5 percent (as compared to 18.9 percent in 1980) whereas the share of light industrial products had shrunk to 40.9 percent (as compared to 71.1 percent in 1980).

South Korea had depended greatly on the United States and Japan as its major trading partners, with 75.6 percent of all exports going to these markets in 1970. Success at diversifying export markets led to a reduction in the United States-Japan export market share to 55.6 percent in 1986. The Middle East accounted for 12 percent of South Korea's export trade from 1972 to 1977, but its share declined to 5.2 percent in 1986 because of the collapse of the construction boom in the Middle East and the Iran-Iraq war (1980–88). Exports to Western Europe declined from 18.8 percent in 1979 to 15 percent in 1986. Exports to developing areas, such as Latin America (0.8 percent in 1972; 3.6 percent in 1986) and Oceania (0.9 percent in 1972; 1.4 percent in 1986), grew.

Indirect Seoul-Moscow trade was estimated at about US$20 million in 1978, with Moscow importing electronics, textiles, and machinery and exporting coal and timber. By the late 1980s, South Korea's global fur trader, Jindo, was expected to produce US$20 million worth of fur garments annually in a joint venture with the Soviet Ministry of Light Industry. South Korean businesspeople were offered such Soviet products as instruments for nuclear engineering and technology for processing mineral ores and concentrates. In the first ten months of 1989, bilateral trade between Seoul and Moscow reportedly increased 156 percent from 1988 figures to US$432 million.

Since the early 1960s, the structural pattern of imports had shown changes, particularly in the relatively decreasing share of imported consumer goods and the accelerated growth of industrial supplies and capital equipment imports. The share of consumer goods imported in 1962 was 24.1 percent of total imports; this share declined to 9.8 percent of total imports in 1986 because of increased South Korean production of these goods for the domestic market. The declining share of raw materials as a percentage of imports during the early 1970s was reversed in 1974 because of the increased value of oil imports (caused by the 1973 war in the Middle East). By 1979 crude oil was 25 percent of South Korea's total import requirements. This figure dropped to 8.4 percent in 1988 because of the use of other sources of energy and the decline in the price of petroleum in the late 1980s.

South Korean exports to the United States in 1988 rose to US$21.5 billion, a 17-percent increase over 1987; imports rose to US$12.8 billion, a 46-percent increase over the 1987 level. The percentage of total South Korean exports destined for the United States market decreased to 35.3 percent in 1988 from 38.7 percent in 1987. At the same time, the United States' share of total South Korean imports rose to 24.6 percent, up from 21.4 percent in 1987. By 1988 Seoul's favorable balance had grown to more than US$8.7 billion.

In 1989 imports rose to US$57 billion (up 18 percent from 1988) whereas exports reached US$61 billion, a 2-percent increase from 1988. The trade surplus was reduced from US$11.5 billion to US$4.3 billion and was projected to decline even more. Invisible receipts rose 10 percent, but payments, mainly reflecting a big increase in South Korean travel abroad, were up 20 percent. Thus, the surplus on invisible trade was reduced from US$1.3 billion to US$400 million.

Korea in the Year 2000

The Setting

South Korea's high GNP growth rate during the 1960s and 1970s was accompanied by growth in the labor supply and a rising share of national product going into capital formation—from 15 percent in the early 1960s to more than 30 percent in the late 1970s. In 1988 South Korean economic planners predicted that in the 1990s the share of the GNP devoted to capital formation would not continue to rise and, in fact, might fall slightly. Lower birthrates and an aging population would result in slow growth of the labor force.

In the late 1980s, South Korean economic planners expected growth to continue at somewhat reduced rates through 2000, a result of slower growth in inputs. Large increases in productivity, however, could be expected to push GNP growth beyond 1988 levels. The rapid growth of exports had enabled the country to specialize in the products it made best and to import those it produced less efficiently. No change in this balance was foreseen. However, domestic producers would have to rely more on the domestic market for growth than in the past. Protection of domestic producers might prompt less productivity; but if competition against foreign products were allowed, a favorable impact on productivity might be expected.

The government borrowed heavily in the 1960s and 1970s to finance economic development. By the mid-1980s, South Korea was one of the world's major debtors. South Korea recorded a favorable balance of trade for the first time in 1986; there was an even more favorable balance in 1987. Funds generated from this trade surplus allowed South Korea to reduce its total foreign debt to US$35.6 billion by 1987 and were expected to allow a further reduction to US$23 billion by 1991. Since 1986 there had been a drastic change in domestic savings, with savings growing to 36 percent in 1987 as compared to 33 percent in 1986. The twin factors of increasing debt and low domestic savings that had threatened growth in the past had been mitigated to a considerable degree.

The Role of Science and Technology

The most important sources of productive growth for South Korean manufacturers had traditionally been directly or indirectly related to the ability of South Korean companies to acquire new technology from abroad and to adapt it to domestic conditions, rather than paying the cost of research and development. However, as Seoul's industry and exports continued to evolve toward higher levels of technology, domestic research and development efforts needed to be increased. Fortunately for South Korea, its high level of well-educated workers, who constitute a formidable brain trust for future research and development, are its major asset.

The Seoul government began investing in technology research institutes soon after the republic was established. The Korean Atomic Energy Commission founded in 1959 was responsible for research and development, production, dissemination, and management of technology for peaceful applications of atomic energy. In the mid-1960s, the government established the Ministry of Science and Technology to oversee all government research and development activities and the Korea Institute of Science and Technology to function as an industrial research laboratory. In the 1970s, in order to better coordinate research and development, two scientific communities were established—one in Seoul, the other near Taejŏn. The Seoul complex included the Korea Institute of Science and Technology, the Korea Development Institute (affiliated with the Economic Planning Board), the Korea Advanced Institute of Science, and the Korea Atomic Energy Research Institute. Plans for the Daeduk Science Town near Taejŏn were far more ambitious. Modeled after the Tsukuba Science City in Japan, by the late 1980s the Daeduk Science Town accommodated laboratories specializing in shipbuilding, nuclear fuel processing, metrology, chemistry, and energy research. The government founded the Korea Advanced Institute of Science to develop and offer graduate science programs, and it also encouraged universities to develop their own undergraduate programs in science.

The tremendous growth of Samsung since the mid-1980s was strong evidence of the high productivity in such modern industries as electronics. The group's total sales nearly doubled (8.4 billion wŏn to 14.6 billion wŏn) between 1984 and 1986, while the number of employees only increased from 122,000 to 147,000. The reason for this high degree of productivity was South Korea's move away from labor-intensive industries to those that were highly automated.

South Korean planners realized that the country needed to advance quickly in such areas as high technology if the economy were to grow while matching foreign competition. POSCO's decisions to build the Pohang Institute of Science and Technology and the Research Institute of Industrial Science and Technology were examples of this trend. POSCO also used a great deal of money to lure back more than 100 top South Korean scientists and researchers who had emigrated abroad.

The Pohang Institute of Science and Technology also maintained a major undergraduate and graduate school. By 1988 the institute had a faculty of 132 teachers, about 500 undergraduate students, and approximately 110 graduate students. Only one of every fifteen applicants was accepted and only those students who scored in the top 2 percent of the nation's college entrance examinations were allowed to apply.

POSCO's efforts represented a great change from the past. As of the late 1980s, many of South Korea's younger scientists, technocrats, and economic planners in had received their graduate education in the United States. Throughout the 1970s and 1980s, the government sponsored the scientific and technical education of many graduate students at prestigious institutions, such as Harvard University and the Massachusetts Institute of Technology. The success of the Pohang Institute of Science and Technology meant that many of South Korea's future scientific and technical leaders would be educated at home.

In 1990 Seoul announced an ambitious plan to promote science and technology so that high-technology activities would dominate the economy by the year 2000. The Ministry of Science and Technology intended to coordinate technology-related projects between government and industry in a variety of fields including semiconductors, computers, chemistry, and new materials.

The anticipated slowdown in economic growth could well be counteracted by the continued high rate of capital formation, increased productivity of labor, and expansion of the education system. Until South Korea's per capita income reached that of the most advanced industrial nations and as long as South Korea remained a "follower" country benefiting from the experiences of others while avoiding their mistakes, it was likely that strong growth would continue.

In 1987 the Korea Development Institute issued a report, *Korea Year 2000,* that profiled South Korean economic development in 2000. The Korea Development Institute noted that the industrial structure would be highly developed and would resemble that of advanced countries inasmuch as high value-added industries, high-technology industries, and soft industries grew relatively rapidly. Further, changes in industrial structure were expected rapidly to reduce the demand for unskilled workers while simultaneously increasing the demand for professional and technical manpower, resulting in further change of the employment structure.

The Korea Development Institute also noted that the Ministry of Science and Technology had prepared a long-range plan of science and technology for the twenty-first century that took into account limited available resources. Accordingly, Seoul selected its comparative advantage areas, including informatics—particularly information storage and retrieval and electronic data processing—, fine chemicals, and precision machinery in the short term; biotechnology, new materials, and public benefit areas, such as the environment, health, and welfare, in the mid-term; and oceanography and aeronautics for the mid- and long term.

The Economic Future

The Korea Development Institute also forecasted in 1988 that South Korea's per capita GNP would exceed US$10,000 early in the twenty-first century. The institute predicted that Seoul would enjoy a higher sustained growth rate than average through the 1990s; that the manufacturing industry would play a pivotal role in the economy in the twenty-first century; and that the service industry would become knowledge-intensive in order to meet the needs of a highly diversified industrialized society. The share of the primary sector (agriculture, forestry, and fisheries) would sink to nearly 5 percent by the turn of the century, whereas the secondary sector (industry) would rise to over 40 percent and the service sector would be at about 55 percent. Major areas of industrial growth would include automobiles, electronics, and machinery.

In 1988 Kim Duk-choong of Sogang University listed five main points that were expected to make the "Korean economic future look bright." He noted that South Korea had drastically reduced its foreign debts since 1985, greatly increased the rate of domestic savings, improved on the equitable distribution of income throughout the population, increased the role of small and medium-sized

193

corporations in the economy, and made the transition from a labor-oriented to a technology-oriented economy. He expected that these positive economic developments would easily outweigh existing problems and lead to real growth in years to come.

Kim's optimism had merit, but there were other important issues that could inhibit economic growth, for example, rising protectionist sentiments in the United States, Japan, and elsewhere. Another problem was the fact that the *chaebŏl* tended to restrict subcontracting and to keep as much production as possible inhouse, which meant that the smaller industries and businesses, which bore the brunt of slowdowns in Japan, would not be able to act as shock absorbers. Moreover, as South Korea moved up the technological ladder, it would face stiff competition from advanced nations like Japan and up-and-coming nations like Thailand. There also was the intangible problem of the resolve of South Korea's workers, who labored six days a week with little vacation time. What effect would a slackening of resolve have on the South Korean worker by the 2000? In general, the future of South Korea's economy looked very bright, but there were enough intangibles to make accurate predictions difficult at best.

*   *   *

There are numerous excellent works on the South Korean economy that offer a variety of perspectives. Historical studies charting the nation's colonial and modernization periods include Andrew C. Nahm's *Korea under Japanese Colonial Rule* and Ramon H. Myers' and Mark R. Peattie's *The Japanese Colonial Empire, 1895-1945.* Donald S. Macdonald's *The Koreans* provides information on the Korean economy from colonial times through contemporary society. Among the general works on the postwar economy are David I. Steinberg's *South Korea's Economy* and *Chaebŏl;* Han Sung-joo and Robert Myers's *Korea;* Edward S. Mason et al.'s *The Economic and Social Modernization of Korea;* Jene K. Kwon's, *Korean Economic Development;* G. Cameron Hurst III's *Korea 1988;* Alice H. Amsden's *Asia's Next Giant;* David S. Bell, Jr., Bun Woong Kim, and Chong Bun Lee's *Administrative Dynamics and Development;* Karl Moskowitz's *From Patron to Partner;* and *The Rise of the Korean Economy* by Byung-Nak Song.

Opposition groups' views of the South Korean economy are best expressed in Minjungsa's *Lost Victory.* The *Far Eastern Economic Review* publishes frequent articles on the economy, as does *Asian Survey.* For a South Korean perspective on the economy, articles in the English-language *Korea Newsreview* and the various publications of the Korean Economic Institute in Washington are valuable. (For further information and complete citations, see Bibliography.)

Chapter 4. Government and Politics

Hwaso Gate, with parapet, Suwŏn Castle

THE CRISIS OF JUNE 1987 brought public dissatisfaction with the Chun Doo Hwan government to a head (see The Demise of the Chun Regime, ch. 1). The next eight months saw the beginning of a compromise between the ruling and opposition camps that marked a potential watershed in South Korean politics. Politicians who had been in exile or under house arrest for many years returned to leadership roles. The media, unleashed from both censorship and official guidance, began a qualitative and quantitative explosion. A newly critical press probed previously hidden aspects of the military, the national security agencies, and the government more aggressively than ever before.

For the first time since the fall of the Syngman Rhee regime in 1960, the Republic of Korea produced a constitution through deliberative processes rather than through military intervention or emergency measures. Moreover, elections for the presidency in December 1987 and for the National Assembly in April 1988 redefined the political process; a minority president leading a minority party began a five-year term with full awareness that, at least in the near term, compromise was necessary for political survival.

The search for the political middle ground was handicapped by external pressures upon ruling and opposition parties alike. On President Roh Tae Woo's right, conservative bureaucrats, military leaders, and Democratic Justice Party members held over from the Chun period watched the president carefully. During the first two years of Roh's rule, the rightists grew increasingly suspicious of the process of compromise and upset with the direction taken by South Korea's emerging left, both within and outside of the political process. The traditional opposition parties—the Reunification Democratic Party and the Party for Peace and Democracy led by Kim Young Sam and Kim Dae Jung, respectively—felt similar pressures from younger and more progressive elements within their parties, as well as from the more radical opposition outside the political process. By mid-1989 the Roh government appeared to have reached its limit of reform and began to return to earlier patterns of political control, including the broad use of the National Security Act and national security agencies to limit dissent.

The National Assembly came into its own in the late 1980s and at least temporarily achieved the balance of powers provided for in the 1987 Constitution. For the first time in South Korea's history, the government party, as a minority in the legislature, was forced to seek procedural and substantive compromises with three opposition parties. Partisan conflict was temporarily muted for the Seoul Olympics in September 1988 but surfaced again at the end of the year in a series of legislative committee hearings concerning corruption under Chun. Further debate in 1989 led to a political compromise late in the year that resolved the question of the ''legacies'' of the Fifth Republic (1980–87) that had animated politics in the legislature since the beginning of the Roh administration.

A judicial revolt in mid-1988 forced the resignation of a chief justice appointed by the Chun administration, the subsequent appointment of a more politically independent successor, and the replacement of several dozen senior judges. An administrative reform commission conducted a surprisingly independent investigation of numerous government agencies, including the national security bodies that had long interfered in the political process.

The pattern of politics outside the formal institutions of government continued to change as the 1990s began. New interest groups, particularly within the intellectual professions, emerged to challenge the government-sponsored professional associations in fields such as journalism, teaching, and the arts. These developments in turn often provoked heavy-handed responses from the government, long accustomed to controlling professional organizations through nationwide umbrella groups. Cause-oriented groups of various political persuasions prepared to launch new parties, stimulated by the prospect of local council elections to be held in 1990.

Many of the political developments of the late 1980s reflected important and irreversible social and economic changes that had occurred during the previous two decades. As the 1990s began, a key question of South Korean politics remained the degree to which the development of a better-educated and more affluent populace—essential to South Korean modernization, yet corrosive of the older style of political leadership—would contribute to greater political liberalization.

The Constitutional Framework

Despite centuries of authoritarian and autocratic rule, reform thinkers in nineteenth-century Korea had debated the subject of government and advocated the rule of law and eventual constitutional government as early as the 1890s. The notion of a government limited by checks and balances under a constitutional order was not entirely new to the Korean political setting in 1945. Organizations such as the Self-Strengthening Society (Chaganghoe) used translations to promote the study of numerous European constitutions and legal codes during the years just before Japan annexed

Korea in 1910. During Japanese rule (1910–45), a self-styled Korean government in exile in China drafted several charters and constitutions. Within colonial Korea, a small Protestant community conducted self-governing denominational meetings in accordance with rules of parliamentary procedure. Japanese rule in Korea, however, was itself largely exempt even from Japanese constitutional constraints (see Korea under Japanese Rule, ch. 1). Despite Korean interest in the idea of constitutionalism, therefore, the colonial experience provided Koreans with little opportunity to experience the practice of limited government.

Since the formation of an independent South Korean republic in 1948, the term *constitutionalism*—as it is popularly understood in Western democracies—has become a major focus of political strife. Although the concept has been interpreted in various ways, there has been at least a nominal consensus that constitutionalism would foster, if not guarantee, a general framework for benevolent and effective government. The constitution would help protect certain individual rights and provide safeguards against the concentration of power in the hands of a dictatorial group.

There have been numerous difficulties in adapting constitutionalism to South Korea, not the least of these being the reluctance of incumbent leaders to step down peacefully and prepare for a transfer of power through the constitutional process. The politics of constitutional manipulation has been deadly serious, calculated to bolster or prolong the tenure of incumbent presidents or to lend an aura of legitimization to a regime brought to power by a coup (see table 8, Appendix). South Korea experienced its first peaceful transfer of power since independence only in 1987 (see Political Dynamics, this ch.). In most of the leadership changes prior to 1987, the incumbents used forceful tactics—including martial law and other surreptitious parliamentary maneuvers—to change the constitution. The 1990s began with discussions of possible further changes in the fundamental law. It appeared that South Korea had yet to escape a pattern in which both powerholders and their political rivals perceived a constitution as a tool for holding power rather than as a framework for long-term governance, and in which each administration required one or more constitutional revisions.

The constitutional framework of the Sixth Republic, which started in 1987, was based on a constitutional bill that was passed by the National Assembly on October 12, 1987, and subsequently approved by 93 percent of the voters in a national referendum on October 28 (see The Legislature, this ch.). The bill was the product of painstaking negotiation and compromise among the major political parties in the National Assembly, unlike the preceding two constitutions, which were essentially unilaterally drafted by the executive branch and then submitted to referendums under emergency measures or martial law. The 1987 Constitution became effective on February 25, 1988, when Roh Tae Woo was inaugurated as president. The new Constitution, which consisted of a preamble, 130 articles, and supplementary provisions, strengthened the power of the National Assembly and considerably reduced the power of the executive. Its adoption marked only the second time that the government and opposition parties had produced a constitutional amendment bill by consensus in South Korea's modern history and the first time that such cooperation had been successful (the first occasion, in 1980, was cut short by a military coup d'état). The new fundamental law, the first since 1960 not intended to extend the rule of the incumbent president, provided for direct election of the president, an issue the opposition parties had campaigned for since 1985. It also eliminated or modified a number of provisions that had come under criticism since the *yusin* (revitalization) constitutional amendment in 1972.

The 1987 Constitution declares South Korea a democratic republic, its territory consisting of "the Korean Peninsula and its adjacent islands." Popular sovereignty is the norm of the state; all public officials are described as servants of the people; and the tenure and political impartiality of these officials are protected by the provisions of law. In language not found in earlier constitutional amendments, the Constitution states that the "Republic of Korea shall seek unification and shall formulate and carry out a policy of peaceful unification based on the principles of freedom and democracy." In another innovation clearly aimed at the past influence of the military on politics and political succession, the Constitution stipulates that "political neutrality shall be maintained" by the armed forces.

The section on fundamental rights reflects continued evolution toward the affirmation of civil rights and due process of law (see Human Rights, this ch.). Individuals may not be punished, placed under preventive restrictions, or subjected to involuntary labor "except as provided by law and through lawful procedures." The protection of habeas corpus, restored in the 1980 constitution but rarely honored in practice in political cases under the Chun government, is further reinforced. People detained or arrested must be informed of the reason and of their right to be assisted by counsel. Family members of those arrested or detained must be informed of the fact "without delay." Prosecutors' failure to indict a criminal suspect or accused person placed under detention might entitle the person to claim compensation for wrongful arrest. Warrants must

*Late nineteenth-century
and early twentieth-century
buildings, Seoul
Courtesy Carpenter Collection,
Library of Congress*

be issued by a judge "through due procedures" rather than at the mere request of prosecutors, as had often occurred, especially in political cases, in the past. Other new provisions include the right of citizens to receive aid from the state if they suffer injury or death because of the criminal acts of others; the autonomy of institutions of higher learning; and recognition of extended labor rights.

The articles on rights, like other portions of the Constitution, originated during a process of political compromise that deferred a number of complex or controversial issues until a later date. A number of new social welfare provisions were left to subsequent legislation. These measures included aspirations to protect working women from unjust discrimination, state protection for citizens incapacitated by disease and old age, environmental protection measures, housing development policies, and "protection for mothers" (see Public Health and Welfare, ch. 2).

As in earlier constitutions, the formal provision of a right was often qualified by other constitutional provisions or by related laws. The most significant of these pre-existing laws was the National Security Act, which severely truncated rights of due process specified in the Constitution and the Code of Criminal Procedure (1954) for persons accused of a variety of political offenses.

The Constitution affirms both the right and the duty to work and requires legislation for minimum wages and standards of working conditions to "guarantee human dignity." Special protection is provided to working women and working children. Except for workers in important defense industries, workers have the right to independent association, collective bargaining, and collective action—a marked change from the 1980 constitution, which stated that collective action could be regulated by law. By 1990, however, not all of the numerous laws that restricted the exercise of labor rights had been thoroughly subjected to the scrutiny of the Constitution Court (see The Judiciary, this ch.).

Chapter Nine of the Constitution, which is concerned with the economy, continues the theme of the previous constitution in committing the state to fostering economic growth and foreign trade. As was the case under the 1980 constitution, tenant farming is technically prohibited, but leasing or proxy management of farmland is recognized in the interest of increasing agricultural productivity and rational land utilization. The new Constitution permits regulations designed to "ensure the proper distribution of income" and prevent "abuse of economic power." In an implicit recognition of severe disparities in regional development in the past, the state is also charged with ensuring balanced development of all regions of the country. The government is responsible for establishing national standards and for developing technical, scientific, and human resources.

Separation of powers came from the political process as well as from the formal structure of government embodied in the Constitution. The Sixth Republic's Constitution provides greater formal balance than earlier constitutions among the three branches of government. In important substantive areas, it strengthens the legislature and the judiciary. In other areas, it sets broad policy guidelines but leaves legislation to the legislators. The resulting formal checks and balances were reinforced by the outcome of the April 1988 general elections, in which the president's party—the Democratic Justice Party—lost a working majority in the legislature for the first time since the establishment of the Republic of Korea.

The process for amending the Constitution received public attention in early 1990 when the Democratic Justice Party and two of the three major opposition parties announced plans to merge and to amend the Constitution to provide for a cabinet-responsibility system. Proposed amendments to the Constitution could be introduced by the president or by a simple majority of members of the National Assembly. A favorable vote of two-thirds of the National Assembly members is required before amendments can be placed before a national referendum. To be successful, amendments require a majority vote by at least one-half of the electorate eligible to vote in general elections. An incumbent president may not benefit from an amendment extending the term of the presidency.

The Government

The Legislature

The unicameral National Assembly consists, according to the Constitution, of at least 200 members. In 1990 the National Assembly had 299 seats, 224 of which were directly elected from single-member districts in the general elections of April 1988. Under applicable laws, the remaining seventy-five representatives were appointed by the political parties in accordance with a proportional formula based on the number of seats won in the election. By law, candidates for election to the National Assembly must be at least thirty years of age. As part of a political compromise in 1987, an earlier requirement that candidates have at least five years' continuous residency in the country was dropped to allow Kim Dae Jung, who had spent several years in exile in Japan and the United States during the 1980s, to return to political life. The National Assembly's term is four years. In a change from the more authoritarian Fourth Republic and Fifth Republic (1972–80 and 1980–87, respectively), under the Sixth Republic, the National Assembly cannot be dissolved by the president.

Legislators are immune from arrest or detention, except in cases of flagrante delicto, while the National Assembly is in session. If an arrest occurs before the National Assembly session begins, the legislator concerned must be released for the duration of the session. National Assembly members also enjoy legal immunity for statements made in that forum. Greater freedom of the media and independence of the courts, combined with the power of the opposition parties in the legislature, gave greater substance to this immunity during the first two years of the Sixth Republic than under the preceding government, when prosecutors and the courts did not honor such immunity.

The position of the National Assembly in the Constitution is much stronger than it had been under the Fifth Republic (see table 9, Appendix). The annual session of the National Assembly was extended to 100 days. Extraordinary sessions of thirty days each might be called by as little as one-quarter of the membership (versus one-third in the 1980 constitution), and there was no limit on the number of such sessions that could be called each year. The power to investigate state affairs also was strengthened. The National Assembly now held the power to remove the prime minister or a cabinet minister at any time, rather than having to wait a year following appointment, as had been the case before. The consent of the National Assembly was required for the appointment of all Supreme Court justices, not just the chief justice. The National Assembly performed a tie-breaking function in presidential elections and was required to approve or to disapprove presidential emergency measures before they took effect, time permitting. Failure to obtain National Assembly approval would void the emergency measures.

The Executive

The president, according to the Constitution, is head of state, chief executive of the government, and commander in chief of the armed forces. The Constitution and the amended Presidential Election Law of 1987 provide for election of the president by direct, secret ballot, ending sixteen years of indirect presidential elections under the preceding two governments. Presidential succession is for a single five-year term by direct election, which must be held at least thirty days before the incumbent president retires. If a presidential vacancy should occur, a successor must be elected within sixty days, during which time presidential duties are to be performed by the prime minister or other senior cabinet members in the order of priority as determined by law. While in office, the chief executive is exempt from criminal liability except for insurrection or treason.

The president may, at his own discretion, refer important policy matters to a national referendum, declare war, conclude peace and other treaties, appoint senior public officials, and grant amnesty (with the concurrence of the National Assembly). In times of serious internal or external turmoil or threat, or economic or financial crises, the president may assume emergency powers "for the maintenance of national security or public peace and order." Emergency measures may be taken only when the National Assembly is not in session and when there is no time for it to convene. The measures are limited to the "minimum necessary."

The 1987 Constitution deleted the 1980 constitution's explicit powers to temporarily suspend the freedoms and rights of the people. However, the president is permitted to take other measures that could amend or abolish existing laws for the duration of a crisis. It is unclear whether such emergency measures could temporarily suspend portions of the Constitution itself. Emergency measures must be referred to the National Assembly for concurrence. If not endorsed by the assembly, the emergency measures can be revoked; laws overridden by presidential orders regain their original effect. In this respect, the power of the legislature is more vigorously asserted than in cases of ratification of treaties or declarations of war, in which the Constitution simply states that the National Assembly "has the right to consent" to the president's actions. In a change from the 1980 constitution, the 1987 Constitution stated that the president is not permitted to dissolve the National Assembly.

The president works out of an official residence called the Blue House, so named because of the building's blue roof tiles. He is assisted by the staff of the Presidential Secretariat, headed by a cabinet-rank secretary general. Apart from the State Council, or cabinet, the chief executive relies on several constitutional organs (see fig. 12).

These constitutional organs include the National Security Council, which provides advice concerning the foreign, military, and domestic policies bearing on national security. Chaired by the president, the council in 1990 had as its statutory members the prime minister, the deputy prime minister, the ministers for foreign affairs, home affairs, finance, and national defense, the director of the Agency for National Security Planning (ANSP, known as the Korean Central Intelligence Agency—KCIA—until December 1980), and others designated by the president. Another body was the Advisory Council for Peaceful Unification Policy, inaugurated in June 1981 under the chairmanship of the president. From its inception, this body had no policy role, but rather appeared to serve as a government sounding board and as a means to disburse political rewards by providing large numbers of dignitaries and others with titles and opportunities to meet periodically with the president and other senior officials.

The president also was assisted in 1990 by the Audit and Inspection Board. In addition to auditing the accounts of all public institutions, the board scrutinized the administrative performance of government agencies and public officials. Its findings were reported to the president and the National Assembly, which itself had broad powers to inspect the work of the bureaucracy under the provisions of the Constitution. Board members were appointed by the president.

One controversial constitutional organ was the Advisory Council of Elder Statesmen, which replaced a smaller body in February 1988, just before Roh Tae Woo was sworn in as president. This body was supposed to be chaired by the immediate former president; its expansion to eighty members, broadened functions, and elevation to cabinet rank made it appear to have been designed, as one Seoul newspaper said, to "preserve the status and position of a. certain individual." The government announced plans to reduce the size and functions of this body immediately after Roh's

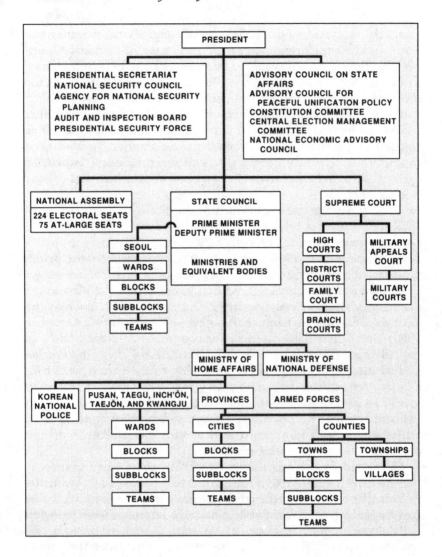

Figure 12. Structure of the Government, 1989

inauguration. Public suspicions that the council might provide former President Chun with a power base within the Sixth Republic were rendered moot when Chun withdrew to an isolated Buddhist temple in self-imposed exile in November 1988.

The State Council

The top executive body assisting the president in 1990 was the

State Council, or cabinet, the members of which in 1990 included the president, the prime minister, and from fifteen to thirty heads of various ministries and their equivalents. More often a technocrat than a politician, the prime minister is appointed by the president with the consent of the National Assembly. Other cabinet members, also presidential appointees, are supposed to be recommended by the prime minister but actually are chosen by the president. As was also true under the 1980 constitution, no member of the military may hold a cabinet post unless he is retired from active service.

The State Council is responsible for the formulation and implementation of basic plans and policies concerning a wide range of government functions. The results of deliberation by the council are conveyed to the Presidential Secretariat and the Office of the Prime Minister, the two principal units responsible for coordination and supervision relating to various government agencies. Given the importance of economic performance to the stability and security of the nation, the Economic Planning Board plays a significant role in the administrative and economic process. The minister of the board by law doubles as deputy prime minister; his senior assistants, many of them holding advanced degrees from foreign universities, have been among the ablest public servants in the country.

As South Korean observers have noted, the president's power to appoint persons to senior and deputy ministerial positions not only has administrative significance but also is an important political tool for balancing factional interests within the president's party and for rewarding loyalty. The South Korean media closely scrutinize high-level appointments for clues to politics within the ruling party. The announcement in early 1990 of plans to merge the ruling party and two of the three major opposition parties and to institute a cabinet-responsibility form of government produced even more intensive interest in cabinet appointments.

In 1989 a presidentially appointed Administration Reform Commission concluded a fourteen-month study concerning the structure of the government. In reporting its findings to the president, the panel proposed a number of changes, including the merger or abolition of several State Council ministries and other government agencies. Faced with strenuous lobbying by officials of the agencies concerned, the ruling party and government administration tabled most of the recommendations. Several proposals were implemented. The new Ministry of Culture, established in late 1989 from the former Ministry of Culture and Information, was placed under the initial direction of Yi O-yŏng, a prominent essayist and literary critic. The new ministry continued the cultural and artistic functions of its predecessor and also took over responsibilities concerning national and public libraries and national language policy from the Ministry of Education. The establishment of the Ministry of Environment, upgraded from the former Office of Environment within the Ministry of Health and Social Affairs, acknowledged that national development over the preceding three decades had often neglected environmental concerns. Its establishment redeemed a pledge made in both the 1980 and 1987 constitutions that the people of South Korea "shall have the right to a healthy and pleasant environment," and that the government would take measures for environmental protection.

The Presidential Secretariat

The Presidential Secretariat, often referred to in the Western media as the Blue House staff, in 1990 included a secretary general of cabinet rank and six or seven senior secretaries with responsibility for political, economic, and other specialized areas. As in other political systems, these top aides enjoyed special presidential confidence. They were widely believed to control access to the chief executive and to influence personnel appointments and policy decisions.

The Judiciary

The administration of justice was the function of the courts as established under the Constitution and the much-amended Court Organization Law of 1949. A number of provisions of the 1987 Constitution were intended to improve judicial independence, which was long held, even within the judiciary itself, to be inadequate (see Events in 1988, this ch.; table 10, Appendix).

At the top of the court system in 1990 was the Supreme Court, whose justices served six-year terms, giving them a measure of independence from the president, whose single term was only five years (lower-level judges served ten-year terms.) All other judges were appointed by the Conference of Supreme Court Justices and the chief justice. This process reverses the more centralized appointment process that had been in place since the *yusin* system of 1972, in which the chief justice (under the direction of the president, in practice) appointed lower court judges. All but the chief justice may be reappointed. The Supreme Court is the final court of appeal in all cases, including courts-martial; except for death sentences, however, military trials under extraordinary martial law may not be appealed.

High Courts in Seoul, Kwangju, and Taegu hear appeals against decisions of lower courts in civil and criminal cases. They also may assume jurisdiction over litigation brought against government agencies or civil officials. Courts of first instance for most civil and criminal matters are the district courts in Seoul and major provincial cities. The Family Court in Seoul handles matrimonial, juvenile, and other family law matters; in other cities such issues are adjudicated in the district courts.

The Constitution divides responsibility for constitutional review of laws and administrative regulations between the Supreme Court and the Constitution Court. The Supreme Court reviews only regulations, decrees, and other enactments issued by the various ministries of other government agencies. The constitutionality or legality of the regulation to be reviewed must be at issue in an ongoing trial. The Constitution Court has much broader powers. It decides on the constitutionality of laws enacted by the National Assembly when requested by a court to aid in the resolution of a trial, or in response to a constitutional petition, which may be brought by any person who has exhausted available legal remedies. The Constitution Court also has exclusive power to rule on the dissolution of political parties and impeachment of the president, cabinet members, and other high officials. All nine members of the Constitution Court must be qualified to be judges. The president, National Assembly, and chief justice each select three members of the court's nine-member panel.

The Constitution Court began operation in late 1988. Unlike its predecessors, which since the early 1960s had made only three rulings, the new body gave rulings in 400 of the more than 500 cases considered during its first year. Most of the cases heard were constitutional petitions. In a series of major decisions, the court declared unconstitutional a law prohibiting creditors from suing the government, directed the National Assembly to revise a portion of the National Assembly Law requiring independent candidates to pay twice the deposit of party-affiliated candidates, declared the Act Concerning Protection of Society unconstitutional, and upheld the constitutionality of a law prohibiting third-party involvement in labor disputes.

The Civil Service

For centuries the most honored profession in Korea was government service, which had been more or less preempted by the scholar-official class (see Traditional Social Structure, ch. 2). In modern South Korea, however, the civil service has lost some of its earlier prestige, partly because financially rewarding jobs have been more

211

plentiful in private industry and commerce. Nonetheless, the upper levels of the civil service, particularly in the economic ministries, generally draw upon some of the best-trained and most technically competent members of the population.

Civil servants have generally enjoyed reputations as competent and dedicated, but the proverbial corruption in the bureaucracy has also unfairly brought disrepute to the profession as a whole. Efforts to eliminate malfeasance have been continuous, although they have been perhaps most pronounced (in the fashion of traditional Chinese and Korean dynastic succession) after the assumption of power by a new regime. The record of reform often has been mixed. In 1980 Chun Doo Hwan announced a far-reaching program intended to "purify" the bureaucracy. Many South Koreans welcomed investigations of former cabinet ministers and the confiscation of large, unexplained fortunes from other leaders, such as Kim Chong-p'il, accused of enriching themselves under the preceding Park Chung Hee regime. Chun also dismissed more than 200 high officials and 1,000 lower-level functionaries. Political motives were clearly evident in the ouster on vague charges of all opposition politicians of any prominence and in the removal of public officials and staff members of state-run corporations likely to remain overly loyal to the late president's political machine.

The anticorruption reforms of Roh Tae Woo, marked by greater attention to due process and broad political participation than those of his predecessor, won considerable public support. In his presidential campaign, Roh had joined other presidential candidates in promising exposure of financial irregularities under the Fifth Republic and had pledged broader disclosure of public officials' assets through the amendment of existing laws. The first promise was largely honored. The question of Fifth Republic corruption was dealt with through vigorous prosecution of former high-level officials and relatives of former President Chun Doo Hwan charged with abuse of power or other irregularities. The opposition parties played a major role in the process by participating in an unprecedented series of National Assembly hearings conducted in late 1988. These riveting sessions, often televised, attracted millions of viewers, emptying the streets of Seoul while the hearings were taking place and drawing greater members even than the broadcast earlier in the year of the Seoul Olympics. By late 1989, the courts had tried and sentenced numerous Chun relatives and former high officials, including a former ANSP chief, on various corruption or influence-peddling charges.

Despite these successes, the disclosure of senior officials' assets remained an elusive goal as the 1980s came to a close, hampered by the lack of legal measures to penalize nondisclosure. The National Assembly had finally passed a law concerning public ownership of property that would require land owners to register property in their true names, but still had not ratified a more controversial bill that would impose stiff penalties for the failure of assemblymen, ministers, and vice-ministerial level officials to report their financial dealings.

The civil service is managed by the Ministry of Government Administration. Recruitment for the most part occurs through competitive examinations held annually in two categories, "ordinary" and "higher" examinations. Those passing the higher tests generally are recognized as bright and able and are loosely known as members of the so-called higher civil service examinations clique. They are given preference in appointment and over the years have become the nucleus of bureaucratic elites scattered in three major government functions—general administration, foreign affairs, and the administration of justice. The foreign service and judiciary are recruited through separate examination systems that are extremely selective. Faculty members at state universities, although selected according to traditional academic criteria rather than solely by examination, also are part of the civil service system, as are those who have passed examinations to become public school teachers.

The Constitution provides that "all public officials shall be servants of the entire people and shall be responsible to the people" and guarantees the political impartiality of public officials. From the perspective of the citizen needing to do some business in a street-level government office, however, the ethos of service sometimes gives way to the traditional self-regard of the official, a situation encapsulated in the traditional phrase *kwanjon minbi* (respect for the official, contempt for the people). Political neutrality also has been undercut by the persistence of political and bureaucratic pressures on civil servants, especially during national elections. These pressures can be especially intense upon low-ranking officials at the bottom of the bureaucratic chain of command and on those officials in the upper five of the nine civil service grades who serve as presidential appointees.

In early 1989, the number of government officials totaled 700,026, most of whom worked for the executive branch of government. About 7,200 civil servants worked for the judiciary. The new importance of the National Assembly under the Sixth Republic was reflected in an increase in staff hired by the legislative branch to some 2,700 employees—500 more than during the final year of the preceding administration. In the 1980s, about one-third of civil service employees worked in local government. The civil service still represents a cross section of society. However, graduates of the so-called big three universities—Seoul National University, Yŏnse University, and Koryŏ University (more commonly called Korea University in English)—continue to enjoy an advantage. Graduates of these schools, all of which are located in Seoul, continue to have an edge in gaining employment in the government as well as in the private sector and are disproportionately represented in the higher civil service grades.

Local Administration

South Korea in 1990 was divided into six provincial-level cities—the special city (*t'ŭkpyŏlsi*) of Seoul (Sŏul-t'ŭkpyŏlsi to Koreans) and the five cities directly governed (*chikhalsi*) by the central government—Pusan, Taegu, Inch'ŏn, Taejŏn, and Kwangju—and nine provinces, or *to* (see Glossary), including Cheju Island (see fig. 1). Major cities were divided into wards (*ku*) and precincts (*tong*). A province was composed of counties (*gun*) and cities (*si*) with a population of more than 50,000. A county consisted of towns (*ŭp*) with a population of 20,000 and more each, townships (*myŏn*), and villages (*ri*). Both cities and towns had further subdivisions designed to facilitate communication between government and people on local community matters.

The need for local self-government was first recognized in 1948; a local autonomy law was enacted in 1949. It was not until December 1960, however, that local elections for the mayors of Seoul and Pusan, provincial governors, and local councils—the first in Korean history—were held. Under the system in operation from the military coup d'état of May 1961 until late 1969, Seoul, Pusan, and the provincial governments were under the direct control of the central government. In view of its special importance, Seoul was controlled by the central government and made subordinate to the Office of the Prime Minister. Provincial administrations and the special cities reported to the Department of Local Affairs of the Ministry of Home Affairs. Likewise, administrative departments of provincial and city governments maintained close contacts with the regional and central offices of the respective cabinet ministries. The police apparatus in each locale also was administratively responsible to the National Police Headquarters in Seoul. The mayor of Seoul was appointed by the president and usually was regarded as his close confidant. Heads of other administrative divisions were recommended by the minister of home affairs for presidential approval. Mayors of ordinary cities and county chiefs—members of the civil service—were recommended by the provincial governor for appointment by the president. Heads of towns and townships were named by county chiefs, heads of wards and precincts by mayors, and village chiefs by heads of townships.

Under the system of proportionality in use in the National Assembly in 1985, the majority of the at-large seats—two-thirds—was given to the party that came in first. This arrangement disproportionately favored the government party, with its traditional advantages of incumbency. Thus, in the 1985 general elections, the government party ended up with a little over 35 percent of the popular vote—the largest share—but held more than 53 percent of the seats in the legislature. Conversely, the second-placed party, with roughly 29 percent of the votes, occupied just over 24 percent of the seats after the at-large seats were distributed. The two-member district system used in 1985 also helped the government party, which had little chance of finishing first in many pro-opposition urban districts, but could hope to win a second-place seat (see table 11, Appendix).

In late 1989, the National Assembly passed legislation designed to increase local autonomy over the following two years. Under the newly amended Act Concerning Local Autonomy, local autonomy was to be introduced in several phases. Local councils would be elected by June 1990. The central government was to continue appointing local administrative heads—including mayors of the six special cities and nine provinces—until elections for those posts, scheduled for 1991, could be held. The government would retain full control over deputy heads of special cities and provinces for the first four years, after which the central government would merely ratify the choices of the mayors and provincial governors. In a last-minute compromise, the National Assembly acceded to the opposition parties' position, permitting political parties to nominate candidates for local elections either individually or in coalition with other parties. Related laws scheduled for National Assembly consideration in 1990 were expected to address other details of local government, including the question of financial autonomy.

Political Dynamics

Compromise and Reform: July–December 1987

The period from late June through December 1987 saw rapid implementation of political reforms in an unusual mood of compromise between the ruling and opposition parties. In July the government paroled 357 political offenders, amnestied more than 2,000 other prisoners, and restored full political rights to prominent opposition figure Kim Dae Jung. In August the National

Assembly established a committee to study constitutional revision. Representatives of four parties took one month to negotiate and propose a draft constitution that incorporated most of the provisions long sought by the opposition parties: greater press freedom and protection for civil rights, a stronger National Assembly, and direct presidential elections. After the bill passed the National Assembly, more than 93 percent of the voters approved the new draft in a plebiscite on October 28, 1987.

Anticipating the presidential election of December 1987, the four major presidential candidates (Roh Tae Woo, Kim Dae Jung, Kim Young Sam, and Kim Chong-p'il, collectively referred to in the media as "one Roh and three Kims") began their informal campaigning with a series of public appearances and speeches in October.

In April 1987, Kim Young Sam and Kim Dae Jung had led their respective factions, who together included seventy-two National Assembly members, out of the New Korea Democratic Party (NKDP) to form the Reunification Democratic Party (RDP). Summer-long efforts to produce a single RDP presidential candidate failed. By late September, Kim Young Sam was finally left in control of the party when Kim Dae Jung and his followers departed to form a new party of their own—the Party for Peace and Democracy (PPD). Kim Young Sam announced his candidacy on October 10, and the RDP convention proclaimed Kim the party's candidate on November 9. Kim Chong-p'il was affiliated with the New Democratic Republican Party (NDRP).

Hoping to benefit from the inability of Kim Dae Jung and Kim Young Sam to agree on a unified candidacy, Roh Tae Woo's Democratic Justice Party (DJP) expected to win the election with a plurality of 1 million votes and sweep about 45 percent of the total vote. The party's strategy was based on the substantive appeal of Roh Tae Woo's June 29 declaration in favor of a new democratic constitution and other reforms, along with a massive public relations campaign. The public relations campaign—roundly scored by Roh's political rivals—portrayed the former four-star general and division commander (he had helped Chun depose the army chief of staff in December 1979) as a simple, "ordinary man" who would bring about a society in which other ordinary people could live comfortably and more affluently. The Roh campaign also avoided the traditionally strident slogans of South Korean politics, preferring promising phrases such as "Commitment to a Bright Future."

DJP strategists seeking the youth vote, which accounted for nearly 60 percent of the electorate, acknowledged the party's likely problem with the more opposition-minded liberal arts college graduates; instead, they focused on segments of the young population believed to be more easily won, such as high-school graduates and technical college graduates. As the campaign continued, Roh increasingly attempted to distance himself from his patron, Chun Doo Hwan, admitting that the government had committed torture and "other mistakes" and affirming that not even the head of state could be exempted in eradicating corruption.

The other conservative candidate, viewed by some of the press as a "spoiler" who would take votes from Roh Tae Woo, was Kim Chong-p'il. Kim's campaign used the "man of experience" theme and was structured around small meetings (especially outside his native South Ch'ungch'ŏng Province), some larger rallies, and carefully chosen television spots financed from the coffers of the Fraternal Association of National Revitalization and by other affluent and conservative South Koreans. In his speeches, Kim criticized Roh's long association with the evils of the Fifth Republic and outlined a tentative program of financial relief for farmers, coal miners, and others.

Like the other major candidates, Kim Young Sam took advantage of the liberalized political climate to begin his presidential campaign with a series of public rallies even before the October 28 national referendum on the new constitution. The failure to agree with Kim Dae Jung on a unified opposition candidacy required a two-pronged offensive, designed both to divert blame for potentially splitting the opposition vote in the election and to attack Roh Tae Woo. The RDP's slogans, "End Military Government with Kim Young Sam" and "A Man for Peace, Harmony, and Honesty," reflected the dual objectives of the campaign. On October 17, 1987, Kim told a home-town audience of 1 million in Pusan that, unlike Roh, he would lead a corruption-free government that would end a "long tradition of military-backed governments" and would make appropriate monetary and symbolic compensation to those killed and wounded in the 1980 "civilian uprising" in Kwangju. In a large rally in Taejŏn on October 24, Kim suggested that a Kim Dae Jung candidacy would "bring about sharp confrontation among Chŏlla and Kyŏngsang people." In keeping with the name of his party, Kim also publicized his plan for "Five Steps to Peaceful Unification" on October 12.

Kim Dae Jung's populist campaign themes were national reconciliation, a just economy, political neutrality of the military, and pursuit of reunification. The platform struck a balance between appeals to Kim Dae Jung's hoped-for constituency among workers, farmers, and lower middle-class voters and reassurances to voters who feared that a Kim Dae Jung candidacy could inflame regional loyalties or result in vindictive purges against those who held power during the Fifth Republic. One of Kim's sons directed specialized party organs such as the United Democratic Youth Association to attract younger voters. Like Roh and Kim Young Sam, Kim Dae Jung was able to assemble 1 million participants in rallies in Seoul and in home-province appearances, while drawing somewhat smaller crowds in other provinces.

In addition to the four principal candidates, several minor parties also offered candidates. These included relative unknowns, such as Kim Sŏn-jok of the Ilche Party (Unified Party), Sin Chong-il of the Hanism Unification Party, and Hong Suk-cha of the Social Democratic Party. Another candidate, Paek Ki-wan, was prominent in dissident circles. Most of these candidates faded as the campaign progressed, eventually withdrawing their candidacy in support of one or another major candidate.

The election results closely followed projections based on the regional origins of the four major candidates, despite protestations by all that regionalism should not divide the country. Of the major candidates, Roh took 36.9 percent of the votes, Kim Young Sam 28 percent, Kim Dae Jung 26.9 percent, and Kim Chong-p'il only 8 percent.

Losers in the election had been charging the government party with illegal electioneering activities ever since it became clear in late September that Kim Dae Jung and Kim Young Sam would not be able to agree on a unified candidacy. The traditional advantages of incumbency were evident early; by October the business pages of Seoul's daily press were already discussing the ''election inflation'' caused by election-related spending, which included government disbursements for development projects. Such spending, common in many countries prior to elections, included a substantial decrease in the price of heating oil, an increase in the official purchase price of rice, and a salary increase for civil servants. Also common, although by no means limited to the ruling party, were customary ''transportation costs'' given to people to attend rallies and the wide distribution of small gifts, such as the cigarette lighters bearing Roh Tae Woo's name, dispensed by the ruling party. Political cartoonists could easily make light of the latter practice, probably because it had been many years since the votes of South Koreans, even in rural areas, had been swayed by simple gifts such as a bowl of rice wine or a pair of rubber shoes. One candidate seemed to sum up the prevailing attitude in remarks at a mid-November rally: ''If they give you money, take it. If they take you to Mount Sorak for sightseeing, then have a nice journey. But on 16 December, be sure to give your vote to me.''

More serious irregularities reported prior to and during the elections included acts of violence or intimidation against election observers, biased television coverage, mobilization of local officials and neighborhood organization officers to encourage people to vote for Roh, and fraudulent handling of ballot boxes. In one working class district in Seoul, for example, election observers seized two ballot boxes being surreptitiously brought in to a polling station on the morning of the election. The government, which removed the observers by force two days later, claimed that the boxes contained absentee ballots, but had no explanation for why they were delivered in commercial trucks carrying fruit, bread, and other consumer goods.

Conversely, few election observers commented on the intimidating effect—no less on potential voters than on candidates—of acts of violence that repeatedly occurred against all major candidates. Candidates were forced to hire phalanxes of bodyguards with plastic shields for protection against flying objects and often were made to cut short public speeches during appearances in regional strongholds of other candidates. In spite of local abuses, it was difficult to estimate what fraction of Roh Tae Woo's plurality of almost 2 million votes, out of 23 million cast, may have been improperly influenced. Extravagant claims of wholesale manipulation in the computerized vote tabulation were made difficult to assess by the failure of those who had made such charges to present convincing evidence. Claims of election rigging also were undercut at the time by the continued insistence of both the Kim Dae Jung and Kim Young Sam camps that their candidate was the one to whom the election rightfully should have gone.

Within a week after the election, public anger at the outcome was divided. Protests continued against election irregularities but were accompanied by increasing criticism of the two major opposition leaders for their failure to produce a unified candidacy that could have defeated the government party candidate. The RDP and PPD, embarrassed by the fact that Kim Dae Jung and Kim Young Sam together received 54 percent of the vote to Roh's 36 percent, both apologized to the public, while vowing to continue disputing the results of the election. Both major opposition parties, together with Kim Chong-p'il's party, gradually turned their attention to the question of upcoming National Assembly elections.

Events in 1988

President-elect Roh Tae Woo outlined his 1988 political goals—both

219

old and new—in a New Year's interview. Some of Roh's comments echoed the authoritarian language of President Chun's 1987 New Year's speech, which had typically called for "grand national harmony" in which transcendent political leadership would see the country through, if only the people would "rid themselves of all vestiges of the old habit of confrontation and strife." Roh made ample reference to traditional themes, speaking of "suprapartisan operation of national affairs," "rooting out corruption," and a mixture of persuasion and "stern measures," if necessary, to bring leftist elements back into the fold. Roh also seemed to promise genuine innovations: to eliminate authoritarian practices, to investigate and punish people guilty of past financial scandals, to protect the press from harassment by law enforcement authorities, to reorganize intelligence agencies, to demilitarize politics, and to resolve the 1980 Kwangju incident by restoring honor to the victims and providing remuneration to the bereaved.

Other leaders and other political forces also had their own agendas for the new year. Under the heading of "Liquidating the Legacy of the Fifth Republic," the opposition parties of Kim Dae Jung and Kim Young Sam sought to investigate corruption in the Fifth Republic, to reexamine the Kwangju incident, and, as well, demanded the release of all political detainees and the reform of numerous laws that had been used to control nonviolent political activity and free expression. Like Roh, Kim Dae Jung's ability to compromise was limited to a degree by his own desire not to lose influence with an offstage constituency, in this case the dissident community and other elements to his left. Kim Chong-p'il's presidential campaign had also made use of these themes in its attacks on the government party's candidate, Roh Tae Woo. Of even greater importance, however, was restoration of the reputations and professional careers of numerous individuals from the Park Chung Hee era who, like Kim himself, had been purged in 1980 during Chun Doo Hwan's takeover. These individuals included more than 8,800 civil servants and officers of state corporations as well as several dozen senior military officers (from the army chief of staff down), who had lost both ranks and pensions. Successful resolution of these issues greatly increased Kim's ability to work with the government party.

Other groups in society had their own expectations. Members of labor unions at many of South Korea's large corporations, fresh from a major campaign of strikes in late 1987, hoped for the right to elect their own leaders and organize outside the framework of the government-sponsored Federation of Korean Trade Unions (see Interest Groups, this ch.). Some dissident organizations hoped that the forthcoming 1988 Seoul Olympics could be held jointly

National Assembly in plenary session, Seoul
Courtesy Korean Overseas Information Service

in P'yŏngyang and Seoul (see Foreign Policy, this ch.). Leftist students also sought opportunities to meet with North Korean students. Some activist students hoped to establish firmer contacts with farmers and the growing labor movement, while at the violence-prone fringe of the radical student movement others planned to continue to dramatize their grievances through arson attacks against United States and South Korean government facilities (see Political Extremism and Political Violence, this ch.). Still other dissidents planned to continue demonstrating against the Roh government out of conviction that it was a simple continuation of the previous militarized regimes.

After his inauguration in February 1988, Roh took steps to honor some of his campaign promises, appointing a woman to his cabinet and approving the rehabilitation of thirty-one generals dismissed in Chun's coups of 1979 and 1980. Another commitment, to appoint members of the opposition parties to cabinet posts, was not met when the two major parties failed to propose names for consideration. Four of the new cabinet appointees, however, were from the Chŏlla provinces.

Negotiations among the major political parties promptly began over amending the National Assembly Election Law, one of the major political issues left unresolved in the 1987 Constitution. At

221

stake were two variables: the size of the electoral districts and the degree of proportionality. Each party took a position that it believed would be to its advantage. Initially, the government party and Kim Chong-p'il's NDRP favored different mixtures of large and small districts. Kim Young Sam's party was divided between its rural members, who also favored multiple-member districts, and the leadership, which argued for single-member districts. Kim Dae Jung's party, which in the presidential election had swept all but two districts in Seoul, hoped to use its heavily concentrated constituency in the Chŏlla provinces to become the largest opposition party with a single-member district system.

The ruling party eventually shifted to a single-member district formula close to that proposed by the PPD, but finally withdrew from the negotiations, claiming that the other parties could not come to agreement in time. In a manner reminiscent of the tactics of the Park Chung Hee era, the ruling party took advantage of its legislative majority to pass unilaterally its own draft amendment in a one-minute session held at 2:00 A.M. on March 8, 1988. The newly amended law reinstated single-member electoral districts, last used in the general election of 1970. It also diluted the element of proportionality somewhat by reducing the number of at-large seats to 75, or about one-fourth of the total of 299, and by more evenly distributing them among the participating parties. The opposition parties strongly protested (Kim Dae Jung's party less vigorously than the others) and then started to prepare their campaigns.

According to most observers, the results of the general election of April 26, 1988, set the stage for a new political drama. For the first time in South Korean history, the government party lost its working majority in the legislature. The government party had hoped to emerge victorious, as the two largest opposition parties again split the antigovernment vote. With 34 percent of the popular vote, however, the DJP held only 125 seats (87 district seats and the remainder at-large), well under the 150 needed for a majority. Kim Chong-p'il's party, the NDRP, ended up with a total of thirty-five seats, enabling it to form its own bargaining group in the National Assembly. Kim Young Sam's RDP gained a small number of seats, but lost in overall ranking in the larger body. Kim Dae Jung's PPD took the senior opposition party position with more than 19 percent of the vote and 23 percent of the total number of seats (see table 12, Appendix).

There were several reasons for the upset. The government party might have made a stronger showing had not Roh, intent upon consolidating his control of a party that still contained many holdovers from the Chun period, replaced one-third of incumbent legislators with political newcomers. Because the new candidates were not able to build up quickly the personal networks necessary for success at the district level, the ruling party in effect gave up one of its strongest campaign assets on the eve of the election. Other factors included the ruling party's lack of a following among younger and better-educated voters and its failure to distance itself sufficiently from the Chun government (the former president's brother was arrested on corruption charges one month before the election). Increasing regionalism also played a role, especially in the Chŏlla provinces, where the government party candidates failed to win a single district seat.

The impact of the new balance of political forces in the National Assembly, characterized by the press as *yŏso yadae* (small ruling power, large opposition power), quickly became evident. Even before the thirteenth National Assembly convened in late May 1988, the floor leaders of the government and opposition parties met to agree upon procedures and to discuss the release of political prisoners. These four-way talks became common during the next two years, especially for routine business matters. Four-way talks also were used to negotiate in advance such political issues as the distribution of committee chairmanships (nine for opposition parties, seven for the government party) and the National Assembly's investigation of dozens of cases of corruption or other irregularities committed under the preceding Fifth Republic.

The judiciary also moved toward greater political independence in 1988. In June one-third of the nation's judges demanded that the chief justice of the Supreme Court, Kim Yŏng-ch'ŏl, resign as a measure to restore public trust in the politicized court system. Two weeks after the chief justice resigned in disgrace, the two major opposition parties abstained from the National Assembly vote to confirm Roh's first choice for the vacancy, thereby causing the nomination to fail. This action resulted in the nomination of Yi Il-kyu, a more independent-minded figure known for not bending to political pressure. A Supreme Court justice during the Chun presidency—until his appointment was not renewed in 1986—Yi had won wide public respect for overturning lower court rulings in political cases. Yi's appointment as chief justice led to National Assembly approval of thirteen new Supreme Court justices and a major reshuffle of the judiciary in July that affected some thirty-five senior District Court and High Court judges. At a meeting of chiefs of all court levels in December 1988 when the Supreme Court was drafting a revision to the Court Organization Law that would give the judiciary full control over its own budgets, Chief

Justice Yi Il-kyu called on the judiciary to "take a hard look at ourselves for the situation in which the public felt distrust for the judiciary" and pledged that he would "never tolerate any outside influence in court proceedings."

Under Yi's leadership, the South Korean judiciary became more independent. This trend continued into 1989, as courts overturned the parliamentary election victories of two government party candidates on charges of illegal campaigning and sentenced numerous former officials and relatives of former President Chun Doo Hwan to prison terms on corruption and power-abuse charges. In another unprecedented action in late 1989, a judge acting on his own initiative granted bail to a student activist charged with violating the National Security Act.

The Seoul Olympics, scheduled to begin in September 1988, contributed to a tacit political truce where the more contentious and difficult political questions, such as the revisions of "bad laws" sought by the two larger opposition parties, were concerned. The primary focus of partisan politics during 1988 was the settling of old accounts concerning the Fifth Republic. These issues, in turn, were divided into two categories: questions related to Chun's seizure of power in late 1979 and early 1980, including the Kwangju incident, and questions concerning corruption and other irregularities during the period of Chun's rule through 1987. In July 1988, following the president's veto of two bills that would have expanded the legislature's inspection powers—for example, enabling the National Assembly to order judicial warrants forcing subpoenaed witnesses, such as former President Chun, to testify—the government party agreed with the three major opposition parties to hold hearings into numerous irregularities of the Fifth Republic. Other special committees established in July were charged with studying reunification policy, democratization issues, problems of regionalism in politics, the conduct of the Seoul Olympics, and irregularities in the recent presidential and general elections.

In twenty meetings held between late September and mid-December 1988, the committee investigating corruption under the Chun government interviewed dozens of witnesses, many of them high-level civilian and military officers. The televised hearings dazzled the public with revelations concerning the suppression of media independence in 1980, the extortion of political funds from large corporations, and improprieties connected with the Ilhae Institute, a charitable foundation established by Chun Doo Hwan (see The Media, this ch).

The hearings had several effects. Pressures against the former president grew as the hearings continued; in late November 1988,

Chun appeared on television to apologize to the nation, taking responsibility for what he termed the "tragic consequences" in Kwangju in 1980. He also stated that he would surrender US$24 million in cash and property and announced that he would seek seclusion in a Buddhist monastery in repentance. The hearings led to subsequent criminal prosecutions of numerous members of Chun's family, as well as former high officials, including the former director of the Agency for National Security Planning, Chang Se-dong. The hearings also gave many South Koreans their first opportunity to see their legislators in action and set a precedent for future broadcasts of National Assembly business.

The drama of the hearings drew attention away from the more prosaic business of the National Assembly, which during the year passed dozens of laws and decided on a 1989 budget. Despite often strong disagreements among parties, these results underscored the role of four-way talks in the process of political compromise, previously a rare commodity in South Korean politics. The resulting de facto coalition foreshadowed the merger of three of the four parties in early 1990.

People dissatisfied with Roh's first year as president overlooked significant political factors, including the restraining impact of world attention prior to the 1988 Seoul Olympics on Roh's conduct. Roh did make effective moves to consolidate his political position during the year, including a series of appointments and reshuffles within the Democratic Justice Party, the cabinet, and the senior ranks of the military. Changed political circumstances in 1989 made it possible for Roh to move more decisively to deal with opponents inside and outside the National Assembly.

Returning to the Politics of National Security, 1989

In his 1989 New Year's address, President Roh promised greater efforts in reaching out to communist bloc countries and in improving relations with the Democratic People's Republic of Korea (North Korea). He also emphasized continued democratization, coupled with stability. The emphasis on stability was shared by the NDRP, which in its New Year's statement noted the need to correct the unbalanced distribution of wealth and to eliminate conflicts based on regionalism but also rejected "any action to undermine political and social stability." Both the RDP and the PPD viewed 1989 as the year for the final resolution of Fifth Republic issues and called for the appointment of a special prosecutor to investigate impartially criminal charges stemming from the National Assembly investigations.

The president's willingness to move toward tighter social controls was given further impetus by developments in the first few months of the year. In February farmers angry over the government's liberalization of agricultural trade staged large-scale, sometimes violent, demonstrations in Seoul. During the same month, the nationwide leftist student organization, the National Association of University Student Councils (Chŏndaehyŏp) challenged the government's desire to retain the initiative between the two Koreas by announcing plans to send members to P'yŏngyang's World Youth and Student Festival scheduled for July. In March a subway workers' strike paralyzed commuter transportation in Seoul for seven days. Nationwide labor unrest continued through April with a violent strike by Hyundai shipyard workers. Student demonstrators continued to match police tear gas with Molotov cocktails through the early months of the year. In May the nation was shocked when students who had taken police officers hostage in a building at Tongŭi University in Pusan set a fire that took the lives of seven police officers who had stormed the facility.

These events were accompanied by signs of uneasiness among advisers of President Roh. In March a cabinet minister, known as a spokesman for those in the military seeking a crackdown on labor union and student radicalism, resigned. A week later, at graduation ceremonies of the Korea Military Academy, the academy superintendent twice failed to salute the president and in his speech complained that "people have such confused perceptions about which are hostile and which are friendly countries that they do not know who our enemy is." Pressures on the president to curb what these and other conservatives in the military and the government party believed was a trend toward deterioration increased further in late March, when it became known that two prominent South Korean dissidents had traveled to P'yŏngyang, where they met with North Korean leader Kim Il Sung and attended a church service. These developments and others, such as the announcement in June that a former opposition legislator had made an unauthorized trip to North Korea in 1988, gave the president the rationale to reverse another trend—the declining involvement of the national security agencies in domestic political life.

During the political openness of 1988, a report of the government's Administration Reform Commission had denigrated the Agency for National Security Planning, on grounds that the agency had in the past "violated human rights on many occasions and interfered in politics, thus incurring the condemnation of the public." As ruling and opposition parties studied ways to limit the agency's role in domestic political surveillance, the ANSP also appeared to take a new approach, announcing that it was scaling back domestic operations, sharing classified documents on external security issues at press conferences, and sending new agency directors to pay respects to the presidents of the opposition parties. By early 1989, political agreement had been reached on a revised ANSP law that would require the agency to observe the right of habeas corpus, remain politically neutral, and end other forms of interference in domestic political life.

The president's response to the growing political crisis of early 1989 was to grant a renewed mandate to the police and security agencies. In view of increasing attacks on police boxes, a longstanding program to provide police with M–16 rifles was stepped up and new rules of engagement issued, permitting police to fire in self-defense on Molotov cocktail-throwing demonstrators. In the aftermath of the Tongŭi University incident, the National Assembly quickly passed a law providing special penalties for the use of Molotov cocktails. In early April, the president established a Joint Security Investigations Headquarters to coordinate the work of police, intelligence, and national security agencies. This organ, which was in existence from early April through late June 1989, investigated student union groups, dissident organizations, and an antigovernment newspaper, eventually arresting more than 500 persons (including the pair who had traveled to North Korea in March) on suspicion of "aiding an antistate organization"—North Korea—under the broad terms of the National Security Act.

The Joint Security Investigations Headquarters was disbanded in June under pressure from the National Assembly. Public prosecutors and the Agency for National Security Planning, however, continued making arrests and pursuing investigations into a variety of political activities on national security grounds. There also was a resumption of the quasi-legal or illegal practices common in national security cases before 1988: breaking into the campaign headquarters of an opposition candidate in a by-election in July; publishing lists of banned "antistate" books even after a civil court ruling that such a ban was illegal; arresting people for reading or possessing books considered to be pro-North Korean; arresting an antigovernment journalist for planning unauthorized coverage of North Korea; and ignoring court orders to allow arrested political detainees to meet with their attorneys. By the end of 1989, all people who had traveled to North Korea without authorization had been convicted and sentenced to lengthy prison terms.

The role of the ANSP was further strengthened during the rest of the year. As part of a cabinet shuffle in July, Roh appointed a former high-school classmate, with a reputation for a hardline approach as a prosecutor under the Fifth Republic, as head of the ANSP. In the National Assembly, discussion of amendments that would ease sections of the National Security Act and restrict the powers of the ANSP were indefinitely postponed. In September the government introduced an amendment that would enable the ANSP to bypass the constitutional guarantees of access to a lawyer in national security cases. In late 1989, the government claimed that 342 people had been charged under the National Security Act during the year.

Parties and Leaders

Unlike the two former military leaders who had preceded him, Roh Tae Woo followed an indirect course to the chairmanship of the Democratic Justice Party (DJP) and the presidency. A Korea Military Academy classmate of Chun Doo Hwan and Chŏng Ho-yong and a 1959 graduate of the United States Army Special Warfare School, Roh had passed through a succession of career-building military commands, including a brigade of the Special Warfare Command, before moving a regiment of his frontline Ninth Division into Seoul to support Chun's forcible removal of the army chief of staff and other senior military leaders on December 12, 1979. As Chun consolidated his political position through the spring and summer of 1980, he placed Roh in the most politically sensitive military posts, naming him to be commander of the Capital Garrison Command and, later, the Defense Security Command. After Chun became president in 1980, however, he retired Roh from the military and used him to fill a series of government posts, beginning with a position as second minister of political affairs, a position that was apparently created especially for Roh. After a short period as minister of sports in the spring of 1982, Roh served for fifteen months as the minister of home affairs.

In retrospect it seems clear that Roh's ability simultaneously to benefit by, yet distance himself politically from, his association with Chun began in mid-1983 when he was moved from the post of minister of home affairs to take the chairmanship of South Korea's Olympic Committee, which he held through 1986. With the Olympic Committee portfolio, Roh was able to avoid entanglement in increasingly tough police handling of the student movement while remaining in the public eye as the person who had successfully managed the campaign to have Seoul selected as the site of the 1988 Games of the XXIV Olympiad. After his election to the National Assembly in April 1985, Roh emerged as a significant figure in the DJP when Chun appointed him to the party presidency.

At the end of the first two years of the Roh presidency, the DJP was a different party from that bequeathed by Chun in 1981. Roh had surprised political observers when he dismissed one-third of the party's local chapter chairmen and denied the party's nomination in the April 1988 National Assembly election to 126 incumbent party members in favor of relatively unknown and new party members. These decisions undoubtedly cost the party heavily in the number of seats won, but they also enabled Roh to begin to reshape the party in his own image. By December 1988, Roh was ready to consolidate his control of the DJP. Within four days, Roh replaced twenty of twenty-three cabinet ministers, eliminating virtually all those carried over from the Chun administration. He also reshuffled the senior DJP leadership, removing Park Chun-kyu, a former adviser to Park Chung Hee's Democratic Republican Party, from the chairmanship.

The numerically dominant membership, or mainstream, of the DJP was made up of figures from the city of Taegu and North Kyŏngsang Province, a group sometimes characterized by the press as the TK Mafia, or TK Division (TK for Taegu and Kyŏngsang). This trend had become evident during the Fifth Republic under Chun and within the Democratic Republican Party under Park Chung Hee before him. Roh also attempted, however, to replace Chun loyalists within the party with individuals who were more likely to owe him their primary loyalty. Roh supporters included some members of an influential subset of the TK group made up of individuals who had graduated from Kyŏngbuk High School, Roh's alma mater. In December 1988, for example, all of the president's senior staff were Roh's fellow high-school alumni. Taegu-Kyŏngsang ties also extended to numerous civil and military posts, most notably all army chiefs of staff after 1980, one-quarter of director-level officers in the Korean National Police, and 120 of 662 prosecutors in 1989.

A second group that supported the president comprised a number of older politicians whom the Seoul press termed the New Elders Group. Members of this group fled from North Korea in the 1940s or during the Korean War, held senior positions in various walks of life, especially journalism, and played an important role in rallying the votes of other former North Koreans in Kyŏnggi and Kangwŏn provinces in the 1987 presidential election. For this service, they were allowed to return to political life, in many cases for the first time since persons of North Korean origin lost political influence following the fall of Syngman Rhee in 1960 and the 1961 coup d'état of Park Chung Hee. As a group, they were strongly anticommunist and favored the restoration of "law and order" in the face of rising dissent in South Korean society.

Political alignments within the ruling party tended to form around personalities rather than ideas because of the importance of personal networks in South Korean society and the fact that under the Constitution Roh could not succeed himself. In August 1989, President Roh removed Yi Chong-ch'an from a senior party post. Yi, the leader of a group of DJP members hailing from the Seoul area, was known to favor greater democracy within the party and to oppose revision of the Constitution to create a cabinet-responsible system. After the announcement in early 1990 that the parties of Kim Young Sam and Kim Chong-p'il would merge with that of Roh Tae Woo, observers expected the roles both of ideas and of personal alignments or factions to be even more significant in the new, enlarged Democratic Liberal Party.

New Democratic Republican Party (NDRP) leader Kim Chong-p'il had been nominated as the presidential candidate of the Democratic Republican Party following Park's assassination in late 1979, but Kim was arrested by Chun on corruption charges during the latter's takeover in 1980. Kim was accused of corruption and stripped of most of his personal assets in South Korea. He spent six years in the United States. In March 1986, he returned to South Korea to attempt to reconstruct Park's old party and restore his own political fortunes. In a series of speeches in 1986 and 1987, Kim spoke of the need to continue the "revitalizing" tasks of the *yusin* phase of Park Chung Hee (see South Korea under Park Chung Hee, 1961–79, ch. 1). His appeal initially was to former officials, cashiered military leaders, and others who had lost their positions in 1980. As Kim's message changed to emphasize his association with the beginnings of South Korea's modern economic development in the 1960s, he began to attract some younger, conservative South Koreans, and many from his native Ch'ungch'ŏng Province. By October 30, 1987, when Kim's NDRP was formally established, people under the age of forty made up more than half of the party's 3,000 charter members. Others included the twenty-one National Assembly members of the now defunct Korea Nationalist Party, which during the 1980s had provided a home for political survivors of Park Chung Hee's party.

Kim Young Sam was a veteran politician with a strong constituency in Pusan and in South Kyŏngsang Province. As a National Assembly member for the opposition New Democratic Party (NDP) in the 1960s, he fought a series of losing battles against Park Chung Hee on such issues as normalization of relations with Japan in 1965. By 1970 he had risen to the top policy-making committee of the NDP. He lost the party's nomination to political rival Kim Dae Jung in the presidential election of 1971 but continued to hold top party posts through 1979, when the government-dominated National Assembly expelled him after he called for the resignation of Park and the abandonment of the *yusin* system. This incident contributed to large-scale unrest in Pusan and nearby Masan and may have indirectly contributed to Park's assassination.

Kim Young Sam, like other well-known political figures, such as Kim Chong-p'il and Kim Dae Jung, was banned from politics in 1980 by Chun Doo Hwan; he spent the early 1980s under house arrest. A Presbyterian elder, Kim used the enforced leisure in well-publicized self-improvement along traditional cultural lines common to exiled South Korean politicians. He was occasionally photographed while practicing calligraphy in his book-lined study, or while on permitted outings with his Democratic Alpine Club. Government censorship prevented detailed press coverage of his twenty-three-day hunger strike against the Chun government in May and June 1983. Although Kim's house arrest was lifted after the hunger strike, his political rights were not restored until after the February 1985 National Assembly elections. Kim subsequently joined his faction members in the newly formed New Korea Democratic Party as an official party adviser; his long-time rival, Kim Dae Jung, directed his own faction in the party from outside it as a member of the Council for Promotion of Democracy.

In the late 1980s, South Korean political observers, increasingly interested in the question of leadership succession within the opposition parties, focused their attention more on generational groupings than on factions. Seen this way, the RDP was broadly divided into old-line Kim Young Sam loyalists and some additional experienced opposition politicians in their fifties and an emergent group of younger politicians, mostly in their forties. Many of the latter group began their first terms in the National Assembly in 1988. They typically brought to their political careers progressive political credentials earned in human rights law, labor relations, or other fields. Several members of this group received nationwide attention for their cogent interrogation techniques during the National Assembly hearings in late 1988.

At the time of the presidential elections in December 1987, sixty-two-year-old opposition leader Kim Dae Jung from the Chŏlla region was in many ways the South Korean political candidate best known outside of South Korea. A one-time newspaper publisher, a Roman Catholic of eclectic views, and a charismatic popular speaker elected to the National Assembly four times in the 1960s,

Kim had an international reputation that stemmed largely from the continuous efforts of the South Korean government to keep him out of the country, in prison, or under house arrest following his near-victory over Park in the 1971 presidential election. He had built active support organizations among South Koreans in Japan and the United States by the time the Korean Central Intelligence Agency kidnapped him at a Tokyo hotel in 1973. Following United States intervention to save his life during the abduction, he was brought back to South Korea to stand trial for alleged violation of the election law and Park's Emergency Measure Number Nine. He served several years of imprisonment and house arrest, then was released and had his civil rights restored in 1980 on the heels of the October 1979 assassination of Park.

Again arrested under martial law in May 1980, Kim Dae Jung was accused of fomenting the Kwangju incident and sentenced to death by a military court on sedition charges that the United States Department of State described at the time as "far-fetched" (see The Kwangju Uprising, ch. 1). Under pressure from the United States government, his death sentence was subsequently reduced to life and then to twenty years' imprisonment. This term was suspended in late 1982 when Kim went to the United States to seek medical treatment. In the United States, Kim divided his time among a research appointment at Harvard University, the Korean Institute for Human Rights in Alexandria, Virginia (informally known as the Kim Dae Jung Embassy), and wide-ranging travels to speak before Korean-American groups and United States civic, academic, and human rights organizations. Kim returned to South Korea in February 1985 on the eve of the National Assembly elections. In March 1985, he was released from the 1980 general ban on political activity, although the suspended criminal charges still in effect meant that he could neither belong to a party nor run for office. He immediately joined with Kim Young Sam, who had also had his ban lifted, to establish the Council for Promotion of Democracy. Although Kim Dae Jung spent most of the next two years under house arrest, he telephonically provided informal guidance to his faction within the New Korea Democratic Party and, after April 1985, within the Reunification Democratic Party (RDP). As part of the political understanding reached in late June 1987, the government dropped all outstanding charges against him and he reemerged to participate fully in politics. After negotiations with the Kim Young Sam faction of the RDP failed to reach agreement concerning a unified candidacy, the Kim Dae Jung faction and its supporters left in October 1987 to form the Party for Peace and Democracy (PPD). The December 16 election was fast approaching when Kim received his party's presidential nomination on November 12.

As the 1990s began, the PPD was made up of at least three discernible groups. The first group comprised old-line Kim Dae Jung followers who occupied the senior positions in the party hierarchy and gave unquestioning loyalty to the party leader. A second group, making up more than one-half of the party's seventy-one National Assembly seats after the April 1988 election, consisted of first-termers obliged by custom to play a low-key role in party affairs until they acquired more political experience. Within this group, however, was a subgroup of activists with long experience in cause-oriented groups and human rights law. Many of these activists had worked for the party in the National Assembly elections in 1985; a few had run as independents in 1988 before formally joining the party. Many of this group, organized as the Study Group for Peaceful and Democratic Reunification (P'yŏngminyŏn) within the party, participated conspicuously in National Assembly hearings in 1988. Collectively, they constituted the party's left wing and its link with the broader dissident movement outside of the National Assembly. Political speculation in late 1989 centered on whether this group would continue to exert a leftward pull, seeking to bring the position of the PPD closer to that of South Korea's emergent left. Observers noted that several PPD members of this group also were members of the Coalition for a National Democratic Movement (Chŏmminyŏn) formed in January 1989 and were likely to be involved with that organization's plans to form a progressive political party to participate in the first local council elections scheduled to take place in 1990.

Chŏmminyŏn was one of a variety of groups that considered plans to form cause-oriented political parties in anticipation of local council elections. These bodies included a group of some fifty former cabinet members and retired generals who believed that the government party was not conservative enough and at least two groups of environmentalists who planned to establish parties dedicated to that issue. A proposed Green Party, like its European counterparts, planned to emphasize antiwar and antinuclear issues as well as the cause of the environment, but also supported a concept of "Oriental humanity" that would promote respect for the elderly and other traditional virtues.

Interest Groups

Despite its Constitution and formal structure, the South Korean government has never fully conformed to the liberal democratic model that sees the state as a simple summation of diverse and competing interests within society. In politics, as in economic life, South Korea has more closely fit the "strong state" model, in which the government has tended to outweigh particular social or group interests. Nonetheless, the balance between the government and various interest groups showed some dramatic changes in the late 1980s; as the 1990s began, observers found it likely that such changes would continue, despite efforts by the government to retain its traditionally strong position.

During most of the postwar period, the South Korean government had encouraged organizations for the communication of economic interests, but had not encouraged professional or occupational interest groups to voice political demands. Independent or unsanctioned interest groups had come into existence from time to time to challenge fundamental policies of the government. In the late 1980s, such challenges accounted for a sizable proportion of extragovernmental political activity.

The relationship between government and business associations in South Korea had its roots in the period of Japanese colonial rule, when the governor general established the Seoul Chamber of Commerce and Industry and other industrial associations as a means of communicating economic policies to the business community. Since 1952 all businesses have been required by South Korean law to belong to the Korean Chamber of Commerce and Industry, the bylaws and initial membership of which closely paralled those of the Seoul Chamber of Commerce and Industry of the colonial period. Since 1961, when the Park government began its economic development plans, the Federation of Korean Industry has represented the major conglomerates. A larger organization, the Federation of Small and Medium Industries, has had much less influence. The Korea Traders' Association and the Korean Federation of Textile Industries round out the four major industrial associations. In 1989 there were some 200 additional business associations licensed by the state (see The Government and Public and Private Corporations, ch. 3).

In most cases, the government recognizes only a single association as the representative of that industry. Major business leaders may have individual access to administrators through personal ties and might be able to influence the government in minor ways, such as obtaining exemptions from specific taxes. For the most part, however, business associations through the 1980s were dominated by the government. As noted by one specialist, "It is through industry associations that the Korean government implements its policies, enforces routine compliance, gathers information, and

National Museum of Korea, Seoul
Courtesy Oren Hadar

monitors performance.'' In the 1980s, this process was sometimes facilitated by the placement of retiring senior military or national security officials in industry association positions.

Institutional changes and pressures toward open markets began to change the traditional government-business relationship in the mid-and late 1980s. Larger corporations became interested in having a role in policy formulation more commensurate with their contribution to more than two decades of economic growth. This interest took several forms, including substantial corporate contributions to all major political parties during elections. As economic ministries grew in influence within a more decentralized economic planning structure in the 1980s, the related industry associations gained a greater voice, just as was true in Japan and the United States. Growing liberalization of the domestic market under foreign pressure also led to greater friction between the interests of specific economic sectors and the need of the government to satisfy its foreign critics or risk a loss of access to vital foreign markets. As the 1990s began, these frictions seemed likely to continue and to lead eventually to further readjustments.

In general, the higher-paid professions establish and administer their own associations and cooperate closely with the appropriate government ministries but receive no government support. These

235

associations are chiefly concerned with maintaining standards and the economic status of the professions concerned and have been traditionally regarded by the government as politically safe. The major exception has been the Korean Bar Association, which became increasingly outspoken on human rights and related legal issues in the 1970s and 1980s.

The government has attempted to keep tight controls on the intellectual professions, sponsoring the formation of the Korean Federation of Education Associations and the Federation of Artistic and Cultural Organizations of Korea. Membership in the Korean Federation of Education Associations was compulsory for all teachers through high-school level. Members of these umbrella groups received significant medical benefits, and they tended to avoid political controversy. The Korean Newspaper Association and Korean Newspaper Editors' Association were politically cautious during the early 1980s, but became much less constrained during the early years of Roh's rule.

Dissident associations have frequently grown from the intellectual sector of society. The Minjung Culture Movement Association (*minjung* means populist) was formed in 1985 by dissident artists and writers who did not want to belong to the state-controlled Federation of Artistic and Cultural Organizations of Korea. Similar organizations of dissident journalists, such as the Association of Journalists Dismissed in 1980, or the Democratic Press Movement Association, often were dealt with harshly under the Fifth Republic. The Association of Korean Journalists, although more broadly based and less ideological, was quick to resist censorship and, after a change in the law in 1988, supported the formation of journalists' unions.

The government has been especially sensitive about unauthorized professional associations among teachers. Many teachers, and some opposition political leaders, have been determined to reduce the state's control over the political views of teachers and the content of education. In early 1989, President Roh vetoed an opposition-sponsored amendment to the Education Law that would have allowed teachers to form independent unions. In spite of the president's veto, activist leftist teachers—numbering about 10 percent of the nation's primary through high-school faculties— announced their intention to form such a union. The National Teachers Union (Chŏn'gyojo), inaugurated in late May 1989, criticized the Korean Federation of Education Associations as progovernment and weak in protecting teachers' rights (see Primary and Secondary Schools, ch. 2). The Ministry of Education responded by dismissing more than 1,000 members of the new union in

the spring and summer of 1989, resulting in the eventual withdrawal of more than 10,000 additional teachers. The Agency for
National Security Planning conducted a well-publicized investigation into the union's ideology, with the implication that members
could be charged with aiding an antistate organization under the
National Security Act. Police broke up pro-National Teachers
Union rallies; members participating in a signature-gathering campaign to support the union were charged with traffic violations.
Eventually, several teachers' union leaders received prison terms
on various charges. The Ministry of Education produced new guidelines that permitted teachers' colleges to deny admission to students with activist records and that allowed district education boards
to screen out ''security risks'' when testing candidates for employment. These measures effectively halted the activities of the National
Teachers Union.

The modern Korean labor movement, including unions of skilled
and unskilled workers, dates to the first decade of Japanese colonial
rule. South Korean law and constitutions since 1948 have recognized the "three rights" of labor: the right to organize, the right
to bargain collectively, and the right to take collective action. In
practice, however, the government has consistently attempted to
control labor and mitigate the effects of unionism through the use
of a variety of legal and customary devices, including company-
supported unions, prohibitions against political activities by unions,
binding arbitration of disputes in public interest industries, which
include 70 percent of all organized labor, and the requirement that
all unions be affiliated with one of the seventeen government-
sponsored industrial unions and with a general coordinating body,
the Federation of Korean Trade Unions (FKTU). In the 1980s,
large companies, often supported by the police and intelligence
agencies of the government, also exerted pressure on unions to prevent strikes, to undermine the development of white-collar unions,
to retain control of union leaders, and to prevent persons with some
college education from attempting to organize workers by taking
positions as industrial laborers.

Despite such measures, the government has never exercised
total control of the labor movement. Even the FKTU occasionally
has been able to file administrative suits against government rulings or to lobby—sometimes successfully—against laws that would
have a negative impact on working conditions or rights of unions.
Through most of its existence, however, the federation has been
able to do little beyond submit proposals for legal reform to the
government. Throughout the postwar period, dissenting labor organizations either have attempted to function apart from the

government-sanctioned structure under the FKTU, or have formed rival umbrella organizations, such as the National Council of Trade Unions, established in 1958.

South Korea experienced an explosion of labor disputes from 1987 through 1989 under the more open political conditions following the crisis of late June 1987 and the pressures created by long-deferred improvements in wages and working conditions (see table 13, Appendix; Social Classes in Contemporary South Korea, ch. 2). More than 3,500 labor disputes occurred from August through November 1987. Most were quickly resolved by negotiated wage increases and by the prospect that another common demand—freer scope for union activities—would be met in forthcoming legislation. In 1988 labor-related laws were amended to make it easier to establish labor unions and to reduce government intervention in labor disputes. Unions were still prohibited, however, from articulating any demands that the government interpreted as political in nature.

In 1988 the number of unions increased from 4,000 to more than 5,700. This figure included numerous new white-collar unions formed at research institutes, in the media, and within the larger corporations.

There was a general privatization of labor-management conflict during 1988 and 1989 as the government adopted a more neutral, hands-off stance. Companies experimented widely with tactics such as lockouts (5 in 1987; 224 in 1988), and labor unions achieved new levels of joint action by workers in different regions and industries. The government's ability to manage organized labor through the traditional means of controlling the FKTU declined. The FKTU, under criticism for the many years it had represented the government more than labor, also began to take a more independent posture as the 1980s came to a close. In 1989 the once-docile umbrella organization prepared to sponsor union candidates in anticipated local elections (an illegal activity under existing law) and held education seminars and rallies to press for "economic democracy" through revision of labor laws and other reforms. Notwithstanding the increasing ability of labor to organize and to present economic demands, however, the government continued to suppress leftist labor groups that appeared to have broad political goals or that questioned the legitimacy of the government, such as the National Council of Labor Unions (Chŏnnohyŏp), which was formally established in early 1990.

In early 1990, the government announced new measures to support its return to more restrictive policies governing strikes. The number of intelligence agents at key industries was more than doubled (from 163 to 337) and a special riot police task force—sixty-three companies in strength—was deployed against "illegal" strikes.

During the postwar period, articulation of workers' interests had been weakest for South Korea's farming population. In 1946 the government used the Korea Federation of Peasants to mobilize the rural population against leftist peasant unions. The Federation of Agricultural Cooperatives, established in 1957, was also largely funded and administered by the state. Its purpose was not to represent farmers' interests but to facilitate government control over the purchase and sale of grain and farmers' purchases of fertilizer.

Although most South Korean farmers continued to belong to cooperatives, two pressures converged in the late 1980s to change the way in which farmers' interests were represented. First, as rural-urban income disparities grew in the late 1970s and 1980s, farmer dissatisfaction with the government cooperatives' role in setting crop prices and the costs of agricultural supplies also increased (see Agriculture, ch. 3). Some farmers turned to independent organizations, such as the Korean Catholic Farmers Association or the Christian Farmers Association. These groups, which were viewed as dissident organizations by the government, performed a variety of services for farmers and also took public positions on government agricultural and price policies, sometimes using mass rallies. The second change, which affected larger numbers of farmers, was the result of South Korea's growing trade surpluses in the late 1980s (see Foreign Trade Policy, ch. 3). As the government responded to pressure from major trading partners, such as the United States, to open South Korea's domestic markets, farmers became increasingly active in large-scale protest rallies against both the government and the major political parties. As the 1990s began, it was clear that the traditional harmony of political interests between a conservative rural population and conservative governments had ended.

Political Extremism and Political Violence

The deliberate use of violence, including occasional assassination, to express or advance political goals was common among both the right and the left in South Korea after liberation in 1945 and up to the outbreak of the Korean War in June 1950. Subsequent political violence up to the 1980s, apart from exchanges between police and participants in political demonstrations or rallies, was largely limited to the illegal government use of violence or the threat of violence to suppress dissent and intimidate political opponents. During the presidency of Syngman Rhee (1948–60), for example, the government mobilized the Anticommunist Youth League and members of street gangs to smash facilities of critical newspapers and intimidate opposition candidates for election (see The Syngman Rhee Era, 1948–60, ch. 1). The Park government continued illegal police practices, including torture of some dissidents, intellectuals, and even members of the National Assembly, and was often indirectly involved in violence. The Korean Central Intelligence Agency (KCIA) also used various means, including physical threats, to intimidate South Korean journalists in the United States. Such methods continued under Chun, occasionally resulting in the deaths of political defendants under police torture. Police were passively present while hired thugs broke up dissident religious services or union meetings. Under Roh Tae Woo, police handling of political suspects retained some of the illegal violence of earlier times, although improved media freedom also meant greater scrutiny of police misconduct. In contrast with earlier regimes, however, the Roh government permitted prosecution and conviction of police officers and even of military personnel in several cases involving violence during its first year in office.

Under a special "afforestation program" administered by the Defense Security Command, more than 400 student activists were punitively induced into the army during the Chun years. According to a Ministry of National Defense report, at least five committed suicide or were killed, and many were forced to become informants (see The Defense Security Command, ch. 5). At least 50 people died (of some 10,000 incarcerated) in the government's "triple purity" (*samch'ŏng*) reeducation camps in the early 1980s. Ten years after the May 1980 Kwangju incident, many South Koreans continued to believe that the initial violence committed by armed Special Forces troops against civilian demonstrators on that occasion was deliberate. The former martial law commander for the region told a National Assembly committee in 1988 that civilian protests were not violent enough at the beginning to justify the use of elite forces and that army brutality aggravated the situation.

Public violence against government institutions was rare from the 1950s through the early 1980s. When students overthrew the Syngman Rhee government in April 1960, mobs destroyed the headquarters of Rhee's Anticommunist Youth League. More spontaneous forms of violence often occurred during student protest rallies in the 1950s, 1960s, and 1970s, when small numbers of rock-throwing students at the edges of large rallies clashed with club-wielding riot police, or security forces dispatched martial arts experts and plainclothes officers to beat or arrest demonstrators. Students also occasionally beat up police informants or plainclothes officers. This pattern changed following the killings of students and other demonstrators in Kwangju in May 1980.

The Kwangju incident permanently stained the legitimacy of the Chun government for subsequent generations of student activists, many of whom also blamed the United States for what they believed to be its supportive role. The use of Molotov cocktails by some elements among student demonstrators, both as a counter to increasingly effective police use of tear gas and as a reflection of increased militancy, became a feature of student demonstrations during the 1980s.

Another threshold was crossed in March 1982, when several students deliberately set a fire in the American Cultural Center in Pusan, causing severe damage and, inadvertently, the death of another South Korean student studying in the building at the time. In a related statement, the students said they were beginning an anti-United States struggle to eliminate United States power from South Korea. The students blamed the United States for causing "the permanent national division of Korea" and for "supporting the military regime that refuses democratization, social revolution, and development."

In April 1985, radical students, together with veteran activists released from prison the year before, formed the Struggle Committee for the Liberation of the Masses, the Attainment of Democracy, and the Unification of the Nation, or Sammint'u. The ideology of this organization borrowed from dependency theory in blaming a "dependent industrialization process" dominated by the United States for South Korea's social and political problems. Sammint'u supported various forms of direct action, including infiltration of labor unions and forcible occupations of United States and South Korean government facilities. Sammint'u activists conducted a number of such actions, including a three-day seizure of the United States Information Service (USIS) building in Seoul in May 1985 and the occupation of two regional offices of the Ministry of Labor in November of the same year. Although Sammint'u was suppressed in 1986 under the National Security Act as an "anti-state" organization, its emphasis on well-organized occupations and other actions (rather than the more spontaneous forms of traditional student protest) and its ability to mobilize students across campus lines marked a permanent change in student protest tactics (see College Student Activism, ch. 2).

By the late 1980s, violence-prone student radicals, although a small minority even among politically active students, demonstrated increasing effectiveness in organizing occupations and arson assaults against facilities. In 1988, under the general guidance of the

241

National Association of University Student Councils (Chŏndae-hyŏp) and the Seoul Area Federation of Student Councils (Sŏch'ongnyŏn), small groups of students armed with Molotov cocktails, metal pipes, and occasionally tear gas grenades or improvised incendiary or explosive devices and staged more than two dozen raids on United States diplomatic and military facilities. Students also conducted a similar number of attacks against offices of the government and ruling party and the suburban Seoul residence of former President Chun (see table 13, Appendix).

Anti-United States attacks in 1989 began in February with a seizure of the USIS library in Seoul and attempted arson at the American Cultural Center in Kwangju. Additional incidents continued through the year at about the same level as in 1988, culminating in the violent occupation of the United States ambassador's residence by six students in December. In the spring of 1989, there were numerous incidents of arson and vandalism against Hyundai automobile showrooms in many cities, as Chŏndaehyŏp mobilized member organizations nationwide to support a strike by Hyundai shipyard workers. Other attacks occurred throughout the year against Democratic Justice Party (DJP) offices and South Korean government facilities.

As the 1980s ended, however, violence-prone radical groups also suffered setbacks and found themselves under increased pressure from the courts, police, and public and student opinion. The deaths of seven police officers in a fire set by student demonstrators in Pusan in May 1989, the arrest of Chŏndaehyŏp leaders on National Security Act charges stemming from the unauthorized travel of a member of the organization to P'yŏngyang over the summer, and the beating to death of a student informer by activists at one university in Seoul in October contributed to this pressure. In student council elections throughout the country in late 1989, students at many campuses defeated student council officers associated with the Chŏndaehyŏp's ''national liberation'' strategy, often replacing them with other leaders who favored a ''people's democracy'' approach, emphasizing organizational work among farmers and the labor movement over violent assaults on symbolic targets, at least for the near term.

Many South Korean commentators interpreted the outcome of the 1989 campus elections as a renunciation of violent methods or as a turn away from radical student activism. Other observers noted, however, the ideological and organizational complexity of ''people's democracy'' elements, some of which had in the past equaled or exceeded Chŏndaehyŏp's commitment to violent activism. As the 1990s began, it seemed likely that at least some radical elements, although perhaps increasingly driven underground like their counterparts in Japan, would remain committed to the use of violence as a political tool.

Human Rights

Traditional Korean political thought, rooted in neo-Confucianism, placed some emphasis on benevolent rule and on the government's paternalistic responsibility to redress grievances of the population. These ideas were carried further in the nineteenth century by the Tonghak Movement (*tonghak* means Eastern Learning), which espoused equality of the sexes and of social classes. Interest among Koreans in modern human rights, however, and especially in civil and political rights protected by law began late in the Chosŏn Dynasty (1392–1910) with the natural rights ideas of enlightenment movement (*kaehwa*) reformers, such as Kim Ok-kyun, Sŏ Chaep'il, and Pak Yŏng-hyo (see The Chosŏn Dynasty, ch. 1).

The Japanese colonial period (1910–45) saw further diffusion of such ideas. In 1919 Koreans who had fled Japanese colonial rule established a government-in-exile in Shanghai that affirmed wide-ranging civil and political rights—freedoms of the ballot, religion, press, movement, property, and social and sexual equality. Within Korea in the 1920s, labor and tenant farmers unions spread the idea of rights and provided experience in organizational and protest techniques. As colonial rule continued, many Korean nationalists came to assume the desirability of a modern legal order and due process of law, especially while experiencing dual legal standards and abuses such as torture and fabrication of evidence in political cases. Meanwhile, Koreans serving in the colonial police and receiving training in the Japanese Imperial Army often absorbed the increasingly stringent and authoritarian perspective of Japanese militarism.

Human rights performance did not immediately improve following the liberation of Korea from Japanese rule in 1945. Many factors—national division, ideological conflict, and violent confrontation even before the outbreak of the Korean War in 1950—contributed to this problem. Japanese-style practices held over from the colonial days also were to blame. The United States Army Military Government in Korea (1945–48), confronted with serious problems of public order, found itself retaining the old colonial police apparatus and its Korean personnel (see South Korea under United States Occupation, 1945–48, ch. 1). United States-sponsored legal reforms, such as an effort to institute habeas corpus in 1946, often failed; attempts by United States advisers to prevent South Korean police from using torture, especially in political cases,

243

also were unsuccessful. Under Syngman Rhee, South Korea continued the prewar pattern of using law and the police for political purposes—intimidating the judiciary, arresting journalists, and applying extralegal pressures against the teaching profession and members of the new National Assembly.

Under the presidencies of Park and Chun such problems worsened, and there were increasing signs of tension between the government and its supporters, who sought to ignore or minimize such rights, and many South Koreans, including some even within the government, who believed that civil, legal, and political rights should be honored. This tension was evident in the affirmations of rights found in most of South Korea's postwar constitutions and especially in the government's need for increasingly stringent measures to control a restive judiciary under the *yusin* constitution. The forced resignations of judges and the resort to military tribunals in some political trials were rationalized on national security grounds, but only served to show that by the mid-1970s the government was, on such matters, no longer able to command the respect and cooperation of a significant part of the country's legal profession.

The Chun government modified some of the worst features of the *yusin* constitution by removing the admissibility of confessions as evidence, for example, but continued most of the abusive police and judicial practices of the Park period with little change. Penal sentences for people found guilty of offenses under certain politically relevant laws—the National Security Act and the Act Concerning Assembly and Demonstration, for example—actually were harsher under Chun than under the preceding *yusin* system.

In addition to the growing disaffection of the legal profession in the 1970s and 1980s, South Korea's modernization had generated two social trends—rapid urbanization and dramatic increases in literacy and education levels—that were essential to industrialization, irreversible, and highly corrosive of traditional authoritarian practices. Public outrage against the police torture and killing of a student during an interrogation in early 1987 helped to fuel the growing political crisis that culminated in the tulmultuous events in June.

The agreement in late 1989 between opposition and government parties concerning the legacy of the Fifth Republic left unresolved the question of what the press and many politicians referred to as revision of *akpŏp* (evil laws). These were laws long used in South Korea to restrict and punish nonviolent political activity. The abolition in 1988 of one such law, the Basic Press Act of December 1980, had important and immediate effects on freedom of the press.

Other laws remained on the statute books and were increasingly used in 1989 as the Roh administration reached the apparent limits of its willingness to tolerate dissent. Despite Roh's initial reputation for moderation, police records reported in the press show that by late 1989 the Roh government had more than doubled the Chun administration's rate of arrests for political offenses.

As measured in numbers of persons under investigation, standing trial, or serving sentences, the Act Concerning Assembly and Demonstration continued under Roh, as under the Fifth Republic, to be the law most frequently used to restrict and control nonviolent political expression. The law gave police chiefs, of whom there were twenty-four in Seoul alone, the authority to deny permission, without appeal, for any proposed demonstration. Police also had wide discretion over treatment of participants in illegal demonstrations, determining whether a given participant was to be charged with sponsoring an illegal demonstration, which carried the threat of a seven-year prison term, or with varying degrees of participation, which could be punished as a misdemeanor or even with a simple warning. Police had on occasion taken actions under the law to prevent persons from attending meetings that the police believed were "likely to breed social unrest."

The National Security Act, as amended in 1980, restricted "antistate activities" that endangered "the state or the lives and freedom of the citizenry." However, Seoul used the law not only against espionage or sabotage, but also to control and punish domestic dissent, such as the publication of unorthodox political commentary, art, or literature, on the grounds that such expressions benefited an "antistate organization." In divided Korea, almost any act of opposition to the South Korean government could be and has been characterized as benefiting North Korea. Arrests under the law have been made for a wide variety of actions, including the sale of cassette tapes containing antigovernment songs; the sale, possession, or reading of books and other publications on the government's banned list; or chanting anti-American slogans at a student rally. Ordinary procedural protections of the Code of Criminal Procedure were not provided for defendants for offenses under this law. Any liaison with antistate organizations was also punishable under the law, although in the late 1980s there was considerable debate concerning the government's selectivity in allowing some politicians and businessmen to travel to North Korea or meet with North Korean officials while severely punishing critics of the government who did the same thing. There was a surge in prosecutions for various offenses under the National Security Act in 1989, despite continuing talk of amending the law to facilitate broader contacts with the north. In early 1990, as the third year of Roh's administration began and as the government mulled over plans to sign several international agreements concerning human rights, it was still unclear whether or when the promise of Roh's 1988 inaugural speech, that ''the day when freedoms and human rights could be slighted in the name of economic growth and national security has ended,'' would be redeemed.

The Media

Modern Korean journalism began after the opening of Korea in 1876. The Korean press had a strong reformist and nationalistic flavor from the beginning but faced efforts at political control or outright censorship during most of the twentieth century. Many Korean journalists established a tradition of remaining independent. They were often critical of the government, zealously protesting any attempts at press censorship. At annexation in 1910, the Japanese governor general assumed direct control of the press along with other public institutions. Following the March First Movement in 1919, Japanese authorities loosened their overt control over cultural activities and permitted several Korean newspapers to function while maintaining some behind-the-scenes direction over politically sensitive topics. During the 1920s, Korean vernacular newspapers, such as *Tonga ilbo* (East Asia Daily), and intellectual journals, such as *Kaebyŏk* (Creation), conducted running skirmishes with Japanese censors. Japanese authorities prohibited sales of individual issues on hundreds of occasions between 1926 and 1932. Japan's war mobilization in the ensuing years ended any semblance of autonomy for the Korean press; all Korean-language publications were outlawed in 1941.

Following the period of the United States Army Military Government in Korea (1945-48), which saw a burgeoning of newspapers and periodicals of every description as well as occasional censorship of the media, almost all subsequent South Korean governments have at times attempted to control the media. Syngman Rhee's government continued the military government's Ordinance Number Eighty-Eight, which outlawed leftist newspapers. Rhee also closed moderate newspapers and arrested reporters and publishers on numerous occasions between 1948 and 1960. On taking power in 1961, Park Chung Hee's Supreme Council for National Reconstruction closed all but fifteen of Seoul's sixty-four daily newspapers and refused to register a comparable percentage of the country's news services, weeklies, and monthly publications while using its own radio and news agencies to promote its official line. The Park government also used the Press Ethics Commission Law of 1964 and, after 1972, emergency decrees that penalized criticism of the government to keep the media in line. In 1974 the government ordered a number of journalists fired and used the KCIA to force *Tonga ilbo* to stop its reporting on popular opposition to the Park government by intimidating the paper's advertisers.

During the Park and Chun years, the government exercised considerable control and surveillance over the media through the comprehensive National Security Act. In late 1980, the Chun government established more thorough control of the news media than had existed in South Korea since the Korean War. Independent news agencies were absorbed into a single state-run agency, numerous provincial newspapers were closed, central newspapers were forbidden to station correspondents in provincial cities, the Christian Broadcasting System network was forbidden to provide news coverage, and two independent broadcasting companies were absorbed into the state-run Korean Broadcasting System (KBS). In addition, the Defense Security Command, then commanded by Roh Tae Woo, and the Ministry of Culture and Information ordered hundreds of South Korean journalists fired and banned from newspaper writing or editing.

The Basic Press Act of December 1980 was the legal capstone of Chun's system of media control and provided for censorship and control of newspapers, periodicals, and broadcast media. It also set the professional qualifications for journalists. Media censorship was coordinated with intelligence officials, representatives of various government agencies, and the presidential staff by the Office of Public Information Policy within the Ministry of Culture and Information using daily "reporting guidelines" (*podo chich'im*) sent to newspaper editors. The guidelines dealt exhaustively with questions of emphasis, topics to be covered or avoided, the use of government press releases, and even the size of headlines. Enforcement methods ranged from telephone calls to editors to more serious forms of intimidation, including interrogations and beatings by police. One former Ministry of Culture and Information official told a National Assembly hearing in 1988 that compliance during his tenure from 1980 to 1982 reached about 70 percent.

By the mid-1980s, censorship of print and broadcast media had become one of the most widely and publicly criticized practices of the Chun government. Even the government-controlled Yonhap News Agency noted in 1989 that "TV companies, scarcely worse than other media, were the main target of bitter public criticism for their distorted reporting for the government in the early 1980s." Editorials called for abolition of the Basic Press Act and related practices, a bill was unsuccessfully introduced in the National

Assembly to the same end, and a public campaign to withhold compulsory viewers' fees in protest against censorship by the KBS network received widespread press attention. By the summer of 1986, even the ruling party was responding to public opinion.

The political liberalization of the late 1980s brought a loosening of press restraints and a new generation of journalists more willing to investigate sensitive subjects, such as the May 1980 Kwangju incident. Roh's eight-point declaration of June 29, 1987, provided for ''a free press, including allowing newspapers to base correspondents in provincial cities and withdrawing security officials from newspaper offices.'' The South Korean media began a rapid expansion. Seoul papers expanded their coverage and resumed the practice of stationing correspondents in provincial cities. Although temporarily still under the management of a former Blue House press spokesman, the MBC television network, a commercial network that had been under control of the state-managed KBS since 1980, resumed independent broadcasting. The number of radio broadcast stations grew from 74 in 1985 to 111 (including both AM and FM stations) by late 1988 and to 125 by late 1989. The number of periodicals rose as the government removed restrictions on the publishing industry (see Transportation and Telecommunications, ch. 3; table 15, Appendix).

There also were qualitative changes in the South Korean media. The Christian Broadcasting System, a radio network, again began to broadcast news as well as religious programming in 1987. In the same year, the government partially lifted a long-standing ban on the works of North Korean artists and musicians, many of whom were of South Korean origin. A newspaper run by dissident journalists began publication in 1988. A number of other new dailies also appeared in 1988. Many of the new weekly and monthly periodicals bypassed the higher profits of the traditional general circulation magazines to provide careful analyses of political, economic, and national security affairs to smaller, specialized audiences. Observers noted a dramatic increase in press coverage of previously taboo subjects such as political-military relations, factions within the military, the role of security agencies in politics, and the activities of dissident organizations. Opinion polls dealing with these and other sensitive issues also began to appear with increasing regularity. Journalists at several of the Seoul dailies organized trade unions in late 1987 and early 1988 and began to press for editorial autonomy and a greater role in newspaper management.

In 1989 South Korea's four largest dailies, *Hanguk ilbo, Chungang ilbo, Chosŏn ilbo,* and *Tonga ilbo,* had a combined circulation of more than 6.5 million readers. The antiestablishment *Hangyŏre sim-mun* (One Nation News) had 450,000 readers—less than the major dailies or smaller papers like *Kyŏnghyang simmun* or *Sŏul simmun* but larger than four more specialized economic dailies. All the major dailies were privately owned, except for the government-controlled *Hanguk ilbo*. Several other daily publications had specialized reader-ships among sport fans and youth. Two English-language news-papers, the government-subsidized *Korea Herald* and the *Korea Times*, which was affiliated with the independent *Sŏul simmun*, were widely read by foreign embassies and businesses. A Chinese-language daily served South Korea's small Chinese population (see Population, ch. 2).

The Yonhap News Agency provided domestic and foreign news to government agencies, newspapers, and broadcasters. Yonhap also provided news on South Korean developments in English by computerized transmission via the Asia-Pacific News Network. Ad-ditional links with world media were facilitated by four satellite link stations. The International Broadcast Center established in June 1988 served some 10,000 broadcasters for the 1988 Seoul Olympics. The government's KBS radio network broadcast over-seas in twelve languages. Two private radio networks, the Asia Broadcasting Company and Far East Broadcasting Company, served a wide regional audience that included the Soviet Far East, China, and Japan.

The South Korean government also supported Naewoe Press, which dealt solely with North Korean affairs. Originally a propagan-da vehicle that followed the government line on unification policy issues, Naewoe Press became increasingly objective and moderate in tone in the mid-1980s in interpreting political, social, and eco-nomic developments in North Korea. *Vantage Point,* an English-language publication of Naewoe Press, provided in-depth studies of North Korean social, economic, and political developments.

Except for two newspapers (one in Korean and one in English) that the government owned or controlled and the state television network, ownership of the media was for the most part distinct from political or economic power. One exception was the conservative daily, *Chungang ilbo*. Under the close oversight of its owner, the late Samsung Group founder and multimillionaire Yi Pyŏng-ch'ŏl, the paper and its affiliated TBC television network generally sup-ported the Park government during the 1970s. Its relations with the government became strained after 1980, however, when Chun Doo Hwan forced TBC to merge with KBS. A journalists' strike at *Chungang ilbo* in 1989, in one of many similar incidents at the major South Korean newspapers, won even greater management and editorial independence.

Most of South Korea's major newspapers derived their financial support from advertising and from their affiliation with major publishing houses. The Tonga Press, for example, published not only the prestigious daily *Tonga ilbo,* but also a variety of other periodicals, including a newspaper for children, the general circulation monthly *Sin tonga* (New East Asia), a women's magazine, and specialized reference books and magazines for students. Throughout the postwar period, *Tonga ilbo* has been noted for its opposition sympathies.

South Korea's principal antiestablishment newspaper, *Hangyŏre simmun,* began publication in May 1988. It was founded by dissident journalists who were purged by the government in the early 1970s or in 1980; many of the paper's reporters and editorial staff left positions on mainstream newspapers to join the new venture. The structure and approach of the paper reflected the founders' view that in the past the South Korean news media had been too easily co-opted by the government. The paper had a human rights department as well as a mass media department to keep an eye on the government's press policy and to critique the ideological and political biases of other newspapers. The paper's nationalism and interest in national reunification were symbolically represented in the logo, which depicted Lake Ch'ŏnji at the peak of Mount Paektu in North Korea; in the exclusive use of the Korean alphabet; and by the type font in which the paper's name was printed—the font dated from a famous Korean publication of the eighteenth century. The paper was printed horizontally, rather than vertically like other Seoul dailies. In other innovations, the *Hangyŏre simmun* relied on sales revenues, private contributions, and the sale of stock, rather than on advertising from major corporations, in line with its claim to be "the first newspaper in the world truly independent of political power and large capital." The newspaper came under increasing government pressure in 1989 (see Political Dynamics, this ch.).

South Korea also had extensive and well-developed visual media. The first Korean film was produced in 1919, and cinemas subsequently were built in the larger cities. The result of the spread of television sets and radios was the dissemination of a homogenized popular culture and the impingement of urban values on rural communities.

Foreign Policy

Organization and Operation

The Constitution of the Sixth Republic vests the conduct of foreign affairs in the presidency and the State Council, subject to the approval of the National Assembly. The president and the State Council, through the prime minister and the minister of foreign affairs, make periodic reports on foreign relations to the legislature. The president receives or dispatches envoys without legislative confirmation; treaties, however, must receive legislative consent. Declarations of war, the dispatch of troops overseas, and the stationing of foreign troops within the national borders also are subject to legislative approval (Article 60 of the Constitution). The National Assembly has a standing Foreign Affairs Committee that reports its deliberations to plenary sessions of the assembly. The assembly may also establish ad hoc committees to consider questions of special importance to the state.

Constitutionally, major foreign policy objectives are established by the president. The chief foreign policy advisers in the State Council are the prime minister, who heads the cabinet, and the minister of foreign affairs. From time to time, these officials may be questioned by the National Assembly; the Assembly may pass a recommendation for the removal from office of the prime minister or a State Council member (Article 63). The president is assisted by the National Security Council in the formulation and execution of foreign, military, and domestic policies related to national security prior to their deliberation by the State Council (Article 91). The Agency for National Security Planning, its mission akin to that of a combined United States Central Intelligence Agency and Federal Bureau of Investigation, has direct access to the president and operates at his personal direction in the overall conduct of foreign policy (see The Agency for National Security Planning, ch. 5).

Diplomatic missions abroad conduct foreign policy. The Ministry of Foreign Affairs was established with functional and area divisions. The foreign ministry staff consists of civil service members and a highly professionalized career foreign service corps, selected on the basis of at least a college education and performance in a highly competitive examination supervised by the Ministry of Government Administration. Regarded as prestigious social positions, diplomatic posts attract ambitious and bright individuals who undergo an intensive training program conducted by the Foreign Affairs Research Institute. The institute in the late 1980s had a very rigorous curriculum in international diplomacy, specialized area training, and intensive language training.

Basic Goals and Accomplishments

The external posture of South Korea in general, and toward North Korea in particular, began a new chapter in the 1980s. While

251

retaining its previous goal—enhancing political legitimacy, military security, and economic development by maintaining close ties with the West—South Korea greatly expanded its diplomatic horizons by launching its ambitious *pukpang chŏngch'aek* (see Glossary), northern policy, or Nordpolitik. Nordpolitik was Seoul's version of the Federal Republic of Germany's (West Germany) Ostpolitik of the early 1970s. Although the policy's origins can be traced back to 1973 under Park, it was greatly invigorated by Roh.

Seoul's Nordpolitik was designed for a number of rather ambitious but initially ill-defined objectives. Seoul's basic dilemma in its Nordpolitik appeared to be how to reconcile its traditional ties with the West with its new opportunities in the East. First, policymakers felt that their economic and military reliance on the West was excessive, mendicant, and too lengthy. Seoul sought to correct this situation by establishing its own self-reliant global posture. This desire to be less dependent became particularly acute as Seoul's Western allies greatly improved relations with Eastern Europe, the Soviet Union, and China.

Second, Nordpolitik was designed to expand and diversify trade relations on a global scale to cope with increasing trade protectionism from the United States. Intentionally or not, the policy aroused anti-Americanism. Ironically enough, the rising anti-United States feeling was accompanied by increasing demands for economic and political democracy, culminating in the Kwangju incident in May 1980.

Finally, Nordpolitik involved the pursuit of wide-ranging relations with socialist countries and contacts and dialogue with North Korea. It had often been observed that political leaders in P'yŏngyang and Seoul utilized their confrontational postures to sustain their political legitimacy. Claiming that P'yŏngyang's response had been far from satisfactory, Seoul's policymakers solicited assistance and cooperation from P'yŏngyang's socialist allies to induce and persuade P'yŏngyang to become more accommodating. Yet Seoul's success in improving relations with P'yŏngyang's socialist allies had not resulted in substantially improved relations with P'yŏngyang by 1990. In fact, for the short term, Seoul even might have lessened its chances for improved relations with P'yŏngyang by having improved its relations with North Korea's socialist allies and by raising the question of whether Nordpolitik was primarily designed to confront and compete with P'yŏngyang. Thus far, Nordpolitik clearly demonstrated the limited power of P'yŏngyang's socialist allies, particularly Moscow and Beijing, vis-à-vis the extremely self-reliant North Korea. In reality, Seoul may have grossly underestimated P'yŏngyang's firmly established independence.

*Twenty-two-story combined government and ministerial building, Seoul
Courtesy Korean Overseas Information Service*

On the whole, however, Nordpolitik was successful, and Seoul's accomplishments could be readily observed in sports, trade, and diplomacy. The 1988 Seoul Olympics was a major catalyst for Nordpolitik. It was the first Olympic Games in twelve years not marred by a bloc-level boycott and had the highest participation ever—159 nations and more than 9,000 athletes. Seoul gained new global recognition and visibility as more than 3 billion people around the world watched the games being televised live.

Had it not been for the North Korean bombing of KAL 858 over the Andaman Sea in November 1987, Seoul might have been more willing to reach out to P'yŏngyang. While the much-feared and predicted North Korean misbehavior over South Korea's staging of the Olympics did not materialize, Seoul probably was relieved by P'yŏngyang's absence from the games.

Seoul's international trade record has been impressive (see Foreign Economic Relations, ch. 3). While encountering, along with other newly industrialized nations, mounting trade friction with the United States and other major markets, Seoul emerged in the late 1980s as the world's tenth-largest trading nation. Economic reforms and the open-door policies of socialist countries, coupled with their recognition of Seoul's economic growth, pushed economic trade and cooperation between South Korea and socialist countries into full swing.

Perhaps Seoul's most impressive success was in diplomacy. Literally implementing the 1988 Olympics slogan, "From Seoul to the World, and from the World to Seoul," by the beginning of 1990 South Korea had established diplomatic relations with 133 countries and had 138 diplomatic missions, including representative offices and a consulate department in Moscow. Conversely, North Korea had diplomatic relations with 102 countries and 85 overseas missions. An impressive number of young South Korean diplomats were trained in the West and actively implemented Nordpolitik. These diplomats were also supported by the aggressive worldwide market diversification programs of South Korea's big business establishments, the *chaebŏl*, and by an increasingly large number of overseas South Koreans, many of whom become salespersons of South Korean products (see The Origins and Development of Chaebŏl, ch. 3).

After Roh's inauguration in February 1988, Nordpolitik was particularly invigorated. In a July 7, 1988, statement primarily aimed at insuring the success of the Olympics, Roh unveiled a six-point plan to ease forty years of bitter confrontation between Seoul and P'yŏngyang and to clear the way for peaceful unification of the divided peninsula. In the afterglow of the Olympics, Roh made his diplomatic debut as the first South Korean president to address the United Nations (UN) General Assembly, on October 18, 1988. Roh's speech called for a six-nation consultative conference to discuss a broad range of issues concerning peace, stability, progress, and prosperity in Northeast Asia. Pledging unilaterally never to use force first against North Korea, Roh proposed to replace the existing 1953 armistice agreement with a peace treaty.

Relations with the United States

South Korea's relations with the United States have been most extensive and intense since 1948. This relation was perhaps inevitable because South Korea was primarily established by the United States and was saved from a total collapse in the course of the Korean War (1950–53) by the United States-initiated, United Nations-sponsored rescue operation. During the subsequent four decades, however, Seoul came of age economically, politically, and even militarily and was no longer as economically or militarily dependent on the United States. Instead, by the 1990s it was seeking to establish a partnership for progress. The Seoul-Washington relationship in this transition was increasingly subject to severe strains.

Trade had become a serious source of friction between the two countries. In 1989 the United States was South Korea's largest and most important trading partner, and South Korea was the seventh-largest market for United States goods and the second-largest market for its agricultural products. Friction, however, had been caused in the late 1980s by South Korea's trade surplus. Correcting and eliminating this trade imbalance became the center of economic controversy between Seoul and Washington. Although Seoul gave in to Washington's demands to avoid being designated as a "priority foreign country" (PFC) under the United States "Super 301" provisions of the Omnibus Trade and Competitiveness Act of 1988, economic policymakers in Seoul greatly resented this unilateral economic threat. They also feared that the PFC designation would fuel anti-Americanism throughout South Korea.

Security was another source of strain. Some policymakers in Seoul and Washington maintained that United States forces should remain in South Korea as long as Seoul wanted and needed them. Not only did 94 percent of South Koreans support the presence of United States forces, but even the vocal opposition parties favored a continued United States military presence in South Korea. Stability in the peninsula, they argued, had been maintained because strong Seoul-Washington military cooperation had deterred further aggression.

Other policymakers, however, felt that United States troops should gradually be leaving South Korea. They argued that South Korea in the late 1980s was more economically, militarily, and politically capable of coping with North Korea. Moreover, they doubted that P'yŏngyang could contemplate another military action, given its acrimonious relationships with Moscow and Beijing. In Washington, meanwhile, an increasing number of United States policymakers advocated gradual troop withdrawal for budgetary reasons. The consultations on restructuring the Washington-Seoul security relationship held during Secretary of Defense Richard B. Cheney's February 1990 visit to South Korea marked the beginning of the change in status of United States forces—from a leading to a supporting role in South Korea's defense. In addition, Seoul was asked to increase substantially its contribution to defense costs. Although the precise amount of savings would be difficult to measure, the United States would likely save at least US$2 billion to US$3 billion annually if defense costs were restructured as the United States wished. Furthermore, disengagement would avoid the potential for American entanglement in complicated internal South Korean politics. In short, it was suggested that it was time for Seoul to be treated as an independent entity responsible for its own security.

Politics also strained relations between Seoul and Washington. An increasingly sensitive South Korean nationalism was faced with what Seoul viewed as a hardened Washington. The United States role in the May 1980 Kwangju uprising was the single most pressing South Korean political issue of the 1980s. Even after a decade, Kwangju citizens and other Koreans still blamed the United States for its perceived involvement in the bloody uprising.

Washington's policymakers applauded Nordpolitik as a necessary adjustment of the relationship between Seoul and Moscow. However, the South Korean press contributed to a distorted zero-sum notion of the situation, suggesting that improving ties with the Soviet Union would cause strains in the relationship with the United States. In his February 1989 speech to the South Korean National Assembly, President George Bush defined continuity and change as the guideposts in Seoul-Washington relations.

Relations with the Soviet Union

Seoul-Moscow relations entered a new era in the 1980s. In many ways, Roh's Nordpolitik and Mikhail Gorbachev's ''New Thinking'' had something in common—they were attempts to reverse their nations' recent histories. Their efforts, while supported by popular longings, still confronted serious resistance from conservative and powerful bureaucracies. In a fundamental sense, the

Soviet economic crisis appeared responsible for Moscow's improved relations with Seoul. Politically, Gorbachev had signaled Soviet interest in improving relations with all countries in the Asia-Pacific region irrespective of sociopolitical system, including South Korea, as was clearly spelled out in his July 1986 Vladivostok and August 1988 Krasnoyarsk speeches.

Improved Seoul-Moscow relations appear to have been carefully and systematically planned in three related stages: sports, trade, and political relations. The Seoul Olympics was a major catalyst. The Soviets were eager to participate in the games, if only for the sake of the athletic competition. Seoul's most honored guests were from the Soviet Union. Moscow sent more than 6,000 Soviets to South Korea. Soviet tourist ships came to Pusan and Inch'ŏn, and Aeroflot planes landed in Seoul. And when the Soviet team headed for home, it also took along thirty-six South Korean television sets, seven minibuses, four large buses, four cars, and one copy machine—all gifts from Daewoo.

Economically, Seoul and Moscow were natural partners. South Korea had been seeking to trade with the Soviet Union even before Gorbachev came to power. Gorbachev desired foreign capital and high technology, as well as Seoul's help in alleviating the Soviet economic crisis through direct investment, joint ventures, and trade. Moreover, with the advantage of geographic proximity, South Korea was an ideal source of badly needed consumer goods and managerial skills. As early as May 1979, during a visit to Helsinki, then South Korean minister of foreign affairs Pak Tong-jin signed an agreement obtaining Finnish assistance in exporting South Korean products to the Soviet Union and Eastern Europe. Seoul has welcomed trade opportunities with Moscow and considers the Soviet Union a significant part of the global market. Moreover, the natural resources Seoul increasingly needs—oil, metals, timber, and fish—are abundant in the Soviet Far East. Trade with the Soviet Union, Eastern Europe, and China would also alleviate South Korea's apprehension over the United States' increasing trade protectionism. Moreover, South Korea's expanding trade with Eastern Europe and the Soviet Union initially was encouraged by the United States, although Washington later became increasingly concerned over possible high-technology transfers.

Because of the lack of diplomatic relations, most South Korean-Soviet trade initially was indirect; Eastern Europe, Hong Kong, Japan, and Singapore served as intermediaries. With an increasing volume of trade, Seoul and Moscow began trading directly, using facilities near Vladivostok and Pusan. Several major South Korean businesses, including Daewoo, Sunkyong, and Lucky-Goldstar, traded directly with the Soviet Union in 1990.

Based on mutual economic interests, the Korean Trade Promotion Corporation (KOTRA) and the Soviet Chamber of Commerce and Industry exchanged a trade memorandum in 1988 pledging mutual assistance in establishing trade offices in 1989. During a six-day visit to Seoul in October 1988, Vladimir Golanov, deputy chairman of the Soviet Chamber of Commerce and Industry, was received by officials of South Korea's major multinationals. KOTRA president Yi Sun-gi signed the trade memorandum in Moscow in December 1988. Seoul's trade office in Moscow opened in July 1989; Moscow's trade office in Seoul opened in April 1989. In December 1989, Seoul invited Soviet officials to attend a trade exhibition where members of the Soviet state-run Tekhsnabeksport displayed impressive high-technology items.

Political relations were developing gradually. South Korea's newfound wealth and technological prowess had been attracting the interest of a growing number of socialist nations. In initiating Nordpolitik, its chief architect Pak Ch'ŏr-ŏn—Roh's confidential foreign policy adviser—was rumored to have visited Moscow to consult with Soviet policymakers. Kim Young Sam visited Moscow from June 2 to June 10, 1989, with the apparent approval of the Roh administration. Selected from among several other South Korean politicians (including Kim Dae Jung, who had reportedly been invited to Moscow) to make certain that the newly emerging Seoul-Moscow relationship would proceed steadily, Kim Young Sam was received as a guest of the Soviet Institute of World Economy and International Relations (IMEMO). He participated in talks with various Soviet officials, including the newly elected chairman of the Supreme Soviet, academician Yevgeni Primakov. In a joint statement, the Reunification Democratic Party (RDP) and IMEMO pledged to promote closer trade and cultural ties between the two nations. While Kim Young Sam was in Moscow, the Kremlin announced that it would allow some 300,000 Soviet-Koreans who had been on the Soviet island of Sahkalin since the end of World War II to return permanently to South Korea—clearly a reflection of the continuing improvement in Seoul-Moscow relations.

Moscow even arranged a Seoul-P'yŏngyang meeting. During the meeting, which was planned by IMEMO, Kim Young Sam, with Roh's prior approval, met with the North Korean ambassador to the Soviet Union, Kwŏn Hŭi-gyŏng, who reportedly proposed a regular exchange between the RDP and the Korean Workers' Party (KWP), as well as a North-South summit meeting. Kim also met with Ho Tam, chairman of the Committee for Peaceful

Reunification of the Fatherland (CPRF), who came to Moscow from P'yŏngyang.

The progress in Seoul-Moscow relations was extraordinary. Given the complementary and parallel interests between Seoul and Moscow, their relations were likely to proceed even if there were temporary setbacks. A highly experienced South Korean diplomat, Kong No-myŏng, was assigned to the Moscow consulate; an equally experienced Soviet diplomat was posted to Seoul. In June 1990, Roh held his first summit with President Mikhail S. Gorbachev in San Francisco. Moscow's "Seoul Rush" may be regarded as an effort to reconcile (and possibly to terminate) its past political-military obligations to P'yŏngyang with the new economic and strategic opportunities in Seoul. Seoul's "Moscow Rush" had been conceived primarily as a way to utilize its growing economic power for political purposes, particularly in its relations with P'yŏngyang. On the other hand, if indeed the final destination of Nordpolitik was P'yŏngyang, Seoul had thus far proved to be less successful than Moscow.

Relations with Japan

Korea is geographically close, yet emotionally distant from Japan. Given the historical relationship between the two countries, the paradoxical nature of their relation is readily understandable. Since normalizing relations in 1965 at the urging of the United States, Seoul and Tokyo have held annual foreign ministerial conferences. The usual issues discussed have been trade, the status of the Korean minority population in Japan, the content of textbooks dealing with the relationship, Tokyo's equidistant policy between P'yŏngyang and Seoul, and the occasional problems (see Foreign Policy, ch. 1).

At the first of three ministerial conferences held in 1987 (in Seoul, New York, and Geneva, respectively), the two countries' foreign ministers discussed pending issues, including Seoul's trade deficit with Tokyo. The Japanese minister of foreign affairs pledged to assist Seoul in its role as host of the Olympics. Seoul and Tokyo signed a bilateral agreement on sea rescue and emergency cooperation.

The 1988 foreign ministerial conference was held in Tokyo. There the two countries agreed to expand exchanges of youths, students, and teachers and to establish the twenty-first century committee between the two nations, as well as a joint security consultative committee for the Seoul Olympics.

Roh's Nordpolitik somewhat relaxed Seoul's vehement opposition to Tokyo's approach to P'yŏngyang. The Japan Socialist Party, in particular, has become active in improving relations not only between P'yŏngyang and Tokyo, but also between itself and Seoul.

As the Japan Socialist Party has abandoned its posture favoring P'yŏngyang, Seoul has welcomed the new equidistant policy, inviting a former secretary general of the Japan Socialist Party, Ishibashi Masashi, to Seoul in October 1988. Ishibashi's visit was unusually productive, not only in improving his party's image in Seoul, but also in his reported willingness to mediate between Seoul and P'yŏngyang. Although Tokyo appeared willing to assist Seoul in improving relations not only with P'yŏngyang but also with Beijing, it did not seem to welcome the much-improved Seoul-Moscow relationship. Further, Seoul-Tokyo relations became somewhat strained when in 1989 Tokyo began steps to improve relations with P'yŏngyang.

Relations with China

Nordpolitik has been viewed as less attractive in Beijing than in Moscow. Beijing's needs for Seoul in the 1980s were hardly matched with those of Moscow, particularly in economic terms. Still, because of complementary economic needs and geographic proximity, South Korea and China began to trade actively. The absence of any official relations, however, made it difficult to expand trade between Seoul and Beijing because South Korea could not legally protect its citizens and business interests in China.

Beijing, in comparison with Moscow, has been politically closer to P'yŏngyang, a situation that has slowed political improvements between Beijing and Seoul despite the increasing volume of trade between the two countries. Furthermore, China has attempted to mediate between North Korea and the United States and North Korea and Japan and also has initiated and promoted tripartite talks among P'yŏngyang, Seoul, and Washington.

Active South Korean-Chinese people-to-people contacts have been encouraged. Academics, journalists, and particularly families divided between South Korea and China were able to exchange visits freely in the late 1980s. Nearly 2 million ethnic Koreans, especially in the Yanbian Korean Autonomous Prefecture in China's Jilin Province, have interacted with South Koreans.

It has been difficult to determine what effect the political turmoil in China will have on Sino-Korean relations. After the military crackdown on demonstrators in Beijing in June 1989, P'yŏngyang predictably came out in support of Beijing's repressive actions. Seoul, on the other hand, produced a more muted response that did not condone the actions in Tiananmen Square but did not condemn them either. Trade between the two countries continued to increase.

Relations with North Korea

Nordpolitik's final destination—P'yŏngyang—has proved difficult to reach. After nearly two decades, inter-Korean relations had not improved measurably. In fact, it may be argued that political leaders in Seoul and P'yŏngyang have skillfully used the perceived mutual threat to maintain and justify their political legitimacy. Their postures may seem reasonable, given that until the precarious 1953 armistice agreement is replaced by a permanent peace treaty, the Korean War cannot be considered completely over. Nevertheless, Seoul and P'yŏngyang have been increasing their contacts across and around the Demilitarized Zone (DMZ) in a gradual and uneven fashion. These expanding contacts appear quite natural because there are an estimated 10 million separated family members. Moreover, South Korean business leaders have been keenly aware of potential economic benefits in improved relations with North Korea. Inasmuch as inter-Korean contacts are gradually becoming a "growth industry," their prospects appear promising.

Inter-Korean relations may be divided into four periods. The first stage covered the period between 1972 and 1973; the second stage was initiated by P'yŏngyang's delivery of relief goods to South Korea after a typhoon caused devastating floods in 1984; and the third stage began with the exchange of home visits and performing artists in 1985. The fourth stage, activated by Nordpolitik under Roh, was represented by expanding public and private contacts between the two Koreas. These working-level contacts have included Red Cross talks aimed at exchanging home visits by divided families and performing artists; sports talks aimed at establishing a unified team for the 1990 Beijing Asian Games; economic trade at the level of premiers; preliminary talks for joint parliamentary meetings; and expanded academic and religious exchanges.

The Nordpolitik blueprint—Roh's declaration of July 7, 1988—opened a new chapter in inter-Korean dialogue. Calling for the building of a single "national commonwealth," Roh solicited the assistance of Washington and Tokyo to improve Seoul's relations with Moscow and Beijing. At the same time, he encouraged Washington and Tokyo to improve relations with P'yŏngyang and to expand inter-Korean exchanges. Roh urged a positive response from P'yŏngyang; North Korea's reaction, however, was not positive.

P'yŏngyang issued an immediate and detailed statement on July 11, 1988. The CPRF dismissed Roh's proposal as old wine in a new bottle, claiming that only the 1972 three basic principles for Korean reunification—reunification by peaceful means, by transcending ideological differences (nationalism), and without external

261

interference (self-determination)—could be the basis to improve inter-Korean dialogue. Seen from P'yŏngyang's perspective, Roh's July 7 proposal was nothing more than a political ploy to cope with increasing radical student agitation that opposed Seoul's hosting of the Olympics without P'yŏngyang's participation. Consequently, Roh's statement angered rather than mollified P'yŏngyang's posture, which was based on Kim Il Sung's proposal to establish a Democratic Confederal Republic of Korea.

Meanwhile, Seoul began to speak more openly about the rising level of direct and indirect inter-Korean trade, much to the displeasure of P'yŏngyang. P'yŏngyang claimed that Seoul had fabricated these trade stories. By 1988, however, Seoul began to reduce tariffs and other duties to liberalize trade with P'yŏngyang. Trade statistics provided by Seoul and P'yŏngyang on north-south trade were largely unreliable inasmuch as each government had its own reasons for reporting high or low figures. Much of the trade was conducted through third parties.

P'yŏngyang's response to Seoul consisted of three points: asking for the repeal of the National Security Act, which designated P'yŏngyang an enemy; making a declaration of nonaggression; and establishing a ''Peaceful Reunification Committee.'' Over the next few months, Roh's government attempted to make progress toward satisfying each of these requirements. In his October 18, 1988, United Nations speech, Roh advocated convening a six-nation consultative conference to achieve a permanent peace settlement in Korea and called for establishing a partnership with P'yŏngyang. In his 1989 New Year's address, Kim Il Sung extended an invitation to the presidents of the major South Korean political parties and religious leaders, including Cardinal Kim Soo Hwan, Reverend Mun Ik-hwan, and Reverend Paek Ki-wan, for a leadership-level inter-Korean reunification meeting to be held in P'yŏngyang. However, any meaningful inter-Korean dialogue bogged down at P'yŏngyang's objections to the annual United States-South Korean Team Spirit military exercises.

Economic relations have demonstrated more promise. An authorized public visit to North Korea by Chŏng Chu-yŏng, honorary chairman of the Hyundai Group, in early 1989 (in technical violation of South Korea's National Security Act) was a remarkable breakthrough. After years of behind-the-scene efforts, Chŏng, through a South Korean intermediary in Japan, was invited by P'yŏngyang and fulfilled his long-cherished dream of seeing his relatives at his native village, near scenic Kŭmgang-san. Chŏng was received in P'yŏngyang by Hŏ Tam, Chairman of the Committee for the Peaceful Reunification of the Fatherland, and by

President Roh Tae Woo
Courtesy Embassy of the
Republic of Korea, Washington

business leaders eager to discuss large-scale economic cooperation, such as joint ventures and development of the tourist industry. Chŏng's visit caused euphoric expectations and also engendered other visits.

Many of Chŏng's expected business dealings, however, suffered temporary setbacks after his return to South Korea. These setbacks were primarily caused by the unauthorized visits to North Korea of Reverend Mun Ik-hwan (March–April 1989), South Korean lawmaker Sŏ Kyŏng-wŏn (who had secretly visited P'yŏngyang in August 1988, had been accused of the visit in June 28, 1989, and had been sentenced in December 1989 to fifteen years in prison), and dissident South Korean student representative, Im Su-kyŏng (who had attended the thirteenth World Youth and Student Festival, July 1–8, 1989, in P'yŏngyang and later had been sentenced to a prison term). The government's harsh handling of these visits clearly showed that it intended to keep the initiative in dealings with North Korea, but the action also appeared to some Koreans to contradict Roh's July 7 statement encouraging free inter-Korean contacts at various levels. That Roh's statement itself seemed to disregard the National Security Act added momentum to dissident calls for the law's abrogation or revision.

Relations with International Organizations and the Third World

South Korea has been very active in the United Nations (UN)

even though, as of 1990, it was not a member. Seoul has taken a vigorous part in the activities of various subsidiary and specialized UN agencies, as well as other international organizations, and has had active permanent missions to the UN, the UN Economic and Social Council and its Economic and Social Commission for Asia and the Pacific, and the European Community. An increasing number of UN Security Council members, including the Soviet Union, tended to consider seriously Seoul's bid for separate entry into the UN. This move was vehemently opposed by North Korea, which claimed that such a recognition would make the division of Korea permanent.

Seoul's activities in the Pacific Economic Cooperation Conference (PECC) were particularly noteworthy. As a founding member of the PECC, South Korea played a key role in liberalizing trade networks throughout the entire Pacific region. The South Korean national committee of the PECC represented academic, business, and government interests. The national committee was extremely useful not only in formulating Seoul's trade policies, but also in communicating these policies to other members' national committees and in successfully negotiating mutually advantageous trade agreements.

Equally impressive has been Seoul's diplomacy toward the developing world. Being a developing nation itself, South Korea has identified with other developing nations. For this reason, and in apparent competition with P'yŏngyang, Seoul has been actively seeking to improve relations, particularly with nonaligned nations, based on the principles of good neighborliness, reciprocity, and equality. As of January 1990, Seoul had full diplomatic relations with seventy-eight members of the Nonaligned Movement, including Yugoslavia and Algeria. To promote economic assistance and expand trade, Seoul established the Economic Development Cooperation Fund in 1987. South Korea signed three loan agreements: US$13 million for a road construction project in Indonesia, US$10 million for modernization of fishing vessels in Peru, and US$10 million for railway projects in Nigeria. To promote better relations with developing countries on the basis of south-south cooperation, Roh made state visits to Malaysia, Indonesia, and Brunei in November 1988.

Future Prospects

Seoul became more globally conscious in the 1980s. South Korean contacts with foreigners have been largely a post-Korean War phenomenon. Indeed, Seoul's expanding foreign business contacts have been greatly stimulated by the fierce rivalry with North Korea. Seoul's basic goals are still to enhance political legitimacy, military security, and economic development vis-à-vis P'yŏngyang. After the

1988 Seoul Olympics, however, South Korea's diplomatic horizon was greatly expanded because of Roh's Nordpolitik, which had successfully transformed South Korea's sports industry, economic relations, and diplomacy (although its success with P'yŏngyang was limited).

Lacking a reconciliation with North Korea—the final destination of Nordpolitik—Roh's remarkable accomplishments will remain incomplete. In his 1990 New Year policy statement, Roh observed that "the East European wave of reform toward freedom and prosperity is bound to teach North Korea before long." He added that he hoped that "similar change will take place in the North in an orderly and peaceful fashion." Roh pledged "[a]ll-out efforts . . . to convince North Korea . . . that it should join the trend of world history and open up."

* * *

A number of introductory books on South Korean domestic politics and foreign relations are available in English. Ki-baik Lee's *A New History of Korea* is a Korean scholar's perspective on Korean political history, valuable chiefly for its examination of the period before 1945. Ramon H. Myers and Mark Peattie's *The Japanese Colonial Empire, 1895-1945* sheds light on the colonial roots of subsequent South Korean political cultural and behavior. Young Whan Kihl's *Politics and Policies in Divided Korea* compares political leadership and styles in the two Koreas, while Ralph N. Clough's *Embattled Korea* is a thorough and cogent treatment of diplomacy and extradiplomatic foreign policies as seen through the prism of rivalry between the two Koreas. Dae-Kyu Yoon's *Law and Political Authority in Korea* is an excellent and detailed study of the interaction between law and politics in the Republic of Korea.

A number of useful articles on South Korean foreign relations and the United States-Korean relationship are contained in Robert A. Scalapino's and Hongkoo Lee's *Korea-U.S. Relations*. Donald Stone Macdonald's *The Koreans*, although not limited to politics, is a useful survey. David I. Steinberg's *The Republic of Korea* contains many insightful observations on South Korean politics. Kim Dae Jung is the only major political figure to have his views published extensively in English. *Mass Participatory Economy* gives his views on South Korean political economy as of the mid-1980s; *Prison Writings* presents his thoughts on South Korean political culture and other subjects. *Human Rights in Korea*, edited by William Shaw, contains several chapters on postwar South Korean political and human rights issues. The United States Department of State's June

1989 "United States Government Statement on the Events in Kwangju, Republic of Korea, in May 1980" also is a valuable document.

Following the abolition of the Basic Press Act in 1988, the South Korean media became a rich source of both factual and interpretive material on politics and government. *Korea Newsreview,* based on coverage of the government-owned *Korea Herald* newspaper, presents weekly articles concerning politics and foreign affairs, generally from a progovernment point of view; beginning in 1987, the publication has also printed the writings of dissenting guest columnists. The full spectrum of Seoul's Korean-language news media coverage on political topics is sampled and translated in the Foreign Broadcast Information Service's *Daily Report: East Asia.* The United States Embassy in Seoul publishes its *Press Translations: Korea* six days each week.

Outside political analysis may be found in monthly periodicals, including *Asian Survey* and *The Journal of Northeast Asian Studies.* The monthly *Korea Update* contains news and commentary on politics and human rights issues. Perceptive accounts of the political scene are found in *Far Eastern Economic Review* and *Asian Wall Street Journal,* as well in major United States dailies such as the *Washington Post, New York Times,* and *Christian Science Monitor.*

Among annual publications are *Korea Annual,* published by the state-sponsored Yonhap News Agency, and the *Asia Yearbook,* published by the *Far Eastern Economic Review.* Amnesty International's *Report on Human Rights* contains a chapter on South Korea in each annual edition, as does the Department of State's *Country Reports on Human Rights Practices.* (For further information and complete citations, see Bibliography.)

Chapter 5. National Security

Signal Fire Tower, Suwŏn Castle, sited with a view of the royal villa. The tower offered an important means of communication.

DURING SOUTH KOREA'S Fifth Republic (1981–87), the modernization of the armed forces was one of the highest priorities of Chun Doo Hwan's administration. As a result, when Chun's term in office ended, he left behind one of the best-equipped military forces in Asia. Army units had been reorganized and equipped with indigenously produced weapons. The improvement of defense fortifications and supply systems along the southern side of the Demilitarized Zone (DMZ) ensured that ground forces were better prepared to defend South Korea than at any time since the end of the Korean War (1950–53). An automated air defense system, jointly managed by the army and air force, reduced the possibility that South Korea would be caught unprepared in the event of a surprise attack. As a by-product of rapid industrialization and coproduction agreements with United States and West European firms, South Korean aircraft producers and shipbuilders were able to supply most of the country's needs for modern fighter aircraft, helicopters, coastal patrol vessels, and other equipment required by the air force and navy.

A tenuous peace held throughout the 1980s on the Korean Peninsula—tenuous because the government of the Democratic People's Republic of Korea (North Korea) in P'yŏngyang continued to expand its armed forces and to deploy two-thirds of all military units—army, navy, and air force—in a combat-ready status close to the DMZ. Moreover, North Korean-directed terrorist activity against South Korea threatened to provoke a renewal of hostilities. In 1980 P'yŏngyang and Seoul each had about 600,000 military personnel on active duty. From 1980 to 1985, the North Korean armed forces increased by 150,000 people, whereas the South Korean armed forces expanded modestly by about 5,000 people. In 1990 North Korea's armed forces had 1.4 million military personnel on active duty. South Korea's armed forces had 650,000 persons on active duty and another 1,240,000 persons in the reserves.

Under Chun's leadership, Seoul cautiously promoted a peaceful dialogue with North Korea and encouraged the expansion of north-south contacts in the early 1980s; P'yŏngyang remained uninterested in these overtures and on at least two occasions perpetrated terrorist attacks that increased tension on the Korean Peninsula. The primary purpose of South Korean peace proposals in 1981 and 1982 was to realize a summit meeting between Chun and North

Korean president Kim Il Sung. South Korean leaders hoped that the establishment of a government-to-government dialogue would lead to agreements reducing the size of the armed forces of both countries and establishing the framework for a peace plan to replace the 1953 armistice.

In October 1983, a P'yŏngyang-directed terrorist attack resulted in the cessation of the peace process. A bomb that exploded in Rangoon, Burma, killed twenty-one people, including seventeen high-ranking officials of the South Korean government then visiting Burma. The bombing was planned and executed by personnel drawn from North Korean army units. Chun's decision not to retaliate with force set a precedent that won him praise from abroad and sympathy for his unpopular regime at home. Seoul's reliance on diplomatic and economic measures to counter terrorism rather than a small-scale attack on a North Korean target, which could be used as an excuse for beginning an all-out war, effectively mobilized international public opinion to limit trade and other contacts with North Korea.

Another terrorist attack occurred in September 1987 when two North Korean saboteurs placed a bomb on a Seoul-bound Korean Air Boeing 707 aircraft carrying ninety-five passengers and twenty crew members. The plane exploded over the Andaman Sea (south of Burma), killing all aboard. Chun, following the precedent set in 1983 after the Rangoon bombing, ruled out military retaliation and asked the international community to condemn North Korea for its continued belligerence.

South Korea also experienced an increase in politically motivated domestic violence during the 1980s. For the first time, a small, vocal segment of the population persistently challenged former and current military leaders, including Chun, to stay out of politics. The 1980 Kwangju rebellion was used by disenfranchised politicians and disillusioned radical students as a rallying cry. Moderates were encouraged to pressure Chun to change the constitution and public security laws to guarantee that soldiers, police, and the intelligence services would never again be turned against the people. Seoul's claims that the radical student organizations were fronts for North Korea gradually lost credibility, particularly in 1985, when student participation in the political process contributed to the high proportion of votes cast for the New Korea Democratic Party in that year's parliamentary elections. Public indignation concerning increasingly brutal attacks on dissidents by police became a major political issue in January 1987 when Pak Chong-ch'ŏl, a Seoul National University student, was tortured and subsequently died while in police custody. From March through June 1987, combat police units of the Korean National Police responsible for crowd control were constantly on the move as antigovernment demonstrations, sometimes including tens of thousands of ordinary citizens, became everyday occurrences in Seoul, Pusan, Kwangju, and other cities.

After the inauguration of Roh Tae Woo as president in February 1988, attention once again reverted to North Korea as the foremost threat to security. Roh made good his promise to ensure the safety of athletes and spectators from around the world who came to Seoul for the 1988 Seoul Olympics. Japan and the United States provided direct security assistance during this period, the former by closely monitoring the thousands of airline flights and visitors passing through Tokyo and other Japanese cities en route to the event, the latter by deploying additional air, naval, and security units in and around South Korea before and during the Olympics. Following the Olympics, Roh relaxed restrictions on South Korean contacts with North Koreans, gave in to increasing demands for social spending, and acknowledged growing skepticism about the threat from P'yŏngyang, all of which resulted in reducing the percentage of the budget spent on defense. These policies were designed to encourage reciprocal moves by North Korea and to reduce tension between the two Koreas.

In 1989 Roh publicized plans to restructure the South Korean armed forces to enhance their defensive capabilities. Seoul also planned to acquire new types of technologically sophisticated weapons to prepare the armed forces for warfare and defense in the twenty-first century.

Development of the Armed Forces
Koguryŏ, Silla, and Koryŏ Kingdoms

Historical records suggest that the Koguryŏ Kingdom was the first Korean state to emphasize the military arts. From the first through the fourth centuries A.D., the Koguryŏ tribes frequently fought with Chinese and other groups for control of the region from the Liao River south to the Yalu River, the latter forming today's international boundary between North Korea and China. Modern South Korean textbooks emphasize an unbroken history of foreign incursions. Like the early warrior kings of Paekche and Silla, however, King Kwanggaet'o, who ruled Koguryŏ from 391 to 412, significantly added to his state's territory by military conquest, absorbing neighboring tribes and fortified towns throughout present-day northeastern China and down into the Korean Peninsula (see Silla;

Koryŏ, ch. 1). The Koguryŏ established military units in each of their five tribes. Each tribal army had about 10,000 men. An elected leader in charge of all military forces in the kingdom headed the chain of command. It was considered an honor for a man to be selected to be a soldier by the council of elders.

In the seventh century, the Silla Kingdom united Korea south of the Taedong River and successfully resisted repeated campaigns by the rulers of Sui (581–617) and Tang (618–907) China to conquer all of Korea. Under Silla rule, the king placed military commanders in charge of civil and military affairs in all of the country's local districts. A military academy was established in the capital city of Kyŏngju and was open to young men of aristocratic birth. Upon completion of their training, these young men were given the title *hwarang,* meaning Flower Knight. Most of the great military leaders of Silla trained at this academy and dedicated their lives to military service.

During the Koryŏ Dynasty (918–1392), Korea remained independent until the kingdom was invaded by the Mongols in 1231. King Taejo (918–39) was a merchant and military leader who reunified the peninsula after the political fragmentation that followed the decline of the Silla Dynasty in the late ninth century. During the reign of King Munjong (1046–83), Korea's northern boundaries once again reached the Yalu and Tumen rivers. King Munjong established two military districts along the northern border and based army units there to defend the kingdom. Following a military coup led by socially and economically disgruntled generals in 1170, Koryŏ kings (most notably those of the Ch'oe family) became virtual puppets of military leaders from 1196 to 1258. In 1259, at the end of several years of warfare with the Mongols, Koryŏ capitulated, becoming a vassal of the Mongol Yuan Dynasty (1279–1364) based in Dadu, which is modern Beijing (see The Evolution of Korean Society, ch. 1). King Kongmin (1351–74), however, increasingly resisted Yuan-imposed institutions and sided with the Ming Dynasty (1368–1644) against the Mongols. Yi Sŏnggye, one of Kongmin's commanders, rebelled against the effort of Kongmin's son to reverse Korea's pro-Ming orientation and in 1392 established the Chosŏn Dynasty.

The Chosŏn Dynasty and the Japanese Colonial Period

In 1592 Japan dispatched a force of approximately 170,000 men in 700 ships to conquer Korea. The Japanese army landed at Pusan in March and controlled most of the Korean Peninsula by July. The small Korean navy under Admiral Yi Sun-sin used ironclad battleships known—because of their appearance—as turtle boats to make frequent attacks on the Japanese fleet attempting to resupply Japanese forces in Korea. King Sŏnjo requested military assistance from Beijing and, as the Chinese and Korean armies gradually pushed the Japanese south, the Korean navy frustrated Japanese efforts to initiate new attacks on the Korean Peninsula. Although Japan's first attempts to subjugate Korea were unsuccessful, many of the central organizations of the Korean imperial military system were weakened by the impact of the invasion.

In the seventeenth and eighteenth centuries, Korean rulers generally devoted little attention to the military, although King Injo (1623–49) did reorganize the army and establish five permanent military bases in the country. Military service became unpopular after the Japanese invasion. The *yangban* (see Glossary) class no longer provided a large source of strong military leaders, and the lower classes generally preferred to pay a tax that exempted them from conscription. Because Korean rulers had little contact with the outside world, the Korean military establishment remained uninformed about developments of new weapons and modern battlefield tactics until the middle of the nineteenth century.

In the late 1860s, the advisers of King Kojong (1864–1907), alarmed by the interest of the United States, France, Russia, and other Western countries in opening Korea to foreign trade, convinced him to modernize the Korean army. During the next two decades, Korean military missions travelled to China and Japan to study modern warfare. King Kojong had neither the money nor the will to establish a large army, and he continued to rely primarily on the Chinese for military protection. In the 1880s, Chinese advisers trained 2,000 Korean troops and organized them into four elite units that were intended to be King Kojong's palace guard. The Tonghak Rebellion in Chŏlla Province in 1894 provided Japan with an excuse to dispatch troops to Korea, and Japanese forces were sent in July with the dual mission of eliminating Chinese influence on the Korean Peninsula and laying the foundation for the eventual colonization of the country.

Japanese victories in the First Sino-Japanese War (1894–95) and the Russo-Japanese War (1904–05)—both partially fought in Korea—left Korea without any foreign powers willing to oppose the Japanese annexation of Korea. Soon after the Treaty of Portsmouth was signed in July 1905, formally ending the Russo-Japanese War, Japan stationed large contingents of police and army units in Korea and disbanded the Korean army. Korea became a Japanese colony in August 1910.

In the 1920s and 1930s, the main staging areas for Korean military groups whose aim was to end Japanese rule in Korea were in Nanjing, China; along the Korean border in Jilin and Liaoning provinces; and in Irkutsk in the Soviet Union. The Nanjing-based groups received military training from and supported Chiang Kai-shek's Guomindang (Kuomintang or KMT—the National People's Party, or Nationalist Party). Until 1939 there were several small Nationalist and communist military groups that used guerrilla tactics to harass the Japanese in Korea and Manchuria (as northeast China was then known). By the end of 1940, the Japanese Imperial Army had destroyed most organized resistance along the Korean border with China; many Korean communists who had belonged to these groups joined the Northeast People's Revolutionary Army of the Chinese Communist Party (see Korea under Japanese Rule, ch. 1). A small number of Soviet-controlled Korean military units were organized in Irkutsk as early as 1921.

The South Korean Army after World War II

In November 1945, the United States Army Military Government in Korea (1945–48) began the task of organizing Korean military and police forces. In December a school for training military officers was established; the South Korean National Constabulary was organized in January 1946. The United States originally had planned to assist South Korea in developing only those police and military organizations necessary to maintain law and order during the period Korea was to be under the five-year Soviet-American trusteeship. By 1948, however, it was apparent that South Korea would need to expand the National Constabulary into a larger and more conventionally organized army to adequately defend itself from a possible invasion by North Korea. For this reason, the United States provided funds and training to expand the eight provincial units and one capital city unit of the National Constabulary from regiments to brigades (see South Korea under United States Occupation, 1945–48, ch. 1).

In November 1948, the Republic of Korea National Assembly passed the Armed Forces Organization Act. Under the provisions of this act, the National Constabulary was reorganized into an army comprising seven divisions. In June 1949, when the last United States Army units deployed in Korea as part of the post-World War II occupation forces withdrew, leaving behind a 500-person military advisory group, the leaders of the South Korean army controlled an organization that had been internally weakened by subversion and political factionalism and that lacked enough trained personnel and modern weapons to prepare adequately for war.

North Korea's effort to win control of the south using guerrilla warfare forced South Korea's military leaders to concentrate on

Korean archer,
late nineteenth century
Courtesy Carpenter Collection,
Library of Congress

counterinsurgency operations. In the fall of 1949, North Korean guerrilla units attempted to gain control of remote areas and small towns in the mountainous areas of eastern and southern South Korea. It was estimated that as many as 5,000 guerrillas trained in North Korea were infiltrated into these areas by the winter of 1949. Two South Korean army divisions and one army brigade were quickly deployed to conduct sweep and destroy missions to eliminate the guerrillas. Counterinsurgency operations were initiated in South Chŏlla Province in October 1949. In some areas, South Korean villages were evacuated both to protect civilians and to assist counterinsurgency units in locating guerrilla bases. By April 1950, less than 500 North Korean guerrillas remained in South Korea. Although the counterinsurgency program succeeded in ending the threat posed by the guerrillas, it had a deleterious effect on the army, necessitating reorganization and retraining for conventional war preparedness.

War on the Korean Peninsula

When North Korea invaded South Korea in June 1950, the poor quality of the South Korean armed forces immediately became apparent. Although South Korea had 94,000 troops when North Korea began its all-out surprise attack, one week later only 20,000 troops could be accounted for. By early September 1950, the

275

invading forces held all of South Korea except for the Pusan-Taegu corridor in the southeast.

The United Nations (UN) Security Council, upon the request of the United States, condemned North Korea's invasion of South Korea and asked members of the UN to assist South Korea. Fifteen nations besides the United States and South Korea eventually provided troops; all forces fought under the UN flag and under the unified command of General Douglas A. MacArthur, commander in chief of UN forces. These combined forces successfully broke North Korea's extended supply lines by landing at Inch'ŏn in September 1950. The invading forces were pushed back to near the Chinese border. Only the massive intervention of the Chinese People's Volunteers (CPV) in October averted the defeat of the North Korean forces. United Nations and communist forces fought to a standstill.

In July 1953, an armistice was signed that in 1990 remained the only agreement preventing the renewal of hostilities on the peninsula. The armistice fixed the boundaries of the 241-kilometer DMZ as the border between North Korea and South Korea. It also established a Military Armistice Commission, comprising China, North Korea, the United States, and South Korea, to resolve armistice violations and prevent the resumption of hostilities. As of 1990, the Chinese representative still was posted to the Military Armistice Commission, attended its plenary sessions, participated in secretarial meetings, officers of the day meetings, language officers meetings, and observed Neutral Nations Supervisory Commission meetings, but deferred to North Korea's representative.

South Korea's Response to the North Korean Military Buildup

In the 1960s, P'yŏngyang began a sustained expansion of its armed forces that continued without interruption through the 1980s (see fig. 13). Under presidents Syngman Rhee and Park Chung Hee, the South Korean military remained largely dependent on the United States to deter a second North Korean invasion and to provide much of the training and equipment needed by the armed forces. When the First Republic (1948–60) fell, South Korea's military institutions were stronger relatively than most of its other government agencies. Each service had a well-established school system and adequate supplies of weapons, ships, and aircraft from World War II and the Korean War.

Because of internal politics and Syngman Rhee's policy of controlling the promotion and assignment of all general rank officers, the military leadership was already at the edge of involvement in the nation's politics. Park Chung Hee and the other military leaders who participated in the May 1961 coup d'état that brought down the Second Republic (1960–61) were motivated largely by dissatisfaction with their corrupt and ineffective military and civilian superiors (see The Democratic Interlude, ch. 1). They believed that South Korea's survival as a nation depended on the reestablishment of social and economic stability. They viewed the strength of the armed forces and the reinstitution of the National Security Act of 1960 and other laws intended to reduce civil disturbances as necessary means to restore order and promote sound economic development. By 1963 when Park won election to the presidency of the Third Republic (1963–72) as a civilian, he already had placed other former military leaders, mostly members of the eighth class of the Officer Candidate School who had graduated in 1949, in key government positions.

Two of Park's major objectives during the Third Republic were to improve defense cooperation with the United States and to modernize the armed forces (see South Korea under Park Chung Hee, 1961–79, ch. 1). In pursuit of these goals, Park devoted one-third of all government spending to defense in 1965. As a sign of support for United States policies in Southeast Asia and in exchange for the substantial financial and material contributions for modernizing the army, Park deployed units of the South Korean army and marine corps to the Republic of Vietnam (South Vietnam).

In the early 1970s, the Park administration, with United States assistance through its Foreign Military Sales program, promoted the establishment of an indigenous defense industry. Park's military advisers were concerned that Kim Il Sung already had built a North Korean arms industry. The Nixon administration was calling for Washington's allies to assume more responsibility for their own defense. Nixon's national security advisors also feared that Seoul might be too weak to deter a North Korean invasion unless it began to manufacture some of its own weapons.

A Defense Industry Bureau was established in the Ministry of National Defense, and planning for a defense industry was incorporated into South Korea's first Force Improvement Plan (1971–76). Some of the weapons were assembled in government-owned plants. Licensed production of the United States-designed Colt M–16 rifle was initiated in 1971, with select South Korean companies supplying the government assembly plant with most of the parts for the weapon. In other cases, coproduction responsibility was entirely delegated to civilian-managed companies, many of which already had produced nonmilitary items with technical assistance from various United States firms. The Tacoma Boatbuilding Company, for example, assisted a South Korean shipbuilding

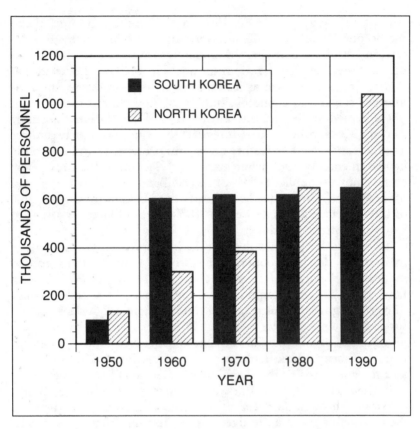

Figure 13. Comparative Growth of the Armed Forces of South Korea and North Korea, 1950–90

company based in Chinhae in constructing several classes of patrol boats, including the Paegu-class derived from the Asheville-class, which was equipped with Harpoon antiship missiles.

Park's assassination in 1979 did not obscure his regime's contributions to improving the armed forces during the eighteen years he was in power. He reorganized the Ministry of National Defense and each of the armed services to enhance the government's capability to manage any military contingency, including an all-out attack by North Korea across the DMZ, small-scale infiltrations along South Korea's extensive 8,640-kilometer coastline, and various types of low-intensity conflict, such as commando raids that targeted industrial, power, and communications facilities, or attempts by terrorists to assassinate key government officials.

President Chun Doo Hwan perpetuated the military's dominance over politics from December 1979 until Roh's inauguration in

February 1988 and protected Park's legacy of simultaneously improving the country's economic and military capabilities. Chun continued Park's policy of devoting one-third of all government spending to the military, outstripping estimated North Korean military expenditures during most of the 1980s. Chun also continued Park's policy of promoting defense-related research and development and commercial agreements with the United States, Japan, and Western Europe—a policy that provided Seoul with access to more advanced defense technologies. Particular emphasis was placed on expanding the air force and establishing a modern air defense network.

Korean Air, then South Korea's only civil airline, began coproduction of Northrop F5-E/F fighter aircraft in 1982. At the end of Chun's term in office, Seoul was considering coproducing either the General Dynamics F-16 or the McDonnell Douglas FA-18. During Chun's administration, South Korean shipbuilders increased production of various types of frigates, missile-equipped fast attack craft, and other, smaller naval vessels. Civilian industries also became more involved in coproduction of defense ordnance, including armored personnel carriers, self-propelled artillery, tanks, and communications equipment.

The Military's Role in Society

As the 1990s began, the armed forces remained the largest and most influential government organization in South Korea. Over 75 percent of South Korean males over the age of twenty had served in the regular army, the reserves, or the Homeland Reserve Force, or had been assigned duties supporting the armed forces under the Conscription Law of 1949. The National Technicians Law gave the Ministry of National Defense the authority to order civilian industrial plants to produce military items and to draft technicians with special skills into military service during wartime. The Act Concerning Protection of Military Secrets limited the freedom of the press to report on military affairs. The Military Installation Protection Law restricted civilian access to areas around military installations.

The *Defense White Paper, 1988,* a report on the armed forces and military preparedness and the first comprehensive document ever prepared by the Ministry of National Defense for the public, noted several initiatives the Roh administration had undertaken to address these concerns. During both the Park and Chun administrations, students who demonstrated against the government had been expelled frequently from school and drafted into the army, where they were treated harshly unless they demonstrated a willingness to accept government doctrine on opposing communism, promoting the common good of society, and showing respect for military and political power figures. In the *Defense White Paper, 1988,* the Roh administration announced that new conscription policies had been formulated that would standardize selection procedures and end past abuses. Officers and noncommissioned officers (NCOs) were under orders to follow a new military protocol that respected the rights of soldiers as citizens. Another measure announced in 1988 was the abolition of the Student Defense Corps, a military training organization established at South Korean colleges in 1969 to provide mandatory lectures on the government's national security policies and mobilization plans and instruction in handling weapons and military tactics.

Changes in the living and working environment on military bases were to include the gradual elimination of barracks and office buildings constructed in the 1950s, expansion of education programs to prepare soldiers for selected jobs in the civilian sector before their discharge, and small increases in pay. Additionally, in order to alleviate civil-military discord, the Roh administration planned to relocate many of the bases in urban areas to suburban or rural areas as soon as possible. Urban growth around military installations in large cities, including Seoul, Pusan, Taejŏn, Inch'ŏn, Ch'unch'ŏn, Masan, Wŏnju, Ŭijŏngbu, and Chinhae, had compromised the security of these bases and day-to-day military activities; in turn, the bases had disturbed the normal commercial and social activities of civilians.

In the 1980s, in addition to their regular military duties, military units continued the traditional practice of aiding farmers in planting and harvesting rice, assisting civil authorities in preventing loss of life and property during and following natural disasters, delivering medical services in rural areas, and providing other social services. In 1987 a total of 561,000 military personnel helped local farmers plant their rice, and 392,000 military personnel were made available for harvesting the crop. The army and the Homeland Reserve Force—more than 1 million troops—were mobilized in July 1987 to perform rescue operations and repair wind and flood damage caused by a typhoon. Stranded civilians were evacuated to safety, temporary dikes were constructed to prevent flood damage, debris was cleared from roads, and temporary shelters were constructed for the homeless.

Government policies on emergency preparedness were designed to quickly mobilize civilian personnel and resources to support the military during wartime. The Military Manpower Law delegated responsibility to the Office of Military Manpower Administration of the Ministry of National Defense for maintaining computerized records on all civilians who were eligible to serve in the Homeland Reserve Force. Men and women between the ages of twenty and sixty who had not been assigned duties in the military reserves but had technical skills needed by the military could also be assigned to support the military during wartime or a national emergency declared by the president and approved by the National Assembly under Article 77 of the 1987 Constitution. As the 1990s began, an estimated 5 million men and women were available for wartime duties in the Homeland Reserve Force and designated civilian industries that would produce, repair, and deliver defense goods to the military in wartime. Another important element of emergency preparedness was a plan to mobilize civilian ships, aircraft, heavy construction equipment, and other types of vehicles and equipment useful to the military in wartime.

Under provisions of the Emergency Prepared Resources Management Law, provincial and local government authorities were responsible for registering civilian assets that were to be included in the plan. Periodic exercises of the plan were conducted to test mobilization procedures. Local governments were required to provide the Ministry of National Defense and other appropriate ministries, including the Ministry of Home Affairs and Ministry of Transportation, with their mobilization plans.

Organization and Equipment of the Armed Forces

The National Security Council and the Ministry of National Defense were the primary executive bodies responsible for military affairs. The former, comprising the prime minister, the director of the Agency for National Security Planning (ANSP), and the ministers of national defense, foreign affairs, home affairs, and finance, was responsible for advising the president on security issues and was convened at the pleasure of the president. The Ministry of National Defense was organized into bureaus responsible for force development, budget, personnel, reserve forces, logistics, military installations, medical affairs, the defense industry, and the military education system.

Army

The ground forces were organized into three armies and several independent operational and functional commands (see fig. 14). The First Army and the Third Army occupied well-fortified positions stretching southward from the DMZ about fifty kilometers. The First Army's mission was to defend the eastern section of the DMZ. The Third Army, South Korea's largest and most diversified

281

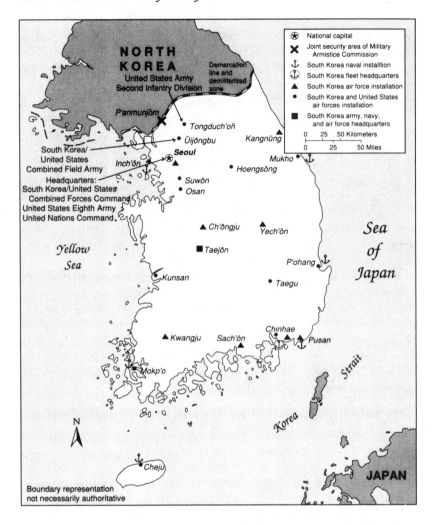

Figure 14. Deployment of South Korean and United States Forces in South Korea, 1990

combat organization, was responsible for guarding the most likely potential attack routes from North Korea to Seoul—the Munsan, Ch'ŏrwŏn, and Tongduch'on corridors. The Second Army had operational command over all army reserve units, the Homeland Reserve Force, logistics, and training bases located in the six southernmost provinces. Select army troops were assigned to the Capital Defense Command (formerly the Capital Garrison Command), whose active duty component, really more a countercoup force than a defensive force, was a little less than a division in 1990, organized into three separate security groups or regiments. They were assigned to defend the Blue House (the presidential residence), major government and Ministry of National Defense buildings, and Kimp'o International Airport. The wartime strength of the Capital Defense Command comes from multiple division reserves, which would be mobilized during a conflict. The Capital Defense Command also was responsible for peacetime training of all Seoul area reserves. Functional commands included the Counterespionage Operations Command, subordinate to the chairman of the Joint Chiefs of Staff and responsible for interdicting North Korean saboteurs and espionage agents; the Defense Security Command, the army's internal security organization; and the Logistics Base Command, which was established to manage the movement of supplies to the frontlines.

Active-duty infantry units were organized as combined armed forces with armor and artillery forces subordinate to the division or brigade commander. The Third Army and First Army controlled nineteen infantry divisions and two mechanized infantry divisions. In 1987 each infantry division had about 14,716 soldiers but in terms of transportation and communications and other equipment was considered "light" by United States standards. Each infantry division had four battalions per regiment, three infantry regiments and one artillery regiment, a reconnaissance/ranger battalion and an armor battalion (some only had armor companies), and a reasonable facsimile of combat support and combat service support units in comparison to United States counterparts. The two mechanized infantry divisions each had three mechanized/maneuver brigade headquarters, a cavalry battalion, and a mix of nine armor and mechanized infantry battalions.

The army was responsible for the ground component of South Korea's air defense network and had two surface-to-surface missile battalions and several antiaircraft gun battalions. The surface-to-surface missile battalions were equipped with United States-produced HAWK and Nike Hercules missiles, the former having a range of 42 kilometers, the latter a range of 140 kilometers. The field armies had small quantities of three types of man-portable, shoulder-launched surface-to-air missiles. These included the British-produced Javelin and the United States-produced Redeye missile. Additionally, there were three types of antiaircraft guns in use: the Swedish-produced Bofors L/70 40mm; the Swiss-produced Oerlikon GDF–002 35mm; and the domestically produced Vulcan 20mm.

The Special Warfare Command had seven brigades trained for wartime missions behind enemy lines. Although information on the organization of these units was unavailable in 1990, they probably were among the best-trained and most combat-ready forces in the army.

A single aviation brigade operated several types of attack and transport helicopters that could be strategically deployed to support combat operations of the infantry divisions and special forces. Some 200 McDonnell Douglas 500–MD helicopters were produced under license by Korean Air between 1976 and 1984. At least fifty of these helicopters were equipped with TOW antitank weapons. The remainder were used as transports and for other support missions. In 1990 South Korea also had about 50 McDonnell Douglas AH–1S attack helicopters and 144 McDonnell Douglas UH–1B/H transport helicopters.

The role of women in the army has changed in the late twentieth century. A small, all-volunteer Women's Army Corps (WAC) was made a separate unit of the army in 1971. Women were required to be high-school graduates, they were enlisted for a two-year tour of duty, and their military occupational specialties were limited to nursing and a few other noncombat positions.

In September 1989, the National Assembly revised the military personnel law which governed the WAC, and the WAC was officially deactivated on December 30, 1989. Female soldiers were formally reassigned to seven branches within the army: infantry, administration, intelligence, finance, education and information, logistics, and medical service. A separate WAC school and personnel center remained.

Between 1980 and 1990, the army increased in size by only a small margin. During this same period, however, new units were formed; the procurement of new tanks, armored personnel carriers, field artillery, antitank guns, air defense missiles, helicopters, and other types of military equipment significantly improved the defensive capabilities of the ground forces (see table 16, Appendix). In 1980 the army had approximately 1,200 United States-produced M–47 and M–48 tanks and 500 mostly United States-produced M–113 armored personnel carriers (also some Fiat 6614 wheeled armored personnel carriers). By 1990 South Korea had manufactured 200 of the domestically produced T–88 tank and had upgraded most of its M–48s to M–48A3s or M–48A5s. During the period from 1980 to 1990, the number of field artillery pieces more than doubled, going from 2,000 to 4,200 pieces, and South Korea began to introduce larger guns to extend the effective range of fire. In 1980 the army was equipped with 57mm, 75mm, 90mm, and

106mm recoilless rifles for antitank use and TOWs. In 1990 the TOW and LAW still were the primary antitank weapons. The 106mm/90mm recoilless rifles increased in numbers and were the basic antitank system for the infantry, although lower caliber weapons still existed. The TOWs were relatively scarce and were organized into independent units separate from the infantry divisions' main organization and equipment. The national air defense network comprised only 100 Vulcan antiaircraft guns and a small number of Nike-Hercules and HAWK surface-to-air missiles in 1980; by 1990 there were 600 antiaircraft guns, and the Nike-Hercules and HAWKs had both increased in number and undergone significant upgrades.

Air Force

The air force was organized into three commands operating approximately 700 aircraft from eight major airbases: the Combat Air Command controlled the bulk of the roughly 500 jet combat aircraft; a small Air Transportation Command had 37 transport aircraft; and the Air Training Command used 7 types of trainers (see table 17, Appendix). In 1990 the air force had 40,000 personnel on active duty. Most of these personnel were stationed at large, well-defended air bases located at Suwŏn, Osan, Ch'ŏngju, Kangnŭng, Taegu, Kunsan, Kwangju, and Sunch'ŏn. The air force also operated an unknown number of smaller airbases. Civilian airfields, including three international airfields at Seoul, Pusan, and Cheju, would be utilized in wartime, as would specially designed sections of major highways.

The Combat Air Command, headquartered at Osan, controlled aircraft that included twenty-two squadrons of ground attack fighters/interceptors, twenty-three counterinsurgency aircraft in one squadron, twenty reconnaissance aircraft in one squadron, and fifteen search-and-rescue helicopters in one squadron. All of these aircraft were produced in the United States, with the exception of sixty-eight Northrop F–5E/Fs that were coproduced with Korean Air. The 294 Northrop F–5s and 36 General Dynamics F–16C/Ds were the primary ground attack aircraft. Approximately 130 McDonnell Douglas F–4s were deployed for air defense but were equally useful in ground attack. All three types of aircraft were capable of being used in either role, depending on their armament. The air force supported army counterinsurgency programs with twenty-three Cessna A–37 aircraft, used as forward air controllers, but which could also be used in ground attack. Eight Northrop F–5s and twelve McDonnell Douglas F–4s were equipped solely for reconnaissance. A total of fifteen Bell UH-1B and UH-1H helicopters were available for search-and-rescue operations.

During the 1980s, the air force modernization program focused primarily on the formation and deployment of twelve new fighter aircraft squadrons and the establishment of an automated air defense network. The F-16 provided South Korea with an aircraft believed to be technologically superior to similarly designed communist aircraft, including the Soviet-produced MiG-29, the most sophisticated aircraft employed by the North Korean air force. South Korea-United States coproduction of F-5 aircraft demonstrated the resolve of South Korean military planners to promote a defense industry that simultaneously utilized advanced United States technology while enhancing indigenous efforts both at establishing an aviation industry and increasing access to Western technology.

The Tactical Air Control Center at Osan became operational in 1983. Reconnaissance aircraft and air defense radar sites informed the center about potentially hostile aircraft before they entered South Korean airspace. In wartime this capability was expected to allow South Korean air controllers more time to assess threat and the ability quickly to communicate orders to interceptor aircraft and surface-to-air missile sites.

Navy and Marine Corps

In 1990 the navy and marine corps remained small forces primarily dedicated to protecting the nation's territorial waters and islands. There was one large naval base at Chinhae, and seven small naval stations located at Cheju, Inch'ŏn, Mokp'o, Mukho, Pukp'yŏng-ni, P'ohang, and Pusan. Both the navy and marine corps were subordinate to the chief of naval operations, who was a member of the Joint Chiefs of Staff. The navy, with 35,000 personnel, was organized into three fleet commands and separate commands for aviation, amphibious operations, mine warfare, training, and logistics—all subordinate to the first vice chief of naval operations. The marine corps, with 25,000 personnel, was organized into two divisions and one brigade under the Marine Corps Command. Although part of the navy, marine units often operated under army control.

During the 1980s, the navy's modernization program focused on antisubmarine warfare and the deployment of new types of indigenously produced submarines, frigates, missile-equipped fast attack craft, and patrol boats. Naval vessels deployed with the Eastern, Western, and Southern fleets were equipped with modern sonar equipment, depth charges, and torpedoes to counter more effectively North Korea's growing submarine force (see table 18, Appendix). Two types of United States-produced and one type of

French-produced shipborne surface-to-surface and surface-to-air missiles were used by the navy on its destroyers, frigates, and fast attack craft. United States-produced Harpoon surface-to-surface missiles, with a ninety-kilometer range, were deployed on Gearing-class destroyers, Ulsan-class frigates, and Paegu-class fast attack craft derived from the Ashville-class. French-produced Exocet surface-to-surface missiles, with a seventy-kilometer range, were employed on Donghae frigates and Kirŏgi-class fast attack craft. Paegu fast attack craft were equipped with United States-produced Standard surface-to-air missiles.

The Naval Aviation Command and the Naval Amphibious Command operated small fleets of aircraft and landing craft, respectively, to support naval fleet and marine corps operations. Twenty-five Grumman S-2 aircraft, twenty-five Hughes 500–MD helicopters, and ten Bell SA–316 helicopters were shore based. They were deployed for surveillance of surface ships and for antisubmarine warfare.

The marine corps was assigned the defense of the Han River estuary and five northwestern islands located close to North Korea. The Naval Amphibious Command operated fifty-two amphibious craft in support of the marine corps.

Reserve and Civil Defense Forces

The reserve forces included mobilization reserve forces for each of the armed services and the Homeland Reserve Force, a paramilitary organization responsible for community and regional defense. Between 1968 and 1988, males between the ages of eighteen and forty were eligible for defense call-up duty; there was no clear policy on the age at which a recruit was eligible for retirement. In January 1988, a new policy was instituted that reduced the age-group of the male population subject to service in the reserves: only males who had been drafted for service between the ages of nineteen and thirty-four were required to serve in the reserves. The period of service was limited to between six and eight years, depending on the individual's age at conscription.

The mission of the mobilization reserves was to provide each of the services with well-trained personnel prepared to enter combat as soon as possible in wartime. In 1990 there were 1,240,000 men in the reserves: 1,100,000 in the army; 60,000 in the marines; 55,000 in the air force; and 25,000 in the navy. Most recruits had served on active duty in their respective services and were assigned to a reserve unit upon completion of their term of enlistment. Units in the reserves probably closely resembled active-duty organizations. Mobilization reserve personnel attended regularly scheduled training about one day a month and also participated in an annual field exercise that lasted about one week. Active-duty officers and NCOs were assigned to command and staff positions in the reserves at battalion and higher levels.

The Homeland Reserve Force was established in April 1968 as part of a nationwide program to increase defense preparedness in the wake of North Korean provocations. In January 1968, a North Korean commando unit infiltrated Seoul and attacked the Blue House in an attempt to assassinate President Park Chung Hee. That same month, two additional North Korean commando units launched attacks on towns on the east coast in attempts to encourage the South Korean populace to overthrow the government. Homeland Reserve Force personnel were given basic training in physical fitness, weapons familiarization, and defense tactics against various types of attacks by enemy forces. In wartime these units would remain close to or in their own cities, villages, or towns, where they would guard roads, power plants, factories, and other potential military targets.

In 1975 the National Assembly passed the Civil Defense Law, which was promulgated to establish organizations in every community to protect lives and property during wartime and natural disasters. Males between the ages of nineteen and fifty who were not drafted for service in the military were recruited for service in civil defense units. In 1980 there were over 90,000 civil defense personnel in the country. By 1990 their numbers were more than 3.5 million. Their missions included air raid defense, search and rescue, and building and road repair.

Recruitment, Training, and Conditions of Service

All males, except for a small percentage of individuals considered physically or socially undesirable for military service, could be drafted into the army. In 1990 there were 407,000 males nineteen years of age who were required to register for military service. Approximately 9.2 percent of these young men were rejected for conscription for one of the following reasons: having a physical or mental disability; possessing a criminal record; being an orphan; and being born out of wedlock or having one parent who was not a South Korean citizen. Conscripts were required to have at least an elementary school education; 77 percent of those drafted had at least a high school education.

The Military Manpower Agency was responsible for assigning recruits to the army, navy, marines, the Korean Augmentation

Army troops participate in offshore training exercise.
Courtesy Republic of Korea Army

of the United States Army (KATUSA), and the combat police units of the Korean National Police. Recruits could request assignment to a particular service and were assigned based on their education, technical skills, and physical condition. About 85 percent of eligible recruits were drafted for periods of between thirty and thirty-six months. Candidates for the KATUSA program were required to be high school graduates with some English-language training. In 1990 approximately 5,000 men in KATUSA served with the United States Army units in South Korea. In 1990 the air force was an all-volunteer force.

The conscription system was flexible and allowed most young men to plan their service in a way that would promote their individual career goals. High school graduates who had been accepted into a college or technical school or who were attending such schools were granted deferments. Conscripts with good education records and aptitudes suited to particular military specialties were selected to be trained as specialists in combat support branches such as signals, ordnance, and engineers. Even conscripts assigned to combat, however, were encouraged to take classes during their terms of duty to prepare for employment when they left the service.

The army, navy, and air force each had a full range of recruit training centers, schools for technical military occupational specialties, and officer training courses. Army recruits were transported from provincial induction centers to one of the Second Army's recruit training centers for basic training. Each branch of the army had one or more schools that offered curricula for enlisted personnel, NCOs, and officers. The large number of schools and the diversified training programs available to servicemen supported the army's need for skilled personnel to use, maintain, repair, and resupply combat forces during wartime. The air force had schools for pilots, air technicians, communication and electronics specialists, aircraft maintenance specialists, and air traffic controllers. The navy had its own schools oriented to the needs of the three fleets and the marine corps.

All officers and enlisted personnel were closely supervised and had to obey strict security regulations that limited their contacts with civilians, including their own families. All military personnel were provided with food, clothing, housing, and medical services. A variety of entertainment and recreational programs were organized on military installations to reduce boredom and promote the physical health and morale of service personnel.

Officers and Noncommissioned Officers

Officers were graduates of army, navy, or air force service academies, reserve officer training cadet programs offered at civilian colleges, or were recruited from enlisted personnel for selected short-term service in noncombat occupational billets. More than 90 percent of the field-grade officers chosen to command combat units at battalion and higher levels were graduates of the Korea Military Academy (in the case of the army), the Air Force Academy, or the Naval Academy. Applicants were chosen on the basis of their academic records, performance in competitive examinations, physical condition, and dedication to the mission of the armed forces. Each academy offered a four-year curriculum to provide the cadet with a bachelor's degree and practical military skills. Graduates of the military academies were required to serve ten years in the military and made up 5 percent of the newly commissioned officers each year. Approximately 40 percent of the new second lieutenants were commissioned from the Reserve Officer Training Corps (ROTC) after two years' training and a two-year, three-month obligation. Another 40 percent of the new second lieutenants were from the Third Military Academy, which had a twenty- to thirty-six week training course. The remaining 15 percent were directly commissioned specialists, including personnel in the medical corps, judge advocates, and chaplains. Most of the recruits of the Third Military Academy were newly graduated from junior colleges or regular colleges. At one time the Third Military Academy was itself a two-year college. Historically, most of the ROTC officers left after completing their obligation, but the graduates of the Third Military Academy often stayed on to field-grade rank and were the dominant source of commission at that rank.

Advanced individual training for officers was provided at the Army's Command and General Staff College, the National Defense College, and military training institutes in other countries. The Command and General Staff College prepared selected field-grade officers for command and staff duties at division, corps, and army levels. The National Defense College trained a limited number of selected senior officers of the three services and some civilian government officials for the highest command and staff positions.

Each army branch, as well as the air force, navy, and marine corps, was responsible for selecting NCOs for training in their occupational specialty. Those selected were required to reenlist for two to seven years, depending on the availability of replacements in their branch. Army staff sergeants were selected from civilian applicants and eligible enlisted personnel who had completed the required courses of studies in branch schools. The navy recruited petty officers through examination at the time of conscription. After finishing basic training, candidates were trained for their duties in a branch school. The air force followed a procedure similar to the navy's. Combat marines were sent to army schools for NCO training, whereas marines in service branches usually attended navy schools.

Enlisted Personnel

Recruit training in each of the services lasted about sixteen weeks and focused on physical conditioning, basic military skills, and the functions of combat and combat support units. Conscripts selected to serve in the army and marine corps were sent to Second Army recruit training centers for basic training. The navy and air force operated their own recruit training centers.

Uniforms, Ranks, and Insignia

The rank and grade structure of the three services corresponded, with minor exceptions, to that of the United States forces, as did the correlation between rank and responsibility (see fig. 15). In peacetime, the army and air force were each commanded by a four-star general; a lieutenant general commanded the marines, and an admiral commanded the navy.

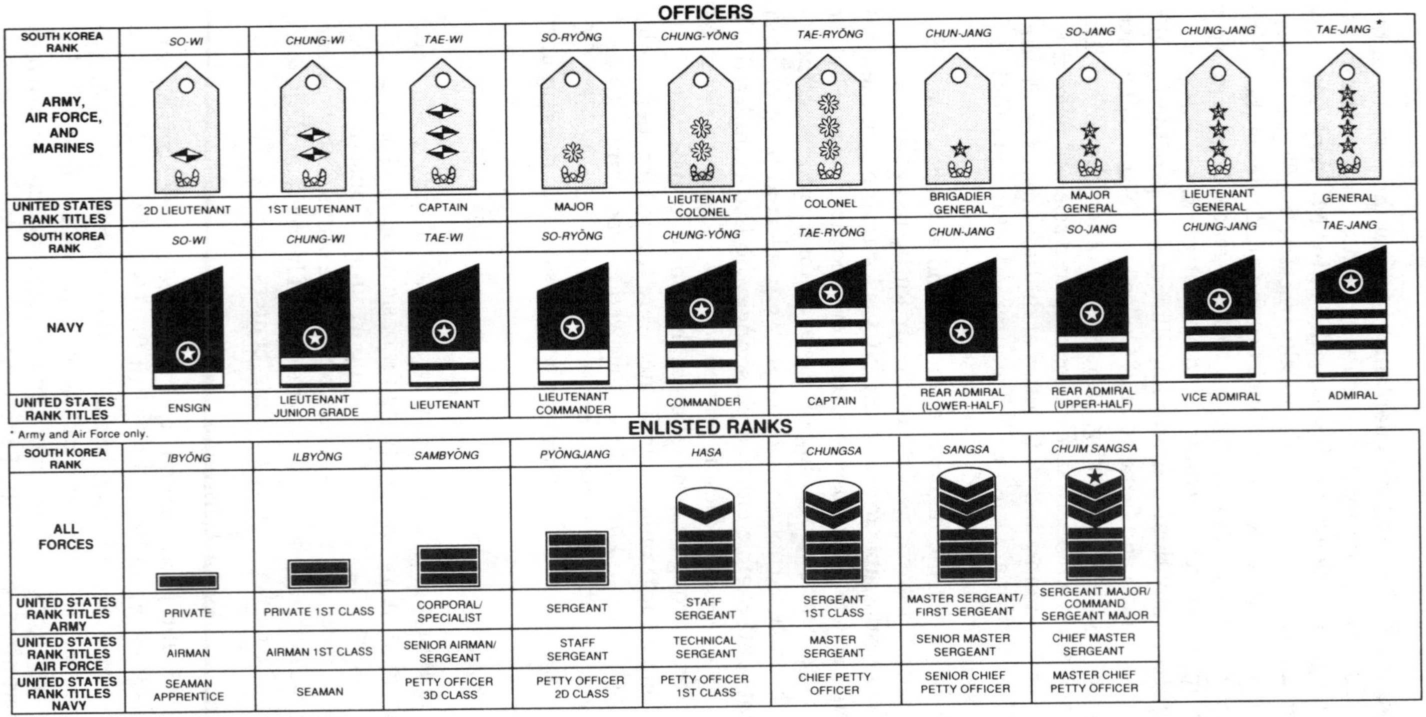

OFFICERS

SOUTH KOREA RANK	SO-WI	CHUNG-WI	TAE-WI	SO-RYONG	CHUNG-YONG	TAE-RYONG	CHUN-JANG	SO-JANG	CHUNG-JANG	TAE-JANG *
ARMY, AIR FORCE, AND MARINES										
UNITED STATES RANK TITLES	2D LIEUTENANT	1ST LIEUTENANT	CAPTAIN	MAJOR	LIEUTENANT COLONEL	COLONEL	BRIGADIER GENERAL	MAJOR GENERAL	LIEUTENANT GENERAL	GENERAL
SOUTH KOREA RANK	SO-WI	CHUNG-WI	TAE-WI	SO-RYONG	CHUNG-YONG	TAE-RYONG	CHUN-JANG	SO-JANG	CHUNG-JANG	TAE-JANG
NAVY										
UNITED STATES RANK TITLES	ENSIGN	LIEUTENANT JUNIOR GRADE	LIEUTENANT	LIEUTENANT COMMANDER	COMMANDER	CAPTAIN	REAR ADMIRAL (LOWER-HALF)	REAR ADMIRAL (UPPER-HALF)	VICE ADMIRAL	ADMIRAL

ENLISTED RANKS

SOUTH KOREA RANK	IBYONG	ILBYONG	SAMBYONG	PYONGJANG	HASA	CHUNGSA	SANGSA	CHUIM SANGSA
ALL FORCES								
UNITED STATES RANK TITLES ARMY	PRIVATE	PRIVATE 1ST CLASS	CORPORAL/ SPECIALIST	SERGEANT	STAFF SERGEANT	SERGEANT 1ST CLASS	MASTER SERGEANT/ FIRST SERGEANT	SERGEANT MAJOR/ COMMAND SERGEANT MAJOR
UNITED STATES RANK TITLES AIR FORCE	AIRMAN	AIRMAN 1ST CLASS	SENIOR AIRMAN/ SERGEANT	STAFF SERGEANT	TECHNICAL SERGEANT	MASTER SERGEANT	SENIOR MASTER SERGEANT	CHIEF MASTER SERGEANT
UNITED STATES RANK TITLES NAVY	SEAMAN APPRENTICE	SEAMAN	PETTY OFFICER 3D CLASS	PETTY OFFICER 2D CLASS	PETTY OFFICER 1ST CLASS	CHIEF PETTY OFFICER	SENIOR CHIEF PETTY OFFICER	MASTER CHIEF PETTY OFFICER

* Army and Air Force only.

Figure 15. Officer and Enlisted Ranks and Insignia, 1990

Service uniforms also resembled those of the United States forces in color and style. Service personnel wore a summer uniform of denim and a winter uniform of wool. Troops in forward areas wore a more expensive padded winter uniform. Noncommissioned officers of the army and air force wore a tunic buttoned to the top; navy noncommissioned officers wore the United States-type seaman's blouse. Officers' uniforms were similar to those worn by officers of the United States.

Defense Spending and Military Production

From the end of the Korean War to 1990, South Korea had evolved from a country dependent on other nations for its national security to a strong and growing nation, increasingly capable of meeting its own defense needs. Civilian industries maintained military assembly lines as a separate, and generally small, part of their corporate activities.

Defense Spending

Seoul's defense budget increased in proportion to the growth of the national economy throughout the 1970s and 1980s, demonstrating how strongly national leaders felt about improving the armed forces (see fig. 16). Between 1971 and 1975, defense spending increased from US$411 million to US$719 million. Defense expenditures averaged about 4.5 percent of the country's gross national product (GNP—see Glossary). In 1976, the first year that the government included proceeds from the defense tax in published figures for military expenditures, the budget for the armed forces and defense industries increased 100 percent over the 1975 figure to US$1.5 billion. The costs involved in initiating weapons production and the loss of military grant aid from the United States were the major reasons for the gradual increase of defense spending from 5.2 percent of GNP in 1979 to 6.2 percent of GNP in 1982. By 1990 defense spending had increased to almost US$10 billion a year, but because of the dramatic growth in the country's economy, this figure was below 30 percent of the government's budget and less than 5 percent of GNP for the first time since 1975.

Annual defense budgets were proposed by the Ministry of National Defense and approved by the president following consultations with the National Assembly. Beginning in fiscal year (FY—see Glossary) 1979, the Ministry of National Defense adopted a budget management system based on the United States Department of Defense project planning budget system. The South Korean system

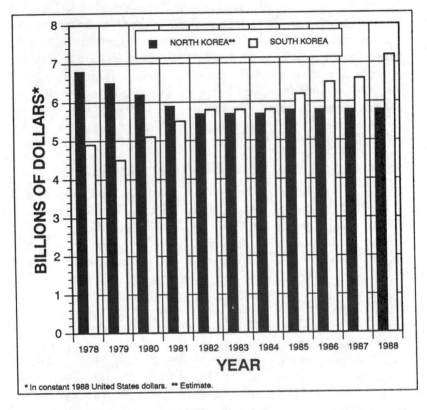

* In constant 1988 United States dollars. ** Estimate.

Source: Based on information from United States, Arms Control and Disarmament
Agency, *World Military Expenditures and Arms Transfers, 1989,* Washington, 1989,
53.

*Figure 16. Comparison of Defense Expenditures, South Korea and North
Korea, 1978–88*

focused on force modernization and the maintenance of military
organizations in peacetime at 70 percent of their wartime strength.
The government's mobilization and resource management plans
for support of the military were designed to bring the armed forces
up to full strength quickly and to maintain the country's capability to supply the military during wartime. Under the 1987 Constitution, the National Assembly was accorded more responsibility
to review the defense budget and to recommend appropriate levels of spending. In 1990, however, the president continued to have
the final say on budget matters.

Approximately 40 percent of the defense budget was devoted
to weapons and equipment modernization in 1990. Defense planners established a number of long-range goals: to establish an

independent reconnaissance system with intelligence satellites and early warning aircraft; to improve the quality of firepower and the accuracy of domestically produced weapons; to deploy indigenously produced surface-to-air and tactical surface-to-surface missiles; and to replace outdated fighter aircraft and naval vessels with technologically advanced models that would neutralize the threat of North Korea's modern weapon systems.

The operational costs of the three armed services constituted approximately 35 percent of the defense budget. Improvements in training, logistical support to combat units, and pay and benefits provided to military personnel were a part of the increased cost of supporting the armed forces. The acquisition of sophisticated new types of weapons, although contributing to national security, also increased operational costs.

The remaining 25 percent of the defense budget was mostly allocated among the armed forces reserves; South Korea's share of the United States-Republic of Korea combined defense improvement program; research into new defense technologies; and construction and maintenance of military installations.

Military Production

The Defense Industry Bureau of the Ministry of National Defense was the government agency responsible for managing the quantity and quality of domestically produced weapons and equipment. In 1990 South Korean industries provided about 70 percent of the weapons, ammunition, communications and other types of equipment, vehicles, clothing, and other supplies needed by the military.

Weapons production for the army began in 1971 when the Ministry of National Defense constructed a plant to assemble United States-designed Colt M–16 rifles. The memorandum of agreement between the United States and the Republic of Korea authorized production of enough rifles to supply South Korean army units. However, the agreement prohibited the production of additional M–16s without the permission of Colt Industries and the United States government. In the mid-1970s, South Korea signed agreements to begin licensed production of many types of United States-designed weapons, including grenades, mortars, mines, and recoilless rifles, with the same stipulations as those for the M–16 rifle. South Korea also began to manufacture ammunition for the weapons it produced for the army.

By 1990 South Korean companies had army contracts to produce tanks, self-propelled and towed field guns, two types of armored vehicles, and two types of helicopters. A division of Hyundai produced the 88 Tank (formerly called the K-1 tank) at Ch'ang-wŏn. The K-1 was the result of a joint United States-South Korean design. The 88 Tank's 105mm gun was an improved version of the same caliber gun that was standard on South Korea's M-48A5 tanks. Although a few components of the tanks' fire control and transmission systems were imported, Hyundai and South Korean subcontractors manufactured most of the systems. One of the Samsung Group's businesses produced 155mm M-109 self-propelled howitzers. Kia Machine Tool was the manufacturer for the KH-178 105mm and the KH-179 155mm towed field guns. The KH-178 and KH-179 guns were derived from United States-designed artillery but were considered indigenously designed. Daewoo Industries and Asia Motors had a coproduction agreement for an Italian-designed wheeled, armored personnel vehicle. Bell Helicopters Textron of the United States and Samsung coproduced UH-1 helicopters. Sikorsky Aircraft Corporation, also of the United States, had a contract with Daewoo to coproduce H-76 helicopters.

In December 1989, the Ministry of National Defense selected the McDonnell Douglas FA-18 to be the second United States-designed fighter aircraft to be coproduced in South Korea. Samsung's aerospace division was awarded a contract to manufacture the airframe and engine; Lucky-Goldstar became the subcontractor for the aircraft's avionics. McDonnell Douglas agreed to deliver twelve FA-18s to the South Korean air force in 1993 and to assist Samsung with the later assembly of 108 aircraft in South Korea. As of 1990, the entire FA-18 program was under review because of increased costs. Korean Air used its depot maintenance facilities at Kimhae to overhaul most types of aircraft in service with the South Korean air force. Additionally, the United States Air Force contracted with Korean Air for the maintenance of its F-4, F-15, A-10, and C-130 aircraft stationed in South Korea, Japan, and the Philippines.

In 1990 South Korean shipbuilders were building two indigenously designed naval vessels, and they had coproduction agreements with United States, Italian, and German companies for several other types of ships. Four shipbuilders—Hyundai, Daewoo, Korea Tacoma, and Korean Shipbuilding and Engineering—constructed South Korean-designed Ulsan-class frigates and Tonghae-class corvettes for the navy. During the 1980s, Korea Tacoma, a South Korean-owned subsidiary of the United States Tacoma Boatbuilding Company, produced one class of patrol gunboat and one class of landing ship for the navy. The Kirŏgi-class patrol boat was a larger model of the Tacoma-designed Schoolboy-class patrol boat manufactured in South Korea during the 1970s. The Kirŏgi-class patrol boat, a 170-ton vessel, required a thirty-one-person crew and was equipped with five guns: one 40mm single-barreled Bofors on the bow, two 30mm twin-barreled Emerson Electrics in the stern, and two 20mm Oerlikon twin-barreled guns behind the bridge. The Kirŏgi-class patrol boat, with a range of 700 kilometers and a maximum speed of 38 knots, was well suited for its inshore patrol mission.

The Mulgae-class landing ship, another naval vessel designed and produced in the United States by Tacoma Boatbuilding Company, was ordered by the navy to augment a small amphibious fleet that comprised several models of obsolescent transport craft produced in the United States during World War II and transferred to the South Korean navy in the 1960s and 1970s. The Mulgae-class landing ship was designed to carry an infantry company with its weapons, mechanized and wheeled vehicles, and other supplies. It had a range of 560 kilometers and a maximum speed of 13 knots. In 1986 South Korea's Kangnam Shipbuilding Corporation began construction of the Swallow/Chebi class minehunter, which was based on the Italian-designed Lerici-class. At that time, the South Korean navy had only eight United States-produced Kunsan-class minesweepers in service with the three fleets. The Swallow-class minehunter had new types of sonar and mine countermeasure equipment that was expected to improve the navy's capability to locate and to eliminate minefields in international shipping lanes during wartime.

In the late 1980s, production of submarines designed by the Federal Republic of Germany (West Germany) was initiated. Three 150-ton submarines designed by the Howaldswerke Shipbuilding Corporation were in service with the navy in 1990. Howaldswerke also had plans to provide technical assistance for the construction of three Type 209 submarines, about 1,400 tons each. South Korean military planners were interested in using submarines to protect critical shipping lanes from North Korean submarines in wartime.

Strategic Planning for War

Under the terms of the 1954 Republic of Korea-United States of America Mutual Defense Treaty, the United States and South Korea agreed to cooperate in defending the security and strategic interests of both countries. South Korea's deployment of army and marine units to South Vietnam in the 1960s and 1970s demonstrated its commitment to meeting its obligations under the treaty. By 1990 the United States had stationed 44,500 military personnel in South Korea—a signal to North Korea and other countries in the region that Washington would meet its security commitments to Seoul under the Mutual Defense Treaty.

United States Forces in Korea

In the confusion of the early days of the Korean War, Seoul placed its armed forces under the command of General Douglas A. MacArthur as United Nations (UN) commander. This arrangement continued after the armistice. For some twenty-five years, the United Nations Command headquarters, which had no South Korean officers in it, was responsible for the defense of South Korea, with operational control over a majority of the units in the South Korean military. The command was the primary peacetime planning organization for allied response to a North Korean invasion of South Korea and the principal wartime command organization for all South Korean and United States forces involved in defending South Korea. In 1978 a binational headquarters, the South Korea-United States Combined Forces Command (CFC), was created, and the South Korean military units with front-line missions were transferred from the United Nations Command to the CFC's operational control. The commander in chief of the CFC, a United States military officer, answered ultimately to the national command authorities of the United States and the Republic of Korea (see fig. 17).

Historically, operational control of South Korea's tactical armed forces has made the United States commander vulnerable to the politics of association. United States commanders have rigidly avoided commentary on South Korean party politics, confining public statements to purely military matters on such issues as arms buildups and threats from North Korea. However, in the complex politics of the Korean Peninsula, the United States commander's military opinions often have been publicly manipulated as support for Seoul's authoritarianism.

In May 1961 and December 1979, the command structure was breached by South Korean troops participating in military coups. A more complex set of circumstances occurred in May 1980, when troops were withdrawn from the CFC under existing procedures and dispatched to Kwangju to respond to the student uprising. Confusion in the South Korean public over the particular circumstances of the incident, the United States position, and the limits of the CFC's control led many South Koreans to believe that the United States fully supported the violent suppression of the uprising. The lack of an accurate historical record for nearly ten years generated widespread misunderstanding, and it has been credited with the rise of anti-Americanism in South Korea, a movement which continues.

Only after President Chun stepped down at the end of 1987, and the opposition in the National Assembly grew stronger, did the United States begin answering the questions concerning United States involvement in Kwangju. On June 19, 1989, Washington issued the "United States Government Statement on Events in Kwangju, Republic of Korea, in May 1980," in response to formal requests from the National Assembly. The statement addressed a series of questions related to the rise to power of then Lieutenant General Chun Doo Hwan. The statement noted no prior knowledge of the assassination of President Park Chung Hee, nor warning of the December 12, 1979, incident, in which a group of South Korean army officers led by Major General Chun seized control of the military. It was revealed that Washington repeatedly protested to the government and the military leadership about the misuse of forces under the Combined Forces Command. The report also stated that South Korean authorities gave the United States two hours advanced warning of the extension of martial law on May 18, 1980, and no prior warning of the military's intention to arrest political leaders or to close both the National Assembly and the universities.

The statement clearly noted that none of the South Korean forces deployed at Kwangju were, during that time, under either the operational control of the CFC or the control of any United States authorities. Additionally, the United States had neither prior knowledge of the deployment of special forces to Kwangju nor responsibility for their actions there. The report addressed the use of the Twentieth Division, CFC, and clarified that the CFC agreement allowed both the United States and South Korea to assert control over its forces at any time without the consent of the other. According to the statement, the United States was informed in advance of intentions to use elements of the Twentieth Division to reenter Kwangju, that United States officials, after cautioning against the use of military force to solve a political crisis, accepted that it would be preferable to use the Twentieth Division rather than Special Forces units (but the latter were also involved). The report further documented that the United States repeatedly protested public distortions of Washington's actions and policy by Seoul and the South Korean press, namely allegations that the United States knew either of the December 12 incident in advance or of the extension of martial law, or that Washington approved of the Special Forces actions in Kwangju.

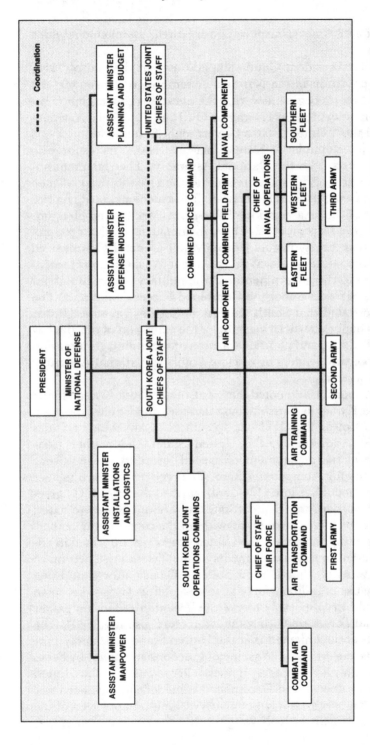

Source: Based on information from Republic of Korea, Ministry of National Defense, *Defense White Paper, 1987*, Seoul, 1988; and Taek-Hyong Rhee, *US-ROK Combined Operations*, Washington, 1986, 31–47.

Figure 17. Organization of South Korean and United States Forces in South Korea, 1988

While the report rebutted most of the myths of American culpability for events in 1979 and 1980, the ten-year delay in issuing the report did little to resolve the misgivings held by many South Koreans, who still persisted in believing that the United States was in some way a party to the military takeover in May 1980, and the harsh suppression of the Kwangju demonstrations that followed.

In 1990 a few hundred United States military personnel were assigned to the United Nations Command headquarters in P'anmunjŏm, in the DMZ, and were responsible for representing the United States at meetings of the Military Armistice Commission. Because the Seoul and P'yŏngyang governments had never negotiated a peace agreement after the Korean War, the sometimes shaky 1953 armistice concluded between the United Nations Command, North Korea, and China remained the only formal channel for handling complaints about violations of the truce.

There were 32,000 United States Army personnel in South Korea in 1990; most were assigned to the Eighth Army, which included the Second Infantry Division, the Seventeenth Aviation Brigade, and other detachments deployed north of Seoul as part of the joint South Korean-United States forward defense strategy. If a conflict were to occur, the Second Infantry Division would be expected to serve as a reserve force for the South Korean army on one of the main invasion routes between the DMZ and Seoul. United States Army personnel with command or planning responsibilities for combat units also were assigned to the headquarters of the CFC and to the headquarters of the Republic of Korea-United States Combined Field Army, of which the Second Infantry Division was the main American component. The remaining United States Army personnel were assigned to support the missions of selected United States and South Korean combat units, serving primarily in communications, logistics, and training positions.

There were 12,000 United States Air Force personnel in South Korea in 1990. They were assigned to units responsible for early warning, air interception, close air support of United States and South Korean ground forces, combat support, aircraft maintenance, and the transportation of personnel and supplies from the United States, Japan, and other United States military installations in the Pacific. The Seventh Air Force, headquartered at Osan Air Base, was the command element for all United States Air Force organizations in South Korea. United States Lockheed U–2 high-altitude reconnaissance and South Korean Grumman E–2C early warning aircraft patrolled the North Korean border and monitored the Soviet Union's air and naval activities in the Sea of Japan area.

Advanced F-16 fighter aircraft were used by tactical fighter squadrons based at Osan and Kunsan. These squadrons operated alongside South Korean air force tactical squadrons in both air interception and close air support roles. South Korea and the United States jointly managed the South Korean tactical air control system, which had wartime responsibility for Korean airspace and the entire South Korean coastline. The United States Military Airlift Command was responsible for transporting United States military personnel, weapons, and supplies from the United States and locations in the Pacific to South Korea.

United States Navy and United States Marine Corps personnel in South Korea consisted of about 500 officers and enlisted personnel who occupied critical staff and liaison positions in the CFC. The United States Pacific Command in Hawaii frequently deployed units of the United States Pacific Fleet, based in Japan, and units of the marine corps, based in Okinawa and other locations in the Pacific, to South Korea for joint training exercises, particularly Team Spirit, held every spring to promote South Korean-United States military cooperation and readiness. During the 1988 Seoul Olympics, the United States Seventh Fleet operated in the Sea of Japan and was assigned specific missions to assist units of the CFC in discouraging P'yŏngyang from attempting to disrupt the Olympic Games.

South Korean and United States Cooperation

In 1968 the United States and South Korea held their first annual Security Consultative Meeting. This meeting provided high-level defense experts from the two countries with an official forum for reassessing the nature of the North Korean threat to South Korea, for agreeing on an overall defense strategy for South Korea, and for outlining the roles of both countries in deterring a North Korean invasion.

During the 1989 Security Consultative Meeting in Washington (the meetings were held in alternate years in Seoul and Washington), the two nations agreed that the Moscow-assisted modernization of P'yŏngyang's air force and army indicated that the military situation in Northeast Asia remained tense and unpredictable. Soviet leader Mikhail S. Gorbachev's Korean policy, focused on promoting unofficial contacts with Seoul though Moscow, continued to bolster P'yŏngyang's military establishment.

South Korean and United States leaders who attended the 1989 Security Consultative Meeting considered it unlikely that the Soviet Union would initiate a military conflict targeting South Korea. They believed, however, that increasing Soviet military support for North

Korea made it highly probable that the Soviet Union would continue to assist North Korea if war broke out. For this reason, United States secretary of defense Richard B. Cheney and South Korean minister of national defense Yi Sang-hun agreed to strengthen strategic planning through existing organizations, such as the CFC.

Internal Security

From the founding of the Republic of Korea, its leaders, while professing liberal democratic ideals, consistently held that the security threat posed by an aggressive, communist North Korea required some modification of Western democracy to fit Korean realities. Confronted with a heavily armed enemy determined to reunify the peninsula on its own terms—by force, if necessary—successive South Korean governments gave top priority to external and internal security, guaranteed by large and well-organized security services. The need for social order and discipline in the face of this threat remained central to the government's approach. Faced with a divided country, even "loyal" opposition often was suppressed as dangerously disruptive. On more than one occasion, political opposition was confused with communist subversion. The communist threat at times provided political justification for authoritarian regimes to maintain power and to suppress public criticism or demands for democracy. In both 1961 and 1980, the military cited these concerns to justify its interventions in South Korean politics.

The Threat from the North

After the division of the peninsula, North Korea used subversion and sabotage against South Korea as part of its effort to achieve reunification. North Korea was unsuccessful at developing a covert political infrastructure in South Korea or forging links with dissidents resident in South Korea, and after the early 1960s P'yŏngyang's efforts were unproductive. Based on available evidence, in 1990 it appeared that P'yŏngyang placed or recruited only a limited number of political agents and sympathizers in the southern part of the peninsula. P'yŏngyang's agents acted individually for the most part, did not maintain regular contact with one another, and received only intermittent support and guidance.

Peacetime infiltration by North Korean agents was a fact of life in South Korea after the armistice in 1953. There were, however, clear shifts both in the number and method of infiltrations over the years and in their goals. Through the mid-1960s, P'yŏngyang sent agents primarily to gather intelligence and to try to build a covert political apparatus. This tactic was followed by a dramatic shift to violent attempts to destabilize South Korea, including commando raids along the DMZ that occasionally escalated into firefights involving artillery. These raids peaked in 1968, when more than 600 infiltrations were reported, including an unsuccessful attempt at a commando attack on the Blue House in Seoul and the infiltration of over 120 commandos on the east coast. In 1969 more than 150 infiltrations were attempted, involving almost 400 agents. In 1970 and 1974, agents attempted unsuccessfully to assassinate President Park. In the 1974 attempt, during an August 15 ceremony marking National Liberation Day at the National Theater in Seoul, the assassin's shots missed President Park but killed Mrs. Park. Subsequently, P'yŏngyang's infiltration efforts abated somewhat, and the emphasis shifted back to intelligence gathering and covert networks.

From the mid-1970s to the early 1980s, most North Korean infiltration was done by heavily armed reconnaissance teams, which increasingly were intercepted and neutralized by South Korean security forces. After shifting to infiltration by sea for a brief period in the 1980s, P'yŏngyang apparently discarded military reconnaissance in favor of inserting agents from third countries. North Korea did not abandon violence, however, as was shown by the abortive 1982 attempt to recruit Canadian criminals to assassinate President Chun Doo Hwan, the 1983 Rangoon assassination attempt that killed seventeen South Korean government officials and four Burmese dignitaries, and the 1987 destruction of a Korean Air airliner with 115 people on board. In the airliner bombing, North Korea broke from its pattern of targeting South Korean government officials, in particular the president, and targeted ordinary citizens.

North Korean propaganda concentrated on weakening the social fabric and sowing discord between the South Korean government and the population. Indirectly, North Korea sought to turn dissident elements within South Korean society into propagandists and agitators who would undermine the government. P'yŏngyang achieved some limited indirect success in this effort, as indicated by the repetition of some of its themes by student dissidents. North Korean coverage of dissident activity in the south was on occasion so timely and accurate as to lead some members of the South Korean government to believe that dissent in the south was directed from the north. However, despite similarities between North Korean propaganda and dissident statements, South Korean security agencies never convincingly established a direct connection between the dissidents and the north, although in the late 1980s some elements among dissident groups increasingly used Marxist-Leninist

Armed Forces Day parade
Courtesy Embassy of the Republic of Korea, Washington

language and North Korean political themes (see Political Extremism and Political Violence, ch. 4).

Seoul's Response

The pre-Korean War period was marked by political turmoil and widespread demands for sweeping political, economic, and social change. As the communists entrenched themselves in the north and right-of-center politicians emerged in control in the south, the possibility for peaceful unification of the peninsula disappeared. In the autumn of 1946, a series of unorchestrated leftist-led labor strikes and rural peasant rebellions were suppressed by the fledgling Korean National Police after some 1,000 deaths and 30,000 arrests. The communist South Korean Workers' Party led a partly indigenous guerrilla movement in the south after a major rebellion on Cheju Island in April 1948 that claimed tens of thousands of lives. South Korea's military and paramilitary forces were beset by mutinies and defections but eventually gained the upper hand. In reaction to the communist-based Yŏsu-Sunch'ŏn rebellion of October 1948, a harsh national security law was passed in December 1949 that made communism a crime. However, the law was so comprehensive and vague that it could be used against any opposition group. Under the law, members of the South Korean Workers'

Party were arrested and some 150,000 persons were barred from political activity. Guerrilla warfare continued until the end of 1949, coupled with skirmishing along the thirty-eighth parallel. North Korea's conventional attack followed when it became clear that the insurgents would not triumph easily.

Recollection of this chaotic period and the invasion from North Korea colored subsequent South Korean government attitudes toward internal security. Domestic opposition, especially from the left, was suspect. President Syngman Rhee's call for national unity provided political justification for limiting the activities of the opposition during the 1950s. Although the regime did not suppress all opposition or independent sources of information, it suppressed some organized opposition and criticism (see The Media, ch. 4).

In the late 1950s, as Rhee became more authoritarian, the government increasingly resorted to using the police force and, to a lesser extent, the military security forces, for political purposes. The Ministry of Home Affairs, whose charter ranged from intelligence and investigative operations to supervision of local and provincial affairs, emerged as a powerful political force. The police, with a strong core of veterans from the Japanese colonial police (approximately 70 percent of the highest ranking officers, 40 percent of the inspectors, and 15 percent of the lieutenants), was both effective and feared. The police used strong-arm tactics to coerce support for the ruling party during elections and harassed the political opposition. The prerogative of the police to call in anyone for questioning was a powerful tool of intimidation. These circumstances inevitably led to police corruption, politicized law enforcement, and exploitation of the populace in the name of internal security. Rhee's political survival became more and more dependent on the police. When police control wavered at the time of the April 19 student revolution in April 1960, his regime fell.

The short-lived Chang Myŏn government (July 1960 to May 1961) did not survive long enough to articulate an internal security policy but was committed to a more open political system. However, because of internal conflict within the ruling party and the obstructions of the conservative opposition, society was in a state of political and social turmoil.

Following the May 16, 1961, military coup, the Korean Central Intelligence Agency (KCIA) was formed on June 19. Directly under the control of the Supreme Council for National Reconstruction, the KCIA, with nearly unlimited power, emerged as the organization most feared during the Park Chung Hee era. Under Kim Chong-p'il's direction, the organization weeded out anti-Park elements and became the prime tool keeping the regime in power.

Under Park, the lack of advancement in civil liberties continued to be justified by referring to the threat from North Korea. The political influence of the Ministry of Home Affairs and the police declined in the face of the KCIA's power. The relationship between the police and general public, however, was not significantly altered. As Se-Jin Kim wrote in 1971: "The former still act with arbitrary arrogance; the latter respond with fear but not respect."

The government often used martial law or garrison decree in response to political unrest. From 1961 to 1979, martial law or a variant was evoked eight times. The October 15, 1971, garrison decree, for example, was triggered by student protests and resulted in the arrest of almost 2,000 students. A year later, on October 17, 1972, Park proclaimed martial law, disbanded the National Assembly, and placed many opposition leaders under arrest (see Constitution; Human Rights, ch. 4). In November the *yusin* constitution (*yusin* means revitalization), which greatly increased presidential power, was ratified by referendum under martial law.

The government grew even more authoritarian, governing by presidential emergency decrees in the immediate aftermath of the establishment of the *yusin* constitution; nine emergency decrees were declared between January 1974 and May 1975. The Park regime strengthened the originally draconian National Security Act of 1960 and added an even more prohibitive Anticommunism Law. Under those two laws and Emergency Measure Number Nine, any kind of antigovernment activity, including critical speeches and writings, was open to interpretation as a criminal act of "sympathizing with communism or communists" or "aiding antigovernment organizations." Political intimidation, arbitrary arrests, preventive detention, and brutal treatment of prisoners were not uncommon.

Opposition to the government and its harsh measures increased as the economy worsened in 1979. Scattered labor unrest and the government's repressive reactions sparked widespread public dissent: mass resignation of the opposition membership in the National Assembly and student and labor riots in Pusan, Masan, and Ch'angwon. The government declared martial law in the cities. In this charged atmosphere, under circumstances that appeared related to dissatisfaction with Park's handling of the unrest, on October 26, 1979, KCIA chief Kim Chae-gyu killed Park and the chief of the Presidential Security Force, Ch'a Chi-ch'ŏl, and then was himself arrested. Emergency martial law was immediately declared to deal with the crisis, placing the head of the Defense Security Command, Major General Chun Doo Hwan, in a position of considerable military and political power.

Popular demand for the restoration of civil liberties after Park's death was immediate and widespread. Acting President Ch'oe Kyu-ha revoked Emergency Measure Number Nine, which had forbidden criticism of the government and the *yusin* constitution. Civil rights were restored to almost 700 people convicted under the emergency decrees. The illegitimacy of the *yusin* constitution was acknowledged, and the process of constitutional revision begun.

The slow pace of reform led to growing popular unrest. In early May 1980, student demonstrators protested a variety of political and social issues, including the government's failure to lift emergency martial law imposed following Park's assassination. The student protests spilled into the streets, reaching their peak during May 13 to 16, at which time the student leaders obtained a promise that the government would attempt to speed up reform. The military's response, however, was political intervention led by Lieutenant General Chun Doo Hwan, then KCIA chief and army chief of staff. Chun, who had forced the resignation of Ch'oe's cabinet, banned political activities, assemblies, and rallies, and arrested many ruling and opposition politicians.

In Kwangju, demonstrations to protest the extension of martial law and the arrest of Kim Dae Jung turned into rebellion as demonstrators reacted to the brutal tactics of the Special Forces sent to the city. The government did not regain control of the city for nine days, after some 200 deaths.

General Chun Doo Hwan, as chairman of the standing committee of the Special Committee for National Security Measures (SCNSM), assumed de facto leadership of the country. The pronouncement of martial law announced as a result of Park's assassination remained in effect until January 24, 1981. Under the Special Committee for National Security Measures and the Legislative Council for National Security that replaced it, sweeping political controls were instituted. Established political parties were disbanded and over 800 people banned from politics; the media were restructured, many journals were abolished, and hundreds of journalists were purged; some 8,000 employees were purged from government or government-controlled companies and some 37,000 people were arrested and "re-educated" in military training camps under the Social Purification Campaign; and military court jurisdiction was extended to such civilian offenses as corruption and participation in antigovernment demonstrations. The new National Assembly Law and the amended National Security Act (which was rewritten to incorporate elements of the 1961 Anticommunist Law) also were passed. On January 10, 1981, the Martial Law Command

Checkpoint at the Demilitarized Zone
Tank trap north of Seoul
Courtesy Robert L. Worden

allowed people to resume limited political activities in preparation for the presidential election.

The Fifth Republic's constitution marked significant progress from the *yusin* constitution. As implemented by the newly elected Chun government, however, it fell far short of popular expectations of democraticization that had been raised after Park's death. The constitution was attacked by students and dissidents as Park's *yusin* system under new trappings. The government attempted to defuse discontent by "decompression" as well as repression, gradually returning civil rights to those banned in 1980. Additionally, the government opened up the political system slightly in 1983 and to a greater degree in 1985, although the dissident movement continued.

Discontent was kept under control until 1987 by the regime's extensive security services—particularly the Agency for National Security Planning (ANSP, the renamed KCIA), the Defense Security Command (DSC), and the Combat Police of the Korean National Police (KNP). Both the civilian ANSP and the military DSC not only collected domestic intelligence but also continued "intelligence politics."

The Act Concerning Assembly and Demonstration was used to limit the expression of political opposition by prohibiting assemblies likely to "undermine" public order. Advanced police notification of all demonstrations was required. Violation carried a maximum sentence of seven years' imprisonment or a fine. Most peaceful nonpolitical assemblies took place without government interference. However, the act was the most frequently used tool to control political activity in the Fifth Republic, and the Chun regime was responsible for over 84 percent of the 6,701 investigations pursued under the act.

The security presence in city centers, near university campuses, government and party offices, and media centers was heavy. Citizens, particularly students and young people, were subject to being stopped, questioned, and searched without due process. The typical response to demonstrations was disruption by large numbers of Combat Police, short-term mass detention of demonstrators, and selective prosecution of the organizers. Arrest warrants—required by law—were not always produced at the time of arrest in political cases.

The National Security Act increasingly was used after 1985 to suppress domestic dissent. Intended to restrict "antistate activities endangering the safety of the state and the lives and freedom of the citizenry," the act also was used to control and punish nonviolent domestic dissent. Its broad definition of offenses allowed enforcement over the widest range, wider than that of any other politically relevant law in South Korea. Along with other politically relevant laws such as the Social Safety Act and the Act Concerning Crimes Against the State, it weakened or removed procedural protection available to defendants in nonpolitical cases.

Questioning by the security services often involved not only psychological or physical abuse, but also outright torture. The 1987 torture and death of Pak Chong-ch'ŏl, a student at Seoul National University being questioned as to the whereabouts of a classmate, played a decisive role in galvanizing public opposition to the government's repressive tactics.

The security services not only detained those accused of violating laws governing political dissent, but also put under various lesser forms of detention—including house arrest—those people, including opposition politicians, who they thought intended to violate the laws. Many political, religious, and other dissidents were subjected to surveillance by government agents. Opposition assembly members later charged in the National Assembly that telephone tapping and the interception of correspondence were prevalent. Ruling party assembly members, government officials, and senior military officials probably also were subjected to this interference although they did not openly complain.

Listening to North Korean radio stations remained illegal in 1990 if it were judged to be for the purpose of "benefiting the antistate organization" (North Korea). Similarly, books or other literature considered subversive, procommunist, or pro-North Korean were illegal; authors, publishers, printers, and distributors of such material were subject to arrest.

Use of tear gas by the police (over 260,000 tear gas shells were used in 1987 to quell demonstrations) increasingly was criticized; the criticism eventually resulted in legal restrictions on tear gas use in 1989. The government continued, however, to block many "illegal" gatherings organized by dissidents that were judged to incite "social unrest." In 1988 government statistics noted 6,552 rallies involving 1.7 million people. There were 2.2 million people who had participated in 6,791 demonstrations in 1989.

Intelligence Agencies

The Agency for National Security Planning

The Agency for National Security Planning (ANSP) was originally established on June 19, 1961 as the Korean Central Intelligence Agency (KCIA) directly under the Supreme Council for

National Reconstruction in the immediate aftermath of the May 16, 1961, military coup. Its duties were to "supervise and coordinate both international and domestic intelligence activities and criminal investigation by all government intelligence agencies, including that of the military." Its mission was akin to that of a combined United States Central Intelligence Agency and Federal Bureau of Investigation.

The first head of the KCIA was Kim Chong-p'il. Kim, utilizing the existing Army Counterintelligence Corps, built a 3,000-member organization—the most powerful intelligence and investigatory agency in the republic. The KCIA maintained a complex set of interlocking institutional links with almost all of the government's key decision-making bodies. The KCIA had a near-monopoly over crucial information concerning national security under the charter of the Act Concerning Protection of Military Secrets and, more importantly, possessed considerable veto power over other agencies through its supervisory and coordination functions.

The KCIA's practically unlimited power to investigate and to detain any person accused of antistate behavior severely restricted the right to dissent or to criticize the regime. The frequent questioning, detention, or even prosecution of dissidents, opposition figures, and reporters seriously jeopardized basic freedoms and created an atmosphere of political repression.

After the 1979 assassination of President Park Chung Hee by the KCIA director, the KCIA was purged and temporarily lost much of its power. Chun Doo Hwan used his tenure as acting director of the KCIA from April to July 1980 to expand his power base beyond the military. The organization was renamed the Agency for National Security Planning, and its powers were redefined in presidential orders and legislation. The ANSP, like its predecessor, was a cabinet-level agency directly accountable to the president. The director of the ANSP continued to have direct presidential access. In March 1981, the ANSP was redesignated as the principal agency for collecting and processing all intelligence. The requirement for all other agencies with intelligence-gathering and analysis functions in their charters to coordinate their activities with the ANSP was reaffirmed.

Legislation passed at the end of 1981 further redefined the ANSP's legally mandated functions to include the collection, compilation, and distribution of foreign and domestic information regarding public safety against communists and plots to overthrow the government. The maintenance of public safety with regard to documents, materials, facilities, and districts designated as secrets of the state was the purview of the ANSP, as was the investigation of crimes of insurrection and foreign aggression, crimes of rebellion, aiding and abetting the enemy, disclosure of military secrets, and crimes provided for in the Act Concerning Protection of Military Secrets and the National Security Act. The investigation of crimes related to duties of intelligence personnel, the supervision of information collection, and the compilation and distribution of information on other agencies' activities designed to maintain public safety also were undertaken by the ANSP. By 1983 the ANSP had rebounded and again was the preeminent foreign and domestic intelligence organization.

As of 1990, the organizational structure of the ANSP was considered classified by Seoul, although earlier organizational information was public knowledge. Despite the social and political changes that came with the Sixth Republic (1987–), the ANSP apparently still considered the support and maintenance of the president in power to be one of its most important roles. In April 1990, for example, ruling Democratic Liberal Party (DLP) coleader Kim Young Sam complained that he and members of his faction within the DLP had been subjected to ''intelligence maneuvering in politics'' that included wiretapping, surveillance, and financial investigations.

Nevertheless, the ANSP's domestic powers were indeed curtailed under the Sixth Republic. Prior to the change, the ANSP had had free access to all government offices and files. The ANSP, Defense Security Command, Office of the Prosecutor General, Korean National Police, and the Ministry of Justice had stationed their agents in the National Assembly to collect information on the activities of politicians. In May 1988, however, overt ANSP agents, along with agents of other intelligence agencies, were withdrawn from the National Assembly building. The ANSP's budget was not made public, nor apparently was it made available in any useful manner to the National Assembly in closed sessions. In July 1989, pressured by opposition parties and public opinion, the ANSP was subjected to inspection and audit by the National Assembly for the first time in eighteen years. The ANSP removed its agents from the chambers of the Seoul Criminal Court and the Supreme Court in 1988.

As of 1990, however, the ANSP remained deeply involved in domestic politics and was not prepared to relinquish the power to prevent radical South Korean ideas—much less North Korean ideas—from circulating in South Korean society. Despite an agreement in September 1989 by the chief policymakers of the ruling and opposition parties to strip the ANSP of its power to investigate pro-North Korean activity (a crime under the National Security Act), the ANSP continued enforcing this aspect of the law rather than limiting itself to countering internal and external attempts to overthrow the government. The ANSP continued to pick up radical student and dissident leaders for questioning without explanation.

In another move to limit the potential for the ANSP to engage in "intelligence politics," the ANSP Information Coordination Committee was disbanded because of its history of unduly influencing other investigating authorities, such as the Office of the Prosecutor General. Additionally, the ANSP, responding to widespread criticism of its alleged human rights violations, set up a "watchdog" office to supervise its domestic investigations and to prevent agents from abusing their powers while interrogating suspects.

Aside from its controversial internal security mission, the ANSP also was known for its foreign intelligence gathering and analysis and for its investigation of offenses involving external subversion and military secrets. The National Unification Board and the ANSP (and the KCIA before it) were the primary sources of government analysis and policy direction for South Korea's reunification strategy and contacts with North Korea. The intelligence service's reputation in pursuing counterespionage cases also was excellent.

The ANSP monitored visitors, particularly from communist and East European countries, to prevent industrial and military espionage. Following the diplomatic successes of the late 1980s—the establishment of diplomatic relations with the Soviet Union and the countries of Eastern Europe, and the increased informal contacts with China, Mongolia, and Vietnam—this mission grew in importance. The security watch list contained 162 out of 3,808 visitors from communist nations in 1988 and 226 out of 6,444 visitors in 1989.

The Defense Security Command

It was Syngman Rhee, not the military, who initiated the political involvement of the military in intelligence activities. The turning point came in 1952 when Rhee proclaimed martial law—and the presence of military police in the chamber of the National Assembly guaranteed passage of the constitutional amendment he sought over the objections of a recalcitrant legislative branch and still-independent judicial branch. Throughout Rhee's administration, two military units—the Joint Military Provost Marshal and the army Counterintelligence Corps (CIC)—engaged in extralegal and violent political tactics, apparently not excluding the outright murder of politically undesirable people. Although the details never

Infantry mobile training exercise
Courtesy Ministry of National Defense, Republic of Korea

were disclosed fully, more than a few minor political figures' disappearances were connected to the two units.

Under Park, the provost marshal's political role declined, while the CIC and its successor, the Army Security Command (ASC), concentrated on internal military security. The CIC/ASC, which was under Park's direct control, maintained strict surveillance over all high-ranking officers. It acted as a deterrent to would-be coup leaders. It tried, less successfully, to prevent the rise of disruptive factions within the military.

The Defense Security Command was formally activated in October 1977. This merger of the Army Security Command, the Navy Security Unit, and the Air Force Office of Special Investigations produced a single, integrated unit under the direct command and operational control of the minister of national defense. Although technically subordinate to the minister, the DSC commander operated semiautonomously and typically had personal, direct access to the president. Given the disparity in service size, the old ASC predominated within the DSC. The strength of the DSC varied over time within a probable range of 5,000 to 7,000 people during the 1980s.

The DSC (and its predecessors) was created to deal with the real question of loyalty within a military on a divided peninsula. It was

315

inspired by the Guomindang model, in which political officers monitored the military services for subversion or disloyalty. The DSC was responsible for monitoring the military for loyalty; for safeguarding military information; for monitoring domestic political, economic, and social activities that might jeopardize military capabilities and national unity; for maintaining defense industrial security—both physically and in terms of counterespionage; for countering North Korean infiltration; for detecting espionage and anticommunist law violations; and for conducting special investigations at the direction of the president.

The DSC assigned small elements to all major military units to monitor security and loyalty. These elements operated outside the unit's chain of command and performed a highly effective independent audit function. The DSC representatives never rivaled unit commanders as political officers occasionally had in communist military units. Their input into officer evaluations, however, often played a decisive role in career progression, giving DSC members influence far beyond their rank and producing friction between them and the "regular" military. Corruption within the DSC was difficult to verify, but political manipulations, misappropriation of operating funds, and undue influencing of promotions certainly occurred and were particularly rampant in the mid- to late 1970s.

For most of the Park regime, the ASC/DSC remained concerned primarily with internal military matters and was involved in the Yun P'il-yong incident in 1972 and removing the army chief of staff, General Yi Se-ho, in 1979 for corruption. Yun P'il-yong, head of the Capital Garrison Command, was court martialed, along with several close followers, on charges of bribery and corruption. His "real" offense, however, was creating a faction among the classes of the four-year graduates of the Korea Military Academy. Yun's faction did not disappear when he was purged. The group of young officers, who called themselves the "Hanahoe" (One Mind Society), had its origins in an alumni group, the Taegu Seven Stars, of seven young officers, including Chun Doo Hwan and Roh Tae Woo, from the first graduating class of the Academy (Class 11). The Hanahoe evolved into a group of some 200 members through ten graduating classes. In 1979 and 1980, Chun drew on the Hanahoe in his ascent to power. The irony of Park's death at the hands of his KCIA chief in 1979, however, was compounded by the rise to power of the commander of the DSC, then Major General Chun Doo Hwan, who used the military's anticoup apparatus to ensure the success of his own coup (see The Chun Regime, ch. 1).

During and following Chun's rise to power, the DSC greatly expanded its charter into domestic politics and during the early

1980s was, perhaps, the dominant domestic intelligence service. The DSC was "credited" with masterminding the media reorganization of 1980 and with being the midwife for the first political parties of the Fifth Republic. Many former DSC members played prominent roles in Chun's administration and in the ruling Democratic Justice Party.

The end of the Fifth Republic brought the DSC under even more pressure than had been brought against the ANSP to cut back on its domestic political activities. Both the DSC and the ANSP withdrew from the National Assembly at the same time in 1988. In October 1988, Minister of National Defense O Cha-bok reported to the National Assembly that the DSC would concentrate on counterespionage activities, preventing the spread of communism, conducting "relevant research," major restructuring, and would discontinue the investigation of civilians. Subsequently, the DSC eliminated the Office of Information that had been charged with collecting information on civilians, whose members had been active in local government offices. As a result of this move, 116 small detachments were disbanded, and the DSC announced plans to cut 860 personnel, or 14 percent of its 1990 strength. Additionally, the DSC curtailed its involvement in security screening of nonmilitary government personnel. An official of the DSC claimed that surveillance of politicians was turned over to "another agency." Given the historically broad interpretation of national security threats espoused by DSC personnel, however, many analysts doubted that the DSC had totally disengaged from domestic political surveillance. Despite the democratic trends of the late 1980s, intelligence and security agencies still were populated by individuals who were both institutionally and personally loyal to the president and ready to use any means at their disposal to support him.

Korean National Police

Organized by the United States Army Military Government in 1945, the Korean National Police (KNP) force was formally activated in 1948 by the new Korean government and placed under the Ministry of Home Affairs. Even after the establishment of a separate military service in 1948, the police force retained a paramilitary role and was employed in military operations during the Korean War.

Attacked in its early years as a remnant of Japanese colonial rule (1910–45), beset by low professionalism, factionalism, endemic corruption, and political manipulation, the Korean National Police nonetheless still evolved into a relatively modern and effective force. Although the police force was used by the Rhee regime in such a flagrantly political way that it was held in low esteem by the citizenry, reforms made after the 1961 military coup began the police force's slow evolution into a professional force. Reorganization, recruitment by examination, merit promotion, and modern concepts of management and training were instituted. Further improvements came during the 1970s when modern communication, data processing, and crime detection practices were introduced.

In 1975 the director general of the KNP was elevated to vice-ministerial rank directly under the minister of home affairs. The KNP reported through its own channels to its headquarters in Seoul. Provincial governors and local officials had no authority over the police.

In addition to the regular police functions of law enforcement, criminal investigation, and public safety, the KNP was responsible for riot control, countering student demonstrations, and other public disorders. Coastal security, including patrolling coastal waters, antismuggling operations, and coordinating counterespionage operations with the navy and the air force, were also its purview. "Combat operations" against small-scale North Korean infiltration attempts; the monitoring of foreign residents in South Korea; anticommunist operations, including counterintelligence activities and monitoring of "security risks" (historically expanded to including monitoring political, labor, economic, academic, religious, and cultural figures); and counterterrorist operations were all part of the mission of the KNP. There sometimes was competitive overlap between the KNP, ANSP, and the DSC.

In 1989 the KNP was a 130,000-person organization that consisted of a headquarters, thirteen metropolitan/provincial police bureaus, the Combat Police, the National Maritime Police, an antiterrorist unit, the Central Police Academy, and other support services, such as a forensics laboratory, a hospital, and other police schools. As of January 1989, there were 201 police stations and 3,220 police substations and detachments throughout the country.

The National Police Headquarters exercised authority over all police components. Metropolitan and provincial police bureaus were responsible for maintaining public order by directing and supervising their own police stations (see fig. 18).

The police station was responsible for maintaining public peace within its own precinct. The police station had seven functioning sections: an administration and public safety section, responsible for operation and supervision of police substations and boxes, litigation of minor offenses, traffic control, and crime prevention; a security section, responsible for maintaining public order; an investigation section, responsible for investigating criminal incidents, lawsuits, booking criminals, custody of suspects, detention-cell management, and transference of cases and suspects involved in criminal cases to prosecution authorities; a criminal section, responsible for crime prevention; a counterespionage section; and an intelligence section, responsible for collection of intelligence and information. The police substation or police box took preliminary actions in all criminal incidents, civic services, and accidents.

Police boxes were the South Korean equivalent of the cop on the beat. They provided direct contact between the people and the police. Police box personnel were supposed to know their areas and the people who lived and worked in them. Police boxes were commanded by lieutenants or sergeants and had reaction vehicles available on a twenty-four-hour basis.

Weighed down by a wide range of administrative duties, KNP personnel spent only 15 percent of their time on routine enforcement duties in 1989. Among other things, the KNP collected fines, approved death certificates, and processed security checks for passport applicants. The personnel shortage was acute; official statistics showed that there was only one police officer (excluding the Combat Police, who accounted for nearly half the strength of the KNP) for every 680 South Koreans, as compared with one police officer for every 390 people in the United States, one for every 318 people in West Germany, and one for every 551 people in Japan (the lowest ratio for any major industrialized noncommunist country). This shortage was compounded by a tight budget and the continued preoccupation with riot control, which left the force ill equipped to deal with the demands of an increasingly affluent and sophisticated society.

Recruitment and training were done through the Central Police Academy, the National Police College, and the Police Consolidated Training School. The Central Police Academy was established in 1987. It had a maximum capacity of 35,000 recruits and was capable of simultaneously offering a six-week training course for police recruits, a two-week training course for draftees of the Combat Police, and a variety of basic specialized training courses for junior police. Officials planned to recruit about 10,000 new police officers a year from 1989 to 1991 to alleviate the personnel shortage, although their ability to maintain the quality of the force, given the low starting pay, was questioned. Only 12 percent of police applicants were university graduates in 1989. Screening unsuitable recruits was problematic because neither psychiatric nor polygraph assessments were administered. (In 1982, for example, an unstable police officer killed fifty-four people in one night following a domestic dispute.)

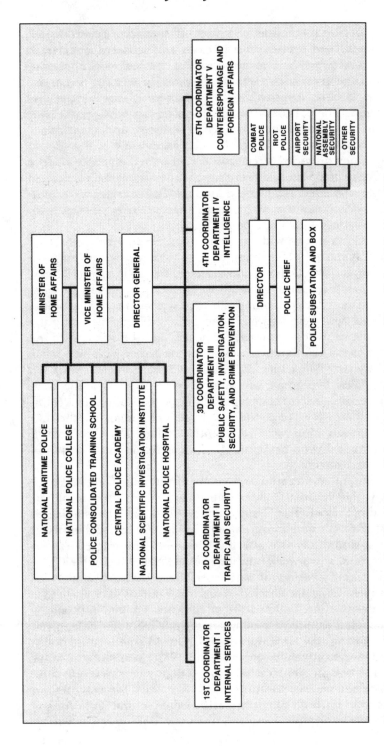

Source: Based on information from Republic of Korea, National Police Headquarters, *Korean National Police*, Seoul, 1989.

Figure 18. Organization of the Korean National Police, 1989

By 1989 the National Police College had graduated some 500 officers since its first class graduated in 1985. Each college class had about 120 police cadets, divided between law and public administration specializations. The National Police College began admitting women in 1989; five women were admitted each year. The cadets shared a collective life for four years at the college. The goal was to establish a career officers corps similar to those created by the military academies.

The Police Consolidated Training School provided advanced studies, basic training for junior police staff, and special practical training courses for security and investigative officers from the counterespionage echelons of police agencies. It also trained Maritime Police instructors, key command personnel for the Combat Police force, and foreign-language staff members.

Revolvers and carbines were the customary weapons; billy clubs were carried by patrol officers. The gradual replacement of carbines by rifles began in 1981. In 1989 the KNP reemphasized the planned replacement of carbines with M–16 rifles. Approximately 4,300 M–16s were to be supplied to police boxes and stations in 1989; by 1999 a total of 110,000 M–16s was scheduled to be distributed. Transportation was by motorcycle, bicycle, jeep, truck, and squad car.

The KNP's special weapons and tactics squad was known as Force 868. Organized in 1982, its members were trained in martial arts and counterterrorist tactics. It received significant support and advice from United States and West European counterterrorist task forces preceding the 1988 Seoul Olympics and was well supplied with the more specialized equipment needed for combating terrorism.

The Combat Police force was technically subordinate to the Ministry of National Defense, but the Ministry of Home Affairs and the Korean National Police were responsible for its operational management and budget. During hostilities, the Combat Police reverted to the Ministry of National Defense. The members of the Combat Police were conscripted at age twenty or older and served for approximately two-and-a-half years. Divided into companies, the Combat Police force was assigned to the metropolitan police bureaus. Except for supervisory personnel who were regular KNP officers, members of the Combat Police were paramilitary; their primary responsibilities were riot control and counterinfiltration. Under normal conditions, they did not have law enforcement powers as did regular KNP officers. In 1967 the Combat Police force was organized to handle counterinfiltration and antiriot duties.

Approximately half of the total strength of the KNP was formed into 350 Combat Police/riot control companies. The percentage of Combat Police in the total force increased during the 1980s. In 1982 there were 39,706 Combat Police, about 40 percent of the police total. By 1987 Combat Police represented 45.8 percent of the total force with 54,100 members. Since service in the Combat Police was regarded as fulfilling a military obligation, young men who did not wish to serve the compulsory minimum thirty-month service in the military could choose instead a thirty-five-month stint with the Korean National Police as combat police. Draftees into military service also could be assigned to the Combat Police force after completion of basic training.

Although the police were relatively well trained and disciplined, illegal police behavior in the conduct of investigations or handling of suspects was occasionally a serious problem. In 1985, for example, as a result of some form of official misconduct, one-fourth of Seoul's detectives were transferred, demoted, or otherwise disciplined. Rough treatment of suspects before a warrant was obtained was a continuing problem. Redress in cases of official misconduct normally was handled internally and rarely resulted in criminal charges against police officials.

Historically, the use of excessive force by the police was pervasive. In violent confrontations with student demonstrators, police units generally remained well disciplined, but rioters were beaten on apprehension, often by plainclothes police. Charges of police beatings in nonpolitical cases were made fairly frequently and sometimes were reported in the press. Antigovernment youth activists were subjected to repeated and severe physical torture, which at times resulted in death during interrogations. Various degrees of physical maltreatment, including sleep and food deprivation, electric shocks, beating, and forced water intake were common during police interrogations under the Rhee, Park, and Chun regimes. With the founding of the Sixth Republic, such reports declined. However, according to the United States Department of State's reports on human rights, some credible allegations of torture were made during the last half of 1989 by persons arrested under the National Security Act. Credible allegations of cruel treatment also continued in 1990. Although political cases received the most publicity, mistreatment of people detained or arrested for nonpolitical crimes is alleged to be widespread.

Criminal Justice

Throughout Korea's history, the assimilation of foreign laws has taken place in waves. Korea assimilated the codes of the Chinese

Qin, Wei, and Tang dynasties in the early Three Kingdoms period, the codes of the Tang, Song, and Yuan dynasties in the Koryŏ period (918–1392), the Ming Code in the Chosŏn Dynasty (1392–1910) period, Western civil law at the close of the Chosŏn Dynasty and during the Japanese occupation, and both Continental Law and Anglo-American law after liberation in 1945. The Chosŏn Dynasty also produced numerous codifications of Korean law and created new laws as necessary to deal with economic, social, and other public policy issues. Confucian values exerted strong influence on Korea's traditional law.

With the end of the Chosŏn Dynasty in 1910, decisive changes occurred in Korean law. Traditional Korean institutions were suddenly replaced. Reform measures, characterized by the introduction of Western institutions, began with the Kabo Reforms (1894–95) forced on Korea by Japan and modeled on the Japanese reforms of the Meiji Restoration (1868). These hasty reforms produced many laws translated from Japanese codes, which in turn had their origins in Roman and Germanic laws. The imposition of institutions by the Japanese and their post-1910 use for repressive colonial control constituted a sharp break with the Korean past.

The Westernized legal system's key features included its origin in the European civil law tradition; prominent roles for legal scholars,

323

university professors, and legislators, rather than judges; codified law rather than precedent as the major source of law; and an inquisitorial rather than adversarial court procedure. In other respects, however, Japanese colonial rule continued several features of the traditional Korean legal order. Under Japanese colonial rule, for example, there was no constitutional law, no guarantee of rights, and no judicial review of the exercise of political power. The legal system of Korea under Japanese rule was composed essentially of rules, duties, and obligations. Further, there was little institutional or procedural separation of powers. The Japanese governor general had even greater executive and legislative power than traditional Korean kings and ruled through a large, efficient, and modern bureaucracy.

After independence, revulsion over the Japanese occupation motivated Korean officials to devise a new codification designed to replace all Japanese laws, decrees, and orders, as well as the regulations and decrees of the United States Army Military Government in Korea (1945–48) with Korean codes. The process took ten years. Eventually, the Criminal Code (1953), the Code of Criminal Procedure (1954), the Civil Code (1958), the Civil Procedure Law (1960), and the Commercial Code (1962), as well as other codes—deliberately distinguished from previous Japanese codes—were adopted. In most substantive areas, however, South Korean law retained the most fundamental principles and procedures of continental jurisprudence as originally received through Japan.

The Code of Criminal Procedure (1954) governed most aspects of the enforcement of criminal justice. The code retained the basic characteristics of the European continental legal system and had some features of Anglo-American law. Among the features adapted from the United States legal system were a requirement for judicial warrants; modification of preliminary examination; strengthening of the system of state-appointed counsel; rejection of hearsay evidence as a matter of rule; and a requirement for corroborating evidence obtained in confessions.

The first exclusionary ruling on a confession in a South Korean court based on the constitutional guarantee of the right to legal counsel occurred in late 1989. Law enforcement and security agency officials, however, did not consider themselves compelled to adhere to legal precedents or court rulings when subsequently investigating other cases. Police and prosecutors, especially in political or espionage cases, still limited the frequency and length of defendants' meetings with counsel, except when taking written statements. Legislative action was needed for the South Korean system to proceed beyond court redress of specific violations in specific cases to the establishment of general guidelines.

Crime

During the late 1980s, South Korea experienced a jump in its traditionally low rates of violent crime. A growing number of violent crimes were directed against women, a fact that drew special public concern.

The Korean National Police authorities denied that there was any "organized crime" in South Korea, although police boxes in Seoul in 1990 posted signs encouraging citizens to report any information concerning *p'ongnyŏkpae*, violent bands of men armed with knives and improvised weapons who contributed to the rise in violent assaults throughout the city. Although there were some ties between Japan's underworld—the *yakuza* (Japanese gangsters)—and South Korean criminal groups through ethnic Koreans residing in Japan, *yakuza* "bosses" did not direct the extension of *yakuza* activities into South Korea. Nevertheless, the disturbing increase in violent crime and apparent disputes between criminal groups suggested that if organized crime did not yet exist in South Korea in 1989, its precursors were evident.

Historically, narcotics abuse in South Korea had been very low; it was confined primarily to marginal urban low-income groups and did not include either heroin or cocaine abuse (see Health Conditions, ch. 2). In the late 1980s, narcotics abuse remained low but had steadily increased, becoming a social and political issue. In reaction to this increase, enforcement responsibility was transferred from the Ministry of Health and Social Affairs to the Narcotics Division of the Supreme Prosecution Administration under the Ministry of Justice. This action gave narcotics enforcement a higher priority, more staffing, and more funding. (Drug-related arrests had increased from 810 in 1985 to 1,227 in 1987 and to 1,606 in 1988.) Most drug-related criminal activity involved the manufacture or abuse of methamphetamine and South Korea's emergence as a major Asian producer of *hirropon*, an illicit methamphetamine. A related problem was transshipment of Asian heroin destined for the United States and other world markets.

Criminal Procedure

In the absence of martial law or emergency decrees, both of which historically had been exercised by the government and provisions for which remained in the 1987 Constitution, criminal procedure in other than political cases followed a set format. Both public prosecutors and the police were authorized to conduct investigations of criminal acts. Public prosecutors were under the direction and supervision of the Office of the Supreme Prosecutor General; the supreme prosecutor general was appointed by the president. In 1990 there were four branches of the Office of the High Prosecutor General and fourteen district offices. Theoretically, police authority to investigate criminal acts was subordinate to the direction and review of the prosecutors. Also, the arrest of a suspect required a judicial warrant except in cases of flagrante delicto or when it was believed that the suspect would flee or commit the act again. The request for a warrant could be made only by the prosecutor.

After an arrest, the suspect had to be transferred to the public prosecutor within ten days and indicted within ten days of the prosecutor's gaining custody. The judge was permitted to extend detention another ten days; the suspect could request court review of the legality of detention.

The public prosecutor initiated legal action. The name of the accused, the alleged crime, the alleged facts of the case, and the applicable laws were stated in the indictment. The prosecutor had significant discretionary power to decide whether or not to bring the case to court based on his interpretation of the law and evidence, or in consideration of a suspect's age, character, motive, or other circumstances, even though a crime had been committed.

Prosecutors normally indicted only when they accumulated what they considered overwhelming evidence of a suspect's guilt. The courts, historically, were predisposed to accept the allegations of fact in an indictment. This predisposition was reflected in both the low acquittal rate—less than 0.5 percent—in criminal cases and in the frequent verbatim repetition of the indictment as the judgment. The principle of "innocent until proven guilty" applied in practice much more to the pre-indictment investigation than to the actual trial.

During the 1980s, there was a dispute within the legal system over the judiciary's power to check prosecution. The prosecution and judiciary differed over whether or not the law gave the judiciary grounds to arraign suspects before issuing warrants. The judiciary tried repeatedly in the 1980s to institutionalize this right and in 1989 asserted it in a proceeding. The judiciary was not able to compel the prosecution to accept this view, however.

At the prosecutor's discretion, a case could be brought before the court by summary indictment if the offense were punishable by fines. In such a case, the judge gave a summary judgment without holding a public hearing. The accused could request an ordinary trial.

Once indicted, the accused had the right to be released on bail. Exceptions could be made if the offense were punishable by death,

life imprisonment, or imprisonment over ten years; if the defendant were a recidivist; if there were suspicion that the defendant would destroy evidence; or if there were reasonable grounds to suspect that the defendant would flee; or if the residence of the defendant were unknown. In 1989 bail was granted in a National Security Act case for the first time.

The constitutional right to representation by an attorney was not interpreted as applying to the investigation and interrogation phases. In National Security Act cases, access to counsel was regularly denied during the investigation phase. In 1989 lawyers sought court orders granting access, but neither the ANSP nor the Prosecutor General's Office felt compelled to comply when the National Security Act was involved.

There was no jury system. Cases that involved offenses punishable by the death penalty, life imprisonment, or imprisonment for not less than one year were tried by three judges of a district or branch court. The remaining cases were heard by a single judge. Political and criminal cases were tried by the same courts; military courts did not try civilians except under martial law.

At least five days before trial, the defendant was served a copy of the indictment. The defendant had to be represented by counsel if the offenses were punishable by death or imprisonment for more than three years. The court appointed defense counsel if the defendant was unable to do so because of age, mental capacity, poverty, or other handicaps that might impair choice or communication.

Hearings generally were open to the public. If danger to national security or prejudice to public peace or good morals were involved, the judge could close the proceedings. Charges against defendants in the courts were declared publicly. Trial documents, however, were not part of the public record. In lengthy and complex indictments, the relationship between specific alleged actions and violations of specific sections of the penal code could become unclear. In cases involving a mixture of political and criminal charges, this situation at times led to charges of unfair proceedings. A defendant had the right to remain silent and free from physical restraint in the courtroom. Judges generally allowed considerable scope for the examination of witnesses.

Either the defendant or the prosecutor could appeal a judgment on the basis of law or fact. Appeals could result in reduced or increased sentences. A Constitution Court was established in 1988 to relieve the burden on the Supreme Court (see The Judiciary, ch. 4). When the constitutionality of a law was at issue in a trial, the Supreme Court requested a decision of the Constitution Court. The president, chief justice, and the National Assembly each named three members of the nine-member Constitution Court.

The Supreme Court retained the power to make final review of the constitutionality or legality of administrative decrees, regulations, or actions when at issue in a trial. Grounds for an appeal to the Supreme Court were limited by the Code of Criminal Procedure to violation of the Constitution, law, or regulation material to the judgment; abolition, alteration, or pardon of penalty; a grave mistake in factfinding; or extreme impropriety in sentencing. An interpretation of law in an appeal had binding effect on the inferior court only when the case was remanded. In other cases, however, a decision of the Supreme Court only had persuasive effect.

Judges were trained professionally and were among the best products of one of the toughest education systems in the world. The qualifications for a judge were the completion of two years of courses at the Judicial Research and Training Institute after passing the national judicial examination, or the possession of qualifications as a prosecutor or an attorney. Judges were members of a tiny elite; the institute had only 3,692 graduates from 1949 to 1988. In 1988 there were only 940 judges, 668 prosecutors, and 1,593 practicing attorneys. There were additional requirements for higher positions: fifteen years of legal experience for the chief justice and justices of the Supreme Court; ten years of experience for the chief judge of an appellate court, the chief judge of a district court, the chief judge of a family court, and the senior judge of an appellate court; and five years of experience for the judge of an appellate court, the senior judge of a district court, and the senior judge of a family court. South Korea's president, with the consent of the National Assembly, appointed both the chief justice and, upon the recommendation of the chief justice, the other justices of the Supreme Court. Under the 1987 Constitution and the Court Organization Law, lower justices were appointed by the chief justice with the consent of the Conference of Supreme Court Justices.

Historically, the executive branch exercised great influence on judicial decisions. However, there were some indications of increased judicial independence in 1989. In a number of cases, the Constitution Court found that the government had violated the constitutional rights of individuals. Moreover, the Supreme Court invalidated the results of the elections for two National Assembly seats, citing election law violations by victorious ruling party candidates.

Penal administration was controlled and supervised by the Ministry of Justice. There were four detention facilities (for unconvicted detainees), twenty-seven correctional institutions, ten juvenile training institutes, and four juvenile classification homes. Conditions in correctional institutions were austere and particularly harsh in winter. Discipline was strict. Prisoners who broke rules or protested conditions sometimes were physically abused. Under normal circumstances, however, convicts were not physically punished. Most accusations of mistreatment involved persons detained or awaiting trial in detention facilities, rather than those who were already convicted and serving their sentences in prison. Visitation was strictly limited to legal counsel and immediate families. Mail was subject to monitoring and occasional censorship. There was no significant difference in the treatment of prisoners on the basis of wealth, social class, race, or sex. The treatment of political prisoners could be better or worse than that of regular prisoners. On some occasions, special provisions were allowed for political prisoners, and as late as 1989 it also was alleged by human rights activists that political prisoners sometimes were subjected to sleep deprivation and psychological pressure.

There were a number of probationary devices that permitted police to supervise suspected or convicted criminals, including deferral of prosecution and suspension of sentence. These measures increased judicial flexibility and were often used to show clemency. Probationary devices also had frequently been used to ensure that released political offenders behaved in a manner acceptable to the government. Criminals who showed repentance regularly were freed in amnesties, often linked to holidays. Amnesty often was declared to showcase the beneficence of the state in forgiving criminals.

* * *

Three excellent sources on the South Korean armed forces are Edward A. Olsen's "The Societal Role of the Republic of Korea Armed Forces" in *The Armed Forces in Contemporary Asian Societies;* Eugene Kim's "The South Korean Military and Its Political Role" in *Political Changes in South Korea;* and Young Woo Lee's insightful article "Birth of the Korean Army, 1945–50" in *Korea and World Affairs.* The *Asian Defence Journal* often has comparative analyses of the military capabilities of the North Korean and South Korean armed forces. Larry A. Niksch's "The Military Balance on the Korean Peninsula" in *Korea and World Affairs* and Richard L. Sneider's *The Political and Social Capabilities of North and South Korea for the Long-Term Military Competition* provide useful information on the Korean arms race. Dae-Kyu Yoon's *Law and Political Authority in Korea* is an excellent and detailed study of the interaction of law and politics in South Korea. Two books by South Korean army officers, Colonel Lee Suk Bok's *The Impact of United States Forces in Korea* and Brigadier General Taek-Hyung Rhee's *U.S.-ROK Combined Operations* provide the South Korean perspective on United States-South Korean military relations. English-language sources on national security issues are published regularly by the Seoul government, South Korean universities, and two daily newspapers, *Korea Herald* and *Korea Times.* The Ministry of National Defense publishes an annual *White Paper* that provides a comprehensive examination of military organization, defense spending, and training in the South Korean armed forces. The National Police Headquarters annually publishes *Korean National Police,* a pictorial and textual description of that organization. Manwoo Lee, Ronald D. McLaurin, and Chung-in Moon's (eds.), *Alliance under Tension: The Evolution of South Korean-U.S. Relations* is another useful source.

The subversive activities of North Korea in South Korea and abroad and the causes for increased domestic violence in South Korea in the 1980s are discussed in official reports published by the United States Department of State and the Committee on Foreign Affairs of the United States House of Representatives. *The Bombing of Korean Airlines Flight KAL-858,* by the United States House Committee on Foreign Relations, provides a comprehensive examination of North Korea's past use of and capabilities for future acts of terrorism targeting South Koreans. Donald N. Clark's *The Kwangju Uprising* examines aspects of the Kwangju incident following Chun Doo Hwan's December 1979 coup. Selig S. Harrison's *The South Korean Political Crisis and American Policy Options* discusses the goals of radical organizations in South Korea in the mid-1980s. For information concerning the history of the Korean legal system, Chun Bong Duck, William Shaw, and Choi Kai-Kwon's *Traditional Korean Legal Attitudes* should be consulted. Articles in the *Far Eastern Economic Review* and *Asian Survey* should also be consulted. (For further information and complete citations, see Bibliography.)

Appendix

Table 1. Metric Conversion Coefficients and Factors

When you know	Multiply by	To find
Millimeters	0.04	inches
Centimeters	0.39	inches
Meters	3.3	feet
Kilometers	0.62	miles
Hectares (10,000 m²)	2.47	acres
Square kilometers	0.39	square miles
Cubic meters	35.3	cubic feet
Liters	0.26	gallons
Kilograms	2.2	pounds
Metric tons	0.98	long tons
....	1.1	short tons
....	2,204	pounds
Degrees Celsius	9	degrees Fahrenheit
(Centigrade)	divide by 5 and add 32	

Table 2. Major Economic Indicators, 1986-89

Indicator	1986	1987	1988	1989
Gross National Product [1]	102.7	128.4	169.2	204.0
Economic growth [2]	12.9	12.8	12.2	6.5
Per capita income [3]	2,503.0	3,098.0	4,040.0	4,830.0
Consumer prices [4]	1.4	6.1	7.2	5.2
Gross savings [5]	33.1	36.3	37.7	35.8
Trade account [6]	4.2	7.7	11.4	4.6
Current account [6]	4.6	9.9	14.2	5.0
Total foreign debt [1]	44.5	35.6	31.2	30.3
Gross investment share [4]	29.3	29.4	29.9	33.4

[1] In billions of United States dollars.
[2] In percentage change.
[3] In United States dollars.
[4] Annual percentage change.
[5] As percentage of gross national product.
[6] In billions of United States dollars, balance of payments basis.

Source: Based on information from Korea Economic Institute of America, *Korea's Economy*, Washington, 1990.

Table 3. Central Government Expenditures, 1984, 1986, and 1987
(in billions of wŏn) *

Expenditure	1984 Amount	1984 Percentage	1986 Amount	1986 Percentage	1987 Amount	1987 Percentage
National defense	3,539.9	28.2	4,335.5	28.3	4,793.5	26.1
General	6,822.1	54.4	8,577.0	56.0	10,009.0	54.5
Fixed capital formation	949.6	7.6	1,284.4	8.4	1,391.5	7.6
Net lending	-2.4	—	9.5	—	0.5	—
Other	1,225.1	9.8	1,113.7	7.3	2,170.7	11.8
TOTAL	12,534.3	100.0	15,320.1	100.0	18,365.2	100.0

—means negligible.
* For value of the wŏn—see Glossary.

Source: Based on information from Bank of Korea, *Annual Report, 1987,* Seoul, 1987, 68; and *The Europa World Year Book, 1989,* 2, London, 1989, 1574.

Table 4. Central Government Revenues, 1984, 1986, and 1988
(in billions of wŏn) *

Source	1984	1986	1988
Internal taxes	6,697.4	8,464.0	12,545.1
Customs duties	1,593.7	1,942.5	2,573.3
Defense surtax	1,511.3	1,878.9	2,978.4
Education surtax	284.8	372.4	512.3
Monopoly profits	866.0	984.0	874.0
Government enterprise receipts (net)	232.3	238.3	340.8
Other	2,012.0	2,398.5	4,185.4
TOTAL	13,197.5	16,278.6	24,009.3

* For value of the wŏn—see Glossary.

Source: Based on information from Bank of Korea, *Annual Report 1987,* Seoul, 1987, 68; and *The Europa World Year Book, 1989,* 2, London, 1989, 1574.

Table 5. Balance of Payments, Selected Years, 1965–88
(in millions of United States dollars)

Year	Current Account Balance	Trade Account Balance	Year	Current Account Balance	Trade Account Balance
1965	9	-240	1985	-887	-19
1970	-623	-922	1986	4,617	4,206
1975	1,887	-1,671	1987	9,854	7,659
1980	-5,321	-4,384	1988	14,266	11,561

Table 6. Trade with the United States, 1982-89
(in billions of United States dollars)

	1982	1983	1984	1985	1986	1987	1988	1989
Exports	6.28	8.26	10.52	10.78	13.92	18.38	21.47	20.64
Imports	5.95	6.27	6.87	6.55	6.54	8.76	12.75	15.91
Trade balance *	0.32	1.98	3.65	4.23	7.37	9.62	8.71	4.73

* Figures may not add because of rounding.

Source: Based on information from United States Department of Commerce, International Trade Administration, *Foreign Economic Trends and Their Implications for the United States: Korea,* Washington, June 1989; United States, Department of Commerce, International Trade Administration, *Foreign Economic Trends and Their Implications for the United States: Korea,* Washington, April 1990; and Korea Economic Institute of America, *Korea Economic Update,* 1, No. 2, Summer 1990, 4.

Table 7. Principal Trading Partners, 1986 and 1988
(in millions of United States dollars)

1986 Exports		1986 Imports	
Country by Rank	Volume	Country by Rank	Volume
United States	13,880	Japan	10,869
Japan	5,426	United States	6,545
Hong Kong	1,691	West Germany	1,216
Canada	1,248	Australia	1,080
West Germany	1,242	Malaysia	902
Britain	1,034	Canada	709
Saudi Arabia	855	France	706
France	543	Saudi Arabia	635
Australia	535	Britain	454
Singapore	532	Oman	440

1988 Exports		1988 Imports	
Country by Rank	Volume	Country by Rank	Volume
United States	21,404,087	Japan	15,975,786
Japan	12,004,068	United States	12,756,657
Hong Kong	3,560,944	West Germany	2,073,987
West Germany	2,367,803	Australia	1,797,390
Britain	1,950,899	Malaysia	1,331,354
Canada	1,692,327	Canada	1,196,816
Singapore	1,355,260	France	1,134,851
Saudi Arabia	1,130,309	Taiwan	1,071,264
France	1,064,886	Britain	914,503
Australia	864,821	Indonesia	905,297

Source: Based on information from Korea Trade Promotion Corporation, *How to Trade with Korea: 1987—A Practical Guide to Trade and Investment,* Seoul, 1987, 20-26; and *The Europa World Year Book, 1989,* 2, London, 1989, 1574.

Table 8. Constitutional Amendments, 1948–90

Date	Description
July 4, 1954 .... (First Republic)	To amend 1948 constitution to allow direct popular election of president rather than election by National Assembly, in which President Syngman Rhee's Liberal Party lacked a stable majority. Passed in late-night National Assembly session under martial law with some opposition members under arrest and others forcibly assembled to form quorum.
November 27, 1954	To eliminate limits on presidential terms in office to permit incumbent president (Rhee) indefinite tenure. Bill carried (after two earlier failures) by fraudulent rounding of fractional number required for two-thirds majority.
June 15, 1960 .... (Second Republic)	To replace presidential system with parliamentary form of government following overthrow of President Rhee. Provided extensive civil rights and established Central Election Management Committee.
November 23, 1960	To allow ex post facto legislation for punishment of rigging of March 1960 presidential elections and other actions by officials under former Rhee government.
December 17, 1962 .... (Third Republic)	To reestablish presidential form of government in civilian form for military leaders under Park Chung Hee, who staged coup d'état in May 1961.
October 17, 1969	To remove two-term restriction to permit President Park indefinite tenure.
November 21, 1972 .... (Fourth Republic—*yusin* constitution)	To increase executive power by permitting broad use of presidential emergency measures, to undercut power of National Assembly, and to restrict many civil rights. Ratified by referendum under martial law.
October 22, 1980 .... (Fifth Republic)	To end *yusin* political order and provide new constitutional framework for military leaders under Chun Doo Hwan, who staged coup d'état in May 1980. Restored some civil rights, which were qualified by accompanying legislation. Ratified by referendum under martial law; coupled with measures barring all major civilian politicians from political participation.
October 28, 1987 .... (Sixth Republic)	To void Fifth Republic constitution and provide for direct popular election of president; coupled with measures restoring rights of political participation to all politicians barred in 1980. Drafted by joint committee of ruling and opposition party representatives following public pledges by ruling party presidential candidate Roh Tae Woo in June 1987. Restored stronger civil rights provisions of 1960 and 1962 constitutions.

Source: Based on information from *Korea Annual, 1988,* Seoul, 1989, 91–94; John Kie-Chiang Oh, *Korea: Democracy on Trial*, Ithaca, 1968, 43, 48; and *Constitution of the Republic of Korea*, Seoul, 1987.

Appendix

Table 9. Status of the National Assembly under the 1987 Constitution

Area of Power	Provision
Symbolic	Text concerning National Assembly precedes text concerning executive.
National Assembly and State Council	National Assembly member apprehended or detained prior to opening of session must be released during session on request of National Assembly (except in cases of flagrante delicto).
	Requires one-quarter of membership to convene extraordinary session (versus one-third in 1980 constitution).
	Deletes provision limiting business in presidentially called extraordinary session to bills introduced by president.
	Deletes 150-day limit on assembly sessions.
	Deletes reference to dissolution of assembly.
	Extends power of inspection or investigation of specific matters of state affairs to include matters under criminal investigation or trial.
	Deletes provision disallowing motion for removal of prime minister or State Council member(s) within first year after appointment.
	Deletes provision for removal of entire State Council if prime minister is removed.
Judicial appointments	Requires consent of National Assembly for all appointments to Supreme Court (not just chief justice).
Presidency	Vote by majority of National Assembly breaks tie in presidential elections.
	Requires convocation of National Assembly if there is time, prior to emergency measures or presidential orders having legal effect. Failure to obtain National Assembly approval voids emergency measures and restores effect of previous laws.

Source: Based on information from Republic of Korea, Ministry of Culture and Information, Korean Overseas Information Service, *Constitution of the Republic of Korea,* Seoul, 1980; and Republic of Korea, Ministry of Culture and Information, Korean Overseas Information Service, *Constitution of the Republic of Korea,* Seoul, 1987.

Table 10. Executive Domination of the Judiciary, 1972–86

Year	Developments
1972	President Park Chung Hee dismisses nine Supreme Court justices who had overturned a law denying relatives of war veterans right to claim compensation from state. Park's 1972 *yusin* constitution rescinds Supreme Court's power to review constitutionality of laws.
1980	Six Supreme Court justices are interrogated by security agency and subsequently forced to step down for their minority views that Kim Chae-gyu, President Park's assassin, had not conspired to overthrow government.
Early 1980s	A number of law students are blacklisted from enrolling in Judicial Training and Research Institute after demonstrating against 1980 Chun Doo Hwan coup d'état.
1985	Two Seoul District Court judges are punitively reassigned to provincial posts after acquitting accused student demonstrators. A third judge is transferred after protesting the reassignment.
	Supreme Court reverses its earlier decision in appeal case of Kang Chong-gŏn, a National Security Act offender under continued detention after his original sentence had expired.
1986	Justice Yi Il-kyu is denied reappointment to Supreme Court. Among his independent decisions are a 1963 determination that voided coerced confession made by suspect on spying charges and questioning jurisdiction of 1980 military court in 1985 appeal by lawyer linked with opposition figure Kim Dae Jung.

Table 11. National Assembly Election Returns, February 1985

Party	Number of Seats		Percentage of Vote	Percentage of Seats
	Direct	Proportional		
Democratic Justice Party	87	61	35.3	53.6
New Korea Democratic Party	50	17	29.2	24.3
Democratic Korea Party	26	9	19.5	12.7
Korea Nationalist Party	15	5	9.2	7.2
Other and independents *	6	0	6.8	2.2
Total	184	92	100.0	100.0

* Most independents subsequently joined one of the four major parties.

Source: Based on information from Byung Chul Koh, "The 1985 Parliamentary Election in South Korea," *Asian Survey*, 25, No. 9, September 1985, 883–97.

Table 12. National Assembly Election Returns, April 1988

Party	Number of Seats Direct	Number of Seats Proportional	Percentage of Vote	Percentage of Seats
Democratic Justice Party	87	38	34.0	41.8
Party for Peace and Democracy	54	16	19.3	23.4
Reunification Democratic Party	46	13	23.8	19.7
New Democratic Republican Party	27	8	15.6	11.7
Other and independents [1]	10	0	7.2	3.3
Total [2]	224	75	100.0	100.0

[1] Most independents subsequently joined one of the four major parties.
[2] Figures may not add to totals because of rounding.

Source: Based on information from Chan Wook Park, "The 1988 National Assembly Election in South Korea: The Ruling Party's Loss of Legislative Majority," *Journal of Northeast Asian Studies*, 7, No. 3, Fall 1988, 65.

Table 13. Strikes and Labor Disputes, 1987–90

Year	Number of Events	Comments
1987	3,749	70.1 percent over pay.
1988	1,873	Average duration 10 days; 51.6 percent over pay, 16.9 percent over the right to bargain collectively, 7.1 percent over working conditions, 5.9 percent over dismissal, 3 percent over employers' unfair acts.
1989 *	1,678	Average duration 17.8 days, 47.6 percent over pay, 25.5 percent over collective bargaining; 69 percent of events ruled illegal under Labor Dispute Adjustment Law.

* January through October.

Table 14. *Principal Radical Organizations, 1985–89*

Date Established	Organization
April 17, 1985	National Federation of Student Associations (Chŏnhangnyŏn). Action wing is Struggle Committee for the Liberation of the Masses, the Attainment of Democracy, and the Unification of the Nation (Sammint'u). Both outlawed as "anti-state organizations" under National Security Act and suppressed in 1986.
March 21, 1986	Struggle Committee Against Imperialism, the Military, and Fascism, and for the Nation and Democracy (Mimmint'u) inaugurated at thirty-eight universities. Mimmint'u ideology emphasizes political linkages and cooperation among students, workers, and farmers.
April 11, 1986	Committee for the Anti-U.S. Struggle for Independence and the Anti-Fascist Struggle for Democracy (Chamint'u) formed at Seoul National University and Korea University. Chamint'u ideology emphasizes struggle and direct action against the government and the United States presence in South Korea.
May 1987	Seoul Area Council of University Student Representatives (Sŏdaehyŏp). Combines Chamint'u and Mimmint'u elements.
August 19, 1987	National Association of University Student Councils (Chŏndaehyŏp) established in Taejŏn. Replaced and enlarged Sŏdaehyŏp.
May 1988	Seoul Area Federation of Student Councils (Sŏch'ongnyŏn).

Source: Based on information from Wonmo Dong, "University Students in South Korean Politics: Patterns of Radicalization in the 1980s," *Journal of International Affairs* [Seoul], 40, No. 2, Winter–Spring 1987, 233–55; and "Monthly Views Two Dissident Groups' Interactions," *Sin tonga* [Seoul], March 1, 1989, 268–85, in Foreign Broadcast Information Service, *Daily Report: East Asia,* April 7, 1989, 26–38.

Table 15. *Media Statistics, 1986, 1988, and 1989*

Media	1986	1988	1989
National newspapers [1]	8	9	18
Local newspapers [1]	10	10	24
News agencies	2	2	2
National radio stations [2]	3	3	3
Affiliated local (rebroadcast) stations	47	49	48
Television stations	2	2	2
Foreign press representatives	40	50	50
Periodicals [3]	2,500	n.a.	3,500

n.a.—not available.
[1] Newspapers are Korean-language dailies, excluding sports newspapers.
[2] Excluding Far Eastern Broadcasting Company.
[3] Estimated.

*Table 16. Orders of Battle and Major Equipment for Ground
Forces of South Korea and North Korea, 1990*

Category		South Korea		North Korea
Active-duty personnel ...		575,000 [1]		930,000
Military units	3	army headquarters	16	corps headquarters
	10	corps headquarters [2]	31	infantry divisions [2]
	2	mechanized infantry divisions [2]	15	armored brigades [2]
	21	infantry divisions [2]	24	infantry brigades [2]
	7	special forces brigades	25	special forces brigades
	8	independent infantry brigades/ armor/infantry/ marine	—	
	1	aviation brigade	—	
	2	surface-to-surface missile battalions		surface-to-surface missile battalions [3]
Equipment	1,560	tanks	3,500	tanks
	1,550	armored personnel carriers	1,960	armored personnel carriers
	4,200	field artillery pieces	7,800	field artillery pieces
	140	multiple rocket launchers	2,500	multiple rocker launchers
	5,300	mortars	11,000	mortars
	12	surface-to-surface missiles	70	surface-to-surface missiles

—means negligible.
[1] Includes 25,000 marines.
[2] Includes subordinate armor and artillery units.
[3] Number of units unknown.

Source: Based on information from *The Military Balance, 1989-1990,* London, 1989, 165-66;
and Republic of Korea, Ministry of National Defense, *Defense White Paper, 1989,*
Seoul, 138-40.

Table 17. Order of Battle and Major Equipment for Air Forces
of South Korea and North Korea, 1990

Category	South Korea		North Korea	
Personnel		40,000 [1]		70,000
Military units [1]	22	ground attack/ interceptor squadrons	3	bomber regiments
	1	reconnaissance squadron	18	ground attack regiments
	1	search-and-rescue squadron		surface-to-surface missile battalions [2]
	4	transport squadrons	6 +	transport regiments
			2	defense artillery divisons
	5	surface-to-surface missile battalions	7	air defense regiments
	2	air defense artillery brigades		
	1	counterinsurgency squadron		
Equipment				
Fighter aircraft	90	F–5A/B	40	J–7
	36	F–16C/D	160	J–6
	204	F–5E/F	100	J–5
	130	F–4	40	Q–5
	20	RF–4/5	10	Su–25
	23	A–37	24	MiG-29
			46	MiG-23
			120	MiG-21
			300	MiG-17
			20	Su-7
Bombers		0	80	H–5
Transport		37	280	
Helicopters		400 [3]	142	

[1] Data on transportation, helicopter, and training units not available.
[2] Number of units unknown.
[3] In army and naval aviation units. The army, navy, and air force have an additional 263 support aircraft, including helicopters, trainers, and transports.

Source: Based on information from *The Military Balance, 1989–1990*, London, 1989, 165–66; and Republic of Korea, Ministry of National Defense, *Defense White Paper, 1989*, Seoul, 1990, 138, 141.

Table 18. *Orders of Battle and Major Equipment for Naval Forces of South Korea and North Korea, 1990*

Category	South Korea		North Korea	
Personnel	35,000 [1]		40,000	
Military units	3	fleet commands		East Coast Fleet
	1	aviation command		West Coast Fleet
	1	amphibious command		
	1	logistics command		
	1	mine-warfare command		
	1	training command		
Equipment	3	minisubmarines	24	submarines
	11	destroyers	2	frigates
	17	frigates	4	corvettes
	11	missile-attack craft	29	missile-attack craft
	68	patrol boats	330	patrol boats
	9	minesweepers	40	minesweepers
	52	amphibious craft	125	amphibious craft
	10	Grumman S-2 aircraft		
	35	Hughes 500-MD helicopters		

Source: Based on information from *The Military Balance, 1989-1990*, 1989, London, 165-66; and Republic of Korea, Ministry of National Defense, *Defense White Paper, 1989*, Seoul, 1990, 141.

Bibliography

Chapter 1

Amsden, Alice H. *Asia's Next Giant: South Korea and Late Industrialization.* New York: Oxford University Press, 1989.

Appleman, Roy E. *South to the Naktong, North to the Yalu.* Washington: Office of the Chief of Military History, Department of the Army, 1961.

Bibliography of Asian Studies, 1985. (Ed., Wayne Surdam.) Ann Arbor, Michigan: Association for Asian Studies, 1990.

Blair, Clay. *The Forgotten War: America in Korea, 1950-1953.* New York: Times Books, 1988.

Buss, Claude A. *The United States and the Republic of Korea: Background for Policy.* Stanford: Hoover Institution Press, 1982.

Chandra, Vipan. *Imperialism, Resistance, and Reform in Late Nineteenth-Century Korea: Enlightenment and the Independence Club.* (Korea Research Monograph No. 13.) Berkeley: Center for Korean Studies, Institute of East Asian Studies, University of California, 1988.

Cho, Soon Sung. *Korea in World Politics, 1940-1950.* Berkeley: University of California Press, 1984.

Ch'oe, Young-ho. *The Civil Examinations and the Social Structure in Early Yi Dynasty Korea, 1392-1600.* Seoul: Korean Research Center, 1987.

Clough, Ralph N. *Embattled Korea: The Rivalry for International Support.* Boulder, Colorado: Westview Press, 1987.

Cole, David C., and Princeton N. Lyman. *Korean Development: The Interplay of Politics and Economics.* Cambridge: Harvard University Press, 1971.

Cumings, Bruce. *The Origins of the Korean War: The Roaring of the Cataract, 1947-1950,* 2. Princeton: Princeton University Press, 1990.

Eckert, Carter J. *Offspring of Empire: The Kŏch'ang Kims and the Colonial Origins of Korean Capitalism, 1876-1945.* Seattle: University of Washington Press, 1991.

Fairbank, John K., Edwin O. Reischauer, and Albert M. Craig. *East Asia: Tradition and Transformation.* Boston: Houghton Mifflin, 1973.

Gleysteen, William H., Jr. "Korea: A Special Target of American Concern." Pages 85-99 in David D. Newsom (ed.), *The Diplomacy of Human Rights.* Lanham, Maryland: University Press of America, 1987.

Grajdanzev, Andrew J. *Modern Korea*. New York: Octagon Books, 1978.

Haboush, JaHyun Kim. *A Heritage of Kings: One Man's Monarch in the Confucian World*. New York: Columbia University Press, 1988.

Han, Sung-Joo. *The Failure of Democracy in South Korea*. Berkeley: University of California Press, 1974.

Han, Woo-keun. *The History of Korea*. (Trans., Lee Kyung-shik; ed., Grafton K. Mintz.) Honolulu: East-West Center Press, 1971.

Henderson, Gregory. *Korea: The Politics of the Vortex*. Cambridge: Harvard University Press, 1968.

Henthorn, William E. *A History of Korea*. New York: Free Press, 1971.

Hinton, Harold C. *Korea under New Leadership: The Fifth Republic*. New York: Praeger, 1983.

Hong, Wontack, and Anne O. Krueger (eds.). *Trade and Development in Korea: Proceedings of a Conference Held by the Korea Development Institute*. Seoul: The Institute, 1975.

Jacobs, Norman. *The Korean Road to Modernization and Development*. Urbana: University of Illinois Press, 1985.

Kihl, Young Whan. *Politics and Policies in Divided Korea: Regimes in Contest*. Boulder, Colorado: Westview Press, 1984.

Kim, Chong-won. *Divided Korea: The Politics of Development: 1945–1972*. Cambridge: East Asia Research Center, Harvard University Press, 1975.

Kim, C.I. Eugene, and Han-Kyo Kim. *Korea and the Politics of Imperialism, 1876–1910*. Berkeley: University of California Press, 1967.

Kim, Han-Kyo (ed.), with the assistance of Hong Kyoo Park. *Studies on Korea: A Scholar's Guide*. Honolulu: Center for Korean Studies, University of Hawaii Press, 1980.

Kim, Se-Jin. *The Politics of Military Revolution in Korea*. Chapel Hill: University of North Carolina Press, 1971.

Koh, Byung Chul. *The Foreign Policy Systems of North and South Korea*. Berkeley: University of California Press, 1984.

Koo, Youngnok, and Sung-Joo Han. *Foreign Policy of the Republic of Korea*. New York: Columbia University Press, 1985.

Lee, Chae-Jin, and Hideo Sato. *U.S. Policy Toward Japan and Korea: A Changing Influence Relationship*. New York: Praeger, 1982.

Lee, Chong-Sik. *Japan and Korea: The Political Dimension*. Stanford: Hoover Institution Press, 1985.

_____. *The Politics of Korean Nationalism*. Berkeley: University of California Press, 1963.

Lee, Hahn-Been. *Korea: Time, Change, and Administration*. Honolulu: East-West Center Press, 1968.

Lee, Ki-baik. *A New History of Korea.* (Trans., Edward W. Wagner, with Edward J. Shultz.) Cambridge: Harvard University Press, 1984.

Lowe, Peter. *The Origins of the Korean War.* New York: Longman, 1986.

Mason, Edward S., et al. *The Economic and Social Modernization of the Republic of Korea.* (Studies in the Modernization of the Republic of Korea, 1945–1975, Harvard East Asian Monographs, No. 92.) Cambridge: Harvard University Press, 1980.

Matray, James Irving. *The Reluctant Crusade: American Foreign Policy in Korea, 1941–1950.* Honolulu: University of Hawaii Press, 1985.

McCune, George McAfee, with Arthur L. Grey, Jr. *Korea Today.* Westport, Connecticut: Greenwood Press, 1982.

McNamara, Dennis L. *The Colonial Origins of Korean Enterprise, 1910–1945.* New York: Cambridge University Press, 1990.

Nam, Joo-Hong. *America's Commitment to South Korea: The First Decade of the Nixon Doctrine.* New York: Cambridge University Press, 1986.

Newsom, David D. (ed.). *The Diplomacy of Human Rights.* Lanham, Maryland: University Press of America for the Institute for the Study of Diplomacy, 1986.

Oh, John Kie-chiang. *Korea: Democracy on Trial.* Ithaca: Cornell University Press, 1968.

Oliver, Robert T. *Syngman Rhee and American Involvement in Korea, 1942–1960: A Personal Narrative.* Seoul: Panmun Book, 1978.

Pak, Chi-Young. *Political Opposition in Korea, 1945–1960.* Seoul: Seoul National University Press, 1980.

Palais, James B. *Politics and Policy in Traditional Korea.* (Harvard East Asian Series, No. 82.) Cambridge: Harvard University Press, 1975.

Rhee, Whee Yung, Bruce Ross-Larson, and Garry Pursell. *Korea's Competitive Edge: Managing the Entry into World Markets.* Baltimore: Johns Hopkins University Press, 1984.

Robinson, Michael Edson. *Cultural Nationalism in Colonial Korea, 1920–1925.* Seattle: University of Washington Press, 1988.

Scalapino, Robert A., and Chong-Sik Lee. *Communism in Korea.* (2 vols.) Berkeley: University of California Press, 1972.

Scalapino, Robert A., and Hongkoo Lee (eds.). *Korea–U.S. Relations: The Politics of Trade and Security.* Berkeley: Institute of East Asian Studies, University of California, 1988.

Shaw, William. *Legal Norms in a Confucian State.* (Korea Research Monograph No. 5.) Berkeley: Center for Korean Studies, Institute of East Asian Studies, University of California, 1981.

Sohn, Pow-Key, Kim Chol-choon, and Hong Yi-sup. *The History of Korea*. Seoul: Korean National Commission for UNESCO, 1970.
Steinberg, David I. *The Republic of Korea: Economic Transformation and Social Change*. Boulder, Colorado: Westview Press, 1989.
United States. Congress. 99th, 2d Session. House of Representatives. Committee on Foreign Affairs. Subcommittee on Human Rights and International Organizations and Subcommittee on Asian and Pacific Affairs. *Political Developments and Human Rights in the Republic of Korea*. Washington: GPO, 1986.
Yang, Sung Chul. *Korea and Two Regimes*. Cambridge, Massachusetts: Schenkman, 1981.

(Various issues of the following publications also were used in the preparation of this chapter: *Asian Survey*, 1980-90; *Asian Wall Street Journal* [Hong Kong], 1980-90; *Far Eastern Economic Review* [Hong Kong], 1980-90; and *Journal of Northeast-Asian Studies*, 1982-90.)

Chapter 2

Ajia Chūtō Dōkō Nempō 1986 (Annual report on developments in Asia and the Middle East, 1986). Tokyo: Ajia Keizai Kenkyūjo (Institute of Developing Economics), 1986.
"Authorities Move to Check Rising Drug Abuse," *Korea Newsreview* [Seoul], 18, No. 43, October 28, 1989, 9.
Beasley, W.G. *Japanese Imperialism, 1894-1945*. Oxford: Clarendon Press, 1987.
Brandt, Vincent S.R. *A Korean Village: Between Farm and Sea*. (Harvard East Asian Monographs, No. 84.) Cambridge: Harvard University Press, 1972.
_____. "Social Trends, Environmental Factors, Political Culture, and National Integration in South Korea." (Paper presented at Hudson Institute Workshop, "Future Prospects for the Korean Peninsula in a World Context," June 12-15, 1982.)
_____. "Sociocultural Aspects of Political Participation in Rural Korea," *Journal of Korean Studies*, 1, 1979, 205-24.
_____. "Some Ways of Looking at Village Values." Pages 84-97 in Andrew C. Nahm (ed.), *Studies in the Developmental Aspects of Korea*. Kalamazoo: Center for Korean Studies, Western Michigan University, 1969.
Ch'oe Yong-ho. "Commoners in Early Yi Dynasty Civil Examinations: An Aspect of Korean Social Structure, 1392-1600,"

Journal of Asian Studies, 33, No. 4, August 1974, 611–31.

Ch'oi Syn-duk. "Korea's Tong-il Movement," *Transactions of the Korea Branch of the Royal Asiatic Society* [Seoul], No. 43, 1967, 167–80.

Chang Dae-hung. "A Study of a Korean Cultural Minority: The Paekchong." Pages 55–88 in Andrew C. Nahm (ed.), *Traditional Korea: Theory and Practice.* Kalamazoo: Center for Korean Studies, Western Michigan University, 1974.

Chang Yunshik. "Colonization as Planned Change: The Korean Case," *Modern Asian Studies* [London], April 1971, 5, No. 2, 161–86.

Chee Ch'angboh. "Shamanism and Folk Beliefs of the Koreans." Pages 141–58 in Andrew C. Nahm (ed.), *Traditional Korea: Theory and Practice.* Kalamazoo: Center for Korean Studies, Western Michigan University, 1974.

Choi Jai-sok. "A Sociological Study of Sindonae," *Transactions of the Korea Branch of the Royal Asiatic Society* [Seoul], No. 43, 1967, 104–56.

Chong Dae-gyun. "Nihonron to Kankokuron no fukōna rentai" (The Unfortunate Connection Between Theories of Japanese and Korean National Identity), *Chuō kōron* (Central Review) [Tokyo], 104, No. 5, May 1989, 248–60.

Chung Young-Iob. "Kye: A Traditional Economic Institution in Korea." Pages 89–112 in Andrew C. Nahm (ed.), *Traditional Korea: Theory and Practice.* Kalamazoo: Center for Korean Studies, Western Michigan University, 1974.

Clark, Donald N. *Christianity in Modern Korea.* Lanham, Maryland: University Press of America, 1986.

Crane, Paul S. *Korean Patterns.* Seoul: Hollym, 1967.

Critchfield, Richard. *The Changing Peasant, Pt. 4. The Confucians.* (American Universities Field Staff, Fieldstaff Reports, Asia, No. 26.) Hanover, New Hampshire: AUFS, 1980.

Curzon, George Nathaniel. *Problems of the Far East: Japan, Korea, China.* New York: Longmans, Green, 1896.

Darlin, Damon. "Humble Span Gains Curious Cachet in South Korea," *Asian Wall Street Journal* [Hong Kong], September 21, 1989, 1, 8.

———. "Sony's Hollywood Move Poses Dilemma for Korea," *Asian Wall Street Journal* [Hong Kong], December 6, 1989, 1.

Dix, Griffin. *Studies on Korea in Transition.* Honolulu: Center for Korean Studies, University of Hawaii Press, 1979.

Dixon, John, and Hyung Shik Kim (eds.). *Social Welfare in Asia.* London: Croom Helm, 1985.

Dong, Wonmo. "Assimilation and Social Mobilization in Korea." Pages 146–82 in Andrew C. Nahm (ed.), *Korea under Japanese Colonial Rule.* Kalamazoo: Center for Korean Studies, Western Michigan University, 1973.

Douglas, James Dixon. *The New International Dictionary of the Christian Church.* Grand Rapids, Michigan: Zondervan, 1974.

Dredge, C. Paul. "Speech Levels and Social Structure in Korea: The Apparent and the Real in a Rural Village." Unpublished paper. N.d.

Earhart, H. Byron. "The New Religions of Korea: A Preliminary Interpretation," *Transactions of the Korea Branch of the Royal Asiatic Society* [Seoul], No. 49, 1974, 7–25.

Fisher, James Earnest. *Democracy and Mission Education in Korea.* (Contributions to Education Series, No. 306.) New York: Teachers College, Columbia University, 1928.

Gale, Jason S. "The Influence of China upon Korea," *Transactions of the Korea Branch of the Royal Asiatic Society* [Seoul], I, 1900, 1–24.

Goldscheider, Calvin (ed.). *Rural Migration in Developing Nations: Comparative Studies of Korea, Sri Lanka, and Mali.* Boulder, Colorado: Westview Press, 1984.

Han Sang-Bok. *Korean Fishermen: Ecological Adaptation in Three Communities.* Seoul: Population and Development Studies Center, Seoul National University, 1977.

Harvey, Youngsook Kim. *Six Korean Women: The Socialization of Shamans.* (American Ethnological Society Monograph No. 65.) St. Paul, Minnesota: West, 1979.

Hurst, G. Cameron. "'Uri Nara-ism': Cultural Nationalism in Contemporary Korea." (Universities Field Staff International, UFSI Reports, Asia, No. 33.) Indianapolis: 1985.

Hyde, Georgie D.M. *South Korea: Education, Culture, and Economy.* Basingstake, Hampshire, United Kingdom: Macmillan Press, 1988.

Itō Abito (ed.). *Motto shiritai Kankoku* (Know More about South Korea). Tokyo: Kobundō, 1985.

Jacobs, Norman. *The Korean Road to Modernization and Development.* Urbana: University of Illinois Press, 1985.

Janelli, Roger L., and Dawnhee Yim Janelli. "Lineage Organization and Social Differentiation in Korea," *Man* [London], 13, No. 2, June 1978, 272–89.

The Japan Year Book, 1938–39. Tokyo: Kenkyusha Press for the Foreign Affairs Association of Japan, 1938.

Ji Moon Suh. "Changing Attitude Toward the National Heritage in Modern Korean Literature," *Asia Quarterly* [Seoul], Summer 1985, 10–16.

Jo, Toshio. "Hall Near Seoul Depicts Colonization," *The Japan Times* [Tokyo], November 23, 1989, 3.

Jones, Leroy P., and Il Sakong. *Government, Business, and Entrepreneurship in Economic Development: The Korean Case.* (Studies in the Modernization of the Republic of Korea, 1945–1975; Harvard East Asian Monographs, No. 91.) Cambridge: Harvard University Press, 1980.

Kalton, Michael C. (trans. and ed.). *To Become a Sage: The 'Ten Diagrams on Sage Learning' by Yi Toegye.* New York: Columbia University Press, 1988.

Kendall, Laurel. *The Life and Hard Times of a Korean Shaman: Of Tales and the Telling of Tales.* Honolulu: University of Hawaii Press, 1988.

Kennedy, Gerald F. "The Korean Kye: Maintaining Human Scale in a Modernizing Form," *Korean Studies*, No. 1, 1977, 197–222.

Kim Chin-wu. *The Making of the Korean Language.* Honolulu: Center for Korean Studies, University of Hawaii Press, 1974.

Kim Kyong-Dong. "Social Change and Societal Development in Korea since 1945—Modernization with Uneven Development," *Korea and World Affairs* [Seoul], 9, No. 4, Winter 1985, 756–88.

Kim Sin-bok. "Recent Development of Higher Education in Korea," *Korea Journal* [Seoul], 23, No. 10, October 1983, 20–30.

Kim Soo-Young. "National Medical Insurance System Comes of Age," *Korea Newsreview* [Seoul], 18, No. 32, August 12, 1989, 4.

———. "Spread of AIDS Harms Health Officials," *Korea Newsreview* [Seoul], 18, No. 41, October 14, 1989, 8.

Kim Young-Oak. "Fallacy of Identity: Barrier to Genuine Understanding," *Japan Foundation Newsletter* [Tokyo], 15, Nos. 5–6, May 1988, 10–15.

Kim Yung-chung. *Women of Korea: A History from Ancient Times to 1945.* Seoul: Ehwa Woman's University Press, 1976.

Kim, C.I. Eugene. "South Korea in 1986: Preparing for a Power Transition," *Asian Survey*, 27, No. 1, January 1987, 64–74.

Kim, Eugene C. "Education in Korea under Japanese Colonial Rule." Pages 137–45 in Andrew C. Nahm (ed.), *Korea under Japanese Colonial Rule.* Kalamazoo: Center for Korean Studies, Western Michigan University, 1973.

Koh, B.C. "North Korea in 1987: Launching a New Seven-Year Plan," *Asian Survey*, 28, No. 1, January 1988, 62–70.

Koh, Hesung Chun. "Characteristics of Korean Culture Through the Arts." (Paper presented at Korea Seminar, November 19, 1982.) New York: Columbia University, 1982.

Koo, Hagen. "The Political Economy of Industrialization in South

Korea and Taiwan," *Korea and World Affairs* [Seoul], 10, No. 1, Spring 1986, 148–80.

Korea Economic Institute of America. *Korea's Economy.* Washington, 1990.

Korea Institute for Population and Health. *Journal of Population and Health Studies* [Seoul], 8, No. 2, December 1988, 11.

Korean National Commission for UNESCO (ed.). *Main Currents of Korean Thought.* Seoul: Si-sa-yong-o-sa, 1983.

Kuroda Katsuhiro. "Kankokuron ni motto 'bunkashugi' " (More "Culturalism" in Theories of Korean Identity), *Chuō kōron* (Central Review) [Tokyo], 104, No. 3, March 1989, 256–63.

Lee Chae-Jin. "South Korea in 1984: Seeking Peace and Prosperity," *Asian Survey,* 25, No. 1, January 1985, 80–89.

Lee Hyo-jae, in collaboration with Choi Syn-duck, et al. "Life in Urban Korea," *Transactions of the Korea Branch of the Royal Asiatic Society* [Seoul], No. 46, 1971, 7–90.

Lee Hyo-jae. "The Changing Family in Korea," *Journal of Social Sciences and Humanities* [Seoul], 29, December 1968, 87–99.

Lee Kwang-kyu. *Kinship System in Korea.* (2 vols.) (HRAFLEX Series.) New Haven, Human Relations Area Files, 1975.

Lee, Byung-jong. "Korea Proposes 19.8. Budget Increase," *Asian Wall Street Journal* [Hong Kong], September 22, 1989, 3.

Lee, Ki-baik. *A New History of Korea.* (Trans. Edward W. Wagner, with Edward J. Shultz). Seoul: Ilchokak, 1984.

Lee, Peter H. (ed.). *The Traditional Culture and Society of Korea: Art and Literature.* (Papers of the International Conference on Traditional Korean Culture and Society.) Honolulu: Center for Korean Studies, University of Hawaii Press, 1975.

Linton, Stephen. *Coverage of the United States in Korean Textbooks: An Analysis of Educational Policy, Tone, and Content.* Washington: United States Information Agency, October 1988.

Manguno, Joseph P. "Korea Faces Prolonged Clash on Education," *Asian Wall Street Journal* [Hong Kong], December 5, 1989, 1, 8.

Maruyama, Masao. *Studies in the Intellectual History of Tokugawa Japan.* (Trans., Mikiso Hane.) Tokyo: University of Tokyo Press, 1974.

Mason, Edward S., et al. *The Economic and Social Modernization of the Republic of Korea.* (Studies in the Modernization of the Republic of Korea, 1945–1975, Harvard East Asian Monographs, No. 92.) Cambridge: Harvard University Press, 1980.

Mattielli, Sandra (ed.). *Virtues in Conflict: Tradition and the Korean Woman Today.* Seoul: Samhwa, 1977.

McBrian, Charles D. "Kinship, Communal, and Class Models of Social Structure in Rising Sun Village." Pages 102–24 in David

R. McCann, John Middleton, and Edward J. Shultz (eds.), *Studies on Korea in Transition.* Honolulu: University of Hawaii Press, 1979.

McCune, Shannon. *Korea's Heritage: A Regional and Social Geography.* Rutland, Vermont: Tuttle, 1956.

McGinn, Noel F., et al. *Education and Development in Korea.* (Studies in the Modernization of the Republic of Korea, 1945–1975. Harvard East Asian Monographs, No. 90.) Cambridge: Harvard University Press, 1980.

McGrane, George A. *Korea's Tragic Hours: The Closing Years of the Yi Dynasty.* Seoul: Taewon, 1973.

McNamara, Dennis. "The Keisho and the Korean Business Elite," *Journal of Asian Studies,* 48, No. 2, May 1989, 310–23.

Mills, Edwin S., and Song Byung-nak. *Urbanization and Urban Problems.* (Studies in the Modernization of the Republic of Korea, 1945–1975, Harvard East Asian Monographs, No. 88.) Cambridge: Harvard University Press, 1979.

Moore, Mick. "Mobilization and Disillusion in Rural Korea: The Saemaŭl Movement in Retrospect," *Pacific Affairs* [Vancouver], 57, No. 4, Winter 1984–85, 577–98.

Moos, Felix. "Leadership and Organization in the Olive Tree Movement," *Transactions of the Korea Branch of the Royal Asiatic Society* [Seoul] No. 43, 1967, 11–27.

Nahm, Andrew C. (ed.). *Korea under Japanese Colonial Rule.* Kalamazoo: Center for Korean Studies, Western Michigan University, 1973.

———. *Studies in the Developmental Aspects of Korea.* Kalamazoo: Center for Korean Studies, Western Michigan University, 1969.

———. *Traditional Korea: Theory and Practice.* Kalamazoo: Center for Korean Studies, Western Michigan University, 1974.

Newman, Anne. "Korean Immigrants in U.S. Struggle Hard for Success," *Asian Wall Street Journal* [Hong Kong], December 15, 1989, 1, 8.

Oh, In-whan, and George Won. "Journalism in Korea: A Short History of the Korean Press," *Transactions of the Korea Branch of the Royal Asiatic Society* [Seoul], No. 51, 1976, 1–55.

Pak Chi-wŏn. *Yangban Chŏn* (Tale of a Yangban: Upperclass Culture in Yi Dynasty Korea). (Trans., Giles Ryan.) Seoul: International Cultural Foundation, 1973.

Palais, James B. *Politics and Policy in Traditional Korea.* (Studies in the Modernization of the Republic of Korea, 1945–1975, Harvard East Asian Monographs, No. 82.) Cambridge: Harvard University Press, 1975.

Park, Moon Kyu. "Interest Representation in South Korea: The Limits of Corporatist Control," *Asian Survey*, 27, No. 8, August 1987, 903–17.

"The Perils of Development," *Economist* [London], 312, No. 18, September 9, 1989, 34.

"The Price of Prosperity," *Asiaweek* [Hong Kong], 12, No. 16, April 20, 1986, 46.

Republic of Korea. Ministry of Culture and Information. Korean Overseas Information Office. *A Handbook of Korea*. Seoul: 1978.

_____. National Bureau of Statistics. Economic Planning Board. *Korea Statistical Handbook, 1987*. Seoul: 1987.

_____. National Bureau of Statistics. Economic Planning Board. *Korea Statistical Handbook, 1989*. Seoul: 1989.

Schoenberger, Karl. "South Korea Seen as Major Source of 'Ice' Narcotic," *Los Angeles Times*, October 14, 1989, A12.

Shupe, Anson. "Sun Myung Moon's Empire Retreats to Asia," *Asian Wall Street Journal* [Hong Kong], November 2, 1989, 10.

Sohn Ho-min (ed.). *The Korean Language: Its Structure and Social Projection*. Honolulu: Center for Korean Studies, University of Hawaii, 1975.

"South Korean Films: Set to Make a Splash by 1988," *Economist* [London], July 13, 1985, 91–99.

The Statesman's Year Book, 1988–1989. (Ed., John Paxton.) New York: St. Martin's Press, 1988.

Steinberg, David I. *The Republic of Korea: Economic Transformation and Social Change*. Boulder, Colorado: Westview Press, 1989.

_____. "Sociopolitical Factors and Korea's Future Economic Policies," *World Development* [London], 16, No. 1, January 1988, 19–34.

Steinberg, David I., and David Kim. *South Korea's Military: Political and Social Roles and Profiles of Korean Leaders*. (Asia Society Media Briefing.) New York: Asia Society, August 1988.

Suh Kuk-sung et al. (eds.). *The Identity of the Korean People*. Seoul: Research Center for Peace and Unification of Korea, 1983.

United Nations. Economic and Social Commission for Asia and the Pacific. *Statistical Yearbook for Asia and the Pacific, 1984*. Bangkok: 1986.

_____. Department of International Economic and Social Affairs. Statistics Office. *1986 Demographic Yearbook*. New York: 1988.

United Nations Educational, Scientific, and Cultural Organization. *Statistical Yearbook, 1988*. Paris: 1988.

Yi Ki-moon. "Language and Writing Systems in Traditional Korea." Pages 15–32 in Peter H. Lee (ed.), *The Traditional Culture and Society of Korea: Art and Literature*. (Papers of the

International Conference on Traditional Korean Culture and Society.) Honolulu: Center for Korean Studies, University of Hawaii, 1975.

(Various issues of the following publications also were used in the preparation of this chapter: *Far Eastern Economic Review* [Hong Kong], 1984–89; Foreign Broadcast Information Service, *Daily Report: Asia and the Pacific; Korea Journal* [Seoul], 1973–87; *Korea Herald* [Seoul], 1988–89; *Korean Studies,* 1985–89; *Social Science Journal* [Seoul], 1985–89; and *Tonga ilbo* [Seoul], 1988–89.)

Chapter 3

Amsden, Alice H. *Asia's Next Giant: South Korea and Late Industrialization.* New York: Oxford University Press, 1989.

Armstrong, Rodney. "Fish and American-Korean Relations," *Korea's Economy,* 2, No. 6, October 1986, 15–17.

Balassa, Bela A., and Marcus Noland. *Japan in the World Economy.* Washington: Institute for International Economics, 1988.

Bank of Korea. *Annual Report: 1987.* Seoul: 1987.

Clifford, Mark. "Junior Partners Promoted," *Far Eastern Economic Review* [Hong Kong], 139, No. 11, March 7, 1988, 67.

Cole, David C., and Princeton N. Lyman. *Korean Development: The Interplay of Politics and Economics.* Cambridge: Harvard University Press, 1971.

Cumings, Bruce. "The Legacy of Japanese Colonialism in Korea." Pages 478–96 in Ramon H. Myers and Mark R. Peattie (eds.), *The Japanese Colonial Empire, 1895–1945.* Princeton: Princeton University Press, 1984.

_____. *The Two Koreas.* (Headline Series, No. 269.) New York: Foreign Policy Association, 1984.

Eckert, Carter J. *Offspring of Empire: The Kŏch'ang Kims and the Colonial Origins of Korean Capitalism, 1876–1945.* Seattle: University of Washington Press, 1991.

The Europa World Year Book, 1989. London: Europa, 1989.

The Europa World Year Book, 1990. London: Europa, 1990.

Farrukh, Iqbal. "Financing Korean Development." Pages 147–56 in Han Sung-joo and Robert J. Myers (eds.), *Korea: The Year 2000.* (Carnegie Council on Ethics and International Affairs. Ethics and Foreign Policy Series, No. 5.) Lanham, Maryland: University Press of America, 1987.

Han, Sung-Joo, and Robert J. Myers (eds.). *Korea: The Year 2000.* (Carnegie Council on Ethics and International Affairs. Ethics

357

and Foreign Policy Series, No. 5.) Lanham, Maryland: University Press of America, 1987.

Ho, Samuel Pao-san. "Colonialism and Development: Korea, Taiwan, and Kwantung." Pages 347–98 in Ramon H. Myers and Mark R. Peattie (eds.), *The Japanese Colonial Empire, 1895–1945*. Princeton: Princeton University Press, 1984.

Hurst, G. Cameron, III (ed.). *Korea 1988: A Nation at the Crossroads*. (Conference and Colloquium Series, No. 3.) Lawrence: Center for East Asian Studies, University of Kansas, 1988.

Jane's World Railways, 1989–90. (Ed., Geoffrey Freeman Allen.) Coulsdon, Surrey, United Kingdom: Jane's Information Group, 1989.

KEPCO Annual Review, 1988. Seoul: KEPCO, 1988.

Kim, Bun Woong, David S. Bell, Jr., and Chong Bun Lee (eds.). *Administrative Dynamics and Development: The Korean Experience*. Seoul: Kyobo, 1985.

Kim, Dae Jung. *Mass-Participatory Economy: A Democratic Alternative for Korea*. Lanham, Maryland: University Press of America, 1985.

Kim, Ilpyong J., and Young Whan Kihl (eds.). *Political Change in South Korea*. New York: Paragon House, 1988.

Kim Kyong-Dong. *Man and Society in Korea's Economic Growth: Sociological Studies*. Seoul: Seoul National University Press, 1984.

Koo, Bon-bo, and Tae-ho Pak. "Government Policies, Recent Trends, and the Economic Input of Direct Foreign Investment in Korea," *Korea's Economy*, 4, No. 4, December 1988, 3–5.

Korea Chamber of Commerce and Industry. *KCCI Quarterly Review* [Seoul], April 1988.

Korea Development Institute. *KDI Quarterly Economic Outlook* [Seoul], Spring 1988.

————. "KDI Forecast: Per Capita GNP to Reach $10,000 in Early 2000s," *Korea Trade and Business* [Seoul], June 1988.

Korea Economic Institute of America. *Korea Economic Update*, 1, No. 2, Summer 1990, 4.

Korea's Economic Policies. Seoul: Federation of Korean Industry, 1987.

Korea Trade Promotion Corporation. *How to Trade with Korea: 1987—A Practical Guide to Trade and Investment*. Seoul: 1987.

Kuznets, Paul W. *Economic Growth and Structure in the Republic of Korea*. New Haven: Yale University Press for Economic Growth Center, Yale University, 1977.

Kwan Suk Kim. "An Analysis of Economic Change in Korea." Pages 99–112 in Andrew C. Nahm (ed.), *Korea under Japanese Colonial Rule*. Kalamazoo: Center for Korean Studies, Western Michigan University, 1973.

Kwon, Jene K. (ed.). *Korean Economic Development.* New York: Greenwood Press, 1990.

Kyong Cho Chung, Phyllis G. Hafner, and Frederic M. Kaplan (eds.). *The Korea Guidebook.* Boston: Houghton Mifflin, 1988.

Lee, Hahn-Been. *The Age of the Common Man in Korea.* Seoul: Bak Young SA, 1987.

Macdonald, Donald Stone. *The Koreans: Contemporary Politics and Society.* Boulder, Colorado: Westview Press, 1988.

"Major Economic Indicators," *Korea's Economy,* 5, No. 1, July 1988, 2.

Mason, Edward S., et al. *The Economic and Social Modernization of the Republic of Korea.* (Studies in the Modernization of the Republic of Korea, 1945–1975, Harvard East Asian Monographs, No. 92.) Cambridge: Harvard University Press, 1980.

Minjungsa. *Lost Victory: An Overview of the Korean People's Struggle for Democracy.* Seoul: Minjungsa Press, 1988.

Moskowitz, Karl. *From Patron to Partner: The Development of U.S.-Korean Business and Trade Relations.* Lexington, Massachusetts: Lexington Books, 1984.

Myers, Ramon H., and Mark R. Peattie (eds.). *The Japanese Colonial Empire, 1895–45.* Princeton: Princeton University Press, 1984.

Nahm, Andrew C. (ed.). *Korea under Japanese Colonial Rule.* Kalamazoo: Center for Korean Studies, Western Michigan University, 1973.

————. *Korea: Tradition and Transformation: A History of the Korean People.* Elizabeth, New Jersey: Hollym, 1988.

"1,000 Hyundai Workers Strike for Free Union Election," *Bi-Weekly Report,* 7, No. 4. March 1, 1988, 5–6.

Pak Duck-Moon. "Changing Prospects for Foreign Direct Investment in Korea and Overseas Investment by Korean Firms." (Paper presented at South East Governors' Association, Third Joint Conference between Southeast United States and Korea, November 14, 1988.)

Park, Yung-chul. "Financial Liberalization and Prospects for Resource Mobilization in Korea." Pages 175–205 in Han Sung-Joo and Robert J. Myers (eds.), *Korea: The Year 2000.* (Carnegie Council on Ethics and Policy. Ethics and Foreign Policy Series, No. 5.) Lanham, Maryland: University Press of America, 1987.

Perkins, Dwight H. "Korea's Economy in the Year 2000." Pages 157–73 in Han Sung-Joo and Robert J. Myers (eds.), *Korea: The Year 2000.* (Carnegie Council on Ethics and International Affairs, Ethics and Policy Series, No. 5.) Lanham, Maryland: University Press of America, 1987.

Platt, Adam, David Bank, and Peter Leydem. "Ending a Battle, but not the War: Labor Unrest at Hyundai," *Newsweek*, 113, No. 15, April 10, 1989, 37.

"POSCO Celebrates 20th Anniversary," *Asian Trade* [Seoul], 2, No. 2, May 1988, 25.

"POSCO: Success Story," *Korea-Europe Economic Report* [Seoul], 3, No. 6, June 1988, 30–31.

"Reborn with Steel," *KCCI Quarterly Review* [Seoul], 4, No. 2, June 1988, 28–29.

Republic of Korea. Economic Planning Board. *The Korean Economy: Past Performance, Current Policies, and Future Prospects.* Seoul: Economic Planning Board, 1988.

_____. Ministry of Culture and Information. Korean Overseas Information Service. *Facts About Korea.* Seoul: Hollym, 1985.

_____. Ministry of Culture and Information. Korean Overseas Information Service. *A Handbook of Korea.* Seoul: Seoul International Publishing House, 1982.

_____. Ministry of Culture and Information. Korean Overseas Information Service. *A Handbook of Korea.* Seoul: Seoul International Publishing House, 1987.

Song Dae Hae. "The Role of the Public Enterprise in the Korean Economy." (Paper presented at seminar on Industrial Development Strategies in Korea, Seoul, April 4–14, 1987.) United States Information Agency.

Song, Byung-Nak. *The Rise of the Korean Economy.* Hong Kong: Oxford University Press, 1990.

Steinberg, David I. *Chaebŏl: Engine of South Korea's Growth. A Background Report.* New York: Asia Society, August 1988.

_____. *South Korea's Economy: Past Successes, Future Prospects. A Background Report.* New York: Asia Society, August 1988.

Sullivan, John, and Roberta Foss (eds.). *Two Koreas—One Future?* Lanham, Maryland: University Press of America for American Friends Service Committee, 1987.

Taiwan Power Company. *Energy Use Trends in Newly Industrialized Countries.* Taipei: Taiwan Power Company, 1987.

United States. Department of Commerce. International Trade Administration. *Foreign Economic Trends and Their Implications for the United States: Korea.* (FET 88–111.) Washington: GPO, March 1988.

_____. Department of Commerce. International Trade Administration. *Foreign Economic Trends and Their Implications for the United States: Korea.* (FET 89–76.) Washington: GPO, June 1989.

_____. Department of Commerce. International Trade Administration. *Foreign Economic Trends and Their Implications for the United States: Korea.* Washington: GPO, April 1990.

Wang, K.P., et al. *Mineral Industries of the Far East and South Asia.* Washington: GPO, 1988.

World of Information. *Asia and Pacific: Review 1985.* Saffron Walden, Essex, United Kingdom: World of Information, 1985.

"World Steel Production," *Korea Businessworld* [Seoul], 4, No. 10, October 1988, 47.

Woronoff, Jon. *Korea's Economy: Man-made Miracle.* Seoul: Si-sa-yong-o-sa, 1983.

(Various issues of the following publications also were used in the preparation of this chapter: *Asian Survey,* 1985–89; *China Post* [Tai-pei], 1985–89; *Far Eastern Economic Review* [Hong Kong], 1985–89; *Korea Newsreview* [Seoul], 1985–89; and *Korea Times* [Seoul], 1988–89.)

Chapter 4

Amnesty International Report, 1991. London: Amnesty International, 1991.

Asia Watch Committee. *A Stern, Steady Crackdown: Legal Process and Human Rights in South Korea.* Washington: Asia Watch, 1987.

Atkin, Rose. "Olympics Seoul '88," *Christian Science Monitor,* October 3, 1988.

Bandow, Doug. "Leaving Korea," *Foreign Policy,* 77, Winter 1989–90, 77–93.

Blum, Andrew A. (ed.). *International Handbook of Industrial Relations: Contemporary Developments and Research.* Westport, Connecticut: Greenwood Press, 1981.

Cho, Myung Hyun. *Korea and the Major Powers.* Seoul: Research Center for Peace and Unification of Korea, 1989.

Clifford, Mark. "A Christian Dialogue," *Far Eastern Economic Review* [Hong Kong], 144, No. 14, April 6, 1989, 11.

Clough, Ralph N. *Embattled Korea: The Rivalry for International Support.* Boulder, Colorado: Westview Press, 1987.

Cumings, Bruce. "The Origins and Development of the Northeast Asian Political Economy: Industrial Sectors, Product Cycles, and Political Consequences," *International Organization,* 38, No. 1, Winter 1984, 1–40.

"Document from Korea: Instances of Ruling Party Campaign Fraud and Irregularities, November 18–28," *Korea Update,* No. 85, December 1987, 13–21.

Dong, Wonmo. "University Students in South Korean Politics: Patterns of Radicalization in the 1980s," *Journal of International Affairs* [Seoul], 40, No. 2, Winter–Spring 1987, 233–55.

Flanz, Gisbert H., and Hakjong Andrew Yoo (eds.). "Republic of Korea." In Albert P. Blaustein and Gisbert H. Flanz (eds.), *Constitutions of the Countries of the World*, 8. Dobbs Ferry, New York: Oceana, November 1980.

Gleysteen, William H., Jr. "Korea: A Special Target of American Concern." Pages 85–99 in David D. Newsom (ed.), *The Diplomacy of Human Rights*. Lanham, Maryland: University Press of America, 1987.

Gorbachev, Mikhail S. *The Coming Century of Peace*. New York: Richardson and Steirman, 1986.

——. Speech by Mikhail S. Gorbachev in Vladivostok. Moscow: Novosti Press, 1986.

Han, Sung-Joo. "South Korea in 1988: A Revolution in the Making," *Asian Survey*, 29, No. 1, January 1989, 29–38.

Hanguk Immyŏngnok (Korean Biographies). Supplement to Yŏnhap Yŏn'gam, 1983 (Yŏnhap Annual, 1983). Seoul: Yŏnhap T'ongsin, 1983.

Hyun, Roy. "Why Seoul Says Don't Fix What Isn't Broken," *New York Times*, September 7, 1989.

Kihl, Young Whan. *Politics and Policies in Divided Korea: Regimes in Contest*. Boulder, Colorado: Westview Press, 1984.

Kim, Chul-Su. "Super 301 and the World Trading System: A Korean View." Paper presented at seminar at Columbia University, New York, December 1989.

Kim, Dae Jung. *Mass-Participatory Economy: A Democratic Alternative for Korea*. Lanham, Maryland: University Press of America, 1985.

——. *Philosophy and Dialogues: Building Peace and Democracy*. New York: Korean Independent Monitor, 1987.

——. *Prison Writings*. (Trans., David R. McCann and Sung-il Choi.) Berkeley: University of California Press, 1987.

Kim, Hong Nack. "The 1988 Parliamentary Election in South Korea," *Asian Survey*, 29, No. 5, May 1989, 480–95.

Kim, Roy U.T. "Moscow-Seoul Relations in a New Era," *Pacific Review*, 2, No. 4, December 1989, 339–49.

Koh, Byung Chul. *The Foreign Policy Systems of North and South Korea*. Berkeley: University of California Press, 1984.

——. "The 1985 Parliamentary Election in South Korea," *Asian Survey*, 25, No. 9, September 1985, 883–97.

Korea Annual, 1988. Seoul: Yonhap News Agency, 1988.

Korea Annual, 1989. Seoul: Yonhap News Agency, 1989.

Lee, Chong-Sik. *Japan and Korea: The Political Dimension*. Stanford: Hoover Institution Press, 1985.

Lee, Kee-bong. "Jung-on" (Witness). Seoul: Wonil Chung-bo, 1989.

Lee, Ki-baik. *A New History of Korea.* (Trans., Edward W. Wagner, with Edward J. Shultz.) Seoul: Ilchokak, 1984.

Lee, Sŏk-ho. "Hanguk ŭi pukpang chŏngch'aek (Korea's Northern Policy)." *Woe-gyo* (Foreign Diplomacy) [Seoul], March 1989, 6-17.

Lu Yun. "The Korean Autonomous Prefecture," *Beijing Review* [Beijing], 30, No. 51, December 21-17, 1987, 27-29.

Maas, Peter. "Seoul Puts Top-Level Corruption Probe on TV," *Washington Post,* November 9, 1988, A21.

Macdonald, Donald Stone. *The Koreans: Contemporary Politics and Society.* Boulder, Colorado: Westview Press, 1988.

"Monthly Views Two Dissident Groups' Interactions," *Sin tonga* (New East Asia), [Seoul], March 1, 1989. Foreign Broadcast Information Service, *Daily Report: East Asia.* (FBIS-EAS-89-066.) April 7, 1989, 26-38.

Moskowitz, Karl. "Limited Partners: Transnational Alliances Between Private Sector Organizations in the U.S.-Korea Trade Relationship." Pages 149-75 in Karl Moskowitz (ed.), *From Patron to Partner: The Development of U.S.-Korean Business and Trade Relations.* Lexington, Massachusetts: Lexington Books, 1984.

Myers, Ramon H., and Mark R. Peattie (eds.). *The Japanese Colonial Empire, 1895-1945.* Princeton: Princeton University Press, 1984.

Newsom, David D. (ed.). *The Diplomacy of Human Rights.* Lanham, Maryland: University Press of America.

Ogle, George. "South Korea." Pages 499-514 in Albert A. Blum (ed.), *International Handbook of Industrial Relations: Contemporary Developments and Research.* Westport, Connecticut: Greenwood Press, 1981.

Oh, John Kie-chiang. *Korea: Democracy on Trial.* Ithaca: Cornell University Press, 1968.

Okonogi, Masao. *North Korea at the Crossroads.* Tokyo: Japan Institute of International Affairs, 1988.

Park, Chan Wook. "The 1988 National Assembly Election in South Korea: The Ruling Party's Loss of Legislative Majority," *Journal of Northeast Asian Studies,* 7, No. 3, Fall 1988, 59-76.

Pak, Ch'ŏr-ŏn. "T'ongil chŏngch'aek (Unification Policy)." *Sin tonga* (New East Asia), [Seoul], September 1988, 204-15.

Republic of Korea. Ministry of Culture and Information. Korean Overseas Information Service. *Constitution of the Republic of Korea.* Seoul: 1980.

_____. Ministry of Culture and Information. Korean Overseas Information Service. *Constitution of the Republic of Korea.* Seoul: 1987.

———. National Unification Board. *A White Paper on South-North Dialogue.* Seoul: 1988.

———. National Unification Board. *To Build a National Community Through the Korean Commonwealth: A Blueprint for Korean Unification.* Seoul: 1989.

Roh Tae-Woo. "Address Before a Joint Meeting of the U.S. Congress." Washington, D.C.: October 18, 1989.

Sanger, David. "Seoul Officials See Accord on U.S. Troop Cut," *New York Times,* February 1, 1990.

Scalapino, Robert A., and Hongkoo Lee (eds.). *Korea-U.S. Relations: The Politics of Trade and Security.* Berkeley: Institute of East Asian Studies, University of California, 1988.

Shaw, William (ed.). *Human Rights in Korea: Historical and Policy Perspectives.* Cambridge: Council on East Asian Studies and East Asian Legal Studies Program, Harvard Law School, 1991.

Shim, Jae Hoon, and Louise de Rosario. "Heart to Heart," *Far Eastern Economic Review* [Hong Kong], 144, No. 15, April 13, 1989, 12–13.

"Statement of Purpose of the Party for Peace and Democracy, 30 October 1987," *Korea Update,* No. 85, December 1987, 54–55.

Ungar, Stanford J. "A Korean Exile's Long Journey Home," *New York Times,* June 23, 1984, A32.

United States. Congress. 101st, 1st Session. Senate. Committee on Armed Services. *A Bill Relating to the Security Relationship Between the United States and the Republic of Korea.* Washington: GPO, 1989.

———. Department of State. *Briefing Paper: South Korean Relations with the Soviet Bloc and China.* Washington: July 1989.

———. Department of State. *Country Reports on Human Rights Practices for 1989.* (Report submitted to United States Congress, 101st, 2d Session, House of Representatives, Committee on Foreign Affairs, and Senate, Committee on Foreign Relations.) Washington: GPO, February 1990.

———. Department of State. "United States Government Statement on the Events in Kwangju, Republic of Korea, in May 1980," Washington: June 19, 1989.

Yoon, Dae-Kyu. *Law and Political Authority in Korea.* Boulder, Colorado: Westview Press and Seoul: Kyungnam University Press, 1990.

(Various issues of the following publications also were used in the preparation of this chapter: *Asian Survey,* 1980–90; *Asian Wall Street Journal* [Hong Kong]; *Asia Yearbook* [Hong Kong], 1980–90; *Christian Science Monitor,* 1980–90; *Far Eastern Economic Review* [Hong Kong], 1980–90; Joint Publications Research Service, *Korean Affairs*

Report, 1985–88; *Journal of Northeast Asian Studies,* 1980–90; *Korea Herald* [Seoul], 1987; *Korea Newsreview* [Seoul], 1987–89; and *Korea Update,* 1980–90).

Chapter 5

Ahn, Byong-man, Soong-hoon Kil, and Kim Kwang-woong. *Elections in Korea.* Seoul: Seoul Computer Press, 1988.

Amnesty International Report (annuals 1980 through 1991). London: Amnesty International, 1980–91.

Amnesty International. *Political Imprisonment in the Republic of Korea.* London: 1987.

————. *Report of an Amnesty International Mission to the Republic of Korea: March 27–April 9, 1975.* London: 1977.

————. *Republic of Korea Violations on Human Rights: An Amnesty International Report.* London: 1981.

————. *South Korea: Violations of Human Rights.* London: 1986.

————. *Violations of Human Rights in South Korea: An Amnesty International Report.* (Excerpts.) London: 1981.

Appleman, Roy E. *South to the Naktong, North to the Yalu.* Washington: Office of the Chief of Military History, Department of the Army, 1961.

Asia Society. *Korea at the Crossroads: Implications for American Policy: A Study Group Report.* New York: Council on Foreign Relations and the Asia Society, 1987.

Asia Watch Committee. *A Stern, Steady Crackdown: Legal Process and Human Rights in South Korea.* Washington: Asia Watch, 1987.

Baker, Edward J. "American Policy and Human Rights in South Korea in the 1980s: Diagnosis and Prognosis." (Paper presented at the Annual Meeting of the Association for Asian Studies, March 1984.) Washington: March 1984.

Billet, Bret L. "South Korea at the Crossroads: An Evolving Democracy or Authoritarianism Revisited?" *Asian Survey,* 30, No. 3, March 1990, 300–11.

Bok, Lee Suk. *The Impact of US Forces in Korea.* Washington: National Defense University Press, 1987.

Bond, Douglas G. "Anti-Americanism and U.S.–ROK Relations: An Assessment of Korean Students' Views," *Asian Perspective* [Seoul], 12, Spring-Summer 1988, 159–90.

Burgess, John. "Protests Turned a New Page in South Korea," *Washington Post,* July 5, 1987, A1, 18.

————. "Seoul Controls the Flow of News with Guidelines, Beatings, Jail," *Washington Post,* March 1, 1987, A41.

Chun Bong Duck, William Shaw, and Dai-kwon Choi. *Traditional Korean Legal Attitudes*. (Korea Research Monograph, No. 2.) Berkeley: Center for Korean Studies, Institute of East Asian Studies, University of California, 1980.

Chuter, Andrew. "Bell Helicopters Textron Signs Korean Agreement," *Jane's Defence Weekly* [London], 6, No. 7, August 23, 1986, 329.

Clark, Donald N. *Christianity in Modern Korea*. Lanham, Maryland: University Press of America, 1986.

_____. *The Kwangju Uprising: Shadows over the Regime in South Korea*. Boulder, Colorado: Westview Press, 1988.

Clough, Ralph N. *Embattled Korea: The Rivalry for International Support*. Boulder, Colorado: Westview Press, 1987.

"Constitution Court's Ruling on National Security Law: Both National Security and Basic Rights of the People Recognized," *Tonga ilbo* [Seoul] (Daily Seoul Press Translations, United States Embassy in Seoul.) Seoul: April 3, 1990.

Cotter, Donald R., and N.F. Wikner. "Korea: Force Imbalances and Remedies," *Strategic Review*, 10, Spring 1982, 63–70.

Cotton, James. "From Authoritarianism to Democracy in South Korea," *Political Studies*, 37, June 1989, 244–59.

Deen, Thalif. "South Korea's Growing Industrial Strength," *Jane's Defence Weekly* [London], 12, No. 4, July 29, 1989, 162–65.

Detrio, Richard T. *Strategic Partners: South Korea and the United States*. Washington: National Defense University Press, 1989.

Gleysteen, William H., Jr. "Korea: Asian Paradox," *Foreign Affairs*, 65, Summer 1987, 1037–54.

Haberman, Clyde. "Is South Korea Ripe for Democracy or More Repression?" *New York Times*, December 13, 1987, 3.

Hahm, Pyong-choon. *Korean Jurisprudence, Politics, and Culture*. Seoul: Yonsei University Press, 1986.

_____. *The Korean Political Tradition and Law: Essays in Korean Law and Legal History*. (Royal Asiatic Society Korea Branch, Monograph Series, No. 1.) Seoul: Hollym, 1982.

Han, Ki-hyong. *Events in Korea and Asia Viewed in 100 Editorials (1970–1979) from the Korea Times*. Seoul: Han'guk ilbosa ch'ulp'an'guk, 1981.

Han, Sung-Joo. "The Emerging Political Process in Korea," *Asian Affairs*, 8, No. 6, November–December 1980, 76–88.

_____. "South Korea in 1987: The Politics of Democratization," *Asian Survey*, 28, No. 1, January 1988, 52–61.

Han, Woo-keun. *The History of Korea*. (Trans., Lee Kyung-shik; ed., Grafton K. Mintz.) Honolulu: East-West Center Press, 1971.

Harrison, Selig S. *The South Korean Political Crisis and American Policy Options.* Washington: Washington Institute Press, 1987.
Hermes, Walter G. *Truce Tent and Fighting Front.* Washington: Office of the Chief of Military History, Department of the Army, 1966.
Hinton, Harold C. *Korea under New Leadership: The Fifth Republic.* New York: Praeger, 1983.
Hyung, Baeg Im. "The Rise of Bureaucratic Authoritarianism in South Korea," *World Politics,* 39, No. 1, January 1987, 231–57.
International Cultural Foundation. *Legal System of Korea.* (Korean Cultural Series, No. 5.) Seoul: Si-sa-yong-o-sa, 1982.
International League of Human Rights and International Human Rights Law Group. *Democracy in South Korea: A Promise Unfulfilled. A Report on Human Rights, 1980–1985.* New York: International League on Human Rights, 1985.
Jacobs, Gordon. "Armed Forces of the Korean Peninsula: A Comparative Study," *Asian Defence Journal* [Kuala Lumpur], 12, No. 11, November 1982, 12–31.
Jane's All the World's Aircraft, 1985–86. (Ed., John Taylor.) London: Jane's Publishing, 1985.
Jane's Armour and Artillery, 1988–89. (Ed., Christopher F. Foss.) London: Jane's Publishing, 1988.
Jane's Fighting Ships, 1983–84. (Ed., John Moore.) London: Jane's Publishing, 1983.
Jane's Infantry Weapons, 1985–86. (Ed., Ian V. Hogg.) London: Jane's Publishing, 1985.
Jane's Weapon Systems, 1987–88. (Ed., Bernard H.L. Blake.) London: Jane's Publishing, 1987.
Jenerette, Vandon E. "The Forgotten DMZ," *Military Review,* 68, No. 5, May 1988, 32–43.
Jho, Sung-do. *Yi Sun-shin: A National Hero of Korea.* Chinhae, Republic of Korea: Naval Academy, 1970.
"KCIA Renamed to have Functions Modified," Foreign Broadcast Information Service, *Daily Report: Asia and Pacific,* No. 248, December 23, 1980, E1–2.
Kihl, Young Whan. *Politics and Policies in Divided Korea: Regimes in Contest.* Boulder, Colorado: Westview Press, 1984.
Kim, Bun Woong, and Wha Joon Rho (eds.). *Korean Public Bureaucracy: Readings.* Seoul: Kyobo, 1982.
Kim, C.I. Eugene. "Civil-Military Relations in the Two Koreas," *Armed Forces and Society,* 11, No. 1, Fall 1984, 9–31.
_____. "Emergency, Development, and Human Rights: South Korea," *Asian Survey,* 18, No. 4, April 1978, 363–78.
_____. "The South Korean Military and Its Political Role." Pages 91–112 in Ilpyong J. Kim and Young Whan Kihl (eds.),

Political Change in South Korea. New York: Paragon House, 1988.

Kim, Chong Lim. *Legislative Process in Korea.* Seoul: Seoul National University Press, 1981.

Kim, Dae Jung. *Building Peace and Democracy.* New York: Korean Independent Monitor, 1987.

_____. *Prison Writings.* (Trans., David R. McCann and Sung-il Choi.) Berkeley: University of California Press, 1987.

Kim, Han-joon. "The American Military Government in South Korea, 1945-48: Its Formation, Policies, and Legacies," *Asian Perspective* [Seoul], 12, Spring-Summer 1988, 51-83.

Kim, Ilpyong J., and Young Whan Kihl (eds.). *Political Change in South Korea.* New York: Paragon House, 1988.

Kim, Jae-Hyup. *The Garrison State in Pre-War Japan and Post-War Korea: A Comparative Analysis of Military Politics.* Lanham, Maryland: University Press of America, 1978.

Kim, Quee-Young. *The Fall of Syngman Rhee.* (Korea Research Monograph No. 7.) Berkeley: Center for Korean Studies, Institute of East Asian Studies, University of California Press, 1983.

Kim, Se-Jin. *Government and Politics of Korea.* Silver Spring, Maryland: Research Institute on Korean Affairs, 1972.

_____. *The Politics of Military Revolution in Korea.* Chapel Hill: University of North Carolina Press, 1971.

Kinney, Robert A. "Students, Intellectuals, and the Churches: Their Roles in Korean Politics," *Asian Affairs,* 8, No. 1, January-February 1981, 180-95.

Korea Annual (annuals 1975 through 1980). Seoul: Hapdong News Agency, 1975-80.

Korea Annual (annuals 1981 through 1989). Seoul: Yonhap News Agency, 1981-89.

"Korean Arms Control," *Korea and World Affairs* [Seoul], 12, No. 3, Fall 1988, 485-95.

Kristof, Nicholas D. "South Korea's Dissatisfied Students: A Battle Is Won: They Want More," *New York Times,* April 4, 1987, A13.

Kristof, Nicholas D., and Sang Ho Woo. "A Moderate Tells Why Students in Korea Fight," *New York Times,* August 2, 1987, A3.

Lachinca, Eduardo. "Two Opposition Leaders Figure Heavily in U.S. Efforts to Quell Chaos in Korea," *Wall Street Journal,* June 24, 1987, 23.

Lee, Chae-Jin. "South Korea in 1983: Crisis Management and Political Legitimacy," *Asian Survey,* 24, No. 1, January 1984, 112-21.

Lee, Changsoo (ed.). *Modernization of Korea and the Impact of the West.* Los Angeles: East Asian Studies Center, University of Southern California, 1981.

Lee, Chong-Sik. "Political Change, Revolution, and Dialogue in the Two Koreas," *Asian Survey*, 29, No. 11, November 1989, 1033-42.

————. "South Korea 1979: Confrontation, Assassination, and Transition." *Asian Survey*, 20, No. 1, January 1980, 63-76.

Lee, Hong Yong. "South Korea: Bipolarity, Multipolarity, and the Northern Threat." Pages 131-51 in Raju G.C. Thomas (ed.), *The Great-Power Triangle and Asian Security*. Lexington, Massachusetts: Lexington Books, 1983.

Lee, Manwoo, Ronald D. McLaurin, and Chung-in Moon (eds.). *Alliance under Tension: The Evolution of South Korean-U.S. Relations*. Boulder, Colorado: Westview Press, 1988.

Lee, Young Woo. "Birth of the Korean Army, 1945-50," *Korea and World Affairs* [Seoul], 4, No. 4, Winter 1980, 639-56.

Lensen, George Alexander. *Korea and Manchuria: Between Russia and Japan, 1895-1904*. Tallahassee, Florida: Diplomatic Press, 1966.

Lerner, Michael. "The Fire of Ice," *Newsweek*, 114, November 27, 1989, 37-40.

Lord, Mary. "Korea's Brave New World: Democracy Waits in the Wings—If the Military Doesn't Have Other Ideas," *U.S. News and World Report*, 103, July 13, 1987, 32-33.

Lovell, John P. "The Military and Politics in Postwar Korea." Pages 155-56 in John P. Lovell (ed.), *Korean Politics in Transition*. Seattle: University of Washington Press, 1975.

Macdonald, Donald Stone. *The Koreans: Contemporary Politics and Society*. Boulder, Colorado: Westview Press, 1988.

Manguno, Joseph P. "Koreans Impatient for Promised Reform: Accumulated Anger Defying Easy Appeasement," *Wall Street Journal*, July 6, 1987, 8.

————. "Seoul's Heir Apparent Must Prove His Political Agility: Former General Faces Both Determined Opposition and Wary Military," *Wall Street Journal*, June 9, 1987, 30.

Marett, James D. "The Republic of Korea Army: The Light Infantry Division," *Military Review*, 67, No. 11, November 1987, 65-71.

Martin, James Robert. "Institutionalization and Professionalization of the Republic of Korea Army: The Impact of United States Military Assistance Through Development of a Military Schools System." (Ph.D. dissertation.) Cambridge: Department of Government, Harvard University, 1973.

McLaurin, Ronald D. "Security Relations: Burden-Sharing in a Changing Strategic Environment." Pages 157-90 in Manwoo Lee, Ronald D. McLaurin, and Chung-in Moon (eds.), *Alliance under Tension: The Evolution of South Korean-U.S. Relations*. Boulder, Colorado: Westview Press, 1988.

Menetrey, Louis C. "The U.S. Military Posture on the Korean Peninsula," *Asian Defence Journal* [Kuala Lumpur], 18, No. 8, August 1988, 12–20.

_____. "World's Attention on ROK Puts U.N. Forces on Alert," *Asia-Pacific Defense Forum*, 12, No. 4, Spring 1988, 18–23.

Merrill, John. *Korea: The Peninsular Origins of the War*. Newark: University of Delaware Press, 1989.

The Military Balance, 1989–1990. London: International Institute for Strategic Studies, 1989.

Minjungsa. *Lost Victory: An Overview of the Korean People's Struggle for Democracy*. Seoul: Minjungsa Press, 1988.

Moon, Chung-in. "U.S. Third Country Arms Sales Regulation and the South Korean Defense Industry: Supplier Control and Recipient Dilemma." Pages 79–102 in Manwoo Lee, Ronald D. McLaurin, and Chung-in Moon (eds.), *Alliance under Tension: The Evolution of South Korean-U.S. Relations*. Boulder, Colorado: Westview Press, 1988.

Morrocco, John D. "South Korea Drives Toward Greater Military Autonomy," *Aviation Week and Space Technology*, 130, No. 24, June 12, 1989, 179–82.

Mueller, Gerhard O.W. (ed.). *The Korean Criminal Code*. (Comparative Criminal Law Project, School of Law, New York University.) London: Sweet & Maxwell, 1961.

Myers, Ramon H. "The Republic of Korea: Great Transition and Coming Crisis," *Vital Speeches of the Day*, 55, May 1, 1989, 418–20.

Nahm, Andrew C. *Korea: Tradition and Transformation: A History of the Korean People*. Elizabeth, New Jersey: Hollym, 1988.

Nahm, Andrew C. (ed.). *Korea under Japanese Colonial Rule*. Kalamazoo: Center for Korean Studies, Western Michigan University, 1973.

Nam, Koon Woo. *South Korean Politics*. Lanham, Maryland: University Press of America, 1989.

Nam, Sunwoo. "The Taming of the Korean Press," *Columbia Journalism Review*, 15, March–April 1978, 43–45.

"New APC From Korea," *Jane's Defence Weekly* [London], 4, No. 14, October 5, 1985, 737.

Niksch, Larry A. "The Military Balance on the Korean Peninsula," *Korea and World Affairs* [Seoul], 10, No. 2, Summer 1986, 253–77.

"North Asian Naval Forces," *Asian Defence Journal* [Kuala Lumpur], 15, No. 1, January 1985, 70–72.

Oka, Takashi. "South Korean Presidential Campaign Shaped by Moral Imperatives," *Christian Science Monitor*, August 7, 1987, 8.

Okonogi, Masao. "South Korea's First Steps in Democracy," *Japan Echo* [Tokyo], 15, Autumn 1988, 26–31.

Oliver, Robert T. *Syngman Rhee and American Involvement in Korea, 1942–1960: A Personal Narrative.* Seoul: Panmun Book, 1978.

Olsen, Edward A. "The Societal Role of the ROK Armed Forces." Pages 87–103 in Edward A. Olsen and Stephen Jurika (eds.), *The Armed Forces in Contemporary Asian Societies.* (Westview Special Studies in Military Affairs.) Boulder, Colorado: Westview Press, 1986.

Oxman, Stephen A. *South Korea: Human Rights in the Emerging Politics.* (Report of an ICJ Mission from 25 March to 12 April 1987.) Geneva: International Commission of Jurists, 1987.

Pae, Sung M. *Testing Democratic Theories in Korea.* Lanham, Maryland: University Press of America, 1986.

Pak, Chi-Young. *Political Opposition in Korea, 1945–1960.* Seoul: Seoul National University Press, 1980.

Park, Anna. "International Election Observation: The 1987 South Korean Presidential Election," *Harvard International Law Journal,* 29, Spring 1988, 423–49.

Park, Joon Young. "The Political and Economic Implications of South Korea's Vietnam Involvement, 1964–1973," *Korea and World Affairs* [Seoul], 5, No. 3, Fall 1981, 471–89.

Pletka, Danielle. "What Do the Students Want? Democracy As They See It," *Insight,* 5, May 22, 1989, 34–35.

"Precedent-setting Ruling on National Security Law Made," Seoul: Yonhap News Agency, April 13, 1990.

Preston, Antony. "Trends in Asian Navies," *Asian Defence Journal* [Kuala Lumpur], 18, No. 8, August 1988, 4–10.

Reese, David. *Crisis and Continuity in South Korea.* London: Institute for the Study of Conflict, 1981.

Republic of Korea. "Article 42 of the Court Organization Law [*Pŏpwŏn chojikpŏp*], Law 3992, December 4, 1987, as last amended by Law No. 4017." Seoul: August 5, 1988.

———. Ministry of Culture and Information. Korean Overseas Information Service. *An International Terrorist Clique: North Korea.* Seoul: 1983.

———. Ministry of Culture and Information. Korean Overseas Information Service. *Korea's Fifth Republic in Perspective.* Seoul: 1984.

———. Ministry of Culture and Information. Korean Overseas Information Service. *Nationwide Martial Law.* Seoul: 1980.

———. Ministry of Court Administration. Supreme Court. *Justice in Korea.* Seoul: 1981.

_____. Ministry of National Defense. *Defense White Paper, 1983.* Seoul: 1984.

_____. Ministry of National Defense. *Defense White Paper, 1987.* Seoul: 1988.

_____. Ministry of National Defense. *Defense White Paper, 1988.* Seoul: 1989.

_____. Ministry of National Defense. *Defense White Paper, 1989.* Seoul: 1990.

_____. Ministry of National Defense. *A Short History of the ROK Armed Forces, 1945-1983.* Seoul: 1983.

_____. National Assembly. *Selected Laws Governing the National Assembly of the Republic of Korea.* Seoul: 1970.

_____. National Assembly. *Selected Laws Governing the National Assembly of the Republic of Korea.* Seoul: 1971.

_____. National Assembly. *Selected Laws Governing the National Assembly of the Republic of Korea.* Seoul: 1981.

_____. National Bureau of Statistics. Economic Planning Board. *Korea Statistical Yearbook: 1988.* Seoul: 1989.

_____. National Bureau of Statistics. Economic Planning Board. *Social Indicators in Korea: 1985.* Seoul: 1986.

_____. National Police Headquarters. *Korean National Police.* Seoul: 1989.

_____. National Police Headquarters. *National Police College: Republic of Korea.* Seoul: 1985.

Rhee, Taek-Hyung. *US-ROK Combined Operations.* Washington: National Defense University Press, 1986.

Rhee, Young-pil. *The Breakdown of Authority Structures in Korea in 1960: A Systems Approach.* Seoul: Seoul National University Press, 1982.

Ro, Kwang H. "The Characteristics of the Praetorian Military in South Korea: 1961-1979," *Asian Profile* [Hong Kong], 17, August 1989, 311-26.

Ropelewski, Robert R. "U.S. Pacific Air Forces Modernization: Revitalization Effort Sparked by New Theater Defense Concepts," *Aviation Week and Space Technology,* February 7, 1983, 38-46.

Shaplen, Robert. "Letter From South Korea," *New Yorker,* 56, November 17, 1980, 174-207.

Shin, Myungsoon. "Political Protest and Government Decision Making: South Korea, 1945-1972," *American Behavioral Scientist,* 26, January-February 1983, 395-416.

Sigur, Gaston. "Korean Political Transition," *Department of State Bulletin,* 87, April 1987, 19-21.

"Sikorsky-Daewoo Deal for AUH-70s in South Korea," *Jane's Defence Weekly* [London], 6, No. 10, September 13, 1986, 570.

Sneider, Daniel. "Push for Democratization in South Korea Shifts to Factories: Mood of Protests Spreads and So Do Strikes," *Christian Science Monitor,* August 13, 1987, 7–8.

Sneider, Richard L. *The Political and Social Capabilities of North and South Korea for the Long-Term Military Competition.* Santa Monica, California: Rand, 1985.

Sohn, Hak-Kyu. *Authoritarianism and Opposition in South Korea.* London: Routledge, 1989.

"South Korea Unveils Its K–1 MBT," *Asian Defence Journal* [Kuala Lumpur], 17, No. 11, November 1987, 82–83.

SRI International. *Korea in the 1980s.* Menlo Park, California: 1982.

Starr, Barbara. "Offsets Key to F/A–18 Deal," *Jane's Defence Weekly* [London], 13, No. 2, January 13, 1990, 47.

Steinberg, David I. "South Korea's Military: Political and Social Roles." Washington: Asia Society, 1988.

Steinberg, David I. *The Republic of Korea: Economic Transformation and Social Change.* Boulder, Colorado: Westview Press, 1989.

Stokes, Henry Scott. "Cracking Down in Korea," *New York Times Magazine,* October 19, 1980, 110–27.

_____. "Korea's Church Militant," *New York Times Magazine,* November 28, 1982, 67–69, 104–08.

Suh, Dae-Sook. "South Korea in 1981: The First Year of the Fifth Republic," *Asian Survey,* 22, No. 1, January 1982, 543–59.

Suk, Chin-Ha. "The Human Rights Issue in South Korea: A Reappraisal," *Asian Thought and Society,* 13, October 1988, 187–94.

Sung, Cheon Kum. *Chun Doo Hwan: Man of Destiny.* Los Angeles: North American Press, 1982.

Szulc, Tad. "Inside South Korea's C.I.A.," *New York Times Magazine,* March 6, 1977, 41–50.

Thomas, Raju G.C. (ed.). *The Great-Power Triangle and Asian Security.* Lexington, Massachusetts: Lexington Books, 1983.

Tracey, Gene D. "U.S. Military Co-Production Programmes: A Case of Skewing the Americans?" *Asian Defence Journal* [Kuala Lumpur], 19, No. 8, August 1989, 50–59.

_____. "US–ROK Co-Production: The Case of the M–16 Rifle," *Asian Defence Journal* [Kuala Lumpur], 19, No. 9, September 1989, 64–69.

United Nations. General Assembly. 39th Session. *Report of the Secretary General: Consideration of Effective Measures to Enhance the Protection, Security and Safety of Diplomatic and Consular Missions and Representatives.* New York: 1984.

United States. Congress. 95th, 1st Session. House of Representatives. Committee on International Relations. Subcommittee on

International Organizations. *Investigation of Korean-American Relations.* Washington: GPO, 1977.

————. Congress. 95th, 1st Session. House of Representatives. Committee on International Relations. Subcommittee on International Organizations. *Rules of the Investigation of Korean-American Relations.* Washington: GPO, 1977.

————. Congress. 95th, 2d Session. House of Representatives. Committee on International Relations. Subcommittee on International Organizations. *Investigation of Korean-American Relations.* Washington: GPO, 1978.

————. Congress. 95th, 2d Session. Senate. Select Committee on Ethics. *Korean Influence Inquiry.* Washington: GPO, 1978.

————. Congress. 99th, 2d Session. House of Representatives. Committee on Foreign Affairs. Subcommittee on Human Rights and International Organizations and Subcommittee on Asian and Pacific Affairs. *Political Developments and Human Rights in the Republic of Korea.* Washington: GPO, 1986.

————. Congress. 100th, 1st Session. House of Representatives. Committee on Foreign Affairs. Subcommittee on Asian and Pacific Affairs. *The Presidential Election in Korea.* Washington: GPO, 1988.

————. Congress. 100th, 1st Session. House of Representatives. Committee on Foreign Affairs. Subcommittee on Asian and Pacific Affairs. *Update on Political Developments in Korea, June 1987.* Washington: GPO, 1987.

————. Congress. 100th, 1st Session. House of Representatives. Committee on Foreign Affairs. Subcommittee on Human Rights and International Organizations. *Assessing the Prospects for Democratization in Korea.* Washington: GPO, 1988.

————. Congress. 100th, 2d Session. House of Representatives. Committee on Foreign Affairs. Subcommittee on Asian and Pacific Affairs. *The Bombing of Korean Airlines Flight KAL-858.* Washington: GPO, 1989.

————. Congress. 100th, 2d Session. House of Representatives. Committee on Foreign Affairs. Subcommittee on Asian and Pacific Affairs. *The Status of Democratization Efforts in the Republic of Korea.* Washington: GPO, 1989.

————. Congress. 101st, 1st Session. House of Representatives. Committee on Foreign Affairs. *Developments in United States-Republic of Korea Relations.* Washington: GPO, 1990.

————. Congress. 101st, 2d Session. House of Representatives. Select Committee on Narcotics Abuse and Control. *Study Mission to Korea, Hong Kong, Thailand, Laos, and Hawaii (January 3–14, 1990).* Washington: GPO, 1990.

_____. Department of State. *Country Reports on Human Rights Practices for 1989.* Washington: GPO, 1990.

_____. Department of State. "Korea: New Beginnings," *Department of State Bulletin,* 87, No. 9, September 1987, 32–34.

_____. Department of State. "United States Government Statement on the Events in Kwangju, Republic of Korea, in May 1980," Washington: June 19, 1989.

Whitaker, Mark. "South Korea's Miracle Week," *Newsweek,* 110, July 13, 1987, 26–28.

Williams, Nick B. "1980 Uprising: Memories of Kwangju Haunt Korea," *Los Angeles Times,* November 3, 1987, 14.

Wilson, Robert W. "Wellsprings of Discontent: Sources of Dissent in South Korean Student Values," *Asian Survey,* 28, No. 10, October 1988, 1066–81.

Wysocki, Bernard. "Growing Disillusionment Fuels Expansion of Korean Opposition," *Wall Street Journal,* June 22, 1987, 23.

_____. "South Korean Election Isn't Only Politics," *Wall Street Journal,* July 31, 1987, 12.

Yang, Sung Chul. "The North and South Korean Arms Race and a New Alternative," *Korean Journal of International Studies* [Seoul], 20, No. 3, Fall 1989, 431–81.

Yi, Sang-u. *Security and Unification in Korea.* Seoul: Sogang University Press, 1983.

Yoon, Dae-Kyu. *Law and Political Authority in Korea.* Boulder, Colorado: Westview Press and Seoul: Kyungnam University Press, 1990.

Yoon, Woo Kon. *Korean Public Bureaucracy.* Seoul: Sung Kyun Kwan University Press, 1982.

Youm, Kyu Ho. "Press Freedom under Constraints: The Case of South Korea," *Asian Survey,* 26, No. 8, August 1986, 868–82.

Youm, Kyu Ho, and Michael B. Salwen. "A Free Press in South Korea: Temporary Phenomenon or Permanent Fixture," *Asian Survey,* 30, No. 3, March 1990, 312–25.

(Various issues of the following publications also were used in the preparation of this chapter: *Asian Defence Journal* [Kuala Lumpur], 1985–89; *Far Eastern Economic Review* [Hong Kong], 1987–88; Foreign Broadcast Information Service, *Daily Report: East Asia,* 1989–90; *Korea Herald* [Seoul], 1985–90; and *Korea Times* [Seoul], 1985–90.)

Glossary

chaebŏl—Korean translation of the Japanese word *zaibatsu,* or business conglomerate. A group of specialized companies with interrelated management servicing each other.

chip (jip)—The household, i.e., family members under one roof; the term *k'ŭnjip* (big house) refers to the main family of the eldest son, while the term *chagŭnjip* (little house) refers to the branch family households of the younger sons.

Ch'ŏndogyo—Teachings of the Heavenly Way, an indigenous monotheistic religion stressing the equality of man and the unity of man and the universe. Formerly Tonghak (*q.v.*), Ch'ŏndogyo had approximately 27,000 followers and 66 churches in South Korea in 1988.

chuch'e (juche)—The political ideology promulgated by Kim Il Sung. The application of Marxism-Leninism to the North Korean experience based on autonomy and self-reliance.

chungin—The "middle people," a small group of technicians and administrators in traditional Korea, subordinate to the *yangban* (*q.v.*), that included astronomers, physicians, interpreters, legal specialists, and artists.

Demarcation Line—Established under the Korean armistice agreement of 1953; marks the actual cease-fire line between South Korea and North Korea.

DMZ (Demilitarized Zone)—The 4-kilometer-wide buffer zone along the approximately 241-kilometer-long Demarcation Line (*q.v.*).

fiscal year—calendar year.

Five Relationships—The Confucian concept of ideal social relationships, formulated by classical Chinese philosophers such as Mencius (372–289 B.C.), which states that there should be affection between father and son, righteousness between ruler and minister, attention to their separate functions between husband and wife, proper order between old and young, and faithfulness between friends.

GDP—gross domestic product. The total value of all final (consumption and investment) goods and services produced by an economy in a given period, usually a year.

GNP—gross national product. GDP (*q.v.*) plus income from overseas investments minus the earnings of foreign investors in the home economy.

han 'gŭl—The Korean phonetic writing system, developed by scholars in the court of King Sejong in the fifteenth century, which is used either by itself or in conjunction with Chinese characters.

International Monetary Fund (IMF)—Established along with the World Bank (*q.v.*) in 1945, the IMF is a specialized agency affiliated with the United Nations and is responsible for stabilizing international exchange rates and payments. The main business of the IMF is the provision of loans to its members (including industrialized and developing countries) when they experience balance of payments difficulties. These loans frequently carry conditions that require substantial internal economic adjustments by the recipients, most of which are developing countries.

p'a—The lineage, a kinship unit consisting of all descendants of a common male ancestor who, in many cases, was the founder of a village. Some *p'a* contain thousands of households—*chip* (*q.v.*)—and members conduct ceremonies at the common ancestral gravesite. In some villages or hamlets in traditional Korea, many or most of the people were members of the same *p'a*.

pukpang chŏngch'aek—Also seen as Nordpolitik, or northern policy. Reconciling traditional ties with the West with new opportunities in the East; establishing self-reliant global posture; expanding and diversifying trade relations on global scale to cope with trade protectionism from the United States; improving relations with P'yŏngyang.

to (*do*)—Province, used in combined form, as Kangwŏn-do for Kangwŏn Province, or Chungch'ŏng-pukto for North Ch'ungch'ŏng Province. There are eight mainland provinces and one island province in the Republic of Korea. *Do,* or *to,* also means island, as in Cheju-do.

Tonghak—Literally, Eastern learning, an indigenous religious movement founded by Ch'oe Che-u in the early 1860s, which spearheaded a popular, anti-foreign rebellion in 1894–95. Later renamed Ch'ŏndogyo (*q.v.*).

wŏn—The monetary unit. In January 1989, the exchange rate was W682.4 per US$1.

World Bank—Informal name used to designate a group of three affiliated international institutions: the International Bank for Reconstruction and Development (IBRD), the International Development Association (IDA), and the International Finance Corporation (IFC). The IBRD, established in 1945, has the primary purpose of providing loans to developing countries for productive projects. The IDA, a legally separate loan fund but administered by the staff of the IBRD, was set up in 1960 to furnish credits to the poorest developing countries on much easier terms than those of conventional IBRD loans. The IFC, founded in 1956, supplements the activities of the IBRD through loans and assistance specifically designed to encourage the growth of productive private enterprises in the less developed countries. The president and certain senior officers of the IBRD hold the same positions in the IFC. The three institutions are owned by the governments of the countries that subscribe their capital. To participate in the World Bank group, member states must first belong to the International Monetary Fund (IMF)—*q.v.*).

yangban—The scholar-official ruling class of traditional Korea, distinguished for its knowledge of neo-Confucianism and its monopoly of high government positions; more broadly, families with lineages descended from scholar-officials and scholars who had passed the civil service examinations even though they had not secured an official post.

Index

abortion, 79
account surpluses, 153, 184
acquired immune deficiency syndrome (AIDS), 129-30
Act Concerning Assembly and Demonstration, 244, 245, 310
Act Concerning Crimes Against the State, 311
Act Concerning Local Autonomy, 215
Act Concerning Protection of Military Secrets, 279, 312, 313
Act Concerning Protection of Society, 211
Administration Reform Commission, 209, 226
Advisory Council of Elder Statesmen, 207-8
Advisory Council for Peaceful Unification Policy, 207
Agency for National Security Planning (ANSP) (*see also* Korean Central Intelligence Agency), 207, 225, 281, 310, 311-14; activities of, 227, 237, 314; conduct of foreign policy by, 251; functions of, 312-13; Information Coordination Committee of, 314; limitations on powers of, 226-27, 228, 313, 314; organizational structure of, 313; origin of, 312; reluctance of, to limit power, 313-14, 327; role of, strengthened, 227-28
Agreement on Reconciliation, Nonaggression, Exchange and Cooperation, xxxvi
agricultural: bank, 171-72; development, 44; subsidies, 47; technology, 47; trade, 226; workforce, 45, 163
agricultural cooperative movement, 141, 167; merged with agricultural bank, 171-72
agricultural economy: government's emphasis on, 142; under Park, 46; pretwentieth century, 139
agricultural productivity, 165, 167, 170; growth of, 165; under Saemaŭl Movement, 47
agricultural products, 165, 167, 255; barley, 165, 167; imports of, xxix, 170; livestock, 167; price supports for, 169; rice, 165

agricultural sector (*see also* farmers): contribution of, to gross domestic product, 165; decline in, xxix, 46; problems in, 163-65; prospects for, 170; share of, in gross national product, 193
Agriculture, Forestry, and Fisheries, Ministry of, xxix
AIDS. *See* acquired immune deficiency syndrome
air defense system, 269; army's responsibility for, 283, 285
air force, 285-86, 289; aircraft, 285-86; base locations, 285; commands in, 285; matériel, xxxix; modernization program, 286; organization of, 285; personnel, 285; role of, xxxix
Air Force Academy, 290
Air Force Office of Special Investigations, 315
airports, 182
Air Training Command, 285
Air Transportation Command, 285
akpŏp (evil laws), 244
Algeria, 264
Allen, Richard V., 60
American Cultural Center, 241, 242
ancestor worship, 11; function of, 100; in kinship system, 100; in urban families, 104
ANSP. *See* Agency for National Security Planning
anti-American sentiment, 55, 62, 221, 241, 255; aroused by Nordpolitik, 252; aroused by Kwangju uprising, 241, 299; fueled by Reagan's support of Chun, 60; violence in, 241, 242
Anticommunism Law, 307
Anticommunist Youth League, 239, 240
April 19 Student Revolution, 34, 306
armed forces. *See* military; *see also under* individual branches
Armed Forces Organization Act, xxxix-xl, 274
army, 281-85; aircraft of, 284; air defense network, 283, 285; Capital Defense Command, xxxix, 282-83; Counterespionage Operations Command, 283; Defense Security Command, 283, 307,

South Korea: A Country Study

9-10; under Rhee, 35, 165; after World War II, 95
land survey, Japanese, 94
language. See Korean language
Latin America, 189
Ledyard, Gari K., 112
Lee, Ki-baik (Yi Ki-baek), 11, 110
Legislative Council for National Security, 57, 308
Liaodong Basin, 4
Liaoning Province, 274
Liao River, 6, 271
Liberal Party, 33, 36
Libya, 161
life expectancy, 120
light industry: exports by, 189; government emphasis on, 142
lineage (p'a), 101-2; continuity of, 100; descent of, 101; importance of, 19, 100; male heir in, 100
literacy, 244; under Japanese occupation, 140; rate, 115
literature: folk tales, 17-18; under Japanese rule, 22; p'ansori, 17; poetry, 16-17; social and political themes in, 22; socialist influence on, 22-23; vernacular, 17
living conditions, 176
living standard: population density as a factor in, 81
Logistics Base Command, 382
Lolang (Nangnang), 4, 5
lower class, 273; rural, 97; urban, 97; women, 108
Lucky-Goldstar, 147, 157, 258; defense production by, 296
Lyuh Woon Hyung (Yŏ Un-hyŏng), 28, 30

MacArthur, Douglas, 32, 276, 298
McCormick, Gavan, 140
Macdonald, Donald S., 139, 154, 185
McDonnell Douglas, 160, 296
Mahan confederation, 4, 5
Malaysia, 264
Manchuria, xxiv; Soviet invasion of, 24
Manchus, 10, 18
Mandate of Heaven, doctrine of, 90
manufacturing sector (see also industrialization; industrial sector; industry), 149; growth in, 44, 137
March First Movement, 20, 246

marine corps, xxxix, 286-87
Marine Corps Command, 286
marriage: arranged, 103; interviews (sŏn pogi) for, 103; love-match (yŏnae), 103; traditional purpose of, 100; women's rights in, 105, 107; women's role in, 104-5
martial law, 307; declared by Park, 40, 307; declared in Pusan, 42; declared by Rhee, 33, 314; demonstrations against, 55
Martial Law Command, 55, 56, 58, 308, 310
Masan: as fishing port, 168; population growth in, 85; student demonstrations in, 42
matériel: air force, xxxix; army, 284-85; coproduction of, 269, 277-78, 279, 285, 286, 295; domestic production of, 295-96
Maternal and Child Health Law (1973), 79
media, 246-50; censorship of, 40, 246, 247, 311; criticism by, of government, 199, 244; government control of, xxx, xxxvii, 39, 246; increased coverage by, 248; opinion polls in, 248; ownership of, 249; purged by Chun, 58; reformist tendencies of, 246
medical: facilities, 131; insurance program, 131-33; personnel, 131
medicine: modern, 130; shamanism as, 122; traditional, 130-31
Mencius, 89; philosophy of, 89, 90, 99, 100
mental health, 129
middle class, 46, 96, 97; average family in, 176-77; necessity of higher education for entering, 116
Middle East: construction projects in, 160, 177, 189
migration, urban, xxv, 81; attempts to stem, 84; effect of, on urban population, 84; under Park, 46, 47; to Seoul, 29; of women, 108; after World War II, 29, 96; of young people, 169
military: academies, 290, 291; academy, in Silla Kingdom, 272; basic training in, 290; under Chun, 278-79; duties, 280; effect of, on social system, 35; elite, 96; equipment, xxxviii; headquarters moved to Taejŏn, xxxix, 85; increase in, 269; insignia, 292; mobilization plans,

Published Country Studies

(Area Handbook Series)

550-65	Afghanistan		550-87	Greece
550-98	Albania		550-78	Guatemala
550-44	Algeria		550-174	Guinea
550-59	Angola		550-82	Guyana and Belize
550-73	Argentina		550-151	Honduras
550-169	Australia		550-165	Hungary
550-176	Austria		550-21	India
550-175	Bangladesh		550-154	Indian Ocean
550-170	Belgium		550-39	Indonesia
550-66	Bolivia		550-68	Iran
550-20	Brazil		550-31	Iraq
550-168	Bulgaria		550-25	Israel
550-61	Burma		550-182	Italy
550-50	Cambodia		550-30	Japan
550-166	Cameroon		550-34	Jordan
550-159	Chad		550-56	Kenya
550-77	Chile		550-81	Korea, North
550-60	China		550-41	Korea, South
550-26	Colombia		550-58	Laos
550-33	Commonwealth Caribbean, Islands of the		550-24	Lebanon
550-91	Congo		550-38	Liberia
550-90	Costa Rica		550-85	Libya
550-69	Côte d'Ivoire (Ivory Coast)		550-172	Malawi
550-152	Cuba		550-45	Malaysia
550-22	Cyprus		550-161	Mauritania
550-158	Czechoslovakia		550-79	Mexico
550-36	Dominican Republic and Haiti		550-76	Mongolia
550-52	Ecuador		550-49	Morocco
550-43	Egypt		550-64	Mozambique
550-150	El Salvador		550-35	Nepal and Bhutan
550-28	Ethiopia		550-88	Nicaragua
550-167	Finland		550-157	Nigeria
550-155	Germany, East		550-94	Oceania
550-173	Germany, Fed. Rep. of		550-48	Pakistan
550-153	Ghana		550-46	Panama

550-156	Paraguay	550-53	Thailand
550-185	Persian Gulf States	550-89	Tunisia
550-42	Peru	550-80	Turkey
550-72	Philippines	550-74	Uganda
550-162	Poland	550-97	Uruguay
550-181	Portugal	550-71	Venezuela
550-160	Romania	550-32	Vietnam
550-37	Rwanda and Burundi	550-183	Yemens, The
550-51	Saudi Arabia	550-99	Yugoslavia
550-70	Senegal	550-67	Zaire
550-180	Sierra Leone	550-75	Zambia
550-184	Singapore	550-171	Zimbabwe
550-86	Somalia		
550-93	South Africa		
550-95	Soviet Union		
550-179	Spain		
550-96	Sri Lanka		
550-27	Sudan		
550-47	Syria		
550-62	Tanzania		

☆ U.S. GOVERNMENT PRINTING OFFICE: 1992   311-824/60005